Global Cooperation and the Human Factor in International Relations

This book aims to pave the way for a new interdisciplinary approach to global cooperation research. It does so by bringing in disciplines whose insights about human behavior might provide a crucial yet hitherto neglected foundation for understanding how and under which conditions global cooperation can succeed.

As the first profoundly interdisciplinary book dealing with global cooperation, it provides the state of the art on human cooperation in selected disciplines (evolutionary anthropology and biology, decision-sciences, social psychology, complex system sciences), written by leading experts. The book argues that scholars in the field of global governance should know and could learn from what other disciplines tell us about the capabilities and limits of humans to cooperate. This new knowledge will generate food for thought and cause creative disturbances, allowing us a different interpretation of the obstacles to cooperation observed in world politics today. It also offers first accounts of interdisciplinary global cooperation research, for instance by exploring the possibilities and consequences of global we-identities, by describing the basic cooperation mechanisms that are valid across disciplines, or by bringing an evolutionary perspective to diplomacy.

This book will be of great interest to scholars and postgraduates in International Relations, Global Governance, and International Development.

Dirk Messner is Co-director of the Centre for Global Cooperation Research, University Duisburg-Essen, Germany, where he is also Professor of Political Science and Director of the German Development Institute/Deutsches Institut für Entwicklungspolitik (DIE), Germany.

Silke Weinlich is Senior Researcher at the German Development Institute/ Deutsches Institut für Entwicklungspolitik (DIE) in Bonn, Germany.

Routledge Global Cooperation Series

This series develops innovative approaches to understanding, explaining, and answering one of the most pressing questions of our time – how can cooperation in a culturally diverse world of nine billion people succeed?

We are rapidly approaching our planet's limits, with trends such as advancing climate change and the destruction of biological diversity jeopardizing our natural life support systems. Accelerated globalization processes lead to an ever-growing interconnectedness of markets, states, societies, and individuals. Many of today's problems cannot be solved by nation states alone. Intensified cooperation at the local, national, international, and global level is needed to tackle current and looming global crises.

Series editors

Tobias Debiel, Claus Leggewie, and Dirk Messner are co-directors of the Käte Hamburger Kolleg/Centre for Global Cooperation Research, University Duisburg-Essen, Germany. Their research areas are, among others, Global Governance, Climate Change, Peacebuilding and Cultural Diversity of Global Citizenship. The three co-directors are at the same time based in their home institutions, which participate in the Centre, namely the German Development Institute/Deutsches Institut für Entwicklungspolitik (DIE, Messner) in Bonn, the Institute for Development and Peace (INEF, Debiel) in Duisburg, and The Institute for Advanced Study in the Humanities (KWI, Leggewie) in Essen.

Titles

Global Cooperation and the Human Factor in International Relations
Edited by Dirk Messner and Silke Weinlich

Global Cooperation and the Human Factor in International Relations

Edited by Dirk Messner
and Silke Weinlich

Routledge
Taylor & Francis Group

LONDON AND NEW YORK

Centre for
**Global
Cooperation
Research**

SPONSORED BY THE

Federal Ministry
of Education
and Research

First published 2016
by Routledge
2 Park Square, Milton Park, Abingdon, Oxon OX14 4RN

and by Routledge
711 Third Avenue, New York, NY 10017

First issued in paperback 2017

Routledge is an imprint of the Taylor & Francis Group, an informa business

British Library Cataloguing in Publication Data
A catalogue record for this book is available from the British Library

Library of Congress Cataloging-in-Publication Data
Names: Messner, Dirk, editor. | Weinlich, Silke, editor.
Title: Global cooperation and the human factor in international relations / edited by Dirk Messner and Silke Weinlich.
Description: New York, NY : Routledge, 2016. | Includes bibliographical references and index.
Identifiers: LCCN 2015023805
Subjects: LCSH: International cooperation. | Cooperation—Social aspects.
Classification: LCC JZ1318 .G556547 2016 | DDC 327.1—dc23
LC record available at http://lccn.loc.gov/2015023805

ISBN: 978-1-138-91299-1 (hbk)
ISBN: 978-0-815-35510-6 (pbk)
ISBN: 978-1-315-69165-7 (ebk)

DOI: 10.4324/9781315691657

Typeset in Goudy
by Deanta Global Publishing Services, Chennai, India

This work and its open access publication has been supported by the Federal Ministry of Education and Research (BMBF) in the context of its funding of the Käte Hamburger Kolleg/Centre for Global Cooperation Research at the University of Duisburg-Essen (grant number 01UK1810).

Contents

Illustrations

Notes on contributors

Lothar Brock is senior professor for International Relations at Goethe-University Frankfurt and also works as a visiting Professor at the Peace Research Institute in Frankfurt (PRIF). In 2013–14 he joined the Centre for Global Cooperation Research in Duisburg as Senior Expert Fellow. Lothar Brock is Head of the Academic Advisory Board of the Development and Peace Foundation in Bonn. His research focuses on normative and institutional aspects of international cooperation. He was involved in PRIF's program on 'Antinomies of the democratic peace' and continues to work on the justification of the use of force at the international level. His areas of expertise include North-South relations, the United Nations, and human rights.

Gianluca Grimalda is Lecturer at the University Jaume I of Castelló de la Plana (Spain) and Research Fellow at the Centre for Global Cooperation Research (University of Duisburg-Essen) and at the Kiel Institute for the World Economy. His research adopts experimental methodologies to study the interaction between individual behavior and socio-economic structures, often adopting a cross-cultural perspective. The topics he has analyzed include globalization, inter-personal cooperation and trust, income redistribution, and individual perceptions of fairness. His work has been published in the *Proceedings of the National Academy of Sciences of the USA*, *Psychological Science*, and the *Journal of Evolutionary Economics*.

Alejandro Guarín is a Senior Researcher at the German Development Institute/ Deutsches Institut für Entwicklungspolitik (DIE), where he works on the relationship between natural resources and development, forest policy, the rise of the new global middle classes, and the behavioral bases of human cooperation. Before joining DIE, he specialized on informal agro-food systems and urban food markets in Latin America and consulted for FAO, MIT, and local governments in Colombia. He studied Biology at the Colombian National University in Bogotá, and later received a Master's in Biogeography from Penn State and a Doctorate in Geography from the University of California at Berkeley.

Daniel Haun is Professor of Early Child Development and Culture at Leipzig University. After studying experimental psychology in Germany, the United States, and England, he completed his PhD in 2007 at the Max Planck Institute for

Psycholinguistics. After a post-doc at the Max Planck Institute for Evolutionary Anthropology he accepted a position as Lecturer in Developmental Psychology at the University of Portsmouth. From 2008 to 2013 he directed the Max Planck Research Group for Comparative Cognitive Anthropology before accepting a position as Professor of Developmental Psychology at Friedrich Schiller University Jena. He joined Leipzig University in April 2015.

Jobst Heitzig is a Senior Researcher at PIK, project lead of an EIT Climate-KIC project and co-speaker of flagship project COPAN on coevolutionary dynamics of coupled physical and socio-economic global systems. He holds a PhD in Mathematics from Hannover University and has worked as a scientific officer with the German National Statistical Office, a data warehouse analyst with the German Development Bank KfW, and a freelance statistical software trainer with SAS. He has also published on dynamical systems theory, complex networks theory, general topology, game theory, environmental economics, social choice, statistical methods, confidentiality protection, and combinatorics.

Eric J. Johnson is the Norman Eig Professor of Business and Co-Director of the Center for Decision Sciences at Columbia Business School. His research on decision processes and their implications for public policy, markets, and marketing has been published in *Science, Psychological Review, Psychological Science, Nature Neuroscience, Harvard Business Review, Journal of Economic Theory*, and many other journals. Honors include the Distinguished Scientific Contribution Award from the Society for Consumer Psychology, Fellow status by the Association for Consumer Research, the TIAA-CREF Institute, and the Association for Psychological Science, and an honorary doctorate in Economics from the University of St. Gallen.

Jürgen Kurths studied Mathematics at the University of Rostock and got his PhD in 1983 at the GDR Academy of Sciences and his Dr. habil. in 1990. He was full Professor at the University of Potsdam from 1994 to 2008 and has been Professor of Nonlinear Dynamics at the Humboldt University, Berlin, and Chair of the research domain Transdisciplinary Concepts of the Potsdam Institute for Climate Impact Research since 2008. He is a Fellow of the American Physical Society and of the Academia Europaea, received an Alexander von Humboldt research award from CSIR (India), two Honorary Doctorates, and was awarded the L.F. Richardson Medal of the EGU. His main research interests are complex synchronization phenomena, complex networks, time series analysis, and their applications.

Claus Leggewie is Director of the Institute for Advanced Study in the Humanities Essen (KWI) since 2007 and Co-Director of the Käte Hamburger Kolleg / Centre for Global Cooperation Research, University of Duisburg-Essen, which was established in 2012. Since December 2008 he has been a member of the German Advisory Council on Global Change (WBGU). His research interests include cultural factors of the adaptation of modern societies to the consequences of climate change; the preconditions and consequences of cultural and religious globalization; and European conflicts of memory and politics of history, as well as political and scientific communication through digital media.

Siddharth Mallavarapu is currently Associate Professor and Chairperson, Department of International Relations, at the South Asian University. His prior publications include a single-author book titled *Banning the Bomb: The Politics of Norm Creation*, and two co-edited books, titled *International Relations in India* (with Kanti Bajpai) and *International Relations: Perspectives for the Global South* (with B.S. Chimni), besides other journal contributions. His research interests include disciplinary histories of International Relations, the politics and episteme of the global south, the theory and practice of global governance, and evaluations of both mainstream and critical approaches to the study of world politics. He was also featured on *Theory Talks* in February 2014.

Norbert Marwan is Senior Researcher and Deputy Chair of the research domain Transdisciplinary Concepts and Methods at the Potsdam Institute for Climate Impact Research (PIK) and speaker of the flagship project Time Series Analysis. He studied Theoretical Physics at the Dresden University of Technology and holds a PhD in Nonlinear Dynamics from the University of Potsdam. His research interests are in the field of nonlinear data analysis, with special focus on recurrence plots, complex networks, and 3D image analysis with applications in Earth and life science.

Alicia P. Melis is Assistant Professor of Behavioral Science at Warwick Business School. She studied Biology at Free University of Berlin and holds a PhD in Psychology from the University of Leipzig. Before joining Warwick University, she worked as Postdoctoral Researcher at the Department of Developmental and Comparative Psychology at the Max Planck Institute for Evolutionary Anthropology in Leipzig. Her research interests include the evolution of cooperation, factors for promotion and stabilization of coordination and cooperation between individuals, and psychological mechanisms supporting human and nonhuman apes' cooperative and pro-social interactions. She works with chimpanzees in African sanctuaries and children.

Dirk Messner is Director of the German Development Institute/Deutsches Institut für Entwicklungspolitik (DIE) and Co-Director of the Käte Hamburger Kolleg/ Centre for Global Cooperation Research, University of Duisburg-Essen, which was established in 2012. He is also Co-Chair (since 2013) of the German Advisory Council on Global Change (WBGU) and member of the China Council on Global Cooperation on Development and Environment (CCICED). His research interests include sustainable development, globalization and global governance, the impact of China's and India's rise on processes of international politics, and interdisciplinary (global) cooperation research.

Iver B. Neumann (b. 1959), D. Phil. (Oxon, Politics, 1992), Dr. Philos. (Oslo, Social Anthropology, 2009) is Montague Burton Professor of International Relations at the London School of Economics and an associate of the Norwegian Institute of International Affairs, where he was formerly Director of

Research. Among his fourteen books are *Russia and Europe: A Study in Identity and International Relations* (Routledge, 1996); *Uses of the Other: 'The East' in European Identity Formation* (University of Minnesota Press, 1999), with Ole Jacob Sending; *Governing the Global Polity* (University of Michigan Press, 2010); *At Home with the Diplomats: Inside A European Foreign Ministry* (Cornell University Press, 2012); and *Diplomatic Sites: A Critical Enquiry* (Oxford University Press, 2013).

Martin A. Nowak is Professor of Biology and Mathematics at Harvard University and Director of the Program for Evolutionary Dynamics. He works on the mathematical description of evolutionary processes, including the evolution of cooperation and human language, as well as the dynamics of virus infections and human cancer. He received his PhD in 1989 from the University of Vienna, then moved to the University of Oxford, where he eventually became head of the mathematical biology group in 1995 and Professor of Mathematical Biology in 1997. A year later he moved to Princeton, and ultimately accepted his present position at Harvard University in 2003.

David G. Rand is Assistant Professor of Psychology, Economics, and Management at Yale University, and the Director of Yale University's Human Cooperation Laboratory. His research combines a range of theoretical and experimental methods in an effort to explain the high levels of cooperation that typify human societies, and to uncover ways to promote cooperation in situations where it is lacking. He received his BA in Computational Biology from Cornell University in 2004 and his PhD in Systems Biology from Harvard University in 2009, and was a post-doctoral research in Harvard University's Psychology Department from 2009 to 2013.

Elke U. Weber is the Jerome A. Chazen Professor of International Business and Professor of Management and Psychology at Columbia University, where she co-directs the Center for Decision Sciences and the Center for Research on Environmental Decisions. Her PhD in Behavior and Decision Analysis is from Harvard. She has served as president for the Society for Mathematical Psychology, the Society for Judgment and Decision Making, and the Society for Neuroeconomics. She is a Fellow of the American Psychological Association, the Association for Psychological Science, the Society for Risk Analysis, and a member of the German National Academy of Sciences.

Silke Weinlich is Senior Researcher in the Department for Bi- and Multilateral Development Cooperation at the German Development Institute / Deutsches Institut für Entwicklungspolitik (DIE) in Bonn. Previously she was head of the research unit '(Im)possibility of Cooperation' at the Käte Hamburger Kolleg / Centre for Global Cooperation Research, University of Duisburg-Essen. She holds a doctorate in political science from Bremen University. Her research interests include Global Governance and the role of international organizations, in particular the United Nations, and multilateral negotiations, as well as the North-South relations and development cooperation 'beyond aid'.

Introduction: Global cooperation research[1]

Dirk Messner and Silke Weinlich

Global challenges such as climate change, the stability of financial markets, or the prevention of pandemics urgently demand coordinated action – indeed they require a new quality of global cooperation (Kennedy, Messner, and Nuscheler 2002; Kaul, Grunberg, and Stern 1999; Barrett 2007). However, instances of successful global cooperation seem to be an exception. Many scholars of international relations draw rather pessimistic conclusions concerning the prospects for a world dealing with its interdependency problems in an effective, legitimate, and peaceful manner. They lament that the rise of new powers makes agreement even more difficult, as does the complexity of the problems to be addressed. Existing institutions, relics of a 250-year long period of Western dominance, fail to deliver (Hale, Held, and Young 2013). At worst, a dark era of ideological contention and geopolitical rivalry might loom ahead, a world in which every state looks out for itself (Bremmer 2012). This pessimism echoes a centuries-old debate about the 'survival of the fittest' (Herbert Spencer) and egoism and greed being the main drivers of human existence. These worldviews stand in surprising contrast to the optimism of other disciplines that have been investigating the foundations of human behavior and civilizations. Novel findings from evolutionary anthropology, evolutionary biology, and related disciplines highlight the cooperative and pro-social capacities of humankind. Cooperation is understood to be one of the vital mechanisms that made possible the emergence of complex social structures (Tomasello 2009, 2014; Benkler 2011; Nowak and Highfield 2011). So far, the disciplinary boundaries have rarely been crossed, and the strands of research mostly exist in isolation. In this book, we want to tap the potential of bringing together these diverse bodies of knowledge in order to develop an innovative approach of global cooperation research. Together with both – disciplines that have and have not been dealing with the global level – we want to initiate a new debate about the abilities and limitations of human beings with regard to (global) cooperation. Our key assumption for this edited volume is that scholars in the field of global governance should know and could learn from what other disciplines tell us about the capabilities and limits of humans to cooperate.

The main objective of this volume is to provide fresh directions and a new impetus to the research on global cooperation by bringing in disciplines whose insights about human behavior might provide a crucial yet hitherto neglected foundation for understanding how and under which conditions global cooperation can succeed. First, the volume offers an innovative take on international politics. As the first profoundly interdisciplinary book dealing with global cooperation, the book adds value to the existing global governance literature by bringing in new perspectives. It provides the state of the art on human cooperation in selected disciplines (evolutionary anthropology, decision sciences, social psychology, complex system sciences), written by leading experts. Second, the book offers first accounts of interdisciplinary global cooperation research. Several authors cross the disciplinary divides; they describe basic cooperation mechanism distilled from an interdisciplinary literature review; they bring together cognitive sciences and institutional design literature to learn more about how 'better' institutions could look like; they use social psychology and experimental economy approaches to find out more about the possibilities of a global we-identity; or they provide an evolutionary perspective on diplomacy. Ultimately, the book aims at paving the way for a new interdisciplinary approach to global cooperation research.

Chapter outlines

The book is divided in three parts. In the first part, 'Why Global Cooperation Research', the chapters spell out in more detail the rational for a new, interdisciplinary research on global cooperation and provide illustrations of the benefits that come with harvesting insights of different disciplines and changing the perspective. In *Chapter 2*, Dirk Messner and Silke Weinlich first build the case as to why global governance research needs to open up towards the astounding findings of humans' abilities to cooperate. They present three sets of findings derived from a reading of this cooperation literature, namely (1) a micro-level perspective on the human ability for cooperation; (2) a macro-level perspective that discusses the relation between cooperation, complexity, and human civilization; and (3) the normative perspective that broaches the issue of the purpose and outcome of cooperation. The authors explore what the history of cooperation looks like when observed through an evolutionary lens and identify four different phases which emerged in the course of the last 400,000 years. Such a perspective gives rise to a different set of explanations as to why there are blockades in today's global cooperation; it also opens up new ways of dealing with these blockades, both in terms of research and practice. In *Chapter 3*, Dirk Messner, Daniel Haun, and Alejandro Guarín look at the behavioral dimension of cooperation. Building on knowledge across academic disciplines about cooperation between individuals and within smaller groups, they develop a 'cooperation hexagon' that consists of the interdisciplinary state of the art of basic cooperation mechanisms. These mechanisms are crucial for whether or not cooperation is successful or sustainable. At the heart of the hexagon lies reciprocity, the most basic mechanism that, many argue, is crucial not only for initiating cooperation but also for its continuation. Similarly important factors are we-identities, trust, enforcement, communication, reputation, and fairness. The more resilient these mechanisms are and the stronger actors invest in them, the better the probabilities of developing and stabilizing cooperation patterns. The authors argue that these basic mechanisms of cooperation are relevant both in small groups and complex systems. This makes them also very relevant for the level of global cooperation. In the last chapter of this section, Lothar Brock critically engages with the evolutionary and behavioral cooperation literature and their relevance for thinking about global cooperation. He introduces some words of caution, arguing that while it is worthwhile to build epistemological bridges, which connect the findings on individual and group behavior to the conditions of cooperation at the global level, since this allows us to confront self-fulfilling prophecies about the selfish human nature, a high degree of reflexivity is needed in order to avoid painting too rosy a picture of the cooperative human nature. His focus in *Chapter 4* is on cooperation in the international system in the context of conflict, which, as he argues, is rather the normal case than the exception. He therefore highlights how closely intertwined cooperation and conflict are and explores the implications of what he terms cooperation in conflict.

Part II of the book, 'Human behavior and cooperation across disciplines', includes disciplinary perspective on cooperation by renowned specialists from evolutionary biology and anthropology, psychology, mathematics, behavioral and decision sciences, and physics. Alicia P. Melis makes a start with writing about the most fundamental topic by searching for the roots of human cooperation and uncovering a natural predisposition of humans to cooperate. In *Chapter 5*, she draws on her research in evolutionary anthropology and reviews a series of psychological studies that explore the similarities and differences between the cooperative behavior of young children and that of our closest primate relatives, the chimpanzees. Melis shows that long before human children have undergone intensive socialization practices cooperation comes naturally to them. This suggests a natural predisposition that most likely has evolved from the last common ancestors of humans and chimpanzees, with whom humans share the basic skills and motivations to cooperate. However, humans seem psychologically better equipped to cooperate with others; from an early age on, children are more tolerant; they have a tendency to share rewards of a cooperative action in an egalitarian way and generally engage in many helpful actions. Nevertheless, it is clear that cooperation, and especially cooperation in large groups, is not easy, even for human beings that are much better at it than any other creature. The next chapter also makes use of experimental studies to find out more about the cooperative abilities of humans. David G. Rand and Martin A. Nowak, however, come from a different angle in *Chapter 6*. Their point of departure is five general mechanisms for the evolution of cooperation that Nowak (2006) derived from theoretical work in the fields of mathematics and evolutionary biology. These mechanisms – direct reciprocity, indirect reciprocity, spatial selection, group selection, and kin selection – explain how cooperation could emerge in the first place and is observable at so many levels, be it between genes, chromosomes, cells, animals – or humans. Human cooperation is the focus of their chapter. The authors review the empirical basis of the five mechanisms by means of laboratory experiments on human behavior. They provide evidence in support of each of the mechanisms and also discuss cooperation that arises in the absence of any of the mechanisms. The authors conclude that direct and indirect reciprocity plays a key role in human cooperation. Reflecting about the relevance of their findings for global cooperation, they in fact argue that as the world becomes increasingly complex and interdependent an ever greater emphasis on reciprocity is expected. In addition, they stress the importance of culture and learning for human cooperation.

In *Chapter 7*, Elke U. Weber and Erik J. Johnson provide yet another perspective on human cooperation by focusing exclusively on the cognitive and motivational processes and constraints that inform human decision making – and thereby cooperation. At the center of their chapter is the question of whether and how human beings are able to take decisions with a long time horizon – something which is at the heart of global cooperation, e.g. in form of addressing issues such as climate change. Building on insights from psychology and behavioral economics about how humans actually make decisions (as opposed to the rational-economic view of how decisions ought to and are assumed to be made), the authors investigate the obstacles and limitations that have an impact on humans' ability to arrive at cooperative plans to ensure future well-being. They argue that the complexity and time scale of current individual, as well as societal, challenges severely challenges the human ability for cooperative and proactive problem solving. When looking at strategic decisions, the authors, however, suggest that some of the cognitive and motivational limitations might actually facilitate the making of future-oriented plans, which is necessary for addressing global problems. The authors conclude by discussing how the decision environments can be changed in order to take advantage of and increase the chances for sustainable cooperative decisions.

Complexity is also the topic of the next chapter, although the authors (physicists and mathematicians) do not investigate the human abilities to cope with complexity but rather focus on how new scientific approaches and methods can help in dealing with complexity and therefore provide new tools and instruments for global cooperation research. In *Chapter 8*, Jürgen Kurths, Jobst Heitzig, and Norbert Marwan provide us with an introduction into complex systems science, highlighting how cooperation and other interaction between systems in general can lead to even greater complexity due to feedback loops. They introduce the complex network approach, which is used to gain a better understanding of systems with irregular, complex structures that change over time. It can be applied to highly divers types of networks, ranging from social networks over infrastructure such as power grids or air traffic to functional networks of the human brain. In contrast to the previous chapter, the authors argue that the complexity of human decision making may very well be captured and explained by rational choice models – if only the models are complex enough. To demonstrate this, they apply a complex system approach to the preference formation in decision making and systems of cooperating humans. Examples of bilateral cooperation problems, the emergence of consensus in decision making in large groups, and the dynamic formation of coalitions in multilateral cooperation are used as illustrations.

Somewhat in contrast to this take on cooperation, which presupposes the matching of interests, tit for tat, or shared benefits of cooperation partners, Claus Leggewie proposes in *Chapter 9* a genuine sociological approach to cooperation theory and something of a counterpoint to the previous assumptions about cooperation. He proposes to take into account the theory of gift exchange as an important approach for addressing the non-utilitarian interaction and reciprocity between groups and communities. Developed in the 1920s by Marcel Maus on the basis of ethnological field studies, a gift involves three obligations: to give, to receive, and to reciprocate – but gifts do not have to be reciprocated directly to the giver. Leggewie employs the notion of the gift to undertake a case study on regional and global debt relief and uses other examples of post-utilitarian interactions to identify empirically and conceptionally promising areas of cooperation research.

Part III of the volume, 'Interdisciplinary approaches to global cooperation', consists of chapters that combine approaches, e.g. research questions, theories, concepts, and methods, from multiple disciplines, and looks through this new lens at global cooperation, offering novel perspectives and ideas. In *Chapter 9*, the economist Gianluca Grimalda zooms in on the possible development of global we-identities which could serve as social glue that makes cooperation within the world society more successful. Does globalization make individuals more accustomed to think of others as being part of their own 'we-group', or does it bring out the attachment to traditional groups and loyalties? The author examines experimentally how social identities at different levels correlate with cooperative attitudes in a study that involved adult populations from six different countries. His findings indeed suggest that globalization seems to favor the construction of an inclusive sense of identities. This in turn leads to a heightened propensity to cooperate. On this basis, Grimalda develops several proposals of action for what he terms globality-minded policy-makers. In *Chapter 10*, Iver B. Neumann, political scientist and anthropologist, brings an evolutionary perspective to the study of diplomacy and thereby allows us to view the failures of contemporary diplomacy, e.g. in multilateral settings, in the context of what he calls the emergence of the institution of diplomacy as a hard-won triumph of the species. Neumann suggests that the birth of diplomacy should not be equaled with the birth of states, as is commonly done. Instead, diplomacy can be regarded as an institution that evolved by and with the human species. Looking for the origins of diplomacy back in time when humans started to cooperate, first within groups and communities, then between communities, cities and states, he brings in a longue durée view on how diplomacy evolved alongside with human civilizations. Introducing the notion of evolutionary tipping points, Neumann describes how diplomacy intensified from small-scale to large-scale, from intermittent to permanent, and from bilateral to multilateral. He identifies six tipping points, ranging from the Pleistocene revolution around 300,000 B.C., when groups started to hunt big game, to the establishment of multilateral institutions in the nineteenth century. He also reflects about the emergence of a seventh tipping point that challenges the present hierarchy of diplomatic agents and gives non-state agents a more important role in arenas of global cooperation. The political scientist Siddharth Mallavarapu puts the design of institutions that might further enhance the possibility of global cooperation at the center of *Chapter 11*, and thereby provides some interesting ideas for further research. He starts from the observation that current global governance discourses are contested and often also challenged with reference to injustices of the past and present. In his chapter, he explores how these 'framings' can be altered and a greater degree of confidence and belief in a global 'we' project be created. For this, he turns to the field of cognitive neurosciences and investigates how novel findings on language, memory, and affect can be factored in to design better institutions. In a way similar to Elke Weber's and Erik Johnson's chapter, Mallavarapu takes the broader human predispositions and flaws as a starting point and looks for ways of both tapping into them creatively while also understanding their role and implications more clearly. Therefore, he raises awareness to biases and prejudices, analogies that humans use to simplify their decision making, or categorizations that lead to exclusions. Mallavarapu highlights the importance of memory or shared amnesia that can bring human collectives closer; he analyzes the role of affect or emotions that, combined with memory and language, may generate a distinctive grammar of cooperation – or resistance.

Note

1 This book was inspired by the intense and stimulating debate at the Masterclass of the Centre for Global Cooperation Research in Duisburg in 2013, titled 'Towards a better understanding of complexity and scale and their relevance for global cooperation'. We would like to thank all participants for their valuable contributions. We would also like to gratefully acknowledge the support of our research assistants, in particular Luis Aue, who tirelessly helped to bring this edited volume towards publication.

References

Barrett, S. (2007). *Why Cooperate? The Incentive to Supply Global Public Goods*, Cambridge, MA: Oxford University Press.

Benkler, Y. (2011). *The Penguin and the Leviathan: How Cooperation Triumphs Over Self-Interest*, New York, NY: Crown Business.

Bremmer, I. (2012). *Every Nation for Itself: Winners and Losers in a G-Zero World*, New York, NY: Penguin.

Hale, T., Held D. and Young, K. (2013). *Gridlock: Why Global Cooperation Is Failing When We Need It Most*, Cambridge, UK: Polity Press.

Kaul, I., Grunberg, I. and Stern, M. (eds.) (1999). *Global Public Goods: International Cooperation in the 21st Century*, New York, NY: Oxford University Press.

Kennedy, P.M., Messner, D. and Nuscheler, F. (2002). *Global Trends and Global Governance*, London: Pluto Press.

Nowak, M.A. (2006). 'Five Rules for the Evolution of Cooperation', *Science*, 314 (5805): 1560–3.

Nowak, M.A. and Highfield, R. (2011). *SuperCooperators: Altruism, Evolution, and Why We Need Each Other to Succeed*, New York NY: Free Press.

Tomasello, M. (2009). *Why We Cooperate*, Cambridge, MA: MIT Press.

Tomasello, M. (2014). 'The Ultra-Social Animal', *European Journal of Social Psychology*, 44 (3): 187–94.

Part I
Why global cooperation research

1 The evolution of human cooperation

Lessons learned for the future of global governance

Dirk Messner and Silke Weinlich

> *Humans putting their heads together in shared cooperative activities are . . . the origina-*
> *tors of human culture.*
>
> (Tomasello 2009: 99)

This chapter is structured as follows: first, we develop the main direction of the book by describing the various crises in world politics that, despite a pressing need for cooperation, are mostly characterized by logjams. We show that many scholars from the discipline of International Relations deem these crises as durable and unchangeable. We then contrast this rather gloomy finding with the optimism concerning cooperation that can be gleaned from the latest knowledge from other academic disciplines on the fundamentals of human behavior and the dynamics of human civilization. At the heart of the edited volume and this chapter is the question of what we can learn from disciplines such as neuroscience, evolutionary anthropology, cognitive psychology, or evolutionary biology that will be of benefit to global cooperation. We therefore subsequently present three sets of findings that emerge from our examination of the literature on cooperation:

- from a micro-perspective, to summarize the state of knowledge on the ability of humans to cooperate;
- from a macro-perspective, to discuss the relationship between complexity and cooperation and to pursue the question of whether global cooperation could fail due to increasing complexity; and
- from a normative perspective, to address whether cooperation can be used for 'good' or 'bad' purposes.

Each of these findings raises new research questions, which we will also outline. A key assumption is that interdisciplinary knowledge on the basics of human cooperation skills can generate food for thought and cause creative disturbances, allowing us a different interpretation of the obstacles to cooperation observed in world politics. We therefore attempt a radical change of perspective in a further step and use instruments and the conceptual apparatus of evolutionary approaches

DOI: 10.4324/9781315691657-2

to look at (1) the four phases of history of human cooperation and (2) the discipline of International Relations. This allows us to identify new patterns of explanation that can help us think about global cooperation in the 21st century beyond some of the constraints of International Relations theories. Precisely which direction these pursuits could take us will be presented at the end of this chapter.

Global cooperation: Where do we stand?

A look into world politics: 'Era of the collapse of world order'?

The global order is not in a good condition. Chairman of the Munich Security Conference Wolfgang Ischinger, former secretary of state of the German foreign ministry, and a serious man not prone to exaggeration or aggravation, warned in February 2015 that we find ourselves in an 'era of the collapse of world order'. The German foreign minister said in March 2015 that he could not remember a period in his political career in which crises and conflicts were as acute as they are today. It would seem as if the international community has failed in its task to manage intensifying global interdependencies through global cooperation, contain global systemic risks, and secure and/or provide the global commons (such as an international legal and security framework, stable international financial markets, regulations for global data traffic, precautionary measures to stabilize the Earth system, climate change) upon which all societies are equally dependent.

In 1989, when the Berlin Wall fell and the East-West conflict came to an end, hopes were high for a new global order (Commission on Global Governance 1995). During the UN world conferences of the 1990s, a 'world domestic policy' for a gradually emerging global society was anticipated (Fues and Hamm 2000; Messner and Nuscheler 1996). And yet 25 years after the end of the Cold War, one can no longer detect a sense of global optimism concerning a cooperation-based global governance. The international community does not shape globalization; it meanders and staggers its way through transnational crisis scenarios in security policy, the global economy, global environmental policy, and the international system as a whole.

The Ukraine war in Europe has led to a new and dangerous freezing of relations between Europe, the West as a whole, and Russia. Russia is violating the basic principles of international law with the annexation of the Crimea, and yet Europe and the US find little support in many parts of the world for their Ukraine policy. This could be attributable to the fact that the West itself has broken or stretched international law in the recent past. For instance, during the invasion of Iraq by the US and its allies in 2003 and in the context of other 'collateral damage' in the wake of 9/11, basic principles of human rights and international law were undermined, such as the treatment of prisoners in Guantanamo and Abu Ghraib. Europe's policy of closed doors in dealing with the refugee catastrophe in the Mediterranean further erodes the West's credibility. In addition to the freezing of relations between Russia and the West, international security is particularly threatened by failing states and civil wars in the Middle East. In Iraq, Syria, Libya, and their neighboring countries, state and societal collapse is accompanied by the spread of transnational jihadism, which also threatens countries in sub-Saharan Africa (e.g. Nigeria, Mali, Somalia) as well as Asian countries (such as the Philippines, Indonesia, Pakistan, and Bangladesh). It even extends to Europe. Like previous totalitarian ideologies – such as Fascism and Stalinism – Islamist jihadism seeks to eradicate its opponents. 2014 was also the year with the largest flows of international refugee since the Second World War – over 50 million people were displaced from their homes by war, violence, and hopelessness. An international order of peace, which seemed within reach in 1989, is now far from the world's grasp.

In the field of global economic governance things look a little better. The financial market crisis of 2008, which began in the OECD states, could at the very least be mitigated (Drezner 2014). In the context of the crisis, the G20 – a club of the most important industrialized and emerging countries – was founded as the central governing body of the global economy, thereby replacing the G8 as the key global governance club, which had brought together Western industrialized countries and Russia. The immediate mutual economic dependencies and vulnerabilities, as well as the legitimate concerns that the international financial system could collapse, led to efforts within the framework of the G20 to gradually create new rules for global financial markets. It also succeeded by way of international appointments and coordination in the G20 to prevent competitive currency devaluations between national economies and protectionist waves on a large scale, thus averting a collapse of the global economy (in contrast to the Great Depression of the 1930s). The G20 acted as a crisis-mitigation body during the financial crisis, yet it still remains silent and ineffective as an alliance to shape the global order (Cooper and Momani 2014).

Progress can hardly be found in the field of global environmental change; if there is progress at all, then it is only in attempts. Over the past two decades, the natural sciences have been able to show in an increasingly systematic manner that humanity will exceed the 'limits of the Earth system' in the 21st century (Rockström et al. 2009) if the world's entrenched resource-intensive and greenhouse-gas-intensive growth pattern continues. Tipping points in the Earth system could then be reached (Lenton et al. 2008; Messner and Rahmstorf 2009), leading to an erosion of the livelihoods of a nine-billion-strong civilization. This is a fundamental change. In this century humanity can bring about an Earth-system change with irreversible consequences. And so we live today, as is increasingly apparent, in the age of the Anthropocene (Crutzen and Stoermer 2000; Messner 2012; Zalasiewicz, Williams, and Waters 2014). This increases the need for global cooperation. Because humans are now able to fundamentally change the Earth system, rules, norms, guidelines, and values need to be developed so that the social and economic activities of people, states, and economies do not jeopardize the stability of the planet (WBGU 2011). The tough climate negotiations symbolize how difficult it is to protect the global commons and to transition to a global economy that is compatible with the planetary boundaries (Keohane 2015).

These fundamental changes are taking place in the context of far-reaching power shifts in the international community. After 250 years of Western dominance in the international system, it seems a new power constellation is emerging (Bremmer 2012; Kaplinsky and Messner 2008; Kupchan, Davidson, and Sucharov 2001). While global structures of interdependence intensify and humanity learns to keep global systemic risk under control, the power vectors in world politics are fundamentally shifting. The 'old' and 'new' powers are far from a common vision of world order (Bremmer 2012; Hale, Held, and Young 2013; Messner 2015a). The rise of new powers could improve the likelihood of a more inclusive world order, and yet historically phases of tectonic power shifts were often times initially characterized as conflicts between rising and declining nations (Kennedy 1987).

The fact remains that accelerated globalization, global systemic risks, and global interdependencies between states, societies, and economies do not automatically lead to more political coordination between global actors and the emergence of common interests, nor to problem-solving-oriented patterns of international cooperation. Although the amount of international cooperation in terms of the intensity of transnational interactions and the number of international institutions exceeds everything that has come before, the quality of that cooperation is insufficient. Against the background of interaction of close to 200 countries, countless private actors and the dominance of national interests against global ones, an effective global governance system has yet to emerge. It would seem as though Hardin's (1968) 'tragedy of the commons', which described the systemic overexploitation of local public goods, might be taking place at the global level. Global cooperation, understood as collective action to achieve common goals to address global problems, is a scarce and fragile commodity at the beginning of the 21st century. Instead of global order, instead of establishing global guiding principles to stabilize the global commons, instead of strengthening multilateral institutions and a global balance of interests, existing patterns of order appear to be dissolving.

Theories of International Relations: Cooperation skepticism everywhere

Neorealist writers such as Mearsheimer feel vindicated by the global political trends described here. He interprets global politics as a power game between major states, predicted the tectonic power shifts towards Asia back in 2001 and reiterates today that a 'peaceful rise of China is impossible' (Mearsheimer 2014). From this perspective, international or even global cooperation based on emerging mutual interests, converging worldviews, and fairness-based compensation mechanisms that make it possible to address global interdependence problems can hardly be expected (Mearsheimer 2011; Morgenthau 1960; Waltz 1959). National interests in the anarchic world order, as well as the pursuit of power, dictate the actions of states. Without an external authority that helps humans overcome their differences, attempts at cooperation are futile. While such an authority exists in the form of a government within nation states, it is absent at the international level. Therefore the question is less under which conditions cooperation can succeed, but rather how anything beyond the most short-lived and instrumental kind of cooperation can ever occur. Based on such assumptions, the degree of global cooperation that can be observed is already more than could be expected – any hopes for a deeper and broader cooperation to tackle common world problems and strengthen the rule-based world order seem rather naive. (Neo)realism arguably remains the dominant frame of reference for many policy-makers and the media when it comes to making sense of world politics.

However, skepticism towards cooperation is also spreading widely among those more closely associated with the global governance school. In 2013 Held, one of the pioneers of a cosmopolitan order, together with Hale and Young published a comprehensive study about 'why global cooperation is failing when we need it most' (Hale, Held, and Young 2013). He and his co-authors lament that the rise of new powers makes agreement more difficult. They argue that it is not yet clear whether countries like China or India will join the existing world order, reshape the rules and institutions in accordance with their own interests, or challenge it. In addition, the complexity of the problems that need to be addressed, ranging from climate change to issues of peace and security or the stability of the financial system, renders global cooperation more intricate. Existing institutions, relics of a period of Western dominance, might fail to deliver (a similar argument was made by Keohane and Victor in 2011 with respect to climate policy). Charles Kupchan (2012), who put forward observations for a 'peaceful power transition' at the beginning of the new century (Kupchan et al. 2001), wrote in a recent book about 'the no one's world', similar to Ian Bremmer's (2012) description of the new world order as 'the G-0 world', who has reached the conclusion that the worst case of a dark era of ideological confrontation and geopolitical rivalries is imminent, one in which each state only looks after itself, thus neglecting the global common good even further.

Dirk Messner, who has highlighted the scope for global governance in different studies (Kennedy, Messner, and Nuscheler 2002; Kumar and Messner 2010), also describes in a recent study a historical constellation in which concepts of world order that are not or hardly compatible collide: (a) ideas of a fair and inclusive global governance architecture that builds on shared sovereignty, the development of common interests and a global balancing of interests; (b) a neo-imperialist world order, which is focused on the classical power game approach à la Putin; (c) the worldviews of many rising powers (e.g. Brazil, China, India) – and also of many followers in the US – that are heavily based on traditional ideas of national sovereignty and a self-centered foreign policy; (d) jihadism, which seeks the destruction of others and which is developing into an internationally networked political force (Messner 2015a).

This ongoing debate in International Relations will not be further explored in the present volume. It serves only as a starting point for the subsequent argument. The fact remains that in the current debate concerning numerous upheavals in world politics, various International Relations theories establish and analyze a comprehensive failure to cooperate and a dramatic collapse of order. Starting points for a cooperation-based form of globalization, which were still front and center in global governance research in the 1990s and during the first decade of the 21st century, can hardly be found in the literature any more (for exceptions, see Ostrom 2009; Scholte 2014; WBGU 2014). The narrowing of perspective on current cooperation crises are undermining clear creative potentials to find ways out of the dilemma of increasing global interdependence with a simultaneous paralysis of global cooperation.

Radical change of perspective: Cooperation as an engine of (the history of) human civilization

In light of this background, we would like to put forward a radical change of perspective in this volume. The focus is on cooperation theories and analysis from various disciplines beyond political science that – contrary to the pessimism towards cooperation that now permeates a broad range of International Relations' approaches – present new insights into the ability of humans to cooperate, as well as the basic dynamics of human civilization. As such they appear to come from another world altogether.

In contrast to the cooperation crises that at present are at the center of attention, Nowak and Highfield (2011) published a volume titled *Super Cooperators. Evolution, Altruism and Why We Need Each Other to Succeed.* In the same vein, Tomasello (2014a) published an article with the paradigm-changing title 'The Ultra-Social Animal' – meaning humans beings. Are we talking about the same species (human beings) and the same planet?

Let us first pay heed to the three wake-up calls from the 'world of cooperation', which do not quite seem to fit into the present global political crisis scenarios and skepticism towards cooperation.

Mathematician and evolutionary biologist Martin Nowak (2006a: 1563) states: 'Perhaps the most remarkable aspect of evolution is its ability to generate cooperation in a competitive world. Thus, we might add "natural cooperation" as a third fundamental principle of evolution beside mutation and natural selection'. Nowak and Highfield (2011: XVIII) argue that '[c]ooperation is the master architect of evolution'.

Michael Tomasello (2014a: 193), director of the Max Planck Institute for Evolutionary Anthropology, sums up his work on the evolution of human thinking and the pro-social behavior engrained in it as follows:

> Human individuals became interdependent with one another in ways that changed not only their social behaviour but also their cognitive processes. . . . Interdependence of the human variety led humans to put their heads together in acts of shared intentionality in which they acted on and understood the world together as a kind of plural subject. Individuals came to feel commitments and obligations towards one another as they worked together. They divided the spoils of their collaborative efforts fairly and justly because they cared about one another, because they wanted to be perceived

as cooperative, and because they were judging themselves in the same way that they were judging others. And all this became even more intense as individuals came to identify with their cultural group in an even larger social context of interdependent collaboration.

Harvard professor for Entrepreneurial Legal Studies, Yochai Benkler (2011: 20, 16), who also draws from evolutionary and cultural studies, asks:

> How do we explain our innate sense of empathy, fairness, or doing the right thing? One answer is that, far from being robots or selfish brutes, we are moral creatures, with moral codes that surpass and triumph over rational calculation and self-interest. . . . human self-interest is only partially true. . . . I believe we are ready to break the selfishness myth and embrace human cooperation as the powerful and potentially positive force that it is.

In disciplines such as neuroscience, cognitive psychology, evolutionary anthropology, and evolutionary biology, new knowledge on the fundamentals of human behavior and the dynamics of human civilization are emerging. At the heart of this knowledge is 'cooperation', i.e. collective action to achieve common goals (see also Bowles and Gintis 2011; Singer and Ricard 2015; Wilson 2012). Cooperation, as it is seen in these strands of research, comes about not only as a result of complementary or easily reconciled individual interests, but rather is an original mode of action that people often resort to, even in social dilemma situations. The basic assumption of the conventional theory of human behavior (that individuals always maximize their short-term, tangible returns, making their decisions independent of others) is hardly tenable from an empirical perspective. Even in one-shot experiments, actors do not behave according to rational choice theories – they often cooperate (Poteete, Janssen, and Ostrom 2010: 215ff.; see also Rand and Nowak, this volume). Alongside self-interest in the strict sense, other preferences and norms also need to be taken into account to explain the behavior of humans and their fundamental ability to cooperate.

'Cooperation' – a good or commodity that is especially scarce and fragile in today's international system and which can only be enforced in the interaction of states through power, hegemony, and dominance, according to many International Relations analysts – would appear to be a central element of human behavior, human societies, and even the history of human civilization. How does this fit together with the pessimistic attitude towards cooperation outlined?

We suggest that scholars of global governance should turn towards the new state of knowledge on the ability of humans to cooperate. Given the enormous cooperation deficit to cope with the dynamics of globalization, global governance scholars should no longer refer solely to political science and economics, but rather ask all disciplines what they can tell us about the ability of humans to cooperate: cooperation in small groups, in local, national, or global negotiation processes, in small or complex organizations, in nations, in transnational networks, in the soon-to-be nine-billion-strong world society, or in the history of human civilization.

Political science and economics research into global governance is currently focused on the here and now, and thus struggles to free itself from the globalization crises outlined previously as from their bleak diagnoses. This 'dictate' of living for the present could, however, lead to false conclusions and distorted perceptions because current dynamics are overvalued, generalized, and hastily projected onto the future. Are the present diagnoses on why global cooperation is failing altering our view on possible failures to cooperate in the future in a globally networked world?

So far the new knowledge on human nature and the complexity of our behavior and motivations has barely reached the world of international politics. The disciplinary boundaries are rarely crossed and the strands of research mostly exist in isolation. On the one hand, researchers who do not deal with global cooperation but who develop new insights into the ability of humans to cooperate only hesitantly engage in thinking about what their discoveries might mean for world politics. While they might reflect on the societal consequences of their findings, they have rarely engaged, until now, in a conversation with those interested in the global level (for exceptions, see Nowak and Coakley 2013; Nowak and Highfield 2011; see also Barrett 2007; Johnson and Levin 2009; Stern 2011; Weber and Johnson 2012). International Relations scholars, on the other hand, mostly ignore the potentially revolutionary findings on human nature and the conditions under which cooperation succeeds.

The importance of the change of perspective that we suggest should not be underestimated; how we frame situations can have real consequences for how we behave (Weber and Johnson 2012). The basic assumptions of the impossibility of cooperation in a time of global power shifts in the 'G-0 world' can become self-fulfilling prophecies if they are internalized as the guiding principle of actions. This is in essence one of the key criticisms that constructivist approaches have developed to demonstrate the limits of (neo)realist thinking (Wendt 1992). In the same way, a perspective that looks at the challenges of international cooperation from the starting principle that people, organizations, and nations can and do cooperate could improve the chances for global cooperation. Moreover, scientific creativity and social fantasy are necessary to chart the spaces of future cooperation. This creativity will probably not emerge from approaches that reduce human societies to utilities, pay-offs, optimal strategies, self-interest, and national interests. The limits of our language, as Wittgenstein argued, are the limits of our worlds (Cooperider, Fry, and Piderit 2007: 420).

We want to take up Wittgenstein's suggestion to expand our horizons and to illuminate the possibilities and conditions of cooperation by introducing perspectives other than those already known to us. This volume brings together authors from various disciplines and makes an attempt at connecting the cooperation dots. We want to collect essential insights on the ability of humans to cooperate from disciplines that are traditionally unaware of each other and to learn from them. The authors in this volume do not present a one-size-fits-all solution to the problems of global cooperation. But the interdisciplinary and multidisciplinary interactions and pursuits that we propose should provoke and lead to new perspectives and questions, and could ultimately contribute to developing theories of global governance. This book is a start in this direction.

We do not want to suggest that we are completely alone in this undertaking. Recently, Shiping Tang (2013) made an interesting contribution by conceptualizing international politics as a system that evolves and has known phases of relatively benign relations, offensive realism, defensive realism, and finally a more institutionally rule-based international system. However, we do believe that our contribution, with its focus on the ability of humans to cooperate, the role of cooperation in the history of human civilization, and global cooperation, is so far quite unique. Previous approaches that selectively addressed the human factor in International Relations can be outlined as follows.

Some scholars working in the realist tradition have indeed looked at findings from evolutionary biology. However, they mostly did so with regard to more traditional interpretations of Darwin, focusing on ideas about natural selection and the 'survival of the fittest', but did not consider novel findings on cooperation (for a critical overview see Bell 2006; Lebow 2013). In general it is probably fair to say that there is considerable unease among political scientists and International Relations scholars with regard to evolutionary and biological explanations. Biological approaches are often associated with privileging individual actions and responsibilities to the detriment of social situations and structures (Sokolowska and Guzzini 2014). Yet there are also a few authors, such as Brown (2013), who argue that the novel findings in evolutionary sciences are too important to be ignored and left to realists alone.

Political psychology approaches that investigate the impact of cognition and emotion on choice and decision making have long been part of International Relations (Gross Stein 2013). More recently the understanding of the relationship between emotion, cognition, and decision has been revolutionized by new findings in neuroscience. This has brought about interesting work on the role of emotions in world politics, often with a particular focus on security issues (for an overview, see the recently published special issue on emotions in world politics, Bleiker and Hutchison 2014). In particular there is a growing body of literature investigating the role of trust in international politics (for a good overview see Ruzicka and Keating 2015).

In political science in general a broader debate on what some call biopolitics some call biopolitics has begun and deals with research at the intersection of political science, psychology, biology, and cognitive neuroscience. In particular the volume edited by Hatemi and Mcdermott (2011) spurred a lively debate in the US (see Isaac 2013). Looking for biological explanations for human behavior that range from evolutionary adaptation to hormonal levels and the genetic transmission of traits, the volume explored how political scientists can utilize biological knowledge and methods to study topics such as civic engagement, corruption, aggression, or political preference formation. Like us, some authors take the special ability of humans to cooperate as their starting point, yet they do not draw any conclusions for cooperation on a global scale, choosing instead to explore national political participation (see Fowler et al. 2011). Closely related to this work is the attempt to develop explanations for international politics and foreign decision-making processes by means of experimental methods (Hafner-Burton, Hughes, and Victor 2013; Hafner-Burton et al. 2014; Mcdermott 2011). Our pursuit in this work distinguishes itself to the extent that we take a broad and radically interdisciplinary approach, one which puts the conditions, possibilities, and limitations of global cooperation front and center.

Behavioral approaches and evolutionary theories of human behavior: Lessons learnt so far?

We present here three outcomes and linked research perspectives that ensue from the interdisciplinary, border-crossing undertaking of this book. They seem to us particularly important for a global cooperation research that fully takes into account the knowledge on the ability of humans to cooperate.

The micro-perspective: The ability of humans to cooperate

Humans are driven by self-interest, yes – but this is only part of the truth. Conventional rational choice theory is based on a simplified model of human behavior, one which reduces human calculations to costs, benefits, pay-offs, and immediate self-interest. This poorly differentiated model is coupled with heroic assumptions about the availability of information and the information processing capacity of humans, in which every situation individuals possess comprehensive information about the respective problems, preferences of other actors, all possible courses of action, and conceivable feedback dynamics that arise from the combination of these factors. From this point of view humans are able to make 'rational decisions'.

In reality humans rely on heuristics and experience, or turn to established practices because they usually do not have full information (Batson 2015; Fehr 2015; Kahneman 2011; Kandell 2012; Ostrom 2003; Simon 1957). They are also influenced by emotions; pure rational calculation does not exist (Lebow 2005). In addition, human are primarily social beings who have diverse cooperative abilities: they can develop shared or even collective intentionalities to create common social systems (Tomasello 2008, 2009, 2014a, 2014b). Humans are even able to be altruistic, understood as a form of cooperation that does not require anything in return (Nowak and Coakley 2013: 4, 5; Leggewie in this volume). Humans also cooperate far more frequently than rational choice theorists would assume (Ostrom and Walker 2003; Rand and Nowak in this volume). Forty to sixty percent of individuals even cooperate in public goods games, in which free riding would be the most prudent strategy from the perspective of conventional rational choice theory. 'Defection [is] by no means the overall default evolutionary pattern . . .; in many circumstances the opposite seems to be the case, against all reason' (Nowak and Coakley 2013: 10). None of this fits in with conventional behavioral theories, which model 'cooperation' and even 'altruism' after game-theory cost-benefit analyses and merely as investments that ultimately have to 'pay off', and which categorize 'true altruism' as an 'evolutionary mistake' (Alexander 1987: 82). The oft-cited *homo economicus*, driven only by his own interest, is only a caricature of real humans – or, as Elke Weber and Eric Johnson formulate in their contribution to this book, 'at best a convenient fiction'.

Such a cooperative behavior could be intuitive and build on the awareness, developed over the course of evolution, that we are dependent on others (when we are young, old, or sick) and others on us (when we look after the youth, the old, or the sick) throughout our lives. Humans have to rely on each other to a considerable extent in order to survive, making cooperation a central survival strategy for *homo sapiens* (de Waal 2009: 36). Based on David Premack's 'theory of mind' (Premack and Woodruff 1978), Marc D. Hauser (2013) argues that this structural dependency of humans on other humans in the evolutionary process led to the ability to identify the senses, feelings, and perceptions of other individuals and to take them into account when formulating own strategies. In this process basic patterns of moral intuitions, or moral principles, could have emerged, which Hauser relates to the basic principles of Rawls (1971), who developed this with the help of his 'veil of ignorance' concept. Basic components of a 'cooperative matrix', an intuitive 'moral grammar', could therefore emerge from these very basic dynamics of human evolution. The ultimate foundation, the basis, the evolutionary starting point of the ability of humans to cooperate would therefore not be 'reason' (as per Kant), emotions (as per Hume), or rational means-goal calculations (as per Bentham; Nowak and Coakley 2013: 17), but rather a 'set of (basic) principles for navigating within the moral domain' based on human actions that reflect the dependency that humans have had on other humans since the beginning of human existence (Hauser 2013: 263).

Homo economicus *exists – and is a great ape*

It is interesting how Tomasello (2014a: 193) differentiates complex interaction patterns of human behavior from apes' behavior: 'Whereas other great apes engage in complex social interactions and cognitive processes, in the end, it is all a kind of instrumental rationality aimed at the individual's personal gain'. In other words: *homo economicus* exists. But unlike what rational choice theorists assume, *homo economicus* belongs to the species of our closest relative: the great ape. Following Tomasello, evolution has led humans past the stage of development of creatures that are only capable of interacting with others out of self-interest or based on purely instrumental rationality. In their contributions in this volume, Alicia Melis, Claus Leggewie, and Elke Weber and Eric Johnson identify more complex action and decision-making patterns that shape human behavior. Humans clearly orient themselves towards given standards and adapt to changing contexts with different norms and preference systems. They are interested in their own interests, but they continuously place these in relation to group interests and the preferences of other actors. Humans can learn cooperation in different contexts. These contexts, which are specific but which can also be changed by humans, therefore play a major role in the norms and value systems that serve as an orientation for individuals and groups.

If one follows these insights into the cooperative skills of individuals, one finds strong evidence that people cooperate more frequently than suspected on the basis of assumptions that humans only look after their direct interests and gains. They do so as diplomats in complex organizations, in international negotiation processes, and also in transnational networks. But people do not – obviously – always cooperate, which raises the important question of under what conditions do humans cooperate and which basic mechanisms favor cooperation. Can we identify factors or contexts that make cooperation more likely to succeed? These questions are discussed and answered in the contributions by Messner, Guarín and Haun, and Rand and Nowak in this volume. The two teams of authors identify similar basic mechanisms of cooperation that are of importance to cooperation in small groups as well as in complex social systems. If one follows the argumentation of Messner et al. and Rand and Nowak, very profound prognoses can be made. Cooperation is likely to fail if the actors do not know each other very well and cannot assess their reputations, if the communication patterns between them are 'thin', if trust and reciprocity are weak, if there are no mechanisms for jointly monitoring agreed-upon rules, and if the actors have not yet been able to develop a common perspective or worldview. As we will see later, this also applies in the context of the G20. The success conditions for cooperation are known to a great extent and they can be influenced, which means we can also think about strategies needed to develop or strengthen them.

From the micro-perspective findings outlined above, our perspective allows us to deduce two sets of research questions that are of particular interest to global governance research. The first set of questions focus on the manner in which international cooperation is conducted today. The emergence of the international community was accompanied by the invention of diplomacy, which established itself as a complex institution with norms, rules, and procedures. Each state has foreign ministers and diplomatic services whose mission is to defend and enforce national interests through peaceful means (see also Neumann in this volume). But are these practices, which date from the conference diplomacy of the 19th century, still relevant today? What would a diplomacy that strengthens the identified basic mechanisms of cooperation look like? What knowledge, skills, and forms of interaction would diplomats need to learn in their training in order to be best prepared to create the conditions that would make it possible to address the protection of a global commons?

The second set of questions deal with the organization of international cooperation. Proponents of the institutionalist school of International Relations assume that international organizations and regimes can help states to cooperate, even under conditions of uncertainty. They reduce transaction costs, provide information, enable repeated interactions that in turn establish reputations, make collective action more efficient, and even engage in enforcement (Abbott and Snidal 1998). Nevertheless, it can be observed that many formal international organizations, and in particular those with universal membership, face obstacles in many areas. Despite regular meetings, supportive secretariats, and strong net-works of interaction between states, social-dilemma situations such as climate change still are not being dealt with in the most constructive manner. Even international problems, in which the dilemma structure is less pronounced (for instance negotiations over multilateral development cooperation or peacekeep-ing), are often overlaid with North-South dynamics that render a problem ori-entation and a balancing of interests more difficult (Weinlich 2014a, 2014b). How can the basic mechanisms of cooperation and insights from cognitive sci-ence be embedded in the design of situations of international negotiations or, going one step further, in the design of international organizations so that they become mutually reinforcing and both encourage and sustain cooperation? What other initiatives, modes, and forms of cooperation could strengthen the basic mechanisms of cooperation in the international system at the beginning of the 21st century? In this volume Siddharth Mallavarapu explores these questions and looks at the implications of cognitive sciences for the design of international institutions that could foster global cooperation.

The macro-perspective: Does cooperation fail in complex systems?

There is a standard argument against any attempts to make use of knowledge on the human cooperative abilities from evolutionary biology, cognitive psychology, or evolutionary anthropology for international politics: these disciplines explore and make statements on individuals and small groups of people. This cannot be applied directly to complex networks and societies, not to mention the inter-actions within the international system. Although it is increasingly acknowl-edged that people in small groups or in laboratory experiments behave in a more cooperative manner than a rational-choice perspective would suggest, it would still be difficult to imagine that this trend could hold for large-scale cooperation. At the heart of this scale problem is that cooperation processes in small groups, local communities, complex organizations, and international system are subject to different dynamics due to their respective structures (Miller and Page 2007; Page 2007; Young 1998). And we agree on that: the before-mentioned, probably universal basic mechanisms of cooperation, e.g. trust, reciprocity, and reputation, obviously have to be 'produced' differently for small group as compared to coop-eration mechanisms for complex organizations.

In addition, the argument that cooperation in small groups is easier to organize and emerges more easily than in larger communities and societies is intuitively convincing (Arrow's famous 'impossibility theorem' precisely refers to this, see Stewart 2000; as well as Kurths, Heitzig, and Marwan in this volume). But the disciplines currently under discussion, such as evolutionary biology and social anthropology, provide an astonishing answer to questions on whether cooperation is impeded by complexity, i.e. whether it is less probable in complex social systems, and whether there is a corresponding natural tension between complexity and cooperation. According to them cooperation does not always become more difficult or less probable with increasing complexity; in fact, the link between cooperation and complexity is quite the opposite. Cooperation is first and foremost the driver, the engine, the evolutionary principle that actually causes complexity to increase (see also Kurth et al. in this volume). For human society, this means that the development of the ability of humans to cooperate is the foundation and starting point for the emergence of increasingly complex groups, communities, and societies. This does not mean that cooperation must *a priori* always succeed or, when it has emerged must then exist forever; cooperation can fail, erode, and collapse. But successful cooperation is a necessary condition for the emergence of increasingly complex structures, and the path from early humans to modern societies is based on cooperation dynamics.

Evolutionary biologists Maynard Smith and Szathmáry (1995: 6) described eight key transitions in the process of evolution and the development of increasing complexity among living creatures. All transitions to higher forms of complexity were marked by two characteristics. First, at each transition, new forms of cooperation with mutual dependencies developed. 'Entities that were capable of independent replication before the transition can replicate only as part of a larger whole after it'. Second, these new forms of cooperation were made possible through new communication patterns, interaction, and exchange: in other words, through 'a change in the method of information transmission'. It is cooperation that enabled the interplay between previously independent units, i.e. the emergence of complex structures, in the first place.

Nowak and Highfield (2011: 15) share this point of view: 'Cooperation is the architect of living complexity'. Nowak argues that since Darwin we have known that reproduction in evolution never proceeds perfectly; mutations produce variation, thus ensuring diversity and variety. This is the first mechanism of evolution. The second mechanism of evolution is selection. Organisms, types, and species disappear and emerge. Darwin showed that this mechanism, combined with the ability to adapt, was related to changing environments and less with what Herbert Spencer later emphasized falsely as 'survival of the fittest' (Spencer 1864) – survival of the strongest, the most powerful and ruthless. The third principle of evolution, according to Martin Nowak (2006a), is cooperation because it actually creates and enables complex forms of organization:

> whenever life discovers a new level of organization (such as the emergence of cells, multicellular organisms, insect societies, or human language), cooperation is involved in one form or another. Mutation and selection alone, without cooperation, may not give rise to complexity.
>
> (Nowak and Coakley 2013: 9)

Evolution is also characterized by the collapse of complex organizations when cooperation fails or erodes. The long history of evolution is, however, a history of increasing complexity based on 'natural cooperation' (Nowak and Highfield 2011: 281). Competition and cooperation are closely related: in human societies, for instance, competition or even conflict between groups generates incentives to cooperate within groups. Groups of cooperating members enjoy advantages vis-à-vis groups functioning at a lower level of cooperation. Groups characterized by cooperation grow, shape their environment, and become drivers of change processes. Cooperation is a success strategy in evolution (especially in humans). A complex picture of the interaction between self-interests and cooperation emerges. For individuals it is one option to try to dominate within a group through their own self-interest for a certain period of time and to assert their interests against the more cooperation-oriented actors. But the group level presents a different picture: cooperation-based groups and cooperation-based networks of groups are superior to groups that are predominantly dominated by actors driven by their self-interest (Nowak and Highfield 2011: 87ff., 270–1; see also de Waal 2009; Nowak and Sigmund 1998, 2005; Traulsen and Nowak 2006). Charles Darwin already recognized this connection. In *The Descent of Man*, published in 1871, he noted:

> There can be no doubt that a tribe including many members who . . . were always ready to give aid to each other and to sacrifice themselves for the common good, would be victorious over most other tribes; and this would be natural selection.
>
> (quoted after Nowak and Highfield 2011: 83)

Joint intentionalities change the course of human history

Tomasello's work (2003, 2008, 2014a, 2014b) also indicates that the ability of humans to cooperate, which developed in the course of evolution, is the basis for the emergence of complex social structures. These in turn gave rise to communities, societies, and then increasingly differentiated cultures over a long period of time. Again, cooperation is the decisive mechanism that allows for complexity. In his evolutionary account of how humans became 'ultra-cooperative', Tomasello (2014a, 2014b) discerns two phases in which the human cooperative abilities developed. In the first phase, early humans began at some point, most likely as a result of changes in the ecological conditions and food shortages, to develop joint intentionalities and to coordinate actions and attentions towards joint goals, namely to hunt large game. Exactly when those first loosely knit human groups developed is still not precisely known, but Tomasello argues that this process began around 400,000 years ago (Tomasello 2014b: 36).

The historic new challenge for early humans in this phase of the development of human behavior and human thought was to negotiate a joint goal and to define roles and the division of labor. Cooperation-oriented communication was needed to this end. Cooperation became a successful adaptation strategy for changing habitats and for a forager niche that early humans could occupy. The significant cognitive challenge for humans as the first loosely knit communities first emerged was, alongside their own perspective, to perceive, consider, and then coordinate the perspective of the cooperation partner with their own. The former fundamentally self-referential human being (who knew and pursued his or her own self-interest, as great apes did and do) learned to see the world not only from his or her perspective but also from the perspective of others (Premack and Wood-ruff 1978). The ability of 'cognitive perspective taking' (Singer and Ricard 2015: 43) that resulted, i.e. perception of the thoughts, perceptions, emotions, and strategies of others set in motion a turning point in human history. This transition from the single to the multiple perspective changed everything. Humans successively learned to supplement the 'I-mode' of perception, thinking, deciding, and acting with the 'we-mode'. As Melis shows in this volume, this already expresses itself in infants at a very early age.

After human ancestors had existed for almost five million years with thinking patterns very similar to that of apes, a previously unknown door opened through the transition to multiple perspectives. It enabled the cultural development of humans into social beings who were able to learn and create together. A process of cumulative cultural evolution had begun, one that has led from early humans to the humans of the 21st century. Tomasello, Kruger, and Ratner (1993) call the mechanism that enabled this process the 'cultural ratchet effect'. Humans started to learn from and with each other to create simple and then increasingly more complex artifacts, to create common cultural practices, to develop them further and to transmit these, triggering a cumulative cultural evolution. This transforma-tion enabled learning and change processes in how humans think and act (as individuals and as groups) that operated on a significantly faster time scale than the processes of organic evolution (Tomasello 2006: 15). The incredible changes in the development of humans that have occurred since then (i.e. over the past 400,000 years) are based – viewed from a historical point of view – on a long cultural learning process. From an evolutionary perspective this period, in which humans set themselves apart from apes and created a unique, global civilization while their nearest relatives have hardly changed since then, is an excitingly brief period of time.

The simultaneity of jointness and individuality, as outlined previously, based on cooperation-oriented communication, led in this phase of human history to the formation of what Tomasello, called 'joint intentionality' (Tomasello 2014b: 32), in line with modern theories of action (Bratman 1992; Gilbert 1992; Searle 1995; Tuomela 2007). 'Intentionality' is understood by Searle (1987) to be the thinking and mental states of humans that relate to situations in the world. Humans are concerned in their thinking with their environment and/or the world. Shared perspectives and developed joint intentionalities mean that humans ('speakers') enter into an exchange with one another, take into account the think-ing and mental states of others, relate them to each other, and in doing so take the step from having a single perspective to being able to take multiple perspec-tives. 'Skills and motivations for shared intentionality thus changed not just the way that humans think about others but also the way they conceptualize and think about the entire world, and their own place in it, in collaboration with others' (Tomasello 2014b: 143–4). Humans begin to form loosely knit groups and com-munities in which they are mutually dependent on another. The ability to share perspectives and develop joint intentionalities, to cooperate, therefore occurs at the very beginning of the development of human cultures and human civilization. This transition to multiple perspectives and the ability to understand the other's point of view and to coordinate activities on jointly agreed goals thus constitutes a first civilizational impetus in the history of humankind. 'Cooperation', mutual activities between humans forming a group, stands at the beginning of the development of human societies and human thinking, because the skills and motivations that were based on joint intentionalities create the opportunity for humans to imagine almost anything that they can communicate with others about almost everything. The cultural ratchet effect is based on this unique ability to undertake 'mental time travel' (Tomasello 2014b: 126).

It is interesting that the reconstruction of the history of human thought and the foundations of human cooperation skills as described by Tomasello is supported by research on the correlation between brain size (which likely reflects cognitive complexity) and population size (Dunbar 1998). Modern humans are an extreme case: their population sizes and brains are many times greater than that of those of their closest relatives, the apes. Gowlett, Gamble, and Dunbar (2012) find a particular leap in human brain size (calculated by the volume of the skull), as well as the size of the group, calculated around 400,000 years ago among *Homo heidelbergensis*. That this coincides with the emergence of joint intentionalities described by Tomasello makes sense, as a larger brain uses a considerable amount of energy. This growing demand for energy may have been the trigger for the common hunting of larger animals that followed, and their success allowed the larger brain to stabilize based on growing group sizes.

Collective intentionalities and wider cooperation based
on competition and conflict between groups

The second phase of the development of human civilization, which occurred around 200,000 years ago, i.e. with the emergence of *Homo sapiens*, was initiated by two pivotal factors (Tomasello 2014b: 82–3). The first factor was that competition and conflict with other groups (the ingroup/outgroup logic) motivated and forced cooperation within the individual groups. We-identities, collective identities, emerged. Tomasello and Nowak are in complete agreement on this point. The *individual's view* of the world (individual intentionality) and the understanding of the *other group members' view* of the world (joint intentionality), which enabled the first achievements in interpersonal coordination and cooperation, were now complemented by an evolving *common, collective worldview* of a community (collective intentionality) that represented the basis for wider cooperation in groups. The group develops its own culture with its own identity.

The second factor is growing group size. The more successfully the group behaves as a result of functioning cooperation and based on collective intentionalities, the larger it becomes. The loosely knit groups of early humans were small communities that had to build joint intentionalities in direct interaction. The scale is now gradually extending to increasingly more complex communities and larger groups. The growing groups differentiate themselves, and humans become cultural beings in that they develop common perspectives on things and values based on collective identities. In larger groups and successively emerging communities and then societies, commonalities between a small number of people, which constituted early human groups, no longer suffice. Collective intentionalities lead to the emergence of cultural conventions, practices, norms, institutions, and social infrastructures that shape the identity of growing communities, create a sense of belonging and make co-existence in growing communities possible in the first place. The group identity is socially and spatially extended even to strangers, so long as they belong to the same group, but also temporally so as to include the group's ancestors and descendants. Long-lasting cultures (with a past, present, and future) emerge.

In summary: cooperation-oriented communication first led to the emergence of joint, interpersonal intentionalities. Early humans learn, alongside their own view of reality, to recognize and understand the perspectives of other individuals and to coordinate the accomplishment of jointly defined goals. They begin to organize themselves in loosely knit groups, and the first problem-solving communities in human history emerge. This evolutionary breakthrough enables the successive emergence of collective intentionalities, which develop in interaction and competition with other groups. Common perceptions, practices, norms, rules, and institutions, i.e. overall culture, emerge. They are the nuclei of evolving and increasingly complex societies. Modern humans 'expand' the first interpersonal model of the interaction between commonality and individuality (joint intentionalities) to more complex forms of living together (collective intentionalities). Cooperation, for Nowak as well as for Tomasello, is the starting point and basic mechanism of the history of human civilization and the development of increasingly complex social structures. 'Human culture is early human cooperation writ large' (Tomasello 2014b: 82).

From the macro-perspective findings outlined previously we can deduce two sets of questions that are of particular interest to global governance research. Empirical findings suggest that humans are particularly good at cooperating if they do so within a group they can identify with. Experimental studies also show that humans form these kinds of group identities very easily and even on the basis of haphazard criteria. Cooperating against outsiders also supports and intensifies cooperation. This hundreds-of-millennia-old ingroup/outgroup mechanism, which first enabled the emergence of human civilization, at the same time contains within itself uncertain outcomes. It creates and strengthens cooperative behavior in groups and is an engine for competition, a diversity of ideas, and thus innovation. And yet ingroup/outgroup dynamics can also lead to exclusion, racism, nationalism, war, and destruction. Less drastic but equally problematic, ingroup vs. outgroup cooperation can lead, for instance, to a hardening of attitudes between groups, as can be seen in the climate talks with 'developing' and 'industrialized' countries. To what extent do group membership and identities offer possible ways out of the logjams in global cooperation, clearly being an essential feature of humanity, against the background of which cooperation in groups and conflict between groups come into existence?

First, more research could be dedicated to the question of to what extent global we-identities could serve as a social glue that make cooperation within the global society more successful. Is the formation of 'global we-identities' possible, and how could it come about? Based on empirical studies, Grimalda's chapter in this volume expresses optimism on this point. Could such we-identities become the basis of a global culture of cooperation? Can they help provide a rule-based and peaceful foundation for the dynamics that spur cooperation within groups on the basis of competition, tensions or even violent conflict with other groups? Could global we-identities help complement the logic of national interests through a logic of common, global interests? How thick or thin could such global we-identities be for expanding areas of global cooperation (Walzer 1994)?

Second, overlapping identities should be taken into consideration (Dunbar 1998). Humans usually belong not only to one but also to many groups. In an age of globalization, this also applies across borders. Interlaced and overlapping identities and their significance for cooperation between groups in and between countries must be better understood. Humans are embedded in diverse social interrelations and have diverse, interconnected identities as citizens of a country, fans of a soccer club, members of parties or civil society groups, participants in global research networks, diplomats acting on behalf of their governments, and so on. The understanding of how these complex identity patterns affect human behavior, cooperation, and conflict is limited (see Leggewie in this volume). In this context, the impact of modern information and communication technologies and virtual realities on ingroup/outgroup dynamics should be examined more closely. Can interpersonal, potentially global network formations, made possible by information and communication technologies, be used to increase the likelihood of cooperation between people, groups, cultures, and nations?

Cooperation: To what end?

It is not just that humans are capable of cooperating; more importantly the ability to cooperate itself is a prerequisite for the emergence of complex societies. Without cooperation there is no culture, no science, no legal system, no social orders, and also no solutions to the many problems that individual people, groups, and states cannot cope with on their own. And yet 'cooperation' is not *a priori* 'good' or 'conflict-free' (Benkler 2011: 57; Dixon 2013; Messner 1997; Tomasello 2009). Humans also cooperate in groups to win conflicts or even wars against other groups: the Islamic State is a community of cooperation; mafias and gangs consist of members who cooperate. The objectives of cooperation must therefore be assessed normatively. One can cooperate for 'noble' or 'base' reasons. Lothar Brock makes reference to this in this volume when he rightly warns: 'we (should) not replace the Hobbesian *homo homini lupus* with a Rousseau-like slogan of *homo homini angelus*'.

Cooperation is therefore a necessary but insufficient condition for 'good solutions' for addressing common problems and social dilemmas. Whether the joint objectives of respective cooperation alliances that address global systemic risks and the way to achieve these objectives are 'fair', 'just', 'adequate', or 'legitimate' goes far beyond the question of whether and under what conditions global cooperation arises. The objectives and results of cooperation must therefore be assessed normatively. One option for this is to undertake an assessment on the basis of 'collective values', which in turn can only come about through cooperation-oriented communication – this is true within societies and in the emerging global society alike. When asked about normative standards, scholars of evolutionary biology and neuroscience, who contribute a great deal to understanding the foundations of human cooperation, reach their disciplinary limits. In order to provide answers as to what constitutes a normatively desirable cooperation endeavor the social sciences and humanities are in demand (Coakley and Nowak 2013).

Concern for protecting the global commons and the search for mechanisms to avoid global systemic risks represent this volume's starting point. We argue that humanity will not be able to solve these challenges without cooperation across borders and agreements on the objective to stabilize the global commons. This point of view opens itself up to moral issues, which in turn lead back to the basic assumptions concerning human behavior. What is 'good'? And are humans even able to behave in a moral manner, transcending their own preferences and interests? Kant differentiates, for instance, between two types of 'goodness' that humans are capable of: the first 'goodness' is from the perspective of the self-interested individual – something that is good for me; the second is an understanding of goodness, which Kant describes as 'moral goodness'. This goes far beyond strategic behavior and self-interests, since the moral good is done for its own sake:

> We do not perform a moral act because it is to our own advantage but because we feel in our consciousness an obligation to do so. . . . the benefit is the good for all (not the pragmatic good for me).
>
> (Lohmann 2013: 281)

Kant therefore describes the ambiguity of human behavior: humans have a tendency first to pursue their own preferences and interests (inclination), but they also have a moral (obligation) involving other people, groups, and societies that contributes to 'domesticating' their own interests. Kant's view in this regard coincides with Tomasello's joint and collective identities. Precisely what this morality consists of depends, of course, on the particular social contexts and historical eras. 'Democracy' and 'human rights' were cognitive 'inventions' of the Enlightenment that became the normative basis, the moral infrastructure of modern societies – which of course also had their dark sides (Mishra 2012). At the beginning of the 21st century it is now about developing an ethic, a global-commons morality, a 'global social contract' (Messner 2015b; WBGU 2011) and establishing this as a (global) social norm aimed at protecting global cooperation. The global discussions on the universal Sustainable Development Goals, which are negotiated under the auspices of the United Nations (UN) in 2015 (despite the global crises happening at the same time), can be interpreted as an effort in this direction (Brandi and Messner 2015; Brock 2015; on norm-building in the international system, see Ehrlich and Levin 2005; Florini 1996). All of this is easier said and written than (globally) done. The challenge of a generally accepted ethics of the global commons would be a 'moral revolution' (Appiah 2011), an achievement of civilization and an 'invention', comparable to the 'invention' of the notion of human rights (Messner 2015b).

For us this gives rise to a large number of possible research perspectives. Can abstract, generally accepted, substantive principles for 'good' cooperation develop that are oriented towards the global commons and take account of the circumstances of complex asymmetries between the participating cooperation actors? Can procedural mechanisms be found to develop processes in which common standards can be negotiated for good cooperation? Empirically and conceptually, it would be a good addition to have studies on global cooperation to address whether and to what extent there can be consensus on the main goal of cooperation, and if consensus is even necessary for cooperation to succeed.

Change of perspective: Global politics from a different angle

These thoughts on the foundations of human behavior and the recapitulation of the possible evolutionary account of the development of the human cooperative abilities stand for themselves. But how can they contribute to a better understanding of the conditions, scope, opportunities, and obstacles for global cooperation in the 21st century?

As a first step we move towards the macro- or even the meta-level. The findings presented here allow us a (possibly) altered perspective on the dynamics of world history – an evolutionary perspective. We would like to try out this perspective more thoroughly and to use the framework developed by Tomasello and his colleagues that, as we argued before, is in line with new insights from evolutionary biology. Of course such an undertaking only works using blatant simplifications. We are aware of the risk of over-generalizations; nonetheless, we believe that such a perspective is rewarding if we want to appropriately understand the history of the cooperation of humankind and its relevance for today's cooperation questions.

As a second step, we interpret the central schools of International Relations in light of our discussions on non-political science cooperation research.

Four phases of the history of human cooperation: An evolutionary perspective

A (very) brief sketch of the history of the world can be described in four phases based on Tomasello's categories. Here we rely on the two previously identified phases and build on them. In the *first phase* early humans got together in small, loosely knit groups around 400,000 years ago. As described, humans overcame the phase of individual intentionalities to develop joint intentionalities in small groups, learned to assert their own perspectives and the perspectives of others in relation to each other, and coordinated activities to achieve common goals. They thus opened the door to cultural learning processes, which led from small groups of early humans to the global society we see evolving today. As humanity evolved, increasingly complex social communities emerged in the *second phase* – around 200,000 years later. Competition between groups and the growing of communities (both results of the success of joint intentionalities) resulted in the emergence of the principle of collective intentionalities, the creation of we-identities, common routines, rules, norms, and culture within communities. Collective intentionalities opened humans trajectories towards the 'invention' of agriculture and the domestication of animals (i.e. the Neolithic Revolution around 10,000 years ago); permanent settlements and village structures appeared. These led to the establishment of the first cities (around 6,000 years ago) and later the great empires (such as the Roman and Chinese), and in Europe, beginning in the Middle Ages, early states were established, after which the 18th century saw the emergence of the modern nation state that had developed specific norms, institutions, practices, cultures, and regulations. *Between* cities, kingdoms, empires, and then nation states, disorder, law of the jungle, violence, and war initially prevailed. Following Tomasello and also Nowak and many other evolutionary biologists and anthropologists, this competition combined with the presence of mutual threat between cities, kingdoms, empires, and states paradoxically led to the development of cooperation-based communication and practices *within* the increasingly complex communities.

It is the constellation of 'anarchy between communities' and, from a certain point, of 'anarchy within the state system' – the continuing dynamics of power and violence between kingdoms, empires, and states not constrained by cooperation – that continues to characterize the (neo)realistic school of International Relations to this day:

> great powers' . . . ultimate aim is to gain a position of dominant power over others, because having dominant power is the best means to ensure one's survival. . . . I also argue that multipolar systems . . . are especially prone to war.
> (Mearsheimer 2001: XI/XIII)

From a (neo)realist worldview, the international community is exactly in a situation in which the joint or even collective intentionalities between states only exist in an instrumental sense (as an alliance), and their development into a community of nations is unlikely.

But the largely unregulated, continuing conflict between cities, kingdoms, empires, and then states was by no means the end of history. It is followed by a *third phase* in the history of human cooperation. The conflict between cities, kingdoms, empires, and states at a certain point became itself the object of collective and cooperation-based rule-making. Humans began to gradually apply the mechanisms of joint and collective intentionality to relations *between* communities. The contribution of Iver B. Neumann in this volume on the development of diplomacy from an evolutionary perspective shows that the origins of the third phase go back to the Pleistocene. Neumann identifies the first continuous contacts *between* culturally very similar nomadic groups several tens of thousands of years ago. He shows how some 5,000 years ago the first institutionalized and formalized relations arose *between* the emerging cities and successively evolved into the complex diplomacy of the 21st century, which came into being over the past 150 years. Overall Neumann presents six key transitions for the evolving diplomacy and the relationships *between* 'groups' and 'societies'. Humans have therefore had the ability for some 10,000 years to develop their individual identity (in conjunction with other humans), to develop collective identities in groups, and to go successively around as 'members' of different groups and communities (first local, then national, and later even on an international or global level) with overlapping identities (Messner 1997). This development of joint intentionalities and incipient collective intentionalities as the bases of cooperation *between* communities creates in the course of history increasingly complex social systems – up to the international system and an evolving global society. At the same time these increasingly complex and increasingly interdependent systems rely on ever closer cooperation for stabilization.

The cooperation mechanisms between communities outlined by Neumann arose historically always first as an idea and only afterwards in actual reality. Today's reality and form of the international system, including the development of international legal structures that one (very optimistically) could interpret as elements or harbingers of a world constitution (Bryde 2003; Habermas 2008), were initially 'cognitively premeditated', 'invented', and then realized in small steps, often accompanied by devastating setbacks. If one were looking for a historical starting point for the application of this cooperation principle to intergovernmental relations, one could refer to the Dutch jurist Hugo Grotius, who in 1625 formulated the first foundations for rule-based dispute resolution between states in his book 'De iure belli ac pacis' (*On the Laws of War and Peace*) (Grotius [1625] 2001). He introduced the concept of 'international law' and thus the first point of departure for joint intentionalities between states. This was a major cognitive innovation: thinking about cooperation and dispute settlement in the evolving system of states based on the ability to appreciate not only the perspective and interests of individual states, but also the perspective and interests of other states. Grotius is considered the spiritual father of the Peace of Westphalia of 1648. In 1795 in his essay 'Perpetual Peace', Immanuel Kant formulated the main features of a comprehensive system of international law and the idea of an order of world citizenship based on peacefully interacting states. Intellectually he went far beyond the joint intentionalities of Hugo Grotius. Conceptually transnational collective identities emerge in Kant's thinking between states and between the people of different states based on a collective 'global we', a common international legal system, common norms, and common culture, which should be open to all states and people. It is interesting that the concept of 'world citizen' was already

Table 1.1 The four phases of cooperation in human history

	Individual intentionality	Joint intentionalities	Collective intentionalities within groups	Joint intentionalities between groups	Collective intentionalities on a global scale
Time	5 million years to around 400,000 years ago	Around 400,000 years ago	Around 200,000 years ago	Between (culturally homogenous) groups several tens of thousands of years ago; between cities around 5,000 years ago; between modern states since the 17th century	Present, 'emerging' since the 20th century
Starting point	Development of human ancestors, closely related to apes	Food supply/hunting larger animals	(1) Competition/conflict between groups (concerning food) – 'Us' against 'them'; (2) increasing group size (emergence of group identities)	Conflict regulation and trade between groups, cities, societies, states	Emergence and intensification of global interdependencies, emergence of global systems and global risks
Interaction forms	Procreation, individual perspectives in the 'world'	Interpersonal awareness: joint goals, humans acquire a 'common background'; emergence of multiple perspectives of the 'world'; social coordination to achieve goals based on cooperative communication; combination of joint awareness and individual perspectives; mutual dependence on cooperation partners	We-identities emerge on the basis of ingroup/outgroup dynamics; lasting group cultures emerge through common practices, conventions, rules, norms, institutions, measures of value; common past, present, and future is created (narrative, culture)	Principles of joint intentionalities, cooperative communication applied to interactions between groups; awareness and recognition of the perspectives of other groups, cities, and states; common goals between groups, cities and states are developed; social coordination to achieve common goals between groups; Interlaced, overlapping identities (in the groups and between the groups) emerge	Principles of 'collective intentionalities' are successively applied to global groups, networks; incipient, global 'we identities' emerge: collectively shared conventions, norms, rules, practices, and institutions; global group identities (e.g. in global epistemic communities); overlapping identities between locally, nationally, and globally networked groups

Organization form	Small groups of 'individuals', raising offspring as 'parents', comparable with groups and herds of apes	Small groups of early humans, interpersonal constellations	Competition/conflict with other groups becomes the starting point for stronger cooperation in groups; interaction 'with strangers' in the group made possible by common identity/ culture; stable, growing groups, small-scale societies emerge	Stable relations between groups, cities and states emerge; 'diplomacy' – relations between groups emerge and level off (on the basis of joint practices, rules, and institutions)	Global networks and communities (sciences, cities, epistemological communities), EU as a regional (transnational) community with comprehensive norms, values, practices, and cultures
Cognitive innovations		Simultaneous individuality and commonality; view of the 'world from one's own perspective as well as the perspectives of 'others'; social coordination and division of labor; emergence of basic infrastructure for interpersonal cooperation	Simultaneous individuality and commonality complemented by group-oriented cognitive models; cooperation in the groups, competition/ conflict between groups intertwined; invention of common social norms and identities (actor-neutral, transpersonal, generic norms and conventions); emergence of 'belongingness', 'identity', stabilizing expectations in the group; cultural 'ratchet effect' is initiated	Simultaneous individuality and commonality as well as group-oriented cognitive models are complemented by commonalities and goal-oriented interactions between groups/cities/states; ingroup/outgroup constellations are complemented by cooperation-oriented relations *between groups*, cities and states; Hugo Grotius 1625: Invention of the concept of international law; Kant 1795: 'Invention' of the concept of world citizen	Simultaneous individuality and commonality; group-oriented cognitive models; commonality and goal-oriented interactions between groups/cities/ states are complemented by 'global we-identities'; increasingly more complex, interlaced, overlapping identities; emergence of global groups; Kant's world society becoming a more elaborate concept: global governance, cosmopolitan democracy, global society

Sources: own adaptation of Tomasello (2014b, 140), Neumann (in this volume) used by Alexander von Humboldt (1769–1859) (Ette 2009). And it was Johann Wolfgang von Goethe (1749–1832), who introduced the concept of 'world literature' (Frick et al. 2010). Intellectually the time was ripe at the end of the 18th century and beginning of the 19th century to think about 'humankind in the singular' and citizens as members of a global community.

In the actual world of modern states, the Hague Peace Conferences of 1899 and 1907 signaled a first attempt to establish rules for dispute settlement between states, i.e. to develop joint intentionalities that recognize and take into account the positions of other states. The historical experiments initially failed, as did the League of Nations, which was established in 1920 after the First World War. After the devastation of World War II, a new attempt was made to create an international order of peace by establishing the United Nations, which at the very least would be based on the principle of joint intentionalities, i.e. the awareness of justified and unjustified perspectives of other states and the idea of rules-based conflict resolution between states. Three hundred and twenty years after Hugo Grotius humans learned to apply joint intentionalities to the relations between states by creating a multilateral institution to secure global peace. Furthermore, the 1948 Universal Declaration of Human Rights carries the seed of the collective intentionalities of all humans, which Kant had already conceived of 150 years earlier. The emergence of the European Union can be seen as an experiment to overcome the centuries-long 'natural state of conflict' between states by gradually developing durable collective intentionalities as a community of nations. Comprehensive common norms, institutions, and practices are emerging in Europe, even if the path to a resilient, common European culture is still far off.

The big question at the beginning of the 21st century is whether a *fourth phase* of human development on the basis of a global culture of cooperation can arise. Can humans develop 'global we-identities' based on collective intentionalities that would lead to global viewpoints, norms, rules, institutions, systems, and cultures, i.e. a (federal) global society that would overcome the 'age of nation states' (Delbrück 1998) and the primacy of national interests in favor of a global community of shared responsibilities? Could the third phase, in which cooperation *between* communities (and states) was gradually established, be transformed into a fourth phase in which cooperation *within a global society* becomes the norm? The emergence of such a global culture of cooperation and institutions to shape globalization, prevent global systemic risks, and stabilize and fairly use the global commons clearly presents a civilizational challenge for humanity.

Theories of International Relations from an evolutionary perspective

Deitelhoff and Zürn (2013) identify an overlapping sequence of three paradigms of the history of the discipline of International Relations. When placed in relation with Tomasello's categories, the following picture emerges: the first paradigm, which emerged in the 1940s to 1960s and in the school of (neo)realism, remains influential to this day and developed from the experiences of the two

World Wars and the dynamics of the Cold War following 1945 (see Morgenthau 1960; Mearsheimer 2014). This perspective focuses in particular on the anarchy of the international system, the 'natural state of war' between countries, i.e. the challenges of war and peace. Dominance and hegemony is the decisive key to averting war and enforcing one's own interests. In this paradigm Tomasello's joint or even collective intentionalities had or have only very limited meaning (e.g. in form of defensive alliances and agreements for avoiding nuclear war). From this point of view blocks (which cooperate against other blocks) only recognize their own self-interests, just like early humans before the 'invention' of multiple perspective taking. Hopes that states will socialize in favor of comprehensive cooperation fail in this perspective because of the basic structure of the anarchic system itself, which only allows socialization effects in form of instrumental and limited cooperation to ensure one's own survival.

The second paradigm, which gained in importance with the European integration of the 1960s and the increasing international interdependencies of the 1970s, brought the conditions and possibilities of intergovernmental cooperation to the foreground (Cooper 1972; Deutsch 1968; Keohane and Nye 1997). In their seminal work *Power and Interdependence. World Politics in Transition*, Keohane and Nye (1977) formulated a perspective on the international system that focuses on the economic- and security-policy interdependencies and vulnerabilities between states. Based on this, they argue for cooperation, joint rule-making, and multilateral institutions. To reduce the potential for conflict between states, they rely on key elements from Hugo Grotius and Immanuel Kant and call for a perspective of joint intentionalities and common interests. This stands in contrast the reductionist views of narrowly self-interested states in the (neo)realistic tradition. The recognition that states (and their societies) are mutually dependent for their survival (just as humans depend on other humans to survive) is therefore a fairly new discovery in the discipline of International Relations.

The third paradigm goes one step further in view of globalization processes, which have been accelerating since the late 1980s. Questions concerning a new global order in the light of a progressive sociation of international relations are at the core of global governance research (Alexandroff and Cooper 2010; Biermann, Pattberg, and van Asselt 2009; Donahue and Nye 2000; Kennedy et al. 2002; Kumar and Messner 2010; Raven, Schot, and Berkhout 2012; WBGU 2011, 2014; Zürn 2004), cosmopolitan approaches (Archibugi 2008; Held 1995; Scholte 2002), and world society theories (Albert, Brock, and Wolf 2000; Kennedy et al. 2002; Stichweh 2000). Ultimately, in a historic phase of 'all-encompassing globalization' (Messner 2015a), the work (which early world citizen and world order theorist Kant had already predicted over 200 years ago, in a world of very 'thin connections' between the societies) is picked up again. Tomasello's concept of collective intentionalities is constitutive for this third paradigm, which looks for leverage points to create global common perspectives, norms, values, institutions, and cultures.

What do these reflections teach us? In light of the new findings on the human ability to cooperate, there is much to indicate that (neo)realism, while providing insightful analysis of collective action problems in the international system, systematically underestimates the room for cooperation. In contrast paradigms two and three outline the potential basic principles and the institutional as well as cognitive innovations that could inform a future global cooperation culture and its institutional architecture. In all three paradigms diverse barriers to cooperation, which we referred to at the beginning of this chapter, are mapped out. Can they be overcome? And what do we learn from the insights gleaned from the study of evolutionary anthropology, evolutionary biology, and other approaches in terms of opportunities, limits, and mechanisms towards the emergence of a global culture of cooperation at the beginning of the 21st century? To this end we suggest the following four search tangents.

Conclusions: Can global cooperation succeed? What we do know and don't know

> . . . humans are not cooperating angels; . . . the best way to motivate people to collaborate and to think like a group is to identify an enemy and charge that 'they' threaten 'us'. . . . Such group mindedness in cooperation is, perhaps ironically, a major cause of strife and suffering in the world today. The solution – more easily described than attained – is to find new ways to define the group.
>
> (Tomasello 2009: 99–100)

Does the radically interdisciplinary view help us to better understand the obstacles to cooperation in current world politics? Furthermore, will humans succeed in gradually implementing the principle of collective intentionalities on a global scale in the context of globalization? Can humans learn to think about humankind in the singular and develop models, norms, institutions, practices, 'we' identities, a culture of global cooperation, and a culture of preserving the Earth system and the global commons? Or is this impossible without competing against each other absent a 'global society'? Will the principle of collective intentionalities, as a key to the emergence of common patterns of order and a shared culture, reach its limits the moment there is no longer any outgroup within the nine-billion-strong human civilization? Or is it 'only' a matter of time until humanity learns a global culture of cooperation based on their fundamental ability to cooperate and on actual global systemic risks? Here are a few final thoughts on what we know, what we know we don't know, and what we are ignorant about with regard to global cooperation.

In principle, we are able to cooperate – but do we learn global cooperation fast enough?

First, a few facts that we know for certain: in the course of human history the ability of humans to cooperate developed in ever larger and increasingly complex contexts. From the very first human groups and communities several 100,000 years ago to the development of today's international institutional systems, humans have exhibited astonishing skills at bringing together different interests in increasingly complex contexts, creating common norms and values, agreeing on common goals, and coordinating joint action in order to achieve these goals. In principle, therefore, there is little point in arguing about whether humans can develop institutions for managing globalization processes and effectively protecting the global commons. Cooperation is the mother of human civilization. It has led to increasingly complex societal forms and incredible cultural achievements.

Historically, humans first developed cognitive answers for new cooperation challenges (such as conflicts between states); the blueprints for the future by Grotius and Kant as outlined above are examples of this. But generally speaking the first attempts to translate such intellectual cooperation innovations into practice typically failed. The failure of the Hague Peace Conferences of 1899 and 1907 and then the League of Nations are examples of this. It was not rare that major crises and disasters, such as the two World Wars, were the basis and starting points for subsequent cooperation successes, such as the establishment of the United Nations and the process of European integration (Buruma 2013; Leggewie and Messner 2012; Morris 2010: 534; WBGU 2011: 94ff.). From an evolutionary perspective, it is not surprising then that the current, historically still 'young' global governance models of today (which build on the first blueprints from Grotius and Kant) are not immediately followed by successful implementation. The historical analogies indicate that possible answers to the challenges of globalization, global risks and the global commons have already been 'imagined', but established routines, heuristics, institutions, norms, values, established paths, and also power structures (still?) impede their use.

It is on this point that we enter the terrain of challenges that we know are important, but we do not know whether humans can overcome them. It is still an open question whether, in light of the current challenges of globalization and global systemic risks, enough time remains for humans, organizations, and societies to learn to address these dynamics with cooperation. In particular, insights from the natural sciences indicate that answers to the major processes of global environmental change must be found in the coming two to four decades to avoid irreparable Earth-system change (Lenton et al. 2008; Messner 2012; Rockström et al. 2009; WBGU 2009, 2011, 2014). Whether humans and their institutions can learn in this short time span to address global risks and to protect the global commons through cooperation, or whether cooperation might only emerge when the global tipping points and systemic risks with somewhat irreversible consequences 'force us to act', is unknown. Lastly, it is about the very fundamental question of whether humans are even capable of replacing the 'crisis mode' as the usual mechanism to effect fundamental change of existing behaviors and patterns (Klinke and Renn 2012; March and Olson 1988; Wiesenthal 1995) with knowledge about future crises, i.e. with the 'knowledge mode' (Messner 2015b) so that preventive action becomes possible.

It is encouraging that human learning processes since the Neolithic Revolution and especially over the past 250 years, i.e. since the Industrial Revolution, have accelerated tremendously. Fogel (1999; similarly Brynjolfsson and McAfee 2014; Morris 2010) argues that the 'greatest innovations', which fundamentally changed human society from the Neolithic revolution on, occurred in approximately one-millennium increments. Examples of this are the first irrigation systems (around 7,000 years ago), the emergence of cities (around 6,000 years ago), the development of mathematics (around 4,000 years ago), and the invention of the printing press (around 550 years ago). Following the Industrial Revolution, breakthrough innovations have taken place in increments of only a few decades (e.g. the invention of the steam engine, the railway, and the car; the development of penicillin, deciphering DNA, and digital technologies). Social innovation processes have also accelerated. After the 'invention' of international law by Grotius [1625] (2001) – a radical accomplishment of cognitive innovation – more than 300 years elapsed until the establishment of a collective security organization in the form of the United Nations. Despite all of the indisputable environmental problems, the gradually emerging knowledge of the limits of the Earth system since the 1970s (Meadows et al. 1972; WCSD 1987) triggered significantly more rapid mental and actual change processes in many societies (Messner 2015b). The cultural ratchet effect, set into motion a good 400,000 years ago, translated itself into accelerated learning processes. Whether they are sufficient to produce accelerated knowledge and innovations for developing global cooperation structures that can prevent global risks, of course, remains to be seen.

The actual obstacles to cooperation as adjustment crises to a 'great transformation'

Again we will begin here with what we know. The micro-perspectives of evolutionary anthropology, psychology, and biology explain why humans cannot adjust in real time to new and greatly changed conditions. Humans are in no way comprehensive information-calculation machines that can easily adjust to any type of novel challenge. People initially orient themselves around established heuristics, proven patterns of behavior, and recognized norms and values. Kahneman (2011; Kahneman and Tversky 1979) and colleagues categorize behavior that is based on such internalized, and therefore not easily modifiable, cognitive, normative, and cultural heuristics and mental maps as 'System 1' of the human mind (experience-based actions; routine actions that enable quick decisions). 'System 1' enables us to position ourselves in a very complex world. 'System 2' of human thinking enables us to make rational decisions, weigh up alternatives, and make calculations. 'System 2' is therefore slower and is generally not used by humans when they encounter (seemingly) known situations that can be intuitively handled by 'System 1'. It is difficult for humans to abandon established patterns of thinking without good reason and being under severe pressure. The above-mentioned 'dictatorship of the present' is based on the stability and importance of 'System 1' for human thinking and action. This makes it difficult to see impending radical, scientifically well-understood changes in the future (such as dangerous climate change) as an opportunity to change behavior (the 'knowledge mode of transformation').

Humans can adapt well to incrementally changing circumstances and contexts by leaving 'System 1' untouched while 'System 2' develops solutions for incremental change. However, if fundamental changes occur that radically devalue existing heuristics, behavior, norms, and institutions, then (adjustment) crises may arise: the old orientation no longer works, and new heuristics, norms, institutions, and cultures must first be developed, proven, accepted, generalized, and implemented. We can also use Kahnemann's concepts to gain insights into the obstacles to global cooperation.

Globalization can then be considered such radical change in the history of humankind that asks too much of the old cooperation instruments of individuals, states, and international institutional systems. Perhaps we are going through a 'great transformation', which in recent human history can only be compared with the Neolithic Revolution and the Industrial Revolution (WBGU 2011). Three parallel, interfering global waves (Messner 2011) have been giving rise to a new historical constellation since the 1980s: first, economic globalization is accelerating. This goes hand in hand with an increasing sociation of International Relations – former national systems, national economies, political systems, societies, cultures, and democracies become global sub-systems. The reach of national policies decreases while the demands for global governance increase. Second, tectonic power shifts are taking place. The 250-year-old Western hegemony in global politics and the global economy are under pressure, and a post-Western order is gradually emerging. The power of established and previously functioning cooperation communities, such as the transatlantic alliance and the G7, are eroding. The third wave of global change arises from the changes to the Earth system, which were gradually set in motion through human production and consumption patterns in the industrialized countries that have manifested themselves with increasing intensity since the end of the 20th century. Human beings are becoming the strongest geological force in the Earth system (Crutzen and Stoermer 2000; Zalasiewicz et al. 2014). The Earth system is becoming humanity's most comprehensive global commons. Humans have to take responsibility for the Earth system and therefore establish new orders, common rules, institutions, and behavioral patterns. These three waves are creating a new global space for action for which an order has yet to be invented.

These major changes, which have emerged over a mere 25 years, require entirely new heuristics of international cooperation based on radically changed norms. Humanity must, as it were, 'reformat' their 'System 1': from national interests and communities of responsibility to global interests and communities of responsibility; from Western to still unclear post-Western norm systems; from concepts of responsibility for the welfare of humans and living generations to welfare concepts that include both responsibility for the Earth system and responsibility for the livelihoods of many generations to come. Humankind is in the middle of a 'great transformation'.

History teaches us that humans can undertake fundamental changes of perspective: for example during the Enlightenment, whose essence, as Kant pointed out, was a radical change in the way humans think about humans, societies, law, state, and human rights. The 'invention' of welfare states as an answer to the volatility of capitalistic economies is likewise an example of comprehensively changing perspectives and models. Radical change is also reflected in the arts, where humans are able over time to see the world through completely different eyes: the transition from Naturalism to Impressionism and Expressionism at the end of the 19th and beginning of the 20th centuries reflects changed worldviews. Even individual artists could radically change their views. The (well-known) almost innocent Art Nouveau paintings by Gustav Klimt from the 1880s to the 1910s and the (lesser known) depictions of female sexuality from the years 1912–1913, which he subsequently painted while in Vienna at the beginning of the 20th century, after he was exposed to the insights from psychology that emerged there at that time, are truly 'worlds apart' (Kandell 2012). Humans are able to respond to profound changes in their environment with corresponding innovations in perception and behavior. But from an evolutionary perspective it is also not surprising that fundamental changes, such as all-encompassing globalization, usually result first in cognitive and intellectual innovations and the developing of new concepts and ideas, which are followed later by real behavioral, societal, economic, and political changes.

From this perspective the currently observed obstacles to cooperation and the possible erosion of the Western-dominated global order would not really be indications of a fundamental inability in humanity to create global cooperation structures. They are far more crises of adjustment, orientation, and transformation in light of radically altered contexts. Traditional diplomacy, nation-state sovereignty, the mindset of Western supremacy – Kahneman's 'System 1' if you will – must first be 'adapted' to the new global realities.

The importance of normative and cognitive heuristics to the process of human decision making indicates just how important it would be to develop a variety of models for global cooperation, to discuss them, and to promote their acceptance in order to open up room for thinking and action (beyond the existing 'System 1' heuristics) that would enable us to gradually replace the established heuristics from the 'era of nation-states'. Changed perspectives and a reinterpretation and remapping of the world are required to overcome the centuries-old models of power games, from hegemony and dominance, even war, as normal states of intergovernmental behavior (Scholte 2014; WBGU 2011, 2014; see also Leggewie in this volume, who proposes embedding the concept of 'gift' and 'forgiveness' in strategies of global cooperation based on the work of the anthropologist Mauss). Such changes in perspective could represent starting points for a global culture of cooperation to address competition and conflicts, to possibly overcome wars, and to create cognitive, emotional, and normative foundations to stabilize the global commons. Humans are creatures of habit who are reluctant, not least in real time, to part from their internalized routines.

From this point of view questions arise that are once again very difficult to answer: how long will this adjustment crisis last? How can learning processes be accelerated in favor of global cooperation? Can such a transition succeed without major international crises? And last but not least, can such an adjustment crisis also fail?

Inadequate basic mechanisms of cooperation in the international system

Let us consider how to deal with the global economic and financial crisis from one such perspective. In the past seven decades, international economic and financial policy has been negotiated primarily in those organizations and clubs in which Western states, due to their voting rights or exclusive membership, called the shots. Tightly knit informal and formal institutional relations emerged, as well as a common cooperation history, crisis-proven mechanisms of cooperation, and other dynamics that generally made the continuation of cooperation more likely. Over the past six decades, the European Union gradually invested in the basic mechanisms and principles of cooperation, without which common interests could not have emerged in international contexts, nor could the containment of power have succeeded.

At the outbreak of the global financial crisis at the end of 2008, the G7/G8 states realized that it was impossible to resolve this crisis without extending their intimate circle. The involvement of emerging countries, and in particular the participation of China, the country with the largest foreign exchange reserves in the global economy at present, was imperative. The G20 was founded, thus more than doubling the size of the club of the major economies. Global interdependencies and immediate global systemic risks (concerns that the global financial system would collapse) thus led to an enlarged cooperation alliance, which had hitherto been rejected by the dominant industrial nations that were organized in the G7. Using Tomasello's terminology, joint intentionalities between old and new powers emerged in a situation of interdependence and from competition between states to avoid an impending financial market meltdown.

The G20 was quite successful in mitigating the imminent crisis symptoms (Drezner 2014). But when it came to dealing with the more fundamental causes, its record was less convincing, nor did the G20 develop into a decisive forum for other policy fields such as climate, trade, or security policy. It proved to have only limited capacity to act. In Tomasello's terms, this means that a development of 'collective intentionality' has not (yet?) occurred.

Explanations derived from political and economic sciences would focus on the power competition between the rising countries from the Global South and the relatively declining industrial economies. They would stress the impact of a redistribution of privileges and the reordering of the international system (Kaplinsky and Messner 2008; Kupchan et al. 2001). Other explanations could be derived from perspectives of evolutionary anthropology and psychology. 'System 1' heuristics, which stem from decades-old power asymmetries, make it very difficult for established states and rising powers to reach an equal footing just in time. The change from 'opposition' (the formerly weak states) to those who set the tone to constructively shaping global politics may also prove difficult

(Stuenkel 2015; Weinlich 2014a). A further explanation is the underprovision of basic mechanisms of cooperation (see Messner, Guarín, and Haun in this volume). To be sure, communication between the members of the G20 does take place. But a common narrative of trust and reciprocity is missing; fairness is not in place, reputations have not been built, the formation of common we-identities are nascent at best. Without this basic mechanism of cooperation, a continuation and intensification of cooperation in as complex a context cannot succeed.

Answers to the obstacles in the international system can be formulated from such a perspective on two levels. First, in light of globalization processes, impending Earth-system change and an emerging post-Western, multi-polar world order, states must 'learn' to reformulate their national interests. This needs to take place in such a way that 'common and collective interests' (synergetic, overlapping interests; interests for the global common good) become an important part. This will allow that the rights to and demands from other societies and future generations for a life of peace and prosperity can be reasonably perceived and ensured. Such a transition to multiple perspective takings is a necessary condition for global cooperation in the 21st century. As Homi Bhabha (1994) argues, in a highly globalized world any individual, local, or national perspective is radically incomplete. Western states, on the one hand, must move away from defending their hegemony in the international system in what is a losing battle. They must accommodate 'new' cooperation partners and be ready for fair cooperation on an equal footing. Emerging and developing countries, on the other hand, must be ready to implement their newly won power multilaterally, together with others, as well as insist that the rules of the game of the international community, which were formulated to their disadvantage for far too long, be changed – not only in terms of power gains, but in the sense of a fair cooperation environment (Brock and Weinlich 2014). In addition to these procedural changes, substantial reorientations and new models of co-existence under the conditions of all-encompassing globalization are necessary. All actors, i.e. industrialized, emerging, and developing countries, must recognize that national welfare can only be sustainable when all states and societies agree on common fundamentals and principles of a global common good to address global systemic risks. Second, cooperation forms and institutions must be found that enable and strengthen the basic mechanisms of cooperation outlined above. These changes need to be driven, embedded, oriented, and triggered by emerging collective intentionalities: multiperspectivity, common points of view, emerging joint norms, rules, routines, and coordinated action, and at the end of the day a global culture, creating the preconditions to protect the global commons.

Disjunctions between inclusive, selective, destructive cooperation alliances in the international system

At this time we are dealing not only with obstacles to cooperation in the international system, but also with complex disjunctions of dynamics – if you bear the full spectrum of intentionalities in mind, from non-shared intentionalities to joint and even collective intentionalities. These disjunctions correspond to the finding that the evolution of the human ability to cooperate is neither a linear nor even a teleological process. Contrary to the traditional game-theory perspective that analyzes stable equilibria like the Nash equilibrium, Nowak (2006b) emphasizes that evolutionary biology is beginning to define evolutionary dynamics, or 'fluid pictures', and evolutionary patterns. Nothing lasts forever. The fluid pattern that emerges from the interplay of self-interest and the ability to cooperate, between individuals and communities as well as between groups, organizations, and states, runs approximately as follows (Imhof, Fudenberg, and Nowak 2005; Nowak and Sigmund 1998; Nowak et al. 2004; Rand, Ohtzuki, and Nowak 2009): cooperation dynamics can arise from competition and conflict; cooperative communities are, generally speaking, superior to other actors and groups; simple, error-prone, and unstable tit-for-tat entities' cooperation patterns can evolve into trust-based and more stable forms of cooperation (generous tit for tat, Nowak 2006a); but successful and broad cooperation can also reduce the attention paid to defectors and lead to the erosion of cooperation. Regression can occur with the result that violence and power are no longer inhibited through cooperation. Civilization collapse is possible, which in human societies is typically followed by renewed cooperation. Although 'war is not the father of all', as Heraclitus once observed, it is possible. The cooperation dilemma 'has no end' (Nowak and Highfield 2011: 49).

At this point we should not attempt to draw a complete picture of the current processes of successful cooperation, cooperation collapse, conflict, and cooperation in international systems and their respective drivers. We will instead sketch a rough map of the world of some of these cooperation disjunctions and obstacles to cooperation, from which it will be evident that a process in the direction of a global culture of cooperation would originate from very different points and levels of cooperation and/or conflict. Cooperation dynamics are not simply a non-linear or non-teleological process. Cooperation areas, the consolidation of cooperation cultures, and the strengths or weaknesses of the basic mechanisms of cooperation are very unevenly distributed in the international system.

In the EU, strong collective intentionalities still dominate, and powerful constellations of actors continue to work towards further developing the closely knit common standards, rules, institutions, and cultures – despite or perhaps because of the European debt crisis. But given all the internal and external turmoil, a disintegration of the EU cannot be fully ruled out at this time.

In recent years, and particularly in the context of the Ukraine, a new freezing of relations has occurred between Europe and Russia; the hope of a 'common European house' (Mikhail Gorbachev), i.e. collective intentionalities in Europe, has not been realized. Even joint intentionalities are not in sight these days. Cautious attempts to entrench 'tit-for-tat strategies', to create at the very least the conditions for new confidence building, can be observed. An escalation of violence cannot be ruled out. This bilateral stalemate between Western countries and Russia blocks attempts to develop common perspectives on global problem dynamics, e.g. within the G20 or the UN Security Council.

The BRICS alliance of Brazil, Russia, India, China, and South Africa is a new cooperation club, an ingroup that seeks to create joint intentionalities. The cooperation within can be viewed as a result of competition with the 'old powers'. This is, as it were, an evolutionary classic. Competition between groups increases the opportunities for cooperation within groups. The G20 then is the coming together of the BRICS ingroup and the old G7 ingroup, opening up at the very least the possibility of creating common viewpoints and cooperation dynamics (Stuenkel 2015).

In addition to these constellations of states there are other networks of actors whose horizons are already directed towards global cooperation and in which collective, global intentionalities (may) indeed emerge: global scientific networks, global networks of cities in the fight against climate change, global human rights networks – contexts in which global viewpoints, norms, rules, institutions, and global cultures emerge. This is where the core of a global civil society forms itself, in whose center protection of the global commons could emerge (Scholte 2014; WBGU 2014).

A radical counterpoint to these non-state nuclei of a global order of peace is the development of the Islamic State: a cooperation alliance that not only has no interest in the development of common or even split intentionalities, viewpoints, and interests with other actors, but even is focused on their destruction.

It is not known whether and how a new dynamic, which succeeds in forming broad cooperation alliances to create a global order, can arise out of these disjunctions and juxtapositions of approaches to global cooperation. We know from complex system science that '[w]hen the system is chaotic, one important observation is that a very small difference between two initial conditions will cause, after some time, rapidly (exponentially) diverging results . . . Such sensitivity to initial conditions is called deterministic chaos. Simple linear relationships or strong causalities are not able to show such behavior; the non-linearity is a necessary condition and it may lead to weak causality' (Kurths, Heitzig, and Marwan in this volume). Complex systems, such as the international system, are therefore sensitive to abrupt perturbations, but are also characterized by the stability of dynamics. '[Complex systems] come back to some kind of "normal" behavior' (Kurths, Heitzig, and Marwan in this volume). What then could a new, future stability of the international system look like? The long history in the development of the ability of humans to cooperate in increasingly complex systems is encouraging. The interpretation of the current upheaval in the international system as a transitional and transformative phase and crisis, in which people, organizations, and states have to develop and learn new heuristics, norms, rules, orders, and cultures, appears plausible. In addition to threatening dynamics of a collapse of world order, there are at the same time examples of learning laboratories for global cooperation in the sciences, in networks of cities, and perhaps to a certain extent in international development cooperation. It is also not known whether there is enough time to avoid global systemic disasters or whether (as is not uncommon in evolutionary processes) global systemic crises first create the pressure and thus possibly the conditions for creating global cooperation spaces and cultures, i.e. broad-based, global, collective intentionalities (as Bremmer 2012 argued). The research on global cooperation can, as the authors of this volume demonstrate, contribute solutions to the major cooperation riddle of humankind and help improve the understanding of the constraints on cooperation on different scales:

- Science can enlarge the area of certain knowledge of the conditions, opportunities, and obstacles to (global) cooperation – this is in the realm of what we know.
- Science can also learn from the past and present and illuminate future perspectives, develop scenarios, and therefore provide foresight into realms of possibility – there are of course uncertainties about their chances of success. This is the realm of what we know we don't know.
- Science cannot, however, 'predict' the future. Evolutionary dynamics can lead to unforeseeable developments. Science cannot therefore abolish the 'unknown unknowns'.

One very simple matter is certain in all the insecurity and uncertainty about the dynamics of globally succeeding and failing cooperation: new planets are hard to find, conclude Nowak and Highfield (2011: 207). Elinor Ostrom (Ostrom et al. 1999: 282) formulated this in a similar manner in her important essay about the systemic commonalities and differences between the local and the global commons:

> We have only one global with which to experiment. Historically, people could migrate to other resources if they made a major error in managing a local common pool resource. Today, we have less leeway for mistakes at the local level, while at the global level there is no place to move.

Could the knowledge about these simple facts help us develop collective intentionalities on a global scale with the requisite speed?

References

Abbott, K. W. and Snidal, D. (1998). 'Why States Act Through Formal International Organizations', *Journal of Conflict Resolution*, 42 (1): 3–32.

Albert, M., Brock, L. and Wolf, K. D. (2000). *Civilizing World Politics. Society and Community Beyond the State*, Lanham, MD: Rowman and Littlefield.

Alexander, R. D. (1987). *The Biology of Moral Systems*, Piscataway, NJ: Transaction Publishers.

Alexandroff, A. S. and Cooper, A. S. (2010). *Rising States, Rising Institutions: Challenges for Global Governance*, Washington, DC: Brookings.

Appiah, K. A. (2011). *The Honor Code: How Moral Revolutions Happen*, New York, NY: W. W. Norton and Co.

Archibugi, D. (2008): *The Global Commonwealth of Citizens: Toward Cosmopolitan Democracy*, Princeton, NJ: Princeton University Press.

Barrett, S. (2007). *Why Cooperate? The Incentive to Supply Global Public Goods*, Cambridge: Oxford University Press.

Batson, D. (2015). 'The Egoism-Altruism Debate: A Psychological Perspective', in T. Singer and M. Ricard (eds.) *Caring Economics: Conversations on Altruism and Compassion, Between Scientists, Economists, and the Dalai Lama*, New York, NY: St. Martin's Press, 15–26.

Bell, D. (2006). 'Beware of False Prophets: Biology, Human Nature and the Future of International Relations Theory', *International Affairs*, 82 (3): 493–510.

Benkler, Y. (2011). *The Penguin and the Leviathan: How Cooperation Triumphs over Self-Interest*, New York, NY: Crown Business.

Bhabha, H. (1994) *The Location of Culture*, London: Routledge.

Biermann, F., Pattberg, P. and van Asselt, H. (2009). 'The Fragmentation of Global Governance Architectures: A Framework for Analysis', *Global Environmental Politics*, 9 (4): 4–40.

Bleiker, R., and Hutchison E. (2014). 'Introduction: Emotions and World Politics', *International Theory*, 6 (3): 490–1.

Bowles, S. and Gintis, H. (2011). *A Cooperative Species: Human Reciprocity and Its Evolution*, Princeton, NJ: Princeton University Press.

Brandi, C. and Messner, D. (2015). 'Was folgt auf die Millenniums-Entwicklungsziele?', *Zeitschrift für Politikwissenschaft*, 24 (4): 513–24.

Bratman, M. E. (1992). 'Shared Cooperative Activity', *The Philosophical Review*, 101 (2): 327–41.

Bremmer, I. (2012). *Every Nation for Itself: Winners and Losers in a G-Zero World*, New York, NY: Portfolio Penguin.

Brock, L. (2015). 'Globale Verantwortung: Von der Entwicklungszusammenarbeit zur Weltgemeinwohlpolitik?', in J. Kursawe, M. Johannsen, C. Baumgart-Ochse, M. von Boemcken and I.-J. Werkner (eds.) *Friedensgutachten 2015*, Berlin: LIT Verlag, 149–60.

Brock, L. and Weinlich, S. (2014). 'Eine Weltordnung mit verlässlichen Regeln: Die Rolle der Vereinten Nationen', in P. Schäfer (eds.) *In einer aus den Fugen geratenen Welt: Linke Außenpolitik, Eröffnung einer überfälligen Debatte*, Hamburg: VSA Verlag, 85–99.

Brown, C. (2013). '"Human Nature", Science and International Political Theory', *Journal of International Relations and Development*, 16 (4): 435–54.

Bryde, B. O. (2003). 'Konstitutionalisierung des Völkerrechts und Internationalisierung des Verfassungsrechts', *Der Staat*, 42: 62–75.

Brynjolfsson, E. and McAfee, A. (2014). *The Second Machine Age: Work, Progress, and Prosperity in a Time of Brilliant Technologies*, New York, NY: W. W. Norton and Company.

Buruma, I. (2013). *Year Zero: A History of 1945*, New York, NY: Penguin.

Coakley, S. and Nowak, M. A. (2013). 'Introduction: Why Cooperation Makes a Difference', in M. A. Nowak and S. Coakley (eds.) *Evolution, Games, and God: The Principle of Cooperation*, Cambridge, MA: Harvard University Press.

Commission on Global Governance (1995). *Our Global Neighbourhood: The Report of the Commission on Global Governance*, Oxford: Oxford University Press.

Cooper, A. F. and Momani, B. (2014). 'Re-Balancing the G-20 from Efficiency to Legitimacy: The 3G Coalition and the Practice of Global Governance', *Global Governance: A Review of Multilateralism and International Organizations*, 20 (2): 213–32.

Cooper, R. N. (1972). 'Economic Interdependence and Foreign Policy', *World Policy*, 24 (2): 159–81.

Cooperider, D.L., Fry, R.E. and Piderit, S.K. (2007). '17 New Designs in Transformative Cooperation', in S.K. Piderit, R.E. Fry, and D.L. Cooperider (eds.) *Handbook of Transformative Cooperation: New Designs and Dynamics*, 418–430.

Crutzen, Paul J. and Stoermer, Eugene F. (2000). The 'Anthropocene'. IGBP Newsletter 41: 17–18.

Darwin, C. ([1871] 2004). *The Descent of Man, and Selection in Relation to Sex*, London: John Murray.

Deitelhoff, N. and Zürn, M. (2013). 'Die internationalen Beziehungen – ein Überblick', in M.G. Schmidt, F. Wolf, and S. Wurster (eds.) *Studienbuch Politikwissenschaft*, 381–410, Wiesbaden: Springer VS.

Delbrück, J. (1998). 'Von der Staatenordnung über die internationale Kooperation zur "supraterritorial oder global governance"', in U. Bartosch and J. Wagner (eds.) *Weltinnenpolitik*, München: LIT-Verlag, 55–66.

Deutsch, K.W. (1968). *The Analysis of International Relations*, Englewood Cliffs, NJ: Prentice-Hall.

de Waal, Frans B.M. (2009). *The Age of Empathy: Nature's Lessons for a Kinder Society*, Toronto: McClelland and Stewart.

Dixon, M. (2013). *Textbook on International Law*, Oxford: Oxford University Press.

Donahue, J. and Nye, J. (eds.) (2000). *Governance in a Globalizing World*, Washington, DC: Brookings.

Drezner, D. (2014). *The System Worked: How the World Stopped Another Great Depression*, Oxford: Oxford University Press.

Dunbar, R.I.M. (1998). 'The Social Brain Hypothesis', *Evolutionary Anthropology: Issues, News, and Reviews*, 6 (5): 178–90.

Ehrlich, P.R. and Levin, S.A. (2005). 'The Evolution of Norms', *PLoS Biology*, 3 (6): e194.

Ette, O. (2009). *Alexander von Humboldt und die Globalisierung. Das Mobile des Wissens*, Frankfurt and Leipzig: Insel Verlag.

Fehr, E. (2015). 'The Social Dilemma Experiment', in T. Singer and M. Ricard (eds.) *Caring Economics: Conversations on Altruism and Compassion, Between Scientists, Economists, and the Dalai Lama*, New York, NY: St. Martin's Press, 77–84.

Florini, A. (1996). 'The Evolution of International Norms', *International Studies Quarterly*, 40 (3): 363–89.

Fogel, R.W. (1999). 'Catching up with the Economy', *The American Economic Review*, 89 (1): 1–21.

Fowler, J.H., Loewn, P.J., Settle, J. and Dawes, C.T. (2011). 'Genes, Games and Political Participation', in P.K. Hatemi and R. Mcdermott (eds.) *Man is by Nature a Political Animal: Evolution, Biology and Politics*, Chicago, IL: University of Chicago Press, 207–223.

Frick, W., Golz, J., Meier, A. and Zehm, E. (eds.) *Goethe Jahrbuch 2009*, Vol. 126, Göttingen: Wallstein Verlag.

Fues, T. and Hamm, B. (2000). 'Die Weltkonferenzen der neunziger Jahre: Spielwiese oder Zukunftsmodell globaler Problemlösung', in U. Ratsch, R. Mutz, and B. Schoch (eds.) *Friedensgutachten 2000*, Münster: LIT, 198–208.

Gilbert, M. (1992). *On Social Facts*, Princeton, NJ, and Oxford: Princeton University Press.

Gowlett, J.A.J., Gamble, C. and Dunbar, R.I.M. (2012). 'Human Evolution and the Archaeology of the Social Brain', *Current Anthropology*, 53 (6): 693–722.

Gross Stein, J. (2013). 'Psychological Explanations of International Decision Making and Collective Behavior', in W. Carlsnaes, T. Risse, and B.A. Simmons (eds.) *Handbook of International Relations*, London: Sage, 195–220.

Grotius, H. ([1625] 2001). *On the Law of War and Piece*, Kitchener: Batoche Books.

Habermas, J. (2008). 'Konstitutionalisierung des Völkerrechts und die Legitimationsprobleme einer verfassten Weltgesellschaft', in W. Brugger, U. Neumann, and S. Kirste (eds.) *Rechtsphilosophie im 21. Jahrhundert*, Frankfurt: Suhrkamp, 360–79.

Hafner-Burton, E. M., Hughes, D. A. and Victor, D. G. (2013). 'The Cognitive Revolution and the Political Psychology of Elite Decision Making', *Perspectives on Politics*, 11 (2): 368–86.

Hafner-Burton, E. M., LeVeck, B. L., Victor D. G., and Fowler, J. H. (2014). 'Decision Maker Preferences for International Legal Cooperation', *International Organization*, 68 (4): 845–76.

Hale, T., Held, D. and Young, K. (2013). *Gridlock: Why Global Cooperation is Failing When We Need It Most*, Cambridge, MA: Polity Press.

Hardin, G. (1968). 'The tragedy of the commons', *Science*, 162 (3859): 1243–8.

Hatemi, P. K. and Mcdermott, R. (eds.) (2011). *Man is by Nature a Political Animal: Evolution, Biology and Politics*, Chicago, IL: University of Chicago Press.

Hauser, M. D. (2013). 'The Moral Organ', in M. A. Nowak and S. Coakley (eds.) *Evolution, Games, and God: The Principle of Cooperation*, Cambridge, MA: Harvard University Press, 253–71.

Held, D. (1995). *Cosmopolitanism: An Agenda for a New World Order*. Cambridge, UK Malden, MA: Polity Press.

Imhof, L. A., Fudenberg, D. and Nowak, M. A. (2005). 'Evolutionary Cycles of Cooperation and Defection', *PNAS*, 102 (31): 10797–800.

Isaac, J. C. (2013). 'Nature and Politics', *Perspectives on Politics*, 11 (2): 363–6.

Johnson, D. and Levin, S. (2009). 'The Tragedy of Cognition: Psychological Biases and Environmental Inaction', *Current Science*, 97 (11): 1593–603.

Kahneman, D. (2011). *Thinking, Fast and Slow*, 1st edition, New York, NY: Farrar Straus and Giroux.

Kahneman, D. and Tversky, A. (1979). 'Prospect Theory: An Analysis of Decision Under Risk', *Econometrica: Journal of the Econometric Society*, 47 (2): 263–91.

Kandell, E. (2012). *Das Zeitalter der Erkenntnis*, München: Siedler Verlag.

Kaplinsky, R. and Messner, D. (2008). 'Introduction: The Impact of Asian Drivers on the Developing World', *World Development*, 36 (2): 197–209.

Kennedy, P. (1987). *The Rise and the Fall of Great Powers*, New York, NY: Random House.

Kennedy, P., Messner, D. and Nuscheler, F. (2002). *Global Trends and Global Governance*, London: Pluto Press.

Keohane, Robert O. and Nye, Joseph S. (1977). Power and Interdependence: World Politics in Transition. Boston: Little; Brown and Company.

Keohane, R. O. (2015). 'The Global Politics of Climate Change: Challenge for Political Science', *PS: Political Science and Politics*, 48 (1): 19–26.

Keohane, R. O., and Nye, J. S. (1977). *Power and Independence*, Essex: TBS.

Keohane, R. and Victor, D. (2011). 'The Regime Complex for Climate Change', *Perspectives on Politics*, 9 (1): 7–23.

Klinke, A., and Renn, O. (2012). 'Adaptive and Integrative Governance on Risk and Uncertainty', *Journal of Risk Research*, 15 (3): 273–92.

Kumar, A., and Messner, D. (eds.) (2010). *Power Shifts and Global Governance: Challenges from South and North*, London: Anthem Press.

Kupchan, C. A. (2012). *No One's World: The West, the Rising Rest and the Coming Global Turn*, Oxford: Oxford University Press.

Kupchan, C., Davidson, J. and Sucharov, M. (2001). *Power in Transition: The Peaceful Change of International Order*, Tokyo: United Nations University Press.

Lebow, R. N. (2005). 'Reason, Emotion and Cooperation', *International Politics*, 42 (3): 283–313.

Lebow, R. N. (2013). 'You Can't Keep a Bad Idea Down: Evolutionary Biology and International Relations', *International Politics Reviews*, 1 (1): 2–10.

Leggewie, C. and Messner, D. (2012). 'The Low-Carbon Transformation: A Social Science Perspective', *Journal of Renewable and Sustainable Energy*, 4: 041404.

Lenton, T. M., Held, H., Kriegler, E., Hall, J. W., Lucht, W., Rahmstorf, S. and Schellnhuber, H. J. (2008). 'Tipping Elements in the Earth's Climate System', *Proceedings of the National Academy of Sciences USA*, 105 (6): 1786–93.

Lohmann, F. (2013). 'A New Case for Kantianism: Evolution, Cooperation, and Deontological Claims in Human Society', in M. A. Nowak and S. Coakley (eds.) *Evolution, Games, and God: The Principle of Cooperation*, Cambridge, MA: Harvard University Press, 273–88.

March, J. G. and Olson, J. (1988). *The Uncertainty of the Past: Organizational Learning under Ambiguity*, Oxford: Oxford University Press.

Maynard Smith, J. and Szathmáry, E. (1995). *The Major Transitions in Evolution*, Oxford: Oxford University Press.

Mcdermott, R. (2011). 'New Directions for Experimental Work in International Relations', *International Studies Quarterly*, 55 (2): 503–20.

Meadows, D., Meadows, D., Randers, J. and Behrens, W. W. (1972). *The Limits to Growth*, New York, NY: Universe Books.

Mearsheimer, J. J. (2001). *The Tragedy of the Great Power Politics*, New York, NY: W. W. Norton and Company.

Mearsheimer, J. J. (2011). *Why Leaders Lie: The Truth about Lying in International Politics*, New York, NY: Oxford University Press.

Mearsheimer, J. J. (2014). *The Tragedy of the Great Power Politics*, Updated edition, New York, NY: W. W. Norton and Company.

Messner, D. (1997). *The Network Society: Economic Development and International Competitiveness as Problems of Social Governance*, London: Routledge.

Messner, D. (2011). 'Three Waves of Global Change: The Dynamics of Global Governance in the First Half of the 21st Century', in T. Fues and L. Youfa (eds.) *Global Governance and Building a Harmonious World: A Comparison of European and Chinese Concepts for International Affairs*, Bonn: Deutsches Institut für Entwicklungspolitik / German Development Institute, Studies 62, 9–38.

Messner, D. (2012). 'Globale Ressourcenknappheiten und Erdsystemgrenzen im Anthropozän: Treiber, Lösungsansätze und Ambitionsniveaus der Transformation zur Nachhaltigkeit', in M. Reder and H. Pfeifer (eds.) *Kampf um Ressourcen: Weltordnung zwischen Konkurrenz und Kooperation*, Stuttgart: Kohlhammer, 138–58.

Messner, D. (2015a). 'Shaping Global Sustainability in the Umbrella of "Comprehensive Globalisation – Germany's Role" ', *Chinese Journal of Global Governance*, 1 (1): 16–35.

Messner, D. (2015b). 'A Social Contract for Low Carbon and Sustainable Development: Reflections of Non-Linear Dynamics of Social Realignments and Technological Innovations in Transformation Processes', *Technological Forecasting and Social Change*. doi:10.1016/j.techfore.2015.05.013.

Messner, D. and Nuscheler, F. (eds.) (1996). *Weltkonferenzen und Weltberichte – Ein Wegweiser durch die internationale Diskussion*, Bonn: J. H. W. Dietz.

Messner, D. and Rahmstorf, S. (2009). 'Kipp-Punkte im Erdsystem und ihre Auswirkungen auf Weltpolitik und Wirtschaft', in T. Debiel, J. Hippler, M. Roth, and C. Ulbert (eds.) *Globale Trends 2010: Frieden – Entwicklung – Umwelt*, Frankfurt: Fischer, 261–80.

Miller, J. H. and Page, S. E. (2007). *Complex Adaptive Systems: An Introduction to Computational Models of Social Life*, Princeton, NJ: Princeton University Press.

Mishra, P. (2012) *From the Ruins of Empire: The Revolt Against the West and the Remaking of Asia*, New York, NY: Farrar, Straus and Giroux.

Morgenthau, H. (1960). *Politics Among Nations: The Struggle for Power and Peace*, New York, NY: Alfred A. Knopf.

Morris, I. (2010). *Why the West Rules-for Now: The Patterns of History and What They Reveal about the Future*, London: Profile Books.

Nowak, M. A. (2006a). 'Five Rules for the Evolution of Cooperation', *Science*, 314 (5805): 1560–3.

Nowak, M. A. (2006b). *Evolutionary Dynamics*, Cambridge, MA: Harvard University Press.

Nowak, M. A. and Coakley, S. (eds.) (2013). *Evolution, Games, and God: The Principle of Cooperation*, Cambridge, MA: Harvard University Press.

Nowak, M. A. and Highfield, R. (2011). *SuperCooperators: Altruism, Evolution, and Why We Need Each Other to Succeed*, New York, NY: Free Press.

Nowak, M. A., Sasaki, A., Taylor, C., and Fudenberg, D. (2004). 'Emergence of Cooperation and Evolutionary Stability in Finite Populations', *Nature*, 428 (6983): 646–50.

Nowak, M. and Sigmund, K. (1998). 'Evolution of Indirect Reciprocity by Image Scoring', *Nature*, 393 (6685): 573–7.

Nowak, M. and Sigmund, K. (2005). 'Evolution and Indirect Reciprocity', *Nature*, 437 (7063): 1291–8.

Ostrom, E. (2003). 'Toward a Behavioral Theory Linking Trust, Reciprocity, and Reputation', in E. Ostrom and J. Walker (eds.) *Trust and Reciprocity: Interdisciplinary Lessons for Experimental Research*, New York, NY: Russell Sage Foundation, 3–18.

Ostrom, E. (2009). *Understanding Institutional Diversity*, Princeton, NJ: Princeton University Press.

Ostrom, E., Burger, J., Field, C. B., Norgaard, R. B. and Policansky, D. (1999). 'Revisiting the Commons: Local Lessons, Global Challenges', *Science*, 284 (5412): 278–82.

Ostrom, E. and Walker, J. (eds.) (2003). *Trust and Reciprocity: Interdisciplinary Lessons from Experimental Research*, New York, NY: Russell Sage Foundation.

Page, S. E. (2007). *The Difference*, Princeton, NJ: Princeton University Press.

Poteete, A. R., Janssen, M. A. and Ostrom, E. (2010). *Working Together: Collective Action, the Commons, and Multiple Methods in Practice*, Princeton, NJ: Princeton University Press.

Premack, D. and Woodruff, G. (1978). 'Does the Chimpanzee Have a Theory of Mind?', *Behavioral and Brain Sciences* 4 (4): 515–629.

Rand, D. G., Ohtsuki, H. and Nowak, M. A. (2009). 'Direct Reciprocity with Costly Punishment: Generous Tit-for-Tat Prevails', *Journal of Theoretical Biology*, 256 (1): 45–57.

Raven, R. P. J. M., Schot, J. W., and Berkhout, F. (2012). 'Space and Scale in Socio-Technical Transitions', *Environmental Innovation and Societal Transitions*, 4: 63–78.

Rawls, J. (1971). *A Theory of Justice*, Cambridge, MA: Harvard University Press.

Rockström, J., Steffen, W. and Noone, K., Persson, Å., Chapin, F. S., Lambin, E. F., Lenton, T. M., Scheffer, M., Folke, C., Schellnhuber, H. J., Nykvist, B., de Wit, C. A., Hughes, T., van der Leeuw, S., Rodhe, H., Sörlin, S., Snyder, P. K., Costanza1, R., Svedin, U., Falkenmark, M., Karlberg, L., Corell, R. W., Fabry, V. J., Hansen, J., Walker, B., Liverman, D., Richardson, K., Crutzen, P. and Foley, J. A. (2009). 'A Safe Operating Space for Humanity', *Nature*, 461 (7263): 472–5.

Ruzicka, J. and Keating, V. C. (2015). 'Going Global: Trust Research and International Relations', *Journal of Trust Research*, 5 (1): 8–26.

Scholte, J. A. (2002): 'Civil Society and Democracy in Global Governance', *Global Governance* 8 (3): 281–304.

Scholte, J. A. (2014). 'Reinventing Global Democracy', *European Journal of International Relations* 20 (1): 3–28.

Searle, J. R. (1987). *Intentionalität: Eine Abhandlung zur Philosophie des Geistes*, Frankfurt: Suhrkamp.

Searle, J. R. (1995). *The Construction of Social Reality*, New York, NY: Simon and Schuster.

Simon, H. A. (1957). *Models of Man: Social and Rational*, Oxford: Wiley.

Singer, T. and Ricard, M. (eds.) (2015). *Caring Economics: Conversations on Altruism and Compassion, Between Scientists, Economists, and the Dalai Lama*, New York, NY: St. Martins Press.

Sokolowska, E. and Guzzini, S. (2014). 'The Open-Endedness and Indeterminacy of Human Nature'. *Journal of International Relations and Development*, 17 (1): 142–6.

Spencer, H. (1864). *Principles of Biology*, London / Edinburgh: Williams and Norgate.

Stern, P. S. (2011). 'Contributions of Psychology to Limiting Climate Change', *American Psychologist*, 66 (4): 303–14.

Stewart, I. (2000). 'Impossibility Theorems', *Scientific American*, 282 (1): 98–9.

Stichweh, R. (2000). *Die Weltgesellschaft: Soziologische Analysen*, Frankfurt: Suhrkamp.

Stuenkel, O. (2015). *The BRICS and the Future of Global Order*, Lanham, MD: Lexington Books.

Tang, S. (2013) *The Social Evolution of International Politics*. Oxford: Oxford University Press.

Tomasello, M. (2003). *Constructing a Language: A Usage-Based Theory of Language Acquisition*, Cambridge, MA: Harvard University Press.

Tomasello, M. (2006). *Die kulturelle Entwicklung des menschlichen Denkens. Zur Evolution der Kognition*, Frankfurt: Suhrkamp.

Tomasello, M. (2008). *Origins of Human Communication*, Cambridge / London: MIT Press.

Tomasello, M. (2009). *Why We Cooperate*, Cambridge: MIT Press.

Tomasello, M. (2014a). 'The Ultra-Social Animal', *European Journal of Social Psychology*, 44 (3): 187–94.

Tomasello, M. (2014b). *A Natural History of Human Thinking*, Cambridge, MA: Harvard University Press.

Tomasello, M., Kruger, A. C. and Ratner, H. H. (1993). 'Cultural Learning', *Behavioral and Brain Sciences*, 16 (3): 495–511.

Traulsen, A. and Nowak, M. (2006). 'Evolution of Cooperation by Multilevel Selection', *Proceedings of the National Academy of Sciences USA*, 103 (29): 10952–5.

Tuomela, R. (2007). *The Philosophy of Sociality: The Shared Point of View*, Oxford: Oxford University Press.

Waltz, K. (1959). *Man, the State, and the State System in Theories of the Causes of War*, New York, NY: Columbia University Press.

Walzer, M. (1994). *Thick and Thin: Moral Argument at Home and Abroad*, Notre Dame, IN: University of Notre Dame Press.

Weber, E. and Johnson, E. (2012). 'Psychology and Behavioral Economics Lessons for the Design of a Green Growth Strategy', White Paper for Green Growth Knowledge Platform (OECD, UNEP, World Bank), *World Bank Policy Research Working Paper*, No. 6240.

Weinlich, S. (2014a). ' Emerging Powers at the UN: Ducking for Cover?', *Third World Quarterly*, 35 (10): 1829–44.

Weinlich, S. (2014b). *The UN Secretariat's Influence on the Evolution of Peacekeeping*, Houndsmill: Palgrave Macmillan.

Wendt, A. (1992). 'Anarchy is What States Make of It: The Social Construction of Power Politics', *International Organization*, 2 (46): 391–425.

Wiesenthal, H. (1995). 'Konventionelles und unkonventionelles Organisationslernen: Literaturreport und Ergänzungsvorschläge', *Zeitschrift für Soziologie*, 24 (2): 137–55.

Wilson, R. K. (2012). 'Elinor Ostrom (1933–2012)', *Science*, 337 (6095): 661.

WBGU (2009). *Solving the Climate Dilemma: The Budget Approach*, Berlin: WBGU.

Wissenschaftlicher Beirat der Bundesregierung Globale Umweltveränderungen (WBGU) (2011). *World in Transition – A Social Contract for Sustainability*, Berlin: WBGU.

WBGU (2014). *Climate Protection as a World Citizen Movement*, Berlin: WBGU.

World Council on Sustainable Development (WCSD) (1987). *Our Common Future: The Brundtland Report*, Oxford: World Council on Sustainable Development.

Young, H. P. (1998). *Individual Strategy and Social Structure. An Evolutionary Theory of Institutions*, Princeton, NJ: Princeton University Press.

Zalasiewicz, J., Williams, M. and Waters, C. N. (2014). 'Can an Anthropocene Series Be Defined and Recognized?', *Geological Society, London, Special Publications*, 395 (1): 39–53.

Zürn, M. (2004). 'Global Governance and Legitimacy Problems', *Government and Opposition*, 39 (2): 260–87.

2 The behavioral dimensions of international cooperation

Dirk Messner, Alejandro Guarín, and Daniel Haun

Introduction

Avoiding catastrophic climate change that can threaten human civilization as we know it may be the ultimate cooperation challenge that our species has yet faced. Harnessing the power contained in fossil fuels has allowed more people to enjoy material well-being than ever before, but these triumphs have been overshadowed by unintended consequences. There is now broad scientific agreement that our carbon-intensive economy has changed global climate in noticeable ways and that further climate change will likely have catastrophic consequences (IPCC 2014), especially for the poorest and most vulnerable people in the world (UNDP 2011; World Bank 2012).

The solution is clear – to stop burning fossil fuels – but this deceivingly simple proposition involves a transformation of the global economy under severe time constraints (WBGU 2011). Such a transformation is only possible if nation states cooperate to protect the atmospheric commons and to develop incentives that shift the economy towards a low-carbon path (Leggewie and Messner 2012; Messner et al. 2010). And yet, even though the science is clear and the options for action are well understood (WBGU 2011; World Bank 2012), getting countries to agree on action to prevent global climate change has proved very difficult. International climate negotiations have failed to reach substantive progress. Similar difficulties arise when dealing with other global problems – such as global financial markets or cross-border migration – that can be addressed only through international cooperation. Embedded in the promise of an increasingly dense globalized network is a paradox: a spreading consensus on the importance and urgency of global problems, together with the rise of seemingly intractable cooperation blockades. Here we aim to address a deceivingly simple question: *why?*

Why is global cooperation hard? The optimistic answer is illustrated by Global Governance theories: international cooperation is possible, but we have not figured out the right way to make it work. Current mechanisms and institutions for international cooperation worked in the bipolar world order, which emerged after 1945, but are not appropriate to deal with a global system in which new configurations such as the G20 – the group of the world's 20 largest economies, including emerging countries like China, India, and Brazil – become more relevant (Messner and Nuscheler 2006; Nye and Donahue 2000; Zürn 2005). The (neo)realist school of

DOI: 10.4324/9781315691657-3

International Relations offers a more pessimistic assessment: it's not a problem with the institutions; the problem is that collective action in the international system beyond the lowest common denominator is impossible. States seek their own interests and will not subordinate their interests to that of other states (Barrett 2005; Bremmer 2012; Mearsheimer 2014). Ultimately, this reflects the assumption that human behavior is driven predominantly by self-interest and the maximization of individual benefits (Buchanan and Tollison 1972; Olson 1965); this behavior scales up to the level of nation states in the form of national interests and competition for dominance in an anarchic world (Morgenthau 1985).

The picture of failed global cooperation is at odds with the body of evidence showing that people are in fact astonishingly cooperative. Research in experimental and evolutionary psychology suggests that children from an early age are inclined to share, to help, and to work together to accomplish common goals. Such a cooperative bias appears to have been part of humans' biological history for a long time, and many of the necessary abilities and motivations heritable (Tomasello 2009). In experiments and field observations, behavioral economists and other social scientists have found robust evidence that people share and cooperate much more than a model of human behavior based on narrow self-interest would predict (Fehr and Schmidt 1999; Kahneman 2011; Ostrom 1990). These findings appear to hold true across many diverse cultural backgrounds (Henrich et al. 2001); they too suggest the existence of a natural human cooperative bias.

Unlike economics, which has used behavioral insights to enrich theories of macro-behavior (e.g. Akerlof and Shiller 2009), in International Relations theories the insights gained by the behavioral sciences beyond rational choice have been so far largely ignored. Here we argue that International Relations theories need to be expanded to accommodate what we know about human cooperation, and that this knowledge could be used to design new and better instruments for global cooperation. The chapter is structured around three central questions that we pose to address the apparent contradiction between the obvious underprovision of cooperation at the global scale and the cooperative bias of individual human beings:

- First, *are we good or bad at cooperating?* We argue that, contrary to the assumptions of many rational choice theories, there is rich evidence that cooperation is widespread and comes naturally to humans. In the second section, we discuss a wealth of experimental and field research suggesting a natural propensity for cooperation that is deeply ingrained in our evolutionary makeup.
- Second, *what are the essential mechanisms that enable cooperation?* In the third section, we show that there is remarkable interdisciplinary convergence about the 'cooperation hexagon' – a relatively small group of factors on which the success or failure of cooperation depends: reciprocity, trust, communication, reputation, fairness, enforcement, and we-identity.
- And third, *what does this knowledge mean for understanding cooperation at an international level?* Taking the behavioral insights about cooperation seriously should prompt a search for a behaviorally sound theory of International

Relations. We propose that this search be geared towards understanding the scaling properties of the mechanisms for cooperation, studying how cooperation works within the groups of people who work in international institutions, and analyzing international cooperation blockades through the prism of the cooperation hexagon.

We end the chapter by addressing some of the theoretical and practical consequences of using a behavioral approach to studying international cooperation.

Are we good or bad at cooperating?

Some of the most influential theories in economics and political science assume that human beings always behave competitively and make rational choices, with the only goal of furthering their narrow interests and maximizing their profits and utilities. They do so in isolation from other actors, based on 'complete information about the structure of the situation they are in, including the preferences of other actors, the full range of possible actions, and the probability associated with each outcome resulting from a combination of actions' (Poteete, Janssen, and Ostrom 2010: 217). From the point of view of such theories cooperation is an 'evolutionary mistake' (Lohman 2013: 280) that occurs due to coercion or to the miscalculation of the costs and benefits of a particular decision. Such cooperation could not be stable in time.

We will show that there is now overwhelming evidence to seriously discredit such a perspective. Before we go any further, it is important to clarify what we mean by cooperation. We use Coakley and Nowak's (2013: 4) definition of cooperation as 'a form of working together in which one individual pays a cost (in terms of fitness, whether genetic or cultural) and another gains a benefit as a result'. This definition emphasizes the distinction between cooperation and other types of interaction that result in a mutual benefit. People commonly collaborate or coordinate to achieve a common aim, but for true cooperation to exist one of the parties must give up something, or give up more, than the other party.

Conventional theories have a hard time explaining this type of behavior. The model of society underpinned by fundamentally uncooperative human behavior is part of a long intellectual tradition stemming from Hobbes's notion that the natural state of humans is war of all against all. Adam Smith also had a vision of a society made up of self-interested individuals, but the aggregate effect of the individual pursuit of happiness would lead to self-organizing prosperity rather than violent anarchy. The concepts (and language) of evolutionary theory such as 'fitness' and 'selection' have been influential in social sciences, and particularly in economics. The rational choice model is founded on the idea that people are egoistical by nature, because otherwise our species would have become extinct.

This model of human behavior is also the basis for understanding International Relations. The realist school, a widely used approach to explaining International Relations, assumes that nations engage in a power game to pursue their own interests (Mearsheimer 2014; Waltz 1979). The absence of a global enforcer creates an anarchic system in which the strongest nations prevail. States can only engage in 'adversarial competition' to defend their sovereignty and their interests (Reinicke 1998: 61), hindering their ability to cooperate. In the context of such theories the idea of global governance – an instance of global cooperation – is naïve at best (Brzezinski 1997).

In what follows we show that cooperation is part of the basic repertoire of human behavior (see also Melis in this volume). This insight has been sidelined by mainstream economics and political science, and it is all but absent from theories of the international system. The fact that people are cooperative in addition to self-interested challenges the idea that behavior is reducible to utility-maximization that responds to punishments and incentives and that it is therefore easily predictable. The power of the rational choice model lies on its simple assumptions and clear predictions. But if it fails to account for a crucial part of human behavior, its validity as a scientific theory must be questioned.

Our perspective on cooperation is not naïve. We do not deny the existence of self-interest, greed, or selfishness – but we do question the assumption that human behavior is reducible to these features. Neither is the outcome of cooperation positive per se: people can cooperate to do very bad things. And yet without cooperation we cannot solve complex social dilemmas or protect the global commons. In the rest of this section we show that the room of possibility for cooperation is much larger than what conventional theories would predict.

The validity of rational choice and related theories has been questioned in recent years. Competitive behavior may not be universal, but instead apply only in specific decision-making settings (Akerlof and Shiller 2009; Kahneman 2003; Poteete et al. 2010). Although the assumption of the self-interested individual is claimed to be grounded on evolutionary theory, mathematical models have shown that natural selection can lead to populations of cooperators (Nowak and Sigmund 2007). If these populations have an advantage over groups of non-cooperators – as is likely to have happened, for example, among early human populations – then cooperative behavior would be selected (see Bowles and Gintis 2011). Rather than a mishap, cooperation could be a key mechanism for evolution on par with mutation and selection (Nowak and Highfield 2011).

This evolutionary perspective is consistent with recent empirical evidence emerging out of the natural and social sciences. Research from multiple disciplines over the last two decades suggests that cooperation is much more common than previously thought, and that this might stem from a natural human predisposition to cooperate. The 'tragedy of the commons' (Hardin 1968), is neither typical nor inevitable: users of common resources such as fisheries and forests can and do self-organize to profit from the common resource while maintaining its integrity in the long run (Acheson and Wilson 1996; Poteete et al. 2010).

Experimental research has also provided a wealth of evidence about the pervasiveness of cooperation (see Cárdenas 2009; see also Rand and Nowak in this volume). Although experiments simplify the complexity of real life and should be thus interpreted cautiously, results indicate that people commonly cooperate (at a cost), even when objectively they could be better off without cooperating.

For example, in prisoner's dilemma games – in which two people have to decide whether to cooperate or to defect, with the best outcome for an individual being to defect – participants routinely decide to cooperate (e.g. Clark and Sefton 2001). In the Ultimatum Game (Güth, Schmittberger, and Schwarze 1982), one participant (the proposer) often gives money to the other participant (the responder) without expecting anything in return (Bowles and Gintis 2011; Camerer 2003). In the trust game, the responder can reciprocate and return a portion of the money to the proposer, and in most cases responders give back a substantial amount (Ostrom and Walker 2005). In so-called public goods experiments, where participants must decide between personal or communal gains, people often opt to contribute to the common pool rather than to free ride (Ahn, Ostrom, and Walker 2003; Benkler 2011; Ostrom and Walker 2005).

Behaviors such as the ones described above appear to stem from a natural predisposition to cooperate; in fact, it seems that in some cases cooperation is our gut reaction (Rand, Greene, and Nowak 2012). Three main lines of evidence suggest the existence of this natural cooperative bias. First, children often cooperate at a very young age, before a great deal of socialization and even before acquiring language (Warneken and Tomasello 2006). Without much adult intervention, children are inclined to help (Hepach, Vaish, and Tomasello 2013) and to provide information to others (Tomasello, Carpenter, and Liszkowski 2007), even in the absence of rewards (Warneken and Tomasello 2008). Importantly, children *like* to cooperate: they prefer doing things together than alone (Rekers, Haun, and Tomasello 2011), and appear to be interested in the social interaction for its own sake, beyond a specific goal (Gräfenhain et al. 2009). From around their second year, children are able to work together to solve problems cooperatively and to achieve mutual goals by assessing other people's intentions (Buttelmann, Carpenter, and Tomasello 2009). This does not imply that children only or always behave cooperatively; when something they really want is at stake, they can be fiercely uncooperative (Rochat 2011). As we grow older, this natural bias for helpfulness is shaped and modulated by socialization. Eventually we start to shift from a more selfless form of cooperation to one that is more influenced by an expectation of what we can receive in return (Tomasello 2009).

Second, evidence for cooperative behavior in other species, particularly primates, suggests that cooperation is well established in our evolutionary lineage (see also Melis in this volume). Other great apes possess many of the cognitive prerequisites necessary for human-like collaboration, at least in controlled settings (Hare et al. 2007; Melis, Hare, and Tomasello 2006; Rekers, Cronin, and Haun submitted). Chimpanzees can recognize when they need help in solving a problem and actively recruit good (over bad) collaborators (Melis et al. 2006). Experiments comparing humans to primates also highlight important differences, such as humans' understanding of common goals and 'shared intentionality', i.e. the awareness of one's own role in a cooperative task (Melis in this volume; Moll and Tomasello 2007; Warneken and Tomasello 2006).

Third, the predisposition to cooperate seems to be independent of culture. Research on cooperation tends to reflect the bias towards what Henrich, Heine, and

Norenzayan (2010) call WEIRD (Western, Educated, Industrialized, Rich, and Democratic) people, but increasing evidence from field experiments in non-Western countries points to some important convergences. In a replication of the Ultimatum Game in 15 small-scale societies (including foragers, hunters and gatherers, and pastoralists), Henrich et al. (2001) found that people in all societies made non-zero offers. Similar results have been reached by researchers in other societies (for a review see Oosterbeek, Sloof, and van de Kuilen 2004) using dictator and public goods games (see Cárdenas and Carpenter 2008 and Cárdenas 2009 for reviews).

In summary, our inclination to cooperate seems to be as much a part of our nature as self-interest, and cooperative behavior is much more common than theories of rational choice would predict. We have argued that this stems from a natural cooperative bias that is reflected in children's interest and ability for cooperation, in similar behavior among related non-human species, and in the ubiquity of cooperative behavior across cultures.

What makes cooperation work?
The cooperation hexagon

Accepting that cooperation is as much a part of human nature as selfishness, why does cooperation emerge in some situations and not in others? Over the last two decades there has been a remarkable convergence by different disciplines around the basic enablers of cooperation: reciprocity, trust, communication, reputation, fairness, enforcement, and we-identity. We call these the cooperation hexagon (Figure 2.1). Just as no one single of these mechanisms is enough to explain why

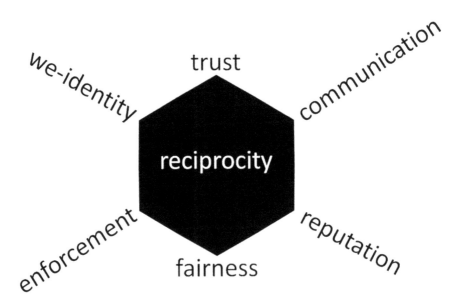

Figure 2.1 The cooperation hexagon.

cooperation occurs, the lack of cooperation cannot be attributed to the absence of any one of them. They work as building blocks that reinforce each other to enable long-term cooperation.

Reciprocity

At the center of the diagram is *reciprocity*, the main evolutionary mechanism underlying cooperation (Nowak and Highfield 2011; Nowak and Sigmund 2007), and one of the basic norms taught in all societies (Ostrom 2005). We do something for others when they do something for us: this is direct reciprocity or 'tit for tat' (Axelrod 1984). Remarkably, we often do something for others when no immediate reward is apparent; this behavior is possible when people interact frequently, live long lives, and co-exist in small groups, and when the cost of cooperating is relatively small. This indirect reciprocity is one of the key building blocks of cooperation in human societies (Nowak and Highfield 2011). In large groups, gossip and reputation allow us to cooperate, knowing that 'I scratch your back and someone else will scratch mine' (Nowak and Highfield 2011: 53). Evidence for the importance of reciprocity for cooperation comes from observations of management of common resources and from experimental data (Ostrom 2005; Poteete et al. 2010). Importantly, when people make themselves vulnerable by making one-sided displays of cooperativeness, partners tend to reciprocate rather than to exploit this behavior (Bowles and Gintis 2011: 21). Reciprocity, however, is not only positive: uncooperative behavior can be paid with the same coin, leading to a downward spiral of anti-cooperation (Nowak 2006).

Trust

Field and experimental research suggests that establishing trust greatly enhances the possibilities of successful cooperation (Ostrom and Walker 2005). Trust can be thought of as the belief about the probability of reciprocation (Rousseau et al. 1998: 395), or the degree to which people allow themselves to be vulnerable in the absence of external enforcement (Ben-Ner and Putterman 2009). But how to know whom to trust? In small groups we can keep track of others' actions and know who is trustworthy or not, but in a world full of strangers we often rely on external clues. Experiments have shown that we make very quick assessments of people's faces to see if they look trustworthy (van't Wout and Sanfey 2008), although this initial impression is modulated through experience (Chang et al. 2010). Ultimately, when the group is too large, we rely on reputation to assess trustworthiness.

Communication

Although cooperation can emerge even in anonymous interactions, it has been well established that communication greatly enhances the chances of more persistent cooperative outcomes. Communications allows us to gauge each other's expectations, devise joint strategies, and make pledges about our future behavior. Face-to-face communication is known to be a key element in the collective management of natural resources in small communities throughout the world (Poteete et al. 2010), and public goods experiments confirm that cooperation is significantly enhanced when participants can communicate (Ben-Ner and Putterman 2009; Brosig, Weimann, and Yang 2004; Ostrom 2005). Communication enhances cooperation even when the interaction is anonymous, suggesting that there is something innately valuable about exchanging pledges independent of reputation (Ben-Ner and Putterman 2009; Cárdenas and Jaramillo 2009). Pledges create a self-enforcing cycle of increasing trust between the cooperating partners that can even overcome initial reluctance to cooperate and that, in public games experiments, result in significantly higher contributions to the public good (Milinski et al. 2008). Communication is thus fundamentally about increasing trust (Ostrom 2005).

Reputation

History matters: we seek information about others' past performance to try to guess how they will behave in the future. In evolutionary biology, reputation-building is a key mechanism for indirect reciprocity. It is important to know in advance if others are trustworthy cooperators or not, and gossip allows this information to be synchronized across populations (Nowak and Sigmund 2005). However, reputations are not static: they can be improved or damaged through our behavior. Decision-making experiments bear out the importance of reputation. Cooperation decreases when participants do not know each other, or when they cannot exchange information with each other, so there is no chance to build reputation (Ebenhöh and Pahl-Wostl 2008). In a public goods game, donations to the common good were increased by publically honoring players who had contributed large sums and shaming those who contributed little (Jacquet et al. 2011).

Fairness

For cooperation to succeed, it is often not enough that acts are reciprocated; reciprocation should also be perceived as fair. Fairness can be thought of as the propensity to be averse to inequality (Fehr and Schmidt 1999). Even though this definition is subjective and relative to some group or outcome of reference, people in a variety of economic experiments consistently state that they want to be fair, they want to be perceived as fair, and they expect others to be fair as well (Akerlof and Kranton 2000). Inequality aversion shapes cooperation, not just in humans from an early age (Castelli, Massaro, and Marchetti 2010) but in other social primates (Cronin and Sánchez 2012). For example, in a public goods game, too much inequality of endowments among the players diminished contributions to the public good, and this was attributed to players' perception of fairness (Tavoni et al. 2011). In ultimatum games, offers that are perceived to be too low are frequently rejected because they are perceived as unfair, despite the fact that doing so is costly for the responder (Almenberg and Dreber 2013). Other experimental and field results suggest that agreement to cooperate may be hampered when the cost and benefits are not fairly distributed (Poteete et al. 2010) or when hierarchical differences constrain communication (Cárdenas and Carpenter 2008).

Enforcement

When trust and reputation are not enough to trigger cooperative behavior, some means of enforcement, such as a punishment or reward, is needed. Punishment enhances cooperation in situations where reputation-building is not possible, such as in one-off interactions (Fehr and Gächter 2002). People actively punish cheaters who do not play by the rules or do not reciprocate, and the very threat of punishment may be enough to deter free-riding. Field and laboratory experiments have shown that the possibility to punish cheaters increases the cooperative outcome (for reviews see Bowles and Gintis 2011 and Ostrom and Walker 2005). Punishment is presumably triggered by the anger felt by the participants towards those who cheat (Fehr and Gächter 2002). Such drive to comply with norms and to make sure that others act in 'the way things are done' appears in children as young as 18 months old (Tomasello 2009). Sometimes positive rewards may be just as effective as punishment for promoting cooperation. For example, contributions to the public pool were as high when people could punish free-riders as when they could reward cooperators (Rand et al. 2009).

We-identity

When seeking partners for cooperation, it is important that we guess correctly which individuals are more likely to reciprocate (Durrett and Levin 2005). Experimental evidence suggests that we tend to cooperate better with those who look like us (Krupp, Debruine, and Barclay 2008; Sigmund 2009), with whom we share other non-physical traits, such as our accent (Haun and Over, in press), or with those who are assigned to our ingroup – even if the group has been defined arbitrarily (Burton-Chellew and West 2012). Observations of actual management of common resources suggest that ethnic or cultural similarity makes it easier to build trust, which then enhances cooperation (Poteete et al. 2010: 44). Similarity is also actively built through language and communication. We learn and build joint narratives that reinforce our sense of belonging and use these narratives – whether around religions, political parties, nation states, or football teams – to expand our common ground (Akerlof and Shiller 2009; Kennedy, Messner, and Nuscheler 2001; Tomasello 2010). A we-identity allows us to perform acts of generosity and kindness within the ingroup, but at the same time allows us to inflict great damage on those outside it (Tomasello 2009: 99).

What does this mean for international cooperation?

We have talked about the capabilities of human beings to cooperate and identified the seven key enablers of cooperation. But how does this knowledge help us to understand the challenges of global governance and international cooperation? If people are fundamentally good at cooperating, the theories of International Relations must be expanded to accommodate assumptions that go beyond power and self-interest. Such a change in perspective could reshape our understanding of historic patterns of social change, challenge received ideas about the nature of the current international 'cooperation crisis', and point in the direction of new lines of empirical research. Such a change could also help us identify the institutional, normative, and cognitive innovations that are necessary to favor global cooperation in the 21st century.

Our review has shown that people are not just 'rational fools' who only optimize their own self-interests (Sen 1977), but that they can cooperate and enjoy doing so. The scope for cooperation at all levels of human organization – including International Relations – is therefore larger than it is assumed. Power, dominance, and self-interest are significant, but evidently nations have cooperated successfully in many ways over the last two centuries – for example in the creation of international law or the establishment of international organizations.

We do not currently have this new, behaviorally sound theory of international cooperation, but below we outline three directions that could help us get there: first, establishing how cooperative behavior 'trickles up' from simple interpersonal relations to larger and more complex forms; second, investigating how cooperation works in the formal and informal institutions and regimes in which nations interact; and third, understanding to what extent current international cooperation challenges are the result of an underprovisioning of the basic elements of the cooperation hexagon.

The history of humankind has been characterized by ever increasing and accelerating complexity (Fogel 1999). This surprisingly rapid cultural evolution – relative to the slow biological one – is based on the ratcheting-up of knowledge by building on what previous generations have learned (Tomasello 1999). All relevant human inventions such as language and other complex social structures are collective cultural products, which are in turn the result of cooperation (Nowak and Highfield 2011; Tomasello and Rakoczy 2003). However, it is not clear exactly how the basic building blocks of interpersonal cooperation come together to build larger and more complex cooperative institutions. Computer models have shown that cooperative populations can and do emerge out of interactions between individuals that are governed by minimal rules such as tit for tat (Nowak and Sigmund 2007), but we don't know whether there are limits to the size or complexity within which these basic mechanisms continue to work. Moreover, simple rules of cooperation do not always lead to stable or persistent cooperative outcomes (Nowak and Highfield 2011: 35). While some properties of cooperation might operate regardless of time or scale, others depend on specific institutional and historical contexts (Ostrom 2005). The mechanisms of the cooperation hexagon emerge and stabilize themselves in different environments and need to be re-established as circumstances change. Where does global governance stand with regard to these cycles of cooperation?

One way to approach this question is by examining how the institutions for international cooperation actually work. Global cooperation is a pretty complex affair, requiring a sophisticated system of decision making and coordination at local, national, and international levels. But it is also something that is carried out by individuals who speak on behalf of others and who work in relatively small groups. How is interaction between these individuals governed, and how is it different from that of other individuals making decisions at local or national levels? The behavioral perspectives discussed in this chapter could help us understand the institutional arrangements for global governance, one of the key concerns of International Regime theory (Rittberger 1995; Zürn 2005). From a behavioral perspective, the question is how a group of people, such as staff of multilateral organizations or civil society organizations, work both as individuals and as representatives of the interests of millions of people.

To understand this particular dynamic from the perspective of our cooperation hexagon, it is important to understand the 'microsituational context' (Poteete et al. 2010: 228). The interaction between the members of these groups is shaped by how well they know or trust each other. But simultaneously they represent the interests of the countries or civil societies to whom they are accountable, and they are influenced by their sense of obligation to the group itself and by their own personal preferences. Some of these individuals may be sympathetic to common global interests, but their decisions are affected by the norms of the institutions that they work in and by the broader institutional and political context. The regimes of international cooperation are thus a point of confluence of interpersonal and inter-institutional dimensions, and the problem of cooperation is not about scale but about different drivers. Understanding how this point of intersection works is a promising area of study for which we currently have very little direct empirical evidence.

Such a behavioral understanding of international cooperation could be advanced by examining the performance of the elements of the cooperation hexagon. In what follows we suggest that, in addition to power, dominance, and self-interest, the current obstacles for international cooperation are related to an underprovisioning of the basic elements of the cooperation hexagon. Many International Relations scholars interpret current blockades in world politics as power games resulting from the transition from world dominated by the G 7/8 – the traditional Western powers – to one in which the G20 – the world's 20 largest economies, including China and India – plays a stronger role (Bremmer 2012; Gu, Humphrey, and Messner 2008; Mearsheimer 2014). Economic, political, and military power resources are being redistributed among old and emerging powers as the 200-year dominance of Western countries erodes. From a realist perspective, power struggles hinder collective action; the only viable policy for the West to prevail is containment. For example, the intense security competition between China and the United States holds considerable potential for war (Mearsheimer

2014). Similarly, the current deadlock in climate negotiations has been attributed to the irreconcilable interests that Western nations and emerging economies have with regard to carbon emissions.

The existence of these power games cannot be denied, but when viewed through the eyes of the cooperation hexagon, the blockades and their possible solutions appear in a new light. Examples of successful international cooperation show that massive investments in generating trust, developing reciprocity, communication, reputation, and a common identity, and establishing enforcement mechanisms were essential to success. After World War II, former enemies of the North Atlantic and Japan created a dense network of cooperation, including the establishment of institutions such as the EU and the OECD despite many opposing interests and power asymmetries. The basic mechanisms of cooperation have been routinized and stabilized in mutual regulations and institutions. Other institutions of international cooperation such as ASEAN (Association of Southeast Asian Nations) show that former foes can cooperate peacefully, but that building up the basic blocks of cooperation requires time (Acharya 2009).

If agreements on climate change and other critical topics are to be reached, these basic mechanisms of cooperation must be rebuilt, redeveloped, and reinvented in new constellations of players such as the G20. Our answer to those who see only power conflicts and blockades is that these forces appear unrestrained in this phase of tectonic power shifts because they have not been embedded and defused by the structures of the cooperation hexagon, i.e. by functional cooperation spaces. The supposed 'clash of civilizations' that threatens the (cooperative) West is replaced by a recognition that we might simply need time and effort to establish mechanisms that enable cooperation to flourish.

A preliminary assessment of the current global cooperation crisis, particularly within the G20, from the point of view of the cooperation hexagon yields important insights:

- *Reciprocity.* OECD countries have developed the type of close, long-standing relations that favor reciprocity over the last 70 years. Old and new powers in the G20 will have to first build up interactions to enable self-strengthening reciprocity to develop before they can engage in certain types of cooperation.
- *Trust.* Trust is a scarce commodity in the new power constellation. Some of the obstacles for cooperation within the G20 could be attributable to persistent mistrust, as emerging countries assume that power-retaining strategies lie behind the political initiatives of the G7 countries. Whereas the G7 is a union based on democratic values, the G20 requires democratic, semi-authoritarian, and authoritarian countries to work together.
- *Communication.* The chances of the emergence of cooperation are increased by communication, but so far communication relationships between G20 societies are still pretty thin compared to, for example, the communication relationships which have been expanding between EU societies over the last seven decades.

- *Reputation.* The lack of trust and the thin communication structures in the G20 suggested previously result in chronic reputation problems within this new power constellation. All involved have to regain a reputation as players who can find solutions in the common interest or to preserve the global commons.
- *Fairness.* Fairness is of enormous importance in international cooperation. The issue of fairness plays a major role regarding the distribution of seats in the control bodies of the IMF and World Bank or burden sharing in climate change negotiations. Developing countries complain about a structural fairness deficit in the international system, and redressing these complaints is a major step towards establishing cooperation to protect global commons.
- *Enforcement.* International agreements to protect the climate and other global commons are unlikely to succeed without sanction mechanisms. And yet, although the WTO has an arbitration court mechanism and sanction option, the G20 has yet to reach a single agreement that is bound by sanctions.
- *We-identities and joint narratives.* Examples of successful international cooperation suggest a key role for a powerful narrative that creates a common identity, such as the European Union as a peace project. Inventing a shared narrative for global cooperation in the G20 is no triviality, both because of the complexity of the problems and the diversity of actors. The development of a common notion about our interdependent future is beyond our current cognitive framework and requires time for nurturing (Weber and Johnson 2012).

The foundations for cooperation in a multipolar world order need to be developed by investing in the institutional, normative, and cognitive innovations that foster the mechanisms of the cooperation hexagon. A view of the current global cooperation blockades such as climate change mitigation through the prism of the cooperation hexagon shows a complicated construction site on which the basic mechanisms of cooperation have to be built and developed by a radically changed constellation of players.

Conclusions

We have argued that the evidence of a human cooperative bias should prompt us to rethink current approaches to International Relations. If we accept that the space for cooperation is larger than dominant theories allow, then we need to reconsider the assumption that national self-interests and competitive struggles will inevitably derail efforts for effective global cooperation. Any theory about human institutions that knowingly ignores the ubiquity of cooperation is inadequate.

Our call for a behaviorally sound theory of International Relations has been based on three key premises. First, we have argued that there is overwhelming evidence to show that cooperation plays a much more important role in human behavior than is predicted by rational choice and related theories. New frontiers in theoretical biology make the case that cooperation is not an evolutionary anomaly but a driver of complex forms of organismic and social organization. Moreover, cooperation has been part of the behavioral repertoire of primates long before our species evolved in Africa; it emerges early in our childhood and occurs across cultures.

Second, cooperation appears to be governed by a relatively small set of basic mechanisms – the cooperation hexagon – that affect whether cooperation persists in time or not. First among these is reciprocity, reflected on our strong aversion to being cheated. Reciprocity is better established when there is trust, when we can communicate to share information, when we can use reputation to assess trustworthiness, and when we perceive the interaction as being fair. An enforcement mechanism such as punishment can help keep free riders at bay and maintain cooperation in larger groups. Finally, cooperation is sustained when people share the physical and intellectual characteristics, ideas, or narratives that create a we-identity.

Third, acknowledging the pervasiveness of cooperative behavior and understanding the basic mechanisms that make it possible prompts us to call for a reformulation of current theories of International Relations. Although we do not claim to have such a theory, we propose to begin this exploration in three different areas:

- Cooperation has been an enabler of society's increasing size and complexity. This suggests that the same basic mechanisms of cooperation operate at different scales and in different contexts, but that they have to be re-established and reworked. To understand the relationship between interpersonal and global cooperation we need to establish the scaling properties of the cooperation hexagon, as well as how these mechanisms perform in times of crisis and transformation.
- Global cooperation is performed by the relatively few people who interact in the institutions and regimes established for International Relations, such as the UN. We hypothesize that the elements of the cooperation hexagon must operate among these groups, with the added complexity that these people interact as both individuals and as representatives of others. We must therefore better understand how cooperation works at this interface between interpersonal and inter-institutional interests.
- Current blockades in international cooperation are attributed to power plays and the narrow pursuit of national interests. Seen through the lens of the cooperative hexagon, an alternative explanation emerges: the current crises in international cooperation could be due to the underprovisioning of the seven basic enablers of cooperation, and any solution should seek to foster them. For example, if agreement on one key issue, such as refugees, is reached and widely seen as fair, this could build up trust among parties and trigger breakthroughs in other issues. Similarly, the setup of international development as a deeply unequal North (donor) – South (recipient) relationship needs to be replaced by one based on a reciprocal perspective of achieving common aims together.

Taking the behavioral insights about cooperation seriously should help shift our perspective of International Relations, and such a shift could have real consequences for how we behave (See Weber and Johnson in this volume; Weber and Johnson 2012). The basic assumption of the impossibility of cooperation in a time of global power shifts can become a self-fulfilling prophecy (see also Brock in this volume). But an alternative perspective that looks at the challenges of international cooperation from the starting principle that people can and do cooperate could improve the chances of global cooperation and maybe break the deadlock in critical cooperation problems, such as avoiding catastrophic climate change. Scientific creativity and social fantasy are necessary to chart the spaces of future cooperation, and this creativity cannot be expected of theorists who reduce human societies to the utilities, payoffs, and self-interest of rational economic people. 'The limits of my language', as Ludwig Wittgenstein (1922: 74) wrote, 'mean the limits of my world'.

References

Acharya, A. (2009). *Constructing a Security Community in Southeast Asia: ASEAN and the Problem of Regional Order*, London: Routledge.

Acheson, J. M. and Wilson, J. A. (1996). 'Order Out of Chaos: The Case for Parametric Fisheries Management', *American Anthropologist*, 98 (3): 579–94.

Ahn, T. K., Ostrom, E. and Walker, J. M. (2003). 'Heterogeneous Preferences and Collective Action', *Public Choice*, 117 (3/4): 295–314.

Akerlof, G. and Kranton, R. (2000). 'Economics and Identity', *The Quarterly Journal of Economics*, 105 (3): 715–53.

Akerlof, G. and Shiller, R. J. (2009). *Animal Spirits: How Human Psychology Drives the Economy, and Why It Matters for Global Capitalism*, Princeton, NJ / Oxford: Princeton University Press.

Almenberg, J. and Dreber, A. (2013). 'Economics and Evolution: Complementary Perspectives on Cooperation', in M. Nowak and S. Coakley (eds.) *Evolution, Games, and God: The Principle of Cooperation*, Cambridge, MA: Harvard University Press, 132–49.

Axelrod, R. (1984). *The Evolution of Cooperation*, New York, NY: Basic Books.

Barrett, S. (2005). *Environment and Statecraft: The Strategy of Environmental Treaty-Making*, Oxford / New York, NY: Oxford University Press.

Benkler, Y. (2011). *The Penguin and the Leviathan: The Triumph of Cooperation over Self-Interest*, New York, NY: Crown Business.

Ben-Ner, A. and Putterman, L. (2009). 'Trust, Communication and Contracts: An Experiment', *Journal of Economic Behavior & Organization*, 70 (1–2): 106–21.

Bowles, S. and Gintis, H. (2011). *A Cooperative Species: Human Reciprocity and Its Evolution*, Princeton, NJ: Princeton University Press.

Bremmer, I. (2012). *Every Nation for Itself: Winners and Losers in a G-Zero World*, New York, NY: Penguin.

Brosig, J., Weimann, J. and Yang, C. (2004). 'Communication, Reputation, and Punishment in Sequential Bargaining Experiments', *Journal of Institutional and Theoretical Economics JITE*, 160 (4): 576–606.

Brzezinski, Z. (1997). *The Grand Chessboard: American Primacy and Its Geostrategic Imperatives*, New York, NY: Basic Books.

Buchanan, J. and Tollison, R. (eds.) (1972). *Theory of Public Choice: Political Applications of Economics*, Ann Arbor, MI: University of Michigan Press.

Burton-Chellew, M. N. and West, S. A. (2012). 'Pseudocompetition Among Groups Increases Human Cooperation in a Public-Goods Game', *Animal Behaviour*, 84 (4): 947–52.

Buttelmann, D., Carpenter, M. and Tomasello, M. (2009). 'Eighteen-Month-Old Infants Show False Belief Understanding in an Active Helping Paradigm', *Cognition*, 112 (2): 337–42.

Camerer, C. (2003). *Behavioral Game Theory*, Princeton, NJ: Princeton University Press.

Cárdenas, J. C. (2009). 'Experiments in Environment and Development', *Annual Review of Resource Economics*, 1 (1): 157–82.

Cárdenas, J. C. and Carpenter, J. (2008). 'Behavioural Development Economics: Lessons from Field Labs in the Developing World', *Journal of Development Studies*, 44 (3): 311–38.

Cárdenas, J. C. and Jaramillo, C. (2009). *Cooperation in Large Networks: An Experimental Approach*, Bogotá, Colombia: Universidad de los Andes.

Castelli, I., Massaro, D. and Marchetti, A. (2010). 'Fairness and Intentionality in Children's Decision-Making', *International Review of Economics*, 57 (3): 269–88.

Chang, L., Doll, B., van't Wout, M., Frank, M. and Sanfey, A. (2010). 'Seeing Is Believing: Trustworthiness as a Dynamic Belief', *Cognitive Psychology*, 61 (2): 87–105.

Clark, K. and Sefton, M. (2001). 'The Sequential Prisoner's Dilemma: Evidence on Reciprocation', *The Economic Journal*, 111 (468): 51–68.

Coakley, S. and Nowak, M. (2013). 'Introduction: Why Cooperation Makes a Difference', in M. Nowak and S. Coakley (eds.) *Evolution, Games, and God: The Principle of Cooperation*, Cambridge, MA: Harvard University Press, 1–34.

Cronin, K. A. and Sánchez, A. (2012). 'Social Dynamics and Cooperation: The Case of Non-Human Primates and Its Implications for Human Behavior', *Advances in Complex Systems*, 15 (suppl. 1): 1250066, 1–21.

Durrett, R. and Levin, S. A. (2005). 'Can Stable Social Groups Be Maintained by Homophilous Imitation Alone?', *Journal of Economic Behavior & Organization*, 57 (3) (July): 267–86.

Ebenhöh, E. and Pahl-Wostl, C. (2008). 'Agent Behavior Between Maximization and Cooperation', *Rationality and Society*, 20 (2): 227–52.

Fehr, E. and Gächter, S. (2002). 'Altruistic Punishment in Humans', *Nature*, 415: 137–40.

Fehr, E. and Schmidt, K. M. (1999). 'A Theory of Fairness, Competition, and Cooperation', *The Quarterly Journal of Economics*, 114 (3) (August 1): 817–68.

Fogel, R. (1999). 'Catching up with the Economy', *American Economic Review*, 89 (1): 1–21.

Gräfenhain, M., Behne, T., Carpenter, M. and Tomasello, M. (2009). 'Young Children's Understanding of Joint Commitments', *Developmental Psychology*, 45 (5): 1430–43.

Gu, J., Humphrey, J. and Messner, D. (2008). 'Global Governance and Developing Countries: The Implications of the Rise of China', *World Development*, 36 (2): 274–92.

Güth, W., Schmittberger, R. and Schwarze, B. (1982). 'An Experimental Analysis of Ultimatum Bargaining', *Journal of Economic Behavior & Organization*, 3 (4): 367–88.

Hardin, Garret (1968). 'The Tragedy of the Commons', *Science*, 162 (3859): 1243–8.

Hare, B., Melis, A., Woods, V., Hastings, S. and Wrangham, R. (2007). 'Tolerance Allows Bonobos to Outperform Chimpanzees on a Cooperative Task', *Current Biology*, 17: 619–23.

Haun, D. B. M. and Over, H. (2013). 'Like Me: A Homophily-Based Account of Human Culture', in P. J. Richerson and M. Christiansen (eds.) *Cultural Evolution*, Cambridge, MA: MIT Press.

Henrich, J., Boyd, R., Bowles, S., Camerer, C., Fehr, E., Gintis, H. and McElreath, R. (2001). 'In Search of Homo Economicus: Behavioral Experiments in 15 Small-Scale Societies', *American Economic Review*, 91 (2): 73–8.

Henrich, J., Heine, S. and Norenzayan, A. (2010). 'The Weirdest People in the World?', *Behavioral and Brain Sciences*, 33 (2–3): 61–135.

Hepach, R., Vaish, A. and Tomasello, M. (2013). 'A New Look at Children's Prosocial Motivation', *Infancy*, 18 (1): 67–90.

Intergovernmental Panel on Climate Change (IPCC) (2014). *Fifth Assessment Report: Synthesis Report. Contributions of Working Groups I, II and III to the Fifths Assessment Report of the Intergovernmental Panel on Climate Change*. Geneva: IPCC.

Jacquet, J., Hauert, C., Traulsen, A. and Milinski, M. (2011). 'Shame and Honour Drive Cooperation', *Biology Letters*, 7 (6): 899–901.

Kahneman, D. (2003). 'A Perspective on Judgment and Choice: Mapping Bounded Rationality', *American Psychologist*, 58 (9): 697–720.

Kahneman, D. (2011). *Thinking, Fast and Slow*, London: Allen Lane.

Kennedy, P., Messner, D. and Nuscheler, F. (2001). *Global Trends and Global Governance*, London: Pluto Press.

Krupp, D., Debruine, L. and Barclay, P. (2008). 'A Cue of Kinship Promotes Cooperation for the Public Good', *Evolution and Human Behavior*, 29 (1): 49–55.

Leggewie, C. and Messner, D. (2012). 'The Low-Carbon Transformation – A Social Science Perspective', *Journal of Renewable and Sustainable Energy*, 4 (4): 041404, 1–17.

Lohman, F. (2013). 'A New Case for Kantianism: Evolution, Cooperation, and Deontological Claims in Human Society', in M. Nowak and S. Coakley (eds.) *Evolution, Games, and God: The Principle of Cooperation*, Cambridge, MA: Harvard University Press, 273–88.

Mearsheimer, J. (2014). *The Tragedy of Great Power Politics*, updated edition, New York, NY: W. W. Norton.

Melis, A. P., Hare, B. and Tomasello, M. (2006). 'Engineering Cooperation in Chimpanzees: Tolerance Constraints on Cooperation', *Animal Behaviour*, 72 (2): 275–86.

Messner, D. and Nuscheler, F. (2006). 'Das Konzept Global Governance: Stand und Perspektiven', in D. Senghaas and M. Roth (eds.) *Global Governance für Entwicklung und Frieden – Perspektiven nach einem Jahrzehnt*, Bonn: Dietz, 18–81.

Messner, D., Schellnhuber, J., Rahmstorf, S. and Klingfield, D. (2010). 'The Budget Approach: A Framework for a Global Transformation Toward a Low-Carbon Economy', *Journal of Renewable and Sustainable Energy*, 2 (3): 031003, 1–14.

Milinski, M., Sommerfeld, R., Krambeck, H., Reed, F. and Marotzke, J. (2008). 'The Collective-Risk Social Dilemma and the Prevention of Simulated Dangerous Climate Change', *Proceedings of the National Academy of Sciences*, 105 (7): 2291–4.

Moll, H. and Tomasello, M. (2007). 'Cooperation and Human Cognition: The Vygotskian Intelligence Hypothesis', *Philosophical Transactions of the Royal Society B: Biological Sciences*, 362 (1480): 639–48.

Morgenthau, H. (1985). *Politics Among Nations: The Struggle for Power and Peace*, sixth edition, revised by Kenneth Thompson, New York, NY: McGraw-Hill.

Nowak, M. (2006). 'Five Rules for the Evolution of Cooperation', *Science*, 314 (5805): 1560–3.

Nowak, M. and Highfield, R. (2011). *Super Cooperators: Evolution, Altruism and Human Behaviour or Why We Need Each Other to Succeed*, Edinburgh, Scotland: Canongate.

Nowak, M. and Sigmund, K. (2005). 'Evolution of Indirect Reciprocity', *Nature*, 437 (7063): 1291–8.

Nowak, M. and Sigmund, K. (2007). 'How Populations Cohere: Five Rules for Cooperation', in R. M. May and A. McLean (eds.) *Theoretical Ecology: Principles and Applications*, Oxford / New York, NY: Oxford University Press, 7–16.

Nye, J. S. and Donahue, J. D. (2000). *Governance in a Globalizing World*, Washington, DC: Brookings Institution Press.

Olson, M. (1965). *The Logic of Collective Action: Public Goods and the Theory of Groups*, second printing with new preface and appendix, Cambridge, MA: Harvard University Press.

Oosterbeek, H., Sloof, R. and van de Kuilen, G. (2004). 'Cultural Differences in Ultimatum Game Experiments: Evidence from a Meta-Analysis', *Experimental Economics*, 7 (2): 171–88.

Ostrom, E. (1990). *Governing the Commons: The Evolution of Institutions for Collective Action*, Cambridge, UK: Cambridge University Press.

Ostrom, E. (2005). 'Toward a Behavioral Theory Linking Trust, Reciprocity, and Reputation', in E. Ostrom and J. Walker (eds.) *Trust and Reciprocity: Interdisciplinary Lessons for Experimental Research*, New York, NY: Russell Sage, 19–79.

Ostrom, E. and Walker, J. (eds.) (2005). *Trust and Reciprocity: Interdisciplinary Lessons for Experimental Research*, New York, NY: Russell Sage.

Poteete, A., Janssen, M. and Ostrom, E. (2010). *Working Together: Collective Action, the Commons and Multiple Methods in Practice*, Princeton, NJ: Princeton University Press.

Rand, D. G., Dreber, A., Ellingsen, T., Fudenberg, D. and Nowak, M. (2009). 'Positive Interactions Promote Public Cooperation', *Science*, 325 (5945): 1272–5.

Rand, D. G., Greene, J. D. and Nowak, M. (2012). 'Spontaneous Giving and Calculated Greed', *Nature*, 489 (7416): 427–30.

Reinicke, W. (1998). *Global Public Policy: Governing Without Government?*, Washington, DC: Brookings Institution Press.

Rekers, Y., Cronin, K. A. and Haun, D. B. M. (submitted). *Spontaneous Cooperation in Sumatran Orangutans*.

Rekers, Y., Haun, D. B. M., and Tomasello, M. (2011). 'Children, but Not Chimpanzees, Prefer to Collaborate', *Current Biology*, 21 (20): 1756–8.

Rittberger, V. (ed.) (1995). *Regime Theory and International Relations*, Oxford: Clarendon Press.

Rochat, P. (2011). 'Possession and Morality in Early Development', *New Directions for Child and Adolescent Development*, 132: 23–38.

Rousseau, D., Sitkin, S., Burt, R. and Camerer, C. (1998). 'Not So Different After All: A Cross-Discipline View of Trust', *Academy of Management Review*, 23 (3): 393–404.

Sen, A. (1977). 'Rational Fools: A Critique of the Behavioural Foundations of Economic Theory', *Philosophy and Public Affairs*, 6 (4): 317–44.

Sigmund, K. (2009). 'Sympathy and Similarity: The Evolutionary Dynamics of Cooperation', *Proceedings of the National Academy of Sciences*, 106 (21): 8405–6.

Tavoni, A., Dannenberg, A., Kallis, G. and Loschel, A. (2011). 'Inequality, Communication, and the Avoidance of Disastrous Climate Change in a Public Goods Game', *Proceedings of the National Academy of Sciences*, 108 (29): 11825–9.

Tomasello, M. (1999). *The Cultural Origins of Human Cognition*, Cambridge, MA: Harvard University Press.

Tomasello, M. (2009). *Why We Cooperate*, Cambridge, MA: MIT Press.

Tomasello, M. (2010). *Origins of Human Communication*, Cambridge, MA: MIT Press.

Tomasello, M., Carpenter M. and Liszkowski, U. (2007). 'A New Look at Infant Pointing', *Child Development*, 78 (3): 705–22.

Tomasello, M. and Rakoczy, H. (2003). 'What Makes Human Cognition Unique? From Individual to Shared to Collective Intentionality', *Mind and Language*, 18 (2): 121–47.

UNDP (2011). *Human Development Report. Sustainability and Equity: A Better Future for All*, New York, NY: United Nations Development Programme.

van't Wout, M. and Sanfey, A. G. (2008). 'Friend or Foe: The Effect of Implicit Trustworthiness Judgments in Social Decision-Making', *Cognition*, 108 (3): 796–803.

Waltz, K. (1979). *Theory of International Politics*, New York, NY: Random House.

Warneken, F. and Tomasello, M. (2006). 'Altruistic Helping in Human Infants and Young Chimpanzees', *Science*, 311 (5765): 1301–3.

Warneken, F. and Tomasello, M. (2008). 'Extrinsic Rewards Undermine Altruistic Tendencies in 20-month-olds', *Developmental Psychology*, 44 (6): 1785–8.

WBGU (2011). *World in Transition: A Social Contract for Sustainability*, Berlin: WBGU.

Weber, E. and Johnson, E. (2012). 'Psychology and Behavioral Economics Lessons for the Design of a Green Growth Strategy', White Paper for Green Growth Knowledge Platform (OECD, UNEP, World Bank), *World Bank Policy Research Working Paper*, No. 6240.

Wittgenstein, L. (1922). *Tractatus Logico-Philosophicus*, London: Kegan Paul, Trench, Trubner & Co.

World Bank (2012). *Inclusive Green Growth: The Pathway to Sustainability*, Washington, DC: World Bank.

Zürn, M. (2005). *Regieren Jenseits des Nationalstaates: Globalisierung und Denationalisierung als Chance*, Frankfurt a. M.: Suhrkamp.

3 Cooperation in conflict
Ubiquity, limits, and potential of working together at the international level

Lothar Brock

Efforts to complete the hitherto prevailing images of the *homo economicus* and the *homo sociologus* with a *homo cooperativus* (Bowles and Gintis 2011; Debiel, Leggewie, and Messner 2014; Messner, Guarín, and Haun 2013) seem to be oddly out of tune with what is going on in the world today. The global agendas for cooperation set up by the post–Cold War World Conferences for the most part have gotten stuck in endless bickering over international responsibilities and national entitlements. States fail to live up to past commitments and hesitate to take on new ones for the future. Globalization, instead of fostering a sense of community, seems to unleash the forces of parochialism and populist thinking. Cosmopolitanism certainly has fewer followers today than in the 1990s. On top of it all, the global constellation of power is shifting. New powers emerge or old ones re-emerge, and there is growing uncertainty about what this will imply for the conduct of International Relations in the future.

Crises like the present one tend to boost the public acceptance of those notions of politics that claim that there is nothing new under the sun, which is to say that all politics can be reduced to a never-ending and never-changing struggle over power. The implications of such thinking have been widely criticized at the academic level, especially with regard to Realism's self-fulfilling prophecies and the issue of reification.[1] Nevertheless, simplistic perceptions of what makes the world go round remain attractive and seem to gain in momentum as things become more confusing than they already are. It is precisely this situation that makes it crucial to come up with alternative frames of reference for sorting out past experiences and reasonable expectations for the future if the future is not to resemble the wartorn past and present.

Addressing the behavioral dimension of international cooperation may serve this purpose well.[2] As Chris Brown states, 'since 1945 the individual has become active in international relations, as both subject and object, to a degree not seen previously in the so-called Westphalia System' (Brown 2013: 435). So it is not only promising, but also useful to address human behavior as a source of knowledge about 'what makes the world go round'.[3] This task goes beyond an empirical verification of the banality that human beings also have the ability to cooperate while committing the worst crimes. What we want to know is how the ability to cooperate comes to bear in specific settings and to what extent cooperation can

DOI: 10.4324/9781315691657-4

become a standard of adequacy for providing public goods. However, cooperation is not only about problem solving in this sense; it is also about who gets what under conditions of multiple asymmetries of capabilities and preferences – this is to say that in our reasoning about the prospects of cooperation in human development we have to address cooperation as it is linked to conflict. So the present chapter is about cooperation *in* conflict, not cooperation *and* conflict.

In common parlance (but also in academic work) cooperation and conflict are mutually exclusive.[4] From this perspective, cooperation stands for pro-social behavior and conflict for some kind of antagonism. In real life, however, cooperation and conflict are closely intertwined (Müller 1993: 4). Cooperation functions as an important way of dealing with conflict and conflict is a major driver of cooperation, up to a point at which Choi and Bowles speak of a co-evolution of cooperation and war (Bowles and Gintis 2011: 133; Choi and Bowles 2007; Neumann in this volume).[5] The positive side of this observation is that the persistence of conflict, which we may take for granted (Coser 1965), does not exclude the possibility of expanding cooperation. For this very reason cooperation is much more common than we may realize when we juxtapose cooperation and conflict. The bad message is that cooperation is not all good (Axelrod and Keohane 1985: 226). It rather is highly ambivalent. This ambivalence may be conveniently addressed in terms of a distinction between self-interested versus altruistic cooperation. However, the distinction is not as clear-cut as it seems to be: on the one hand, even self-interested (and therefore limited) cooperation can produce public goods. On the other hand, even seemingly altruistic cooperation is not distinctly separated from the power game that constitutes the dark side of International Relations, as will be explained later. Thus the crucial question from the viewpoint of peace research is not only whether and how cooperation comes about, but also how exactly it interacts with conflict.

I want to deal with this issue in the following way. I will first elaborate my understanding of cooperation in conflict at the international level, with special attention to the normative ambivalence of cooperation. Second, I will explore the implications of cooperation in conflict for a behavioral approach to cooperation. Third, I will present an attempt to provide a quasi-evolutionary account of global cooperation that emphasizes the interaction between adaptation and change of the environment. Finally I will ponder the question of whether it makes sense to talk of an ongoing evolution of international (global) cooperation or whether we are witnessing mere variations of the same old power games.

Cooperation in conflict: What does it mean?

Bowles and Gintis define cooperation in a parsimonious manner as the 'engagement with others in a mutually beneficial activity' (Bowles and Gintis 2011: 2). The authors combine this definition with two theses: '*First*, people cooperate not only for self-interested reasons but also because they are genuinely concerned about the well-being of others, try to uphold social norms and value behaving ethically for its own sake.' At the same time 'people punish those who exploit the cooperative behavior of others for the same reasons'. *Second*, these predispositions result from the fact that those of our ancestors who cooperated and upheld ethical norms were more successful than those who did not (Bowles and Gintis 2011: 2). Cooperation thus understood carries a clear message: cooperate and you will be successful *and* happy. This way of looking at cooperation fits well with the plea of Messner, Guarín, and Haun (this volume) for a fundamental change of perspective on International Relations.

Confirming the findings of Nowak and Highfield (2011), Messner et al. (2013: 8) state that cooperation 'may be a third mechanism of evolution, on par with mutation and selection'. However, cooperation is multifaceted and works in quite different directions. This is all well known. But the expectations tied to a normative understanding of cooperation merit some second thoughts:

(1) What we learn from the first thesis of Bowles and Gintis (2011) is that cooperation can be the source of confrontation in the form of punishment for non-cooperation. Beyond this observation, cooperation may even *produce* non-cooperation. Thus, as part of their first thesis, Bowles and Gintis (2011: 1) state, 'Contributing to the success of a joint project for the benefit of one's group, even at a personal cost, evokes feelings of satisfaction, pride, even elation'. This wording reminds us that the evolution of cooperation (i.e. the selection of cooperative behavior as superior to non-cooperation) is closely tied to life in distinctive communities. The positive experience of cooperation within these communities, however, was not automatically transferred to inter-group relations. To take an example from International Relations, the formation of nation states from the 19th century onward can be described as a process of inclusion that was based on 'othering' in the form of identifying 'strangers' who did not belong and therefore had to be excluded and/or kept in check (by police or military means) (Anderson 1991; Gellner 1983; Smith 2001). So cooperation of people as a nation went along with nationalism and even chauvinism and war.[6] To take another example, empirical research on the 'democratic peace' has shown that democracies can be expected to cooperate peacefully with each other, but not with non-democracies. To the contrary, they can behave in a quite militant manner not only *in spite* of the positive experience with cooperation among their own ranks, but also *because* this positive experience makes them suspicious of non-democracies (Geis, Brock, and Müller 2006).

(2) Such militant behavior can be aggravated through cooperation and can even become a threat to peace and security in general. At the international level, the classical example for this kind of cooperation is alliance politics. Alliances can be quite counterproductive with regard to international or global peace and security. The alliance politics of the late 19th and early 20th centuries were understood by US President Wilson as practices feeding into the run-up to the First World War. In Wilson's understanding, the League of Nations was founded to replace alliances with collective security and

the concomitant secret diplomacy with open parliamentary discussion. The League certainly did not live up to these expectations, but the message was clear: certain forms of cooperation are a threat to peace. Therefore, exclusive cooperation in alliances was to be replaced by inclusive cooperation in the form of collective security.

(3) The 'engagement with others in a mutually beneficial way' can go along with quite different notions of what constitutes the benefits of cooperation, as long as all involved think that they get something out of cooperation that is important *to them*. So actors may cooperate on the basis of spurious reciprocity. An example of this practice is 'antagonistic cooperation'. The term was introduced by the early US-American sociology of conflict. It referred to instances in which two social entities that otherwise competed joined in order to pursue a common goal. Lewis Coser took up this term in his sociology of conflict (Coser 1965: 166–8). International Relations scholars used it with reference to the Second World War and the Cold War either to characterize the wartime cooperation between the Allies or to distinguish a form of international cooperation that reduced the risks involved in deterrence, but that thereby helped to perpetuate the deterrence system.[7]

(4) International cooperation may even jeopardize the already 'thin' democratic control of foreign policy. This happens when democratic governments seek consensus at the intergovernmental level in order to present the outcome as an external given that has to be accepted by the respective parliaments lest the reputation of the state as a reliable partner would suffer (Wolf 2000).

(5) Finally, partial cooperation can be used to legitimize the harshest form of confrontation: the use of force. This case refers to international intervention in intra-state armed conflict on the basis of a Security Council resolution. In accordance with Chapter VII of the United Nations (UN) Charter, the Security Council can authorize the member states to take all action that they deem appropriate to cope with the threat to international peace emanating from an intra-state armed conflict. In virtually all the cases in which such an authorization was granted, which presupposed cooperation of the permanent members, collective action in line with Chapter VII of the UN Charter turned into wars of the intervening countries that were beyond Security Council control. Russia and China expressly blamed those members of the North Atlantic Treaty Organization who intervened in Libya in March 2011 as misapplying Security Council authorization to legitimize the application of force for their own goals (regime change). This critique was then used by the two permanent members of the Security Council to block all collective action in the case of Syria.

In a more systematic way we can identify various types of negative linkages between international cooperation and conflict. Social entities may cooperate in order to enhance their power vis-à-vis other social entities, as happens when states form an alliance that is directed against a third state or a group of states (*strategic cooperation*). There may be *tactical cooperation* within strategic confrontation, as in the Cold War, designed to reduce the risks of all-out confrontation but with the unintended consequence of perpetuating a system of 'mutually assured destruction'. Finally, cooperation may turn collective security institutions into an instrument for legitimizing war (*cooperation as surreptitious legitimization of non-cooperation*).

All of these examples may be ranked as self-interested cooperation. But that will not do. First of all, altruistic cooperation is also tied into the international power game, and second, even self-interested and therefore limited cooperation can lead to more overall well-being, the improvement of social institutions, and the affirmation and universalization of standards of adequate behavior. As to the first point, the call by the Western democracies for international cooperation in the fight against terrorism, climate change, state fragility, or corruption has been interpreted in large parts of the global South as camouflage for Western hegemonic ambitions. The same goes for Western policies of humanitarian aid and peace building, the international protection of civilians from mass atrocities, or the protection of human rights in general (Cunliffe 2011; Jahn 2012). All of the respective activities have been criticized as part of a grand hegemonic design directed against the emancipation of the global South.[8]

The second point refers to the observation that even self-interested and therefore limited cooperation in conflict can have far-reaching positive effects. It can contribute to the mitigation of the conflict in which it comes to bear and it may (if inadvertently) help to universalize standards of adequacy that, in a Kantian sense, can serve as general guideline for living together peacefully in a world loaded with conflict. A much debated example is the emergence of a Western security community in the context of the Cold War (Adler and Barnett 1998; Deutsch 1957). Here cooperation which was directed against a third party, the Soviet Union (and initially also Germany), interacted with the emergence of a regional system (the Western security community) from which war as an option of international power politics disappeared. The emergence of international humanitarian law (and the ongoing differentiation of international law in general) can also be considered as an example of self-interested cooperation with far-reaching consequences. International humanitarian law was invented in the mid-19th century under the impression of the growing destructiveness of war. It was to cut down on its human, social, and also infrastructural costs in the context of the upcoming second industrial revolution. But it did not question war as such. Nevertheless, the invention of international humanitarian law unleashed a normative dynamic that lead from the first Geneva agreement in 1864 to the Geneva conventions of 1948 and the Protocols of 1977, thereby raising the standards of acceptable behavior in 'armed conflict'. This was achieved in close interaction with the emergence of the general prohibition of the unilateral use of force (Pictet 1985).

These examples show how even 'limited cooperation' in conflict can change the overarching normative order.[9] Cooperation within the Western security community and the invention of international humanitarian law both reflect the emergence of a community of values modifying identity and interests in a constellation of conflict. The same holds true for the United Nations. The creation of the UN certainly reflected the interests of the great powers to preserve their status in the post-war constellation. However, under the impression of the horrors of war the founding of the UN also reflected a sense of responsibility beyond mere calculations of costs and benefits for each of the major actors (see below). Functionally, in these examples self-interested and altruistic cooperation merged.[10]

Thus it is necessary to look closely at who is cooperating with whom, under which conditions, for which purpose, and with which (unintended) effects. Take for instance the cooperation between Mafia clans, who divide up the turf in order to enhance their prospects for more booty. Compare this with the tactical cooperation between the main antagonists of the Cold War in the issue areas of arms control and the avoidance of a military confrontation by default. While it is difficult to see how cooperation among Mafia clans could ever serve the common good, the type of 'antagonistic cooperation' practiced during the Cold War did. It helped to mitigate immediate tensions, and it changed the overarching framework of reference for the interaction between East and West. The establishment of the Conference on Security and Cooperation in Europe symbolized and promoted this change.

Therefore, cooperation should be assessed not only for its immediate causes and effects in specific situations but also with regard to its general impact on the normative framework and practice of International Relations. Under a *realist* perspective, cooperation will always remain under the reservation of power-political calculations (Waltz 1979). In contrast, the present chapter claims that even limited cooperation may generate a substantial modification in the way that interests and adequate behavior are being defined and that *intended*[11] rationality comes into play.

In order to accommodate the various linkages between cooperation and conflict in our reasoning about the evolution of cooperation, I suggest untangling cooperation and pro-social behavior. 'Pro-social behavior' burdens cooperation with a normative load that is unwarranted, as the previous examples show. Cooperation can be defined in a more neutral way as the pooling of resources, both material and immaterial, for specific, but not necessarily common, ends. What qualifies the pooling of resources as cooperation is the consensus underlying the pooling. This consensus can be quite limited (agreement to disagree), but over time it can grow. It can become fairly strong, but it also may break down. No matter whether it is based on the joy of achieving something together or on a self-interested calculation, I suggest labeling cooperation that provides public goods as *constructive* rather than altruistic cooperation because altruism points to *motivation*, whereas constructive behavior refers to *effects*. This does not exclude a preference-based definition of altruism (Bowles and Gintis 2011: 201). But it disburdens us from the task of showing in each case what the motivation (and possibly even the 'true' motivation) behind a certain kind of behavior may be. In the social world, all action can be regarded as being based on mixed motives. This is so because the borderline between self-interested and altruistic behavior is 'structurally' fuzzy, if it can be drawn at all.

At the international level, constructive cooperation can be understood as a pattern of behavior that produces public goods in the absence of a central institution capable of executing an authoritative allocation of rights, duties, and resources. The production of public goods is what we usually have in mind when we talk about 'international cooperation'. But, as pointed out previously, international cooperation, just as any other form of cooperation, is ambivalent. There can be constructive und destructive, inclusionary and exclusionary international cooperation. In this regard, reference to 'international cooperation' is confronted with the same dilemma as reference to the 'international community' (Vetterlein and Wiener 2013).[12] Just as in the case of the 'international community', there is a universalistic claim inherent in the term 'international cooperation' that is not always warranted. Thus the critique of Western humanitarian assistance or human rights policy as a hegemonic design points to a basic dilemma: we cannot do without the idea that there is something which transcends the narrow self-interests of states and which comes to bear in international cooperation. But what is in the international or universal interest by necessity can only be defined from a particularistic perspective, since no actor can claim to represent the universal, not even the United Nations, as they are composed of individual states all pursuing specific interests in a highly competitive environment.

This dilemma also applies to '*global* cooperation'. Global cooperation, just as international cooperation, may be understood as referring to 'the norms and institutions (of varying degrees of formality) and processes by means of which social goods – including wealth, power, knowledge, health and authority – are constantly being generated and allocated' (Farer and Sisk 2010: 1). But the generation and allocation of social goods is loaded with conflict. So we have to be careful in our talk about global cooperation, lest we overlook that even at the global level the challenge consists not only of 'global problems' to be solved, but also of intractable interests waiting to be pushed. At the global level there may be no outside against which cooperation would be directed, thus reproducing existing patterns of exclusion or creating new ones. Yet there certainly is an inside – the people in their various communities. The critique of international cooperation as a means to thwart democratic pressures from within (Wolf 2000) could also become relevant for cooperation at the global level – for instance, when a global political elite decides on legitimate standards in international trade, which would then be sold to the people as a global consensus that the national governments are forced to adhere to. In sum, there is 'rule' (*Herrschaft*) involved and not only 'authority' (Cronin and Hurd 2008; Fin 2010; Gemko and Zürn 2012).

Implications for the behavioral study of international cooperation

We may conclude from the findings of evolutionary biology that cooperation, in all cultures, comes natural with humans (Messner et al. this volume; Melis, this volume; Nowak 2006). This is a strong appeal not to follow the popular short-cut from Hobbes's observation that life is 'brutish, nasty and short', to the inference that we are living in a cage of human nature that we can only leave without killing each other under the strong hand of a leviathan. The popularity of Hobbesian images increased with the advent of Social Darwinism. However, the behavioral approach to cooperation should not be used for simply reversing this fad and opening up another shortcut, this time leading from a redefinition of human nature to the expectation that conflict could be overcome by cooperation. As Ned Lebow observes, Robert Axelrod's research 'has given hope to some that cooperation will ultimately triumph over conflict' (Lebow 2013: 3). Burdening cooperation with such an expectation can only end in disappointment and resignation. Cooperation may change conflict, but it will never overcome it. To the contrary, because of its entanglement with conflict, cooperation will always be limited and insufficient. Nevertheless, cooperation is crucial for the future of mankind, as it has been crucial for its past. What is needed, then, is a sober assessment of cooperation considering its entanglement with conflict.

Such an assessment calls for a high degree of reflexivity on the part of those who engage in narratives about the evolution of cooperation and the part that human nature is supposed to be playing in it. As Chris Brown (2013) summarizes, speaking of human nature has had a totalizing effect in Western thinking: there were those who denied 'difference' under the perspective of enlightened universalism and those who denied difference under the veil of standards which helped to exclude those from civilization who did not fit. The first version of the denial of difference came to bear in the definition of colonialism as a civilizing mission. The second version surfaced in a profane version of Darwinian reasoning and the 'scientific racism' of the late 19th century, which, again, helped to level the ground for fascism and National Socialism in the first half of the 20th century. Today, 'scientific racism' is (almost) dead. But a crude mixture of enlightened universalism and the colonial heritage of superiority has survived for quite some time and thus became an object of the post-colonial critique of Western hegemony, the feminist critique of patriarchy, and the scientific (anthropology-based) rejection of essentialism (Brown 2013: 438–9). Brown does not conclude that we finally should turn away from human nature. His observations rather serve as preemptive defense for the ensuing attempt to bring human nature (back) in. This attempt reflects the growing importance of the individual both as subject and object of world politics – for instance through the international recognition of human rights, the emergence of an international criminal law, or the ongoing discourse on global justice. Brown stresses the need to clarify what the 'human' stands for. He is confident that the newer works of evolutionary psychology, experimental economics, neurosciences, game theory, etc., can help find an answer. His own preliminary answer to the question of what the 'human' stands for in human rights is twofold. On the one hand he asserts that there are certain uncooperative features of human behavior that have to be taken into account when setting up the institutional framework in which politics unfold. On the other hand, he specifically refers to the work of Binmore and Gintis on altruism as offering new perspectives on understanding International Relations as a 'corrective to the work of those evolutionary economists whose work is essentially designed to show that the norms of capitalism correspond to our "animal spirits" ' (Brown 2013: 449).

This somewhat contradictory handling of the issue has provoked some critical commentaries. Ewelina Sokolowska and Stefano Guzzini bemoan that Chris Brown is unwittingly 'following a certain determinism in which political institutions can be designed to adapt to a given, and hence determining, Human Nature: people are free to disregard these human constants, but only at their own peril' (Sokolowska and Guzzini 2014: 143). With this reading, Brown's argument would indeed come close to the logic of *quasi*-deterministic thinking that can be spotted in Hans Joachim Morgenthau's six laws of international politics derived from human nature (Morgenthau 1954) or the socialization model presented by Kenneth Waltz, in which human nature is replaced by the inescapable imperatives emanating from anarchy as the constituting feature of the international (Waltz 1979; Wilson 2013). In both cases there are certain givens that have to be considered. For ignoring them there is a price to pay. Referring to new empirical and conceptual advances in developmental biology and cognitive neuroscience, Sokolowska and Guzzini (2014: 145–6) make the point that evolution should be taken more seriously in order to break away from any determinism because what evolution has to offer is a better solution: 'a highly plastic brain that is capable of adapting to particular environmental demands'. It is this plasticity of the human brain, the authors claim, that is our distinctive and universal human nature.

In another response to Chris Brown, Stephen Rosow (2014: 151–2) states that Brown seems

> torn between appeals to a weaker ontological position – in which assumptions about the nature of the body and mind are linked to human behavior but remain provisional and contestable – and a stronger ontology in which certain fixed, universal attributes, capacities and proclivities of human psychology determine, if not behavior *per se*, at least the parameters of 'normal' human behavior.

I think that Rosow makes an important point. His statement applies not only to Chris Brown's argument but also to the entire endeavor to counter Hobbesian (or profane Social Darwinian) ideas about human nature and to replace them with the notion of *homo cooperatives*. The scientific critique of a Hobbesian world should offer an alternative without opening up another pathway to deterministic thinking, which could then again be used by politics in a way that 'limits contestation and pluralism' (Rosow 2014: 155). These observations shed a new light on what evolution may be about. It is not about the successive replacement of confrontation (conflict) by cooperation, but rather about opening up our own minds to the human ability to adapt to changing circumstances.

This is in line with scientific thinking in other disciplines. Thus genetics today are complemented by epigenetics. The latter basically deals with the observation that DNA sequences do not *determine* outcomes, but that these sequences can be read in different ways and that the resulting pattern can be inherited by offspring.

It follows that there is much more leeway for learning than deterministic theories on the social implications of human nature would have it. Recent research in physics, biochemistry, and medicine, too, confirms the need to open up to non-linear systems. In this context, quantum physics played a pioneering role. Quantum physics in a nutshell stands for a change of perspective from constructing causality as sequences of events that move along fixed tracks (the laws of Newtonian physics) to dealing with processes of communication on a spread-out maneuvering area (Görnitz and Görnitz 2008). In the social sciences, *constructivism* goes into the same direction, while 'scientific' or 'critical realism' at least accepts that the observation of a world external to the observer is conditioned by socially constructed beliefs (Bennett 2013: 446). In sum, various scientific endeavors converge around the observation that the 'hard facts of life' that populist notions of international politics like to refer to merit a second look because they may not be as hard as they appear to be.

Opening up these new heuristic spaces, then, has to be understood as a warning not to replace the Hobbesian 'homo homini lupus' with a Rousseau-ish slogan of 'homo homini angelus'. Apart from the fact that wolves are great in cooperating (especially when they hunt) and that angels helped to chase Adam and Eve from paradise, the important point is that people in situations of conflict can be both: nice neighbors who help each other and not-so-nice neighbors who kill each other. What is more, the behavior of neighbors can change from one pattern to the next in a very short time. Stories to this avail have been told over and over again – for instance, about the war in Bosnia-Herzegowina, or the armed conflict in the Central African Republic, or, for that matter, about any civil war. Yet it is not a matter of pure chance whether people cooperate or go for confrontation. Thus it is worthwhile to reflect upon the circumstances under which they tend to act as helpful neighbors or utterly unhelpful enemies, or as a precarious mixture of both. The evolutionary approach to cooperation can help in this endeavor.

For instance, in the analysis of present International Relations it is important to know more about the effect of globalization on the behavior of people. To this avail, Buchan et al. (2009) conducted experimental games in six different countries, offering a representative environment (see Grimalda in this volume). The aim of the study was to test two competing hypotheses. The first one is 'that globalization prompts reactionary movements that reinforce parochial distinctions between people'. The second hypothesis suggests 'that globalization strengthens cosmopolitan attitudes by weakening the relevancy of ethnicity, locality or nationhood as sources of identification'. The authors of the study wanted to know to what extent individuals 'are self-interested, willing to cooperate exclusively with people from their own locality, or, alternatively, to cooperate with groups from around the world' (Buchan et al. 2009, 4138–9). The research produced findings that, as interpreted by the authors, support the cosmopolitan hypothesis. The findings suggest that 'humans' basic "tribal instincts" may be highly malleable to the influence of the processes of connectedness embedded in globalization. (Buchan et al. 2009: 4141). This means that globalization may enhance large-scale cooperation rather than foster parochial confrontation.

Yet in spite of the preferences expressed in the experiment, there is an obvious upsurge of parochialism in word politics today.[13] How do we account for this puzzle? One answer is offered by Ned Lebow, who alerts us to the shortcomings of experimental research. Focusing on 'tit-for-tat' arrangements, as in Axelrod's tournaments of the 1980s, he claims that none of the conditions arranged in an experimental situation can be replicated in the real world, 'where "tits" are readily interpreted as "tats", cooperation as defection and either dismissed as noise' (Lebow 2013: 4). To the extent that this observation can be applied in general to games that test the preferences of players against an experimental pay-off structure, it would follow that the explanatory power of experiments is smaller than the scientific pretense would suggest. To cite Lebow once more: outside the experiment, 'outcomes and their payoffs can only be estimated imperfectly as policies not infrequently bring about outcomes the reverse of those intended'. He goes on: 'The real world is characterized by opacity with regard to actor motives as well as outcomes' (Lebow 2013: 5). In my reading of the issue it does not follow that experimental research is doomed from the beginning. Experimental research can help to question seemingly self-serving assumptions about what is going on in the world. Accordingly, I read the findings of Buchan et al. (2009, 2011) as confirming that globalization as such does not diminish the chances for cooperation. But, as Buchan et al. concede themselves, their research also reveals that we know very little about the connection between globalization and large-scale cooperation. And, we may add, we know very little about how people become cosmopolitan minded and how stable this state of mind is in crises.

A second answer to the puzzle could be that perhaps we are misinterpreting 'parochialism'. Perhaps what we see is not substantive parochialism but the expression of discontent with the way globalization is being handled by those who are (deemed to be) responsible for its social, economic, and environmental outcomes. Under this perspective, the findings of Buchan et al. (2009, 2011) could be interpreted as calling for an investigation of the notion of 'tribal instincts' used by the authors. There is an interesting parallel with regard to the role of religion or ethnicity in conflict. In the 1990s there was a lot of talk about 'ethnic conflict'. In the meantime, the role of religion has come to the fore. Today, there is a broad consensus that religion as such (just like ethnicity) is rarely a cause of armed conflict. Only if religion and ethnicity are being politicized do they tend to attain a powerful influence on the dynamics of conflict. The same could hold true for 'tribal instincts', which may help a group to survive but also can be politicized in such a way that it turns into a force of social disintegration or political separatism.

A third answer is provided by Messner et al. in this volume. Their recreation of Dieter Senghaas's peace hexagon (Senghaas 1995) in the shape of a cooperation hexagon identifies six causal mechanisms that, taken together, ensure 'reciprocity' as 'the main evolutionary mechanism underlying cooperation' (Messner et al. in this volume). While Senghaas understood his hexagon as the quintessence of historic experience in Europe, Messner et al. offer a more systematic account of what enables people to cooperate. The six causal mechanisms they identify are supposed to work 'scale-free', though in different ways depending on the context. The fact that today the causal mechanisms are not working so well at the international or global level the authors attribute to the global power shift, which goes hand in hand with a new constellation of players. With regard to these developments, they state, 'If agreements on climate change and other critical topics are to be reached, these basic mechanisms of cooperation must be rebuilt, redeveloped, and reinvented in new constellations of players such as the G20' (Messner et al. in this volume). So the present crisis of international cooperation comes to bear as a change in the environment to which existing patterns of cooperation have to adjust. This argument implies that cooperation has been evolving all through human history. But this is not a linear process. There may be ups and downs and even catastrophic breakdowns. Thus there are multiple cooperation blockades today, which, however, do not result from timeless power games: the forces of confrontation 'appear unrestrained in this phase of tectonic power shifts because they have not (yet) been embedded and defused by structures of the cooperation hexagon, i.e. the functional cooperation spaces' (Messner et al. in this volume).

This leads to the question about the long-term impact of cooperation on the environment to which it has to adjust under an evolutionary perspective. I will take up this question in two steps. First I will look into theoretical issues involved in thinking about the interaction between cooperation and a changing environment. In a second step I will try to sketch a narrative of environmental change through cooperation and to check this against the experience of a breakdown of cooperation.

Selection and socialization in International Relations

The international cooperation problems addressed in behavioral studies deal with the choice between cooperative and non-cooperative behavior in changing settings of conflicting interests (Axelrod and Keohane 1985). Under the perspective of natural selection, cooperation can be expected to spread as a preferred way of dealing with 'fierce competition' (Nowak 2006: 1560) to the extent that it increases fitness. From the viewpoint of International Relations two questions arise: (1) Does natural selection work between states? (2) What is the impact of cooperation on the nature of competition (conflict)? Or to put it differently, to what extent is there not just a unidirectional process of adaption to externally pre-given circumstances, but also an *interaction* between cooperation (as a form of adjustment) and the environment (towards which adjustment takes place)? In the following I want to address these questions. I will start out with a brief reference to the issue of natural selection in International Relations and the role of socialization as an alternative focus, and then proceed from there to the question of which way we could conceive the interaction between cooperation and conflict (as a changing environment of international politics).

In his review of literature on the contribution of evolutionary biology to the analysis of International Relations Ned Lebow states that 'natural selection is universally accepted within the scientific community'. Yet he poses the question of whether natural selection is 'an appropriate mechanism in politics'. At least for the analysis of International Relations his answer is a clear 'no' (Lebow 2013: 3). His argument is as follows: in politics outcomes depend on political skills. Political skills, however, are not being passed on through natural selection. There are those who manage to build great nations, and there are those who ruin them in no time. This may result in a pattern of ups and downs that is 'more typical of international relations than the kind of development associated with evolution' (Lebow 2013: 4). A second reason given is that 'selection' does not account for the increase in the numbers of independent states in the past 100 years and the survival of so many weak, fragile, or even collapsed states among them (Lebow 2013: 4; see also Brock et al. 2012). With a focus on identities Alexander Wendt, in his 'Social Theory of International Politics', comes to a comparable assessment: 'While natural selection may help explain the emergence of Hobbesian identities 3,000 years ago, however, it is of only marginal relevance to explain state identities today'. The reason given is that in order for selection to work survival must be difficult, 'which for modern states it is manifestly not': despite continuing warfare and inequalities of power, the death rate of states is going down. Wendt therefore suggests turning to 'cultural selection' as an evolutionary mechanism, involving the transmission of behavior among units and over time. Thus socialization via imitation or social learning comes into play (Wendt 2005: 323–4).

The cultural-selection approach is promising for the analysis of a possible interaction between adaption and the environment. In the words of Wendt: 'Rather than working behind the backs of actors through reproductive failure, cultural selection works directly through their capacities for cognition, rationality, and intentionality' (Wendt 1999: 324).

However, what is being selected remains an open question. As Waltz sees it, states are free to choose any policy they like. But under anarchy only a certain pattern of behavior will assure their 'survival' (understood as their ability to retain power and avoid political marginalization). This pattern is characterized by a constant but prudent[14] quest for power. Since this quest for power is essential for the 'survival' of states, it trumps all other interests. It follows, first, that cooperation will only take place to the extent that it resonates with the dominant quest for power as a condition of 'survival'. A state that chooses cooperation as its dominant strategy would 'fall by the wayside' (Waltz 1979: 118). Second, cooperation to the extent that it occurs does not change the basic environment. Rather, the dominant pattern of behavior would reproduce anarchy.

Presuming that cultural selection/socialization works in International Relations, what are the chances for overcoming anarchy, understood as a Hobbesian culture of self-help, through cooperation? And if cooperation changes the environment, which calls for new adjustment, what is international politics heading for? As Wendt proclaimed in his seminal essay under the same title, 'anarchy is what states make of it' (Wendt 1992). This statement became a formidable rock around which the various ships of theory building in International Relations cruised in the choppy seas of Constructivism (Fierke and Joergensen 2001).

Constructivist thinking in International Relations converges around the idea that 'reality' is not out there to be discovered; we rather construct 'reality' through our shared perceptions of the world and our practical experience in dealing with it. Applied to the argument forwarded by Waltz, this would mean that there is no fixed response to the decentralized power structure that constitutes the international system. Waltz himself talks about a *prudent* quest for power. But what is *prudent*? In Waltz's view, a quest for power is prudent to the degree that it assures survival (understood as avoiding marginalization and becoming an object of the power games of others) without upsetting the apple cart of the existing balance of power and thus becoming a threat to the imprudent actor. A prudent choice, however, is difficult to make. There is a high danger of cultural selection by imitating other states' imprudent behavior: 'Behaviors might seem appealing and be widely imitated, even if they are bad for the survival prospects of the state that imitates them'. Nevertheless, Waltz 'makes the far-from-trivial case that the system would cause less suffering *if* states behaved *as if* the system compelled them to be prudent' (Wilson 2013: 427–3).

Where do we take it from here? In Waltz's (defensive) concept of prudent power politics, cooperation is not precluded. To the contrary, it can be considered as an essential element of prudence in international politics. However, in realist thinking (including Waltz's *defensive realism*) cooperation remains marginal. There may be ups and down in international cooperation, but in the end the quest for relative power will prevail. From a constructivist reading of politics in a decentralized political system, there are no systemic limits to cooperation. If we regard cooperation as a strategy of adapting to a changing environment, then cooperation also changes our understanding of what the 'environment' is and calls for. This way, the environment is not an external given which favors a certain mode of behavior. Rather, the perception of the environment and of what it stands for would change as we adapt.

Can the recent history of International Relations plausibly be told in such a way that cultural selection would appear to favor cooperation as the dominant mechanism of assuring 'survival', thus making the environment itself less 'fiercely competitive'?

The long-term impact of international cooperation on conflict

The recent history of international cooperation can be told as a story of progress from modest beginnings of exclusionary control in Europe to an elaborated system of (partly) inclusionary interaction at the global level. Cooperation in the form of exclusionary control was practiced by the Holy Alliance, which emanated from the Congress of Vienna and tried to restore or defend the old system of feudal legitimacy against the revolutionary movements that came up in Europe and the European colonies in the Americas in the late 18th and the early 19th centuries. While the Vienna Congress gave birth to the Holy Alliance, it can by no means be reduced to a midwife service for reactionary policies.

Rather, the Congress constituted the first attempt to coordinate policies among the great powers at a continental scale and to introduce the idea of international regulation of the use of international resources.[15] Furthermore, by creating the German Confederation (Staatenbund), which was big enough to check French ambitions but small enough to leave the constellation of big powers unaffected, it practiced some kind of *prudent* security policy as envisaged by Kenneth Waltz. It reacted to 25 years of revolutionary unrest and war and is commonly valued as the beginning of an unprecedented period of peace in Europe (Durchhardt 2013). Nevertheless, even though the Concert of Europe constituted a fledgling form of collective security, it was exclusionary not only with regard to domestic politics but also at the international level. It rested on political coordination among the five great powers (the Pentarchy, which included France after the second defeat of Napoleon). The smaller powers were politically marginalized, though they profited to the extent that the 'Concert' guaranteed their existence.

The road beyond the Concert of Europe was outlined by the very intellectual movement the political heritage of which the Holy Alliance wanted to control: 'of the Enlightenment'. The Enlightenment offered ideas not only for civil emancipation but also for progress at the international level. While keen thinkers like William Pen, the Abbé de St. Pièrre or Adam Smith had tried to convince the ruling elites that war no longer paid for the modernizing countries of Europe, but that productive interchange was much more profitable, Kant went a decisive step further by calling for a universalist perspective on international order, which was to be accompanied by a paradigm shift in international law, from regulating war in a state of nature to leaving the state of nature in favor of cooperation-based inter-state and inter-societal relations. This new normative order was to be built on international organizations, world citizens law (Weltbürgerrecht), and the inclusion of the people in the decision making on war and peace (Republicanism).

Kant was way ahead of his time. But eventually, leaving the state of nature – if not in these words and without reference to Kant – became the agenda behind first attempts to facilitate international trade with the help of a functional international organization, the invention of international humanitarian law, the upgrading of international mediation as a standard for dealing with international conflict (at the Hague Peace Conferences), and, finally, with the transformation of exclusionary cooperation in the form of alliance politics into inclusionary cooperation in a universal collective security system (League of Nations). So the standards of adequate behavior became more inclusionary in three ways: by enhancing functional cooperation, by universalizing international law (which formally had been a European affair until the mid-19th century), and by reducing the exclusionary effect of international security cooperation (collective security).

A major normative push to continue down this road came with the Kellog-Briand Pact of 1928 and – much more forcefully – with the negotiation and adoption of the United Nations Charter. The Kellog-Briand Pact was originally designed as an attempt to institutionalize cooperation in the form of exclusionary control directed against German re-armament. But as it turned out, it became a point of reference for the transformation of international law from a law of war to a law of peace. Outlawing wars of aggression paved the way for the general prohibition of the unilateral use of force through the UN Charter (Art. 2/4). The concept of collective action to restore or secure international peace under the UN Charter combined universalism with remnants of the old system of big-power cooperation. Thus the Security Council was marked by a hierarchy among the membership, which offered a voice to the international community at large but reserved the last word for the five permanent members.

The practice of collective action to secure or restore international peace under the UN Charter was largely blocked during the Cold War. Nevertheless, the UN Charter stands for a new normative order[16] of International Relations, which offered a framework for reorganizing world politics when Real Socialism broke down and the Cold War ended. In the early 1990s, the series of world conferences and the UN Secretariat formulated new agendas for global cooperation that were unprecedented in scope and ambition. While these agendas were confronted with 'new' intra-state wars, the number of 'old' inter-state wars has gone down since the end of the Second World War to all but zero (Themnér and Wallensteen 2013). 'Old' wars have largely been replaced by external intervention in intra-state armed conflict.

As a special feature of the UN system, direct cooperation for preserving or restoring peace was combined with extensive non-military cooperation, which was to advance global well-being, promote human rights, and enable people to solve conflicts peacefully – and thus provide the material, spiritual, and procedural basis for overcoming the 'scourge of war'. In this sense the UN were conceived as a 'working peace system'. Along this line one can speak of the emergence of a normative order that constituted a considerable step away from the Hobbesian logic of dealing with conflict and a step towards a Grotian and even a Kantian logic (Buzan 2004; Brock 2004; Brock 2011: 53–7). I suggest to understand this process as resulting from an interaction between the international environment to which actors have to adjust and the various practices of cooperation among these actors. This dynamic is driven by an increasing connectivity of the fate of people and states and the emergence of a fragile identity of people as members of world society. Within the UN system cooperation provides reputation, and this in turn enhances cooperation. With regard to the interaction between the change of the environment and cooperation at the international and global level (state and non-state), one can speak of the evolution of global cooperation as a spreading practice in dealing with conflict and transforming it.

This is all fine. The crux of the matter is that cooperation, in the context of the Hague Peace Conferences, the League of Nations, the Kellog-Briand Pact, and finally the United Nations, was driven not by the cumulative effects of enlightened thinking but rather by the run-up to, and the actual experience of, two world wars. So it took repeated breakdowns of international cooperation in the form of an unprecedented escalation of collective violence to advance global cooperation. Put differently, global cooperation was fostered by global confrontation. From a realist viewpoint this can be interpreted as demonstrating that no matter how far states move in their efforts to cooperate, they will eventually end up in confrontation – all the more so if their cooperative ambitions get out of touch with the logic of anarchy.

Against this interpretation it can be argued that the drive towards global coop-eration was stronger than the disruptive forces of war or fascism, and more recently the confrontation between capitalism and socialism. It is indeed remarkable that the lessons drawn from the disaster of the First World War were not perceived as suggesting a retreat from the agenda set by the Hague Peace Conferences, but rather as necessitating a follow-up that would transcend the original agenda. Like-wise, the Second World War could have led to a retreat from multilateral coopera-tion. Instead, already during the war, the Allies came up with the idea of a further institutionalization of global cooperation in the framework of a 'working peace system'. Renewed confrontation followed in the shape of the Cold War. But it did not relegate the idea of global cooperation to oblivion; rather the UN system served as an arena in which the confrontation proceeded. Also, after the Cold War, during the 'unipolar moment' of the one remaining superpower, the US and their coalitions of the willing did not discard international law altogether as a mere shackle to be thrown off; rather the US tried to influence the development of international law in such a way that it would widen their leeway of action while raising the substantive standards that other states had to meet (especially in the protection of human rights and the fight against terrorism).[17] So there is some-thing to build on in the present crisis of cooperation, which is unfolding in the context of a global power shift and a new constellation of players all demanding to have a say in shaping the future world order. And it is not entirely out of place to claim that the present crisis can be understood as a process of adjustment in which 'basic mechanisms of cooperation must be rebuilt, redeveloped, and rein-vented' (Messner et al. in this volume). What are the prospects for such rebuilding and reinventing?

At the end of the First World War, the British government ordered a study to be made on the European Concert of Powers as a pool of ideas for a post-war order. In the present crisis, Müller et al. (2014) suggest to repeat the same move and to look into the prospects of a 'concert of powers for the 21st century'. Is our thinking moving in circles? Looking back at the Concert of Powers in Europe is not neces-sarily a nostalgic undertaking. What Müller et al. have in mind is an idea to overcome new blockades in the Security Council that have come up with the present power shift and the new constellation of players driven by rivaling notions of justice. The authors suggest the formation of some kind of a standing group of leading powers (including representatives of regional organizations), which would prepare major decisions of the Security Council that otherwise would not mate-rialize. The standing group would thus function as an informal institution designed not to replace but to innervate the UN as the central arena of global cooperation. It would be designed to build trust, empathy, and respect for the vital interests of those belonging and not belonging to the group, to foster the principle of the non-use of force in dealing with disputes, to strengthen respect for international law, and to mitigate the quest for military superiority. These are all aims that the

UN as a formal institution also stands for. They are not to be duplicated through the Concert of Powers. Rather the idea is that the combination of formal and informal communication can enhance these aims in a better way than their ritualized invocation in the UN (Daase 2009).

Müller et al. (2014) expressly state that all the good things that are to come out of the Concert of Powers should not be expected to constitute a necessary input. So, again, the emergence of such an informal institution would not constitute a mere adjustment to a changing environment. It rather is expected to change the environment as adjustment in its initial form (at the beginning of the concert) goes on. Accordingly, the answer to the question whether our thinking is moving in circles would be 'no'. But it all depends on the possibility to transform conflict in such a way that it can be handled without the use of force. The magnitude of this task is demonstrated by the failures of the liberal democracies to make use of the window of opportunity that opened up with the peaceful ending of the Cold War. Instead of expanding inclusionary cooperation in dealing with the great agendas put forward by the world conferences of the early 1990s, they practiced exclusionary control in order to enforce their notions of justice and order – if deemed necessary, by the use of force. So the issue is not only how to improve problem solving and to create new authorities to this avail, but how to balance problem solving and authority formation with changing patterns of rule at the international level.

Conclusion

The fact that the UN has survived the Cold War and Western hegemonic ambitions after the Cold War can be interpreted as evidence of a general agreement that global cooperation is needed and feasible in spite of the prevailing failures of the international community to practice it consistently and effectively. The UN and the idea that there is something 'out there' that is persistently being called the 'international community' stands for an aspiration that was spelled out in the Charter: to free the world from the scourge of war and to improve the well-being of all. This aspiration has to be located in the continuing and perhaps deepening worldwide struggle over the accessibility and distribution of resources (material and immaterial, including recognition). But the struggle as such does not repudiate the aspiration; it rather confirms it.

The findings of evolutionary biology, anthropology, and psychology can help to ground the aspiration that the UN stands for in solid research on human behavior (Messner et al. 2013). On this ground one can build an epistemological bridge that connects the findings on individual and group behavior to the conditions of cooperation at the global level (scaling up). This perspective is crucial in order to confront the old self-fulfilling prophecies of 'power breeds power' with a closer look at human capabilities. However, scaling up what we learn about the behavior of human beings and the communities they live in to the international and global level has to be matched with a high degree of reflexivity in order to avoid the trap of observing that which matches the preferred worldviews of the observer. Within this context, this chapter suggests to take a closer look at the linkages between cooperation and conflict. It suggests defining cooperation in a non-normative way as a pooling of resources for specific (but not necessarily common) purposes. The normative aspect of cooperation can then be addressed with a view to the positive 'side effects' of cooperation, i.e. the mitigation of conflict and the production of standards of adequate behavior. The task of building a normative order at the global level would then foster by way of cultural selection those standards that – in a Kantian sense – are suited to serve as general (global) guidelines for doing politics. If in a rudimentary way, the UN fulfills this function as it converts the aspiration of global cooperation under international law into a practice that can be measured against these standards. The record of cooperation in the UN system, however, is modest. It is to be feared that existing patterns of cooperation within the UN system do not suffice to mitigate serious big-power clashes. Under this perspective it is worthwhile to ponder the possibility of combining the formal set-up of the UN with an informal set-up that would help to keep up the political space needed to channel emotions and to come up with ideas for compromise. Diplomacy as a formal institution for the practice of informality remains crucial in this respect (Neumann in this volume). However, since informal institutions can undermine formal ones, the real challenge would be to use informal communication for overcoming blockades at the formal level (in this case most likely the Security Council) *and* to advance the international rule of law. Put differently, diplomacy has a role to play, but it remains a precarious role since it works at the intersection of rule and authority.

Notes

1 The *New York Times International Weekly* aptly paraphrased a form of 'reification' as 'Reality TV's Influence on Reality' (February 28th, 2014, p. 1).
2 For the controversies which the behavioral approach is generating in International Relations, cf. Brown 2013; Hall 2006; Lebow 2013; Sokolowska and Guzzini 2014.
3 Wilson (2013: 418) speaks of tapping 'into 100 years of biological thinking on Darwin's legacy' for the benefit of theory building in international relations.
4 In his seminal study of war, Quincy Wright, borrowing from the US sociology of conflict, defines cooperation as a process in which social entities profit from one another and conflict as a process in which the parties interact to their mutual disadvantage (Wright 1965: 1439).
5 Thus the behavioral approach to cooperation focuses on the evolution of altruistic cooperation in a competitive environment (Nowak 2006: 1560). Messner et al. in this volume mention that it makes a difference whether the causal mechanisms that foster cooperation unfold in a charitable institution or in a competitive environment.
6 In this sense, the co-evolution of cooperation and war (Choi and Bowles 2007) is an issue of not only the history of the hunters and gatherers, but also of human development in the context of the second industrial revolution.
7 Cf. Lothar Brock 1973: 13–32.
8 Another example for the way humanitarian motives and self-interest can be fused was offered by the international search for the passenger plane that went missing on its flight from Malaysia to China in March 2014. International participation in the search was clearly not only motivated by trying to ease the pain of the passengers' relatives,

but also by attempts to demonstrate geopolitical presence and technological competence in an area adjacent to the tension-loaded South China Sea.

9 Normative orders are here understood as orders of justification. Cf. Cluster of Excellence 'The Emergence of Normative Orders', Goethe University Frankfurt; Forst and Günther 2010.

10 For the distinction between a functional and a substantive definition of altruism, cf. Bowles and Gintis 2011: 201.

11 Behavioral approaches in various scientific undertakings (organizational theory, decision theory, or experimental economics) underline the failure of rational choice as a descriptive model of human behavior. Still, rationality plays an important role in politics. This comes to bear in the concept of bounded rationality. Bounded rationality asserts that decision makers *intend* to be rational, in the sense that their behavior is goal oriented and adaptive, 'but because of human cognitive and emotional architecture, they sometimes fail' (Jones 1999: 297–8).

12 A theory-based reflection on community at the international level can be found in Vetterlein and Wiener 2013.

13 Thus the present crisis of the EU as the most advanced case of international cooperation interacts with the spread of populism, which responds to the intensity of European cooperation.

14 'Prudent' refers to the categorization of Waltz (1979) as a 'defensive realist'. Striving for absolute power would constitute a threat to others, which in turn would become a security threat to the imprudent actor.

15 The first of these functional organizations, which regulated international shipping on the Rhine river, was created in the context of the Vienna Congress.

16 Cf. Forst and Günther 2010 for a definition.

17 Even the Iraq war of 2003 was justified as enforcement of Security Council resolutions of 1991. For the norm politics involved cf. i.a. Reus-Smith 2004; in connection with discursive processes Deitelhoff 2009.

References

Adler, E. and Barnett, M. (eds.) (1998). *Security Communities*, Cambridge: Cambridge University Press.

Anderson, B. (1991). *Imagined Communities: Reflections on the Origin and Spread of Nationalism*, second edition, London: Verso.

Axelrod, R. and Keohane, R. O. (1985). 'Achieving Cooperation under Anarchy', *World Politics*, 38 (1): 226–54.

Bennett, A. (2013). 'The Mother of All Isms: Causal Mechanism and Structured Pluralism in International Relations Theory', *European Journal of International Relations*, 19 (3): 459–82.

Bowles, S. and Gintis, H. (2011). *A Cooperative Species: Human Reciprocity and Its Evolution*, Princeton, NJ: Princeton University Press.

Brock, L. (1973). 'Problemlösung und Interessenpolitik. Friedenspolitische Funktionen einer gesamteuropäischen Zusammenarbeit', in U. Albrecht, W. v. Bredow, L. Brock, V. Hornung, H. Recke, U. Rehfeldt, J. Rodejohann, and C. Wörmann (eds.) *Durch Kooperation zum Frieden?*, München: Hanser, 13–32.

Brock, L. (2004). 'World Society from the Bottom Up', in M. Albert and L. Hilkermeier (eds.) *Observing International Relations: Niklas Luhmann and World Politics*, London: Routledge, 86–102.

Brock, L. (2011). 'Staatenordnung und Weltgesellschaft', in T. ten Brink (ed.) *Globale Rivalitäten. Staaten und Staatensystem im globalen Kapitalismus*, Stuttgart: Franz Steiner, 45–65.

Brock, L., Holm, H.-H., Soerensen, G. and Stohl, M. (2012). *Fragile States: Violence and the Failure of Intervention*, Cambridge: Polity.

Brown, C. (2013). '"Human Nature", Science and International Political Theory', *Journal of International Relations and Development*, 16 (4): 435–54.

Buchan, N. R., Brewer, M. B., Grimalda, G., Wilson, R. K., Fatas, E. and Foddy, M. (2011). 'Global Social Identity and Global Cooperation', *Psychological Science Online First*, 22 (6): 821–8, May 17 (reformulation of Buchan 2009).

Buchan, N. R., Grimalda, G., Wilson, R. K., Brewer, M. B., Fatas, E. and Foddy, M. (2009). 'Globalization and Human Cooperation', *PNAS*, 106 (11): 4138–42.

Buzan, B. (2004). *From International to World Society? English School Theory and the Social Structure of Globalization*, Cambridge: Cambridge University Press.

Choi, Y.-K. and Bowles, S. (2007). 'The Coevolution of Altruism and War', *Science*, 318 (5850): 636–40.

Coser, L. A. (1965). *Theorie sozialer Konflikte*, Neuwied / Berlin: Luchterhand.

Cronin, B. and Hurd, I. (eds.) (2008). *The UN Security Council and the Politics of International Authority*, New York, NY: Routledge.

Cunliffe, P. (ed.) (2011). *Critical Studies on the Responsibility to Protect*, New York, NY: Routledge.

Daase, C. (2009). 'The ILC and Informalization', in G. Nolte (ed.) *Peace through International Law. The Role of the International Law Commission. A Colloquium at the Occasion of Its Sixtieth Anniversary*, Heidelberg: Springer, 179–83.

Debiel, T., Leggewie, C. and Messner, D. (2014). 'Homo Cooperativus: Fusion als Strategie zur Erforschung globaler Problemlösungen', *Unikate* 45: 134–45.

Deitelhoff, N. (2009). 'The Discursive Process of Legalization: Charting Islands of Persuasion in the ICC Case', *International Organization*, 63(1): 33–66.

Deutsch, K. W. (1957). *Political Community and the North Atlantic Area: International Organization in the Light of Historical Experience*, New York, NY: Greenwood Press.

Durchhardt, H. (2013). *Der Wiener Kongress. Die Neugestaltung Europas 1814/15*, München: C.H. Beck.

Farer, T. and Sisk, T. D (2010), 'Enhancing International Cooperation: Between History and Necessity', *Global Governance*, 16 (1): 1–12.

Fierke, K. M. and Joergensen, K.-E. (eds.) (2001). *Constructing International Relations: The Next Generation*, Armonk, New York, and London: M. E. Sharpe.

Fin, D. (2010). 'International Authority, Deliberative Legitimacy, and the Responsibility of States', *Global Governance*, 16 (4): 549–58.

Forst, R. and Günther, K. (2010). 'Die Herausbildung normative Ordnungen. Zur Idee eines interdisziplinären Forschungsprogramms', *Normative Orders Working Paper*, No. 01/2010.

Geis, A., Brock, L. and Müller, H. (eds.) (2006). *Democratic Wars: Looking at the Dark Side of Democratic Peace*, Houndmills: Macmillan.

Gellner, E. (1983). *Nations and Nationalism*, Blackwell: Oxford University Press.

Gemko, T. and Zürn, M. (2012). 'Constraining Authority through the Rule of Law: Legitimatory Potential and Political Dynamics', in A. Nollkaemper, R. Peerenboom, and M. Zürn (eds.) *Rule of Law Dynamics*, Cambridge: Cambridge University Press, 68–89.

Görnitz, B. and Görnitz, T. (2008). *Die Evolution des Geistes. Quantenphysik – Bewusstsein – Religion*, Göttingen: Vandenhoek und Ruprecht.

Hall, R. B. (2006). 'Human Nature as Behavior and Action in Economics and International Relations Theory', *Journal of International Relations and Development*, 9 (3): 269–87.

Jahn, B. (2012). 'Humanitarian Intervention. What's in a Name?' *International Politics*, 49 (1): 36–58.

Jones, B. D. (1999). 'Bounded Rationality', *American Review of Political Science*, 2 (1): 297–321.

Lebow, N. (2013). 'You Can't Keep a Good Idea Down: Evolutionary Biology and International Relations', *International Political Reviews*, 1: 2–10.

Messner, D., Guarín, A. and Haun, D. (2013). 'The Behavior Dimensions of International Cooperation', *Global Cooperation Research Papers*, No.1, Duisburg: Käte Hamburger Kolleg/Global Cooperation Research.

Morgenthau, H. J. (1954). *Politics among Nations*, second edition, New York, NY: Knopf.

Müller, H. (1993). *Die Chance der Kooperation: Regime in den internationalen Beziehungen*, Darmstadt: Wissenschaftliche Buchgesellschaft.

Müller, H., Jüngling, K., Müller, D. and Rauch, C. (2014). *Ein Mächtekonzert für das 21. Jahrhundert*, HSFK-Report 1, Frankfurt: Peace Research Institute Frankfurt.

Nowak, M. (2006). 'Five Rules for the Evolution of Cooperation', *Science*, 314 (5805): 1560–3.

Nowak, M. and Highfield, R. (2011). *SuperCooperators: Evolution, Altruism and Human Behavior or Why We Need Each Other to Succeed*, Edinburgh: Canongate.

Pictet, J. (1985). *Development and Principles of International Humanitarian Law*, Dordrecht: Nijhoff.

Reus-Smith, C. (ed.) (2004). *The Politics of International Law*, Cambridge: Cambridge University Press.

Rosow, S. J. (2014). 'The Cosmopolitan Aspiration', *Journal of International Relations and Development*, 17 (1): 151–6.

Senghaas, D. (1995). 'Frieden als Zivilisierungsprojekt', in D. Senghaas (ed.) *Den Frieden denken*, Frankfurt: Suhrkamp, 196–223.

Smith, A. D. (2001). *Nationalism: Theory, Ideology, History*, Cambridge: Polity.

Sokolowska, E. and Guzzini, S. (2014). 'The Open-Endedness and Indeterminacy of Human Nature', *Journal of International Relations and Development*, 17 (1): 142–56.

Themnér, L. and Wallensteen, P. (2013). 'Armed Conflict 1946–2012', *Journal of Peace Research*, 50 (4): 509–21.

Vetterlein, A. and Wiener, A. (2013). 'Gemeinschaft revisited. Die sozialen Grundlagen internationaler Ordnung', *Leviathan*, 41 (28): 78–103.

Waltz, K. (1979). *Theory of International Politics*, Boston, MA: McGraw-Hill.

Wendt, A. (1992). 'Anarchy Is What States Make of It', *International Organization*, 46: 391–425.

Wendt, A. (1999). *Social Theory of International Politics*, Cambridge: Cambridge University Press.

Wendt, A. (2005). *Social Theory of International Politics*, Cambridge: Cambridge University Press.

Wilson, I. (2013). 'Darwinian Reasoning and Waltz's Theory of International Politics: Elimination, Imitation and the Selection of Behaviours', *International Relations*, 27 (4): 417–38.

Wolf, K.-D. (2000). 'The New Raison d'Etat. International Cooperation Against Societies?', in M. Albert, L. Brock, and K.-D. Wolf (eds.) *Civilizing World Politics? Society and Community at the International Level*, Lanham, Boulder, New York, and Oxford: Rowman and Littlefield, 119–32.

Wright, Q. (1965). *The Study of War*, Chicago; IL: University of Chicago Press.

Part II

Human behavior and cooperation across disciplines

4 The cooperative bias in humans' biological history

Alicia P. Melis

Introduction

Humankind faces enormous challenges. Our growing human population in combination with the damaging impact of our societies on the environment pose a serious threat to our own future existence. Increased energy demand, depletion of natural resources, global warming and climate disruption, or increased antibiotic resistances are some examples of the global-scale problems we need to solve to avoid otherwise devastating consequences for all (Ehrlich and Ehrlich 2013; Walker et al. 2009). Luckily, we are at a much better position than ever before to tackle some of these problems. Research and technology advances allow us to monitor better the existing problems and to come up with alternatives and solutions. However, technological advances alone are not enough, and solving these problems will depend heavily on our ability to cooperate and negotiate at a global scale.

Our success as a species is thought to rely (together with our capacity for cumulative culture) on our capacity to cooperate (Boyd and Richerson 2009; Tomasello 2008; Tomasello et al. 2012). Although many animal species cooperate in various ways, human cooperation is special with regard to the range and scale of our cooperative activities. All human societies, from small-scale to large-scale, are based on cooperation between individuals. From cooperative hunting and food sharing among hunter-gatherers to paying taxes in our modern and complex societies, all humans' social and economic interactions depend in one way or another on collaboration between individuals. However, despite the urgent need for international cooperation, efforts to cooperate at a global scale are often fruitless. The selfish interests of individual states and our incapacity to come to mutually beneficial agreements currently block attempts to solve the serious problems we face (e.g. climate change).

Notwithstanding the limitations of human global cooperation, recent comparative and developmental psychological research suggests that there is strong cooperative bias in humans. Humans share with our closest living primate relatives some cooperative traits, but have in addition evolved many other mechanisms that support cooperation across a wide range of contexts and in large groups of individuals. Interestingly, some of these cooperative skills emerge relatively early

DOI: 10.4324/9781315691657-6

in ontogeny and years before children have undergone intense socialization by teachers and parents (Tomasello et al. 2012; Tomasello and Vaish 2013). Furthermore, research from behavioral economics suggests that adult humans behave more cooperatively than traditional economic views of rational decision making would predict (e.g. Camerer and Fehr 2006; Henrich et al. 2005, see also Rand and Nowak, this volume; Weber and Johnson, this volume). So, humans do behave cooperatively at an interpersonal level, and the evolution of large-scale societies and the emergence of complex regulatory institutions shows that we have also found ways to maintain cooperation in large groups of individuals. However, the necessity to cooperate at a global scale is something relatively new, since it is only in the last 60 years when the human population has more than doubled and economies have reached such a level of internationalization and globalization.

There are different types of cooperative interactions, and different challenges associated with each of them. Based on their influence on the immediate payoffs for actor and recipient, we can distinguish (1) mutually beneficial cooperative behaviors and (2) altruistic or investing behaviors (Melis and Semmann 2010). In mutually beneficial cooperative behaviors (from now on *collaborative* activities), two or more individuals coordinate their actions to produce outcomes from which participants benefit immediately, such as obtaining a common resource. From a proximate perspective, this type of cooperative behavior is therefore not incompatible with individuals' selfish motives and maximization of individual profits. In fact, cooperation is often a strategy to achieve higher or otherwise inaccessible payoffs. The main two problems of collaborative activities are coordination and group-level collective actions where free-riders can thrive. Even if individuals are motivated by the higher payoffs associated with cooperation, participants may not know or cannot agree on how to coordinate because of not completely aligned interests. At the group level, if individuals can profit from the benefits produced by others, there is a high incentive not to collaborate and to free-ride on others' work. Here mechanisms to enforce cooperation become critical.

In addition to mutually beneficial forms of cooperation, individuals also engage in altruistic or investing behaviors in which only the recipient obtains immediate benefits, and actors' motivation is to intervene towards another person's goal, problem, need, emotion, etc. (Warneken and Melis 2012). Altruistic behavior can be maintained over time via reciprocity (direct or indirect), so that from a long-term pay-off perspective an exchange of altruistic behaviors would also be mutually beneficial. I am choosing the distinction based on immediate benefits for the actor, since the time-delay factor creates new psychological – cognitive and motivational – challenges. When adult humans behave altruistically toward others, expecting future reciprocation (which is not always necessarily the case), trust and reputation mechanisms become important factors.

In the following, I review using the typology above (collaborative interactions and altruistic behavior) a series of psychological studies investigating the similarities and differences between young children's and one of our closest primate relatives', the chimpanzees', cooperative behavior. This twofold approach, comparative and developmental, offers a unique opportunity to identify those aspects of our cooperative behavior that have deeper phylogenetic roots from those aspects that are derived in humans and/or the result of socialization practices and culture. A better understanding of our natural predisposition to cooperate with others—and the exact contexts that best elicit cooperation (or hinder its emergence)—is key to overcoming the limitations of human cooperation.

Chimpanzees are a crucial species for the study of human cooperation because (1) they are our closest primate relatives (together with bonobos) and (2) they live in a complex social world in which there is competition and cooperation in a wide range of contexts (Muller and Mitani 2005). They cooperate in the context of grooming, when forming coalitions and alliances within their social groups, in the context of coalitionary behavior in intergroup aggressive encounters, and when hunting monkeys or other mammals and sharing the meat afterwards. Furthermore, there is good evidence suggesting that some of these behaviors are probably maintained via reciprocity (Gomes, Mundry, and Boesch 2009; Langergraber et al. 2007; Mitani 2006). However, until recent experimental approaches to the study of cooperation, little was known about the proximate mechanisms underlying chimpanzees' or other nonhuman primates' cooperative behavior.

The results from the studies reviewed next suggest that we share with chimpanzees basic skills and motivations to cooperate with others. However, from a very young age humans seem psychologically better equipped to cooperate with others, in particular in the context of joint collaborative activities. These studies also show the importance of distinguishing between different types and contexts of cooperation. Cooperation is not a uniform trait, since the payoff structure (and therefore underlying motivation), as well as the cognitive requirements to achieve successful cooperation, varies between contexts.

Collaborative interactions

Collaboration or working together with others to achieve common goals is a fundamental aspect of all human social interactions. Our capacity to join and coordinate efforts with others allows us to solve a wide range of problems and constitutes the basis of some of the greatest achievements of human civilizations. From removing a heavy log blocking the road, to building a bridge, to playing an instrument in an orchestra – these are all activities that involve collaboration between two or more individuals. These human activities are possible because we have evolved a set of psychological skills that allow us to plan, coordinate actions, communicate, and if necessary assist each other when performing our different roles to achieve the common goal. From a fairly young age children understand how the different roles in a collaborative task are interconnected and can employ different means to facilitate coordination with a partner (e.g. Warneken, Chen, and Tomasello 2006).

Recent comparative research suggests that we share with chimpanzees some of the capacities necessary for collaboration, whereas at the same time from a very young age children exhibit some other capacities extremely important for the emergence and maintenance of collaborative interactions that we do not find in chimpanzees. So, despite some similarities, young children seem psychologically better equipped to solve problems collaboratively with others than chimpanzees do.

I will first review the similarities between the two species, which relate to the more cognitive basis necessary for collaboration, and then will proceed with the differences in the mechanisms facilitating the emergence and maintenance of collaboration in the long run.

Several different studies suggest that chimpanzees can quickly learn the instrumental role that a partner plays in a collaborative interaction and can employ different non-communicative means to guarantee successful coordination with the partner. They have shown to be flexible problem solvers, capable of overcoming different new obstacles in order to coordinate their actions with those of the partner and ultimately to benefit themselves.

In a first study, Melis, Hare, and Tomasello (2006a) asked whether chimpanzees who had previously succeeded in a collaborative food-retrieval task (Melis, Hare, and Tomasello, 2006b) had some understanding about the role that the partner played in the collaborative interaction. The goal was to investigate whether chimpanzees' successful collaboration was the by-product of simultaneous but independent actions or the result of truly intentionally coordinated actions between partners. The collaboration task was a pulling task in which two individuals were required to pull simultaneously on two ends of a rope in order to obtain a tray of food that had been placed outside the testing room (Figure 4.1). The critical measure was whether or not chimpanzees would recruit the partner, who had been locked in an adjacent room, to initiate the collaborative activity and obtain the baited tray. Subjects were presented with two conditions: (1) the collaboration condition in which the two ends of the rope were too far from each other for one chimpanzee to pull both ends simultaneously, and (2) the solo condition, in which one individual alone could reach both ends of the rope and pull the tray within reach. The results showed that subjects recruited the partner – opening a door and allowing the partner to join them – significantly more often in the collaboration than in the solo condition (Figure 4.1). This suggests that chimpanzees have some knowledge about how the partner's actions (or at the very least the partner's presence), in addition to their own actions, are necessary for success in collaborative food-retrieval tasks. This experiment was followed by another one in which the same subjects were allowed to choose between two partners. The two potential partners differed in their collaboration skills: one of them was able to inhibit pulling and waited for the subject so that they were able to succeed, whereas the other partner was more impulsive and did not wait for the subject, ineffectually pulling the rope out of the tray. In the first session subjects chose equally often both partners, but in the second session, conducted one or two days later, all subjects preferentially chose the skillful partner, showing that they had quickly identified and now remembered the partner who could best perform the role and with whom they were able to benefit the most. These results show that chimpanzees not only know that the partner's presence is necessary for success, but also that the partner needs to be skillful at his/her role.

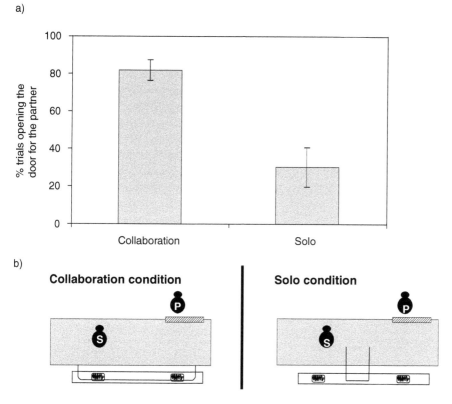

Figure 4.1 Chimpanzees recruit a partner when needed. Experimental set-up and results.

(a) Mean percentage of trials (± SEM) in which subjects recruited the partner. (b) Set-up of the collaboration and solo conditions: the subject was released from an adjacent room into the testing room, while the partner was "locked" in another adjacent room that only the subject could open with a key from inside the testing room. In the collaboration condition the two ends of the rope were 3.4 m apart, whereas in the solo condition the two ends of the rope were close to each other so that the subject did not need the partner. From Melis (2013) (adapted from Melis, Warneken, and Hare (2010))

A more recent study by Melis and Tomasello (2013) demonstrates further the flexibility of chimpanzees' behavior when it comes to coordinating actions with a partner. The goal of this study was to investigate whether chimpanzees show some knowledge regarding the specific action that the partner needs to perform and whether they are willing to help their partner perform his/her role. For this purpose, Melis and Tomasello (2013) presented a new group of chimpanzees with a different collaborative food-retrieval task requiring two different and complementary roles. Each role required a specific tool, and the two tools were not interchangeable. As is typical in other collaboration studies, one individual alone could not perform both roles and needed the partner's action. However, the critical manipulation in this study was that only one of the subjects in the dyad was given the necessary tools. That is, the subject had her own tool and the partner's tool, whereas the partner had none. In order for them to succeed, the subject had to transfer the correct tool to the partner. The results showed that most subjects helped their partners and transferred not just any tool, but the specific tool that the partners needed, and they did this irrespectively of which role they had to perform themselves. That is, chimpanzees transferred the partners' tool and kept and used the one they needed. This study suggests that chimpanzees know that the partner needs to perform the complementary action. Together the results from these two different studies, Melis et al. (2006a) and Melis and Tomasello (2013), suggest that chimpanzees have some knowledge regarding how the different roles in a collaborative activity are interrelated and are part of the action plan to achieve the goal.

Importantly, collaboration requires, in addition to coordination skills, that individuals distribute the acquired resources in a way that partners are incentivized to continue helping each other in future interactions. The main constraint that hinders chimpanzees' collaborative capacities is precisely that: poor mechanisms promoting the distribution of the resources at the end, which leads to unhappy partners and the breakdown of collaboration long term. This does not mean that chimpanzees cannot collaborate at all. As reviewed before, chimpanzees are sophisticated collaborators under certain circumstances. More importantly, we know that in the wild chimpanzees cooperate in various contexts: when building coalitions and alliances, during inter-group aggression and defense, and possibly when hunting monkeys or other mammals (Boesch and Boesch 1989; Muller and Mitani 2005). What our experimental studies show is that chimpanzees are constrained in the context of joint food acquisition. Collaborative hunts in the wild are probably an exception, facilitated by the difficulty of catching prey and the difficulty of monopolizing the spoils (the big carcasses and the fact that meat is difficult and slow to process). In the following, I review the line of studies that shows that, in comparison to humans, chimpanzees lack some psychological traits crucial for collaboration, whereas from a very young age children are psychologically well adapted to collaborate and share the acquired resources with their collaborative partners.

In pioneering experimental studies investigating chimpanzees' collaborative skills, dyads of chimpanzees were presented with a heavy baited box that they had to pull together within reach (Crawford 1937; Povinelli and O'Neill 2000). Critically, the task required subjects to work very close to each other, the resources they could obtain were few and clumped, and subjects were paired without paying attention to the relationship between them. The main result from these studies was that success hardly emerged spontaneously and that dyads required extensive training before they were capable of collaborating, leading authors to conclude that chimpanzees lack the cognitive skills to collaborate with others. However, years later we have learned that the main constraint in these studies was not the inability to coordinate actions with the partner but the lack of motivation to cooperate when resources were hardly sharable and the most dominant partner in the dyad could monopolize all rewards (Melis et al. 2006b; see also Chalmeau and Gallo 1996). In the study by Melis et al. (2006b), dyads were confronted with highly sharable and dispersed rewards, and the working space between partners was maximized. However, even in such a set-up collaboration only emerged among highly tolerant pairs (tolerance levels were assessed in a different feeding context). In fact, we observed how the same individuals collaborated and stopped collaborating depending on which partner they were paired with, showing that it was not inability to work jointly with others but instead ability to anticipate potential conflict over the acquired resources with the partner. In a follow-up study we presented the successful dyads from Melis et al. (2006b) and naïve bonobo dyads with the same collaborative task and manipulated whether the rewards were clumped in one dish or dispersed in two separate dishes (Hare et al. 2007). The rewards' distribution had no effect on bonobos' collaboration levels but strongly influenced chimpanzees' performance; chimpanzees cooperated less frequently when the rewards were clumped because dominant individuals monopolized the totality of the rewards and subordinates increasingly lost interest in the task.

Low levels of social tolerance and competition over food limits chimpanzees' capacity to solve problems with others. Furthermore, they do not possess mechanisms to reward partners' contribution to the collaborative activity. That is, individuals capable of monopolizing the resources do not share more after partners have helped acquiring the resources than when they have not. Some observations from chimpanzees in the wild have reported that chimpanzees share meat after collaborative hunts, taking into account who has and who hasn't participated in the hunt, suggesting a 'fair meat distribution' (Boesch 1994; Boesch and Boesch-Achermann 2000). However, in an experimental study in which we manipulated whether subjects obtained the resources alone or in collaboration with a partner and then measured sharing levels, we found no evidence supporting this claim (Melis, Schneider, and Tomasello 2011; see also Hamann et al. 2011). We found, though, that another variable, proximity to the resources at the time of acquisition (variable which could be confounded with collaboration during natural observations), did influence levels of sharing. Non-possessors were able to feed more if there were together with the food-possessor from the moment on that this one gained access to the food, but got less food if they joined the food-possessor later. The exact proximate mechanism is still unclear, but one possibility is that non-possessors tend to beg more when they are nearby at the moment of capture, maybe because they are more aroused (Melis et al. 2011). So, although chimpanzees understand that the partner plays a role in their own success obtaining the resources, chimpanzees do not incentivize their partners' sharing more after collaboration than after individual food acquisition (Melis et al. 2011; Hamann et al. 2011). Studies that have investigated chimpanzees' sense of fairness, or inequity aversion, by looking at their tendency to reject unequal and disadvantageous deals have found that they behave rationally and accept anything (Brauer, Call, and Tomasello 2006; Jensen, Call, and Tomasello 2007; but see Brosnan, Schiff, and de Waal 2005). Even when subordinate individuals do reject the unequal and disadvantageous deal (10–1) in an open-ended mini-ultimatum game because there is a second and better alternative option (5–5), dominant proposers do not learn to offer equal splits (Melis, Hare, and Tomasello 2009). A variety of studies suggest that there are several factors (dominance, age: Boesch and Boesch-Achermann 2000; harassment: Gilby 2006; reciprocal exchange: Mitani and Watts 1999, 2001; proximity: Melis et al. 2011) that probably influence how much food chimpanzees share after collaborative food acquisition, but there is no evidence for a mechanism specifically adapted to reward partner's participation in a collaborative activity.

The results from these studies with chimpanzees contrast with the results from similar studies with young children. From a very young age humans are much more egalitarian and reward partners' participation in the collaborative activity. Although the traditional view was that equality develops in the school years when children reach seven to eight years of age (Damon 1977, 1980), several new studies have shown that in the context of joint collaborative activities equality emerges at a much younger age (Hamann et al. 2011; Melis, Altrichter, and Tomasello 2013; Warneken et al. 2011).

First, children can successfully collaborate with peers to acquire clumped resources. Warneken et al. (2011) presented dyads of three-year-olds with a collaborative pulling task like the one from the chimpanzees and manipulated the distribution of rewards – clumped and dispersed – as in Hare et al. (2007) and Melis et al.(2006b). Children knew each other but were not necessarily good friends. Overall children collaborated successfully in both conditions and tended to split the rewards fairly, showing that the opportunity to monopolize resources does not constitute a constraint for young children as it does for our primate relatives. But why did children in this situation share equally when a large number of previous studies found that equality emerges later in ontogeny? Two further studies confirmed what Warneken et al. (2011) already suggested: collaboration encourages equal sharing in children. Hamann et al. (2011) measured children's and chimpanzees' tendency to restore equality in three different situations: a collaborative, a parallel-work, and a windfall situation. Pairs of two- and three-year-old children encountered a board with four marbles bunched together out of their reach. To make the marbles accessible subjects were required to pull a block that hit the marbles. Once the marbles were hit by the block, they rolled down to the access points, but they always split in an unequal fashion: three marbles for one lucky kid and one marble for the unlucky kid. In the collaboration condition the two children had to pull simultaneously from two ropes; in the parallel-work each child could pull independently on his/her own rope; and in the windfall situation they didn't have to do anything since the marbles were already accessible. The results showed that three-year-olds, but not two-year-olds and chimpanzees, restored equality (giving one marble to the unlucky kid) much more often in the collaborative than in the windfall or parallel-work situations, suggesting that collaborative interactions positively influence sharing towards equality. In another study, Melis et al. (2013) measured three-year-olds' sharing behavior with a puppet, who had or had not contributed to acquiring the resources (gummy bears). Children shared equally significantly more often when the puppet had helped obtaining the rewards that when the puppet lagged behind, saying that he/she 'preferred to do something else'. These three studies show that at this young age children can already keep track of how the resources were acquired and have a natural tendency to share equally after collaborative effort with others (Hamann et al. 2011; Melis et al. 2013; Warneken et al. 2011). These results also replicate the large number of studies in which children across cultures behaved mainly selfishly when they received windfall resources (e.g. Benenson, Pascoe, and Radmore 2007; Birch and Billman 1986; Rochat et al. 2009). This suggests potentially two different developmental trajectories for sharing collaboratively produced resources and non-collaboratively produced resources, and a higher natural predisposition to share equally in the former case. Tomasello et al. (2012) argued that humans' cooperative tendencies probably evolved in the context of mutualistic collaborative foraging or hunting, so that skills to facilitate and maintain successful collaboration with partners were crucial in our evolutionary history. Interestingly, although the collaborative context is a context that enhances equal sharing, at three to five years of age children's behavior is still strongly biased towards self-interest in other sharing contexts. That is, children at these young ages are sensitive to and willing to pay a cost to reject disadvantageous deals (Blake and McAuliffe 2011; LoBue et al. 2011); they are also capable of rewarding a collaborative partner by splitting the rewards evenly with her/him, but this is the best it can get at these young ages (Hamann et al. 2011; Kanngiesser and Warneken 2012; Melis et al. 2013; Warneken et al. 2011). It is only later in ontogeny, around seven to eight years of age, when children consistently incorporate fairness norms in their interactions with others, becoming averse to both disadvantageous and advantageous inequity in a wider range of contexts and showing a consistent willingness to pay costs to maintain equality (Blake and McAuliffe 2011; Fehr, Bernhard, and Rockenbach 2008).

The studies reviewed here show that, in comparison to chimpanzees, children seem from a young age psychologically well equipped to engage in joint collaborative activities with others. Their more tolerant nature allows them to work with others, even not-close friends, to obtain mutually beneficial outcomes in a wider range of situations. The opportunity to monopolize resources does not constrain their collaborative skills, as it does in chimpanzees, and in addition they recognize their partners' contribution to the joint activity and tend to share rewards equally with them, which incentivizes partners to continue collaborating.

In addition, another line of studies suggests that children, but not chimpanzees, find the joint collaborative activity enjoyable and gratifying in itself. Bullinger, Melis, and Tomasello (2011) gave chimpanzees the opportunity to choose between accessing a reward by working alone or in collaboration with a partner. The subjects could choose between a room in which they could pull a baited tray within reach and obtain a banana, or another room in which they could pull the baited tray together with a partner and also obtain a banana (the partner obtained a banana as well). That is, they would obtain the exact same amount of food in the individual and collaborative option, the only difference being that they would do something together with the partner (who, in addition, would also benefit) in the collaborative option. The results showed that

(a)

(b)

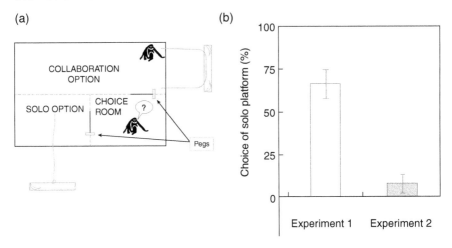

Figure 4.2 Chimpanzees prefer to work alone unless collaboration leads to higher payoffs.
Experimental set-up and results.

(a) Set-up of the study showing that the subject could choose to obtain the reward pulling alone or collaborating with a tolerant partner, (b) In experiment 1, when the payoffs in the solo and the collaboration option were identical, subjects preferentially chose the solo option. In experiment 2, when the rewards in the collaboration option were slightly higher, subjects preferentially chose to collaborate with the partner. From Melis (2013), adapted from Bullinger et al. (2011).

overall subjects preferentially chose to work alone. However, in a second experiment when the amount of food in the collaborative option was slightly increased, subjects altered their preference, choosing almost exclusively to collaborate with the partner (Figure 4.2). This shows that chimpanzees tactically choose collaboration when it is associated with higher payoffs, but otherwise prefer to work alone and probably do not find the collaborative interaction intrinsically rewarding. In a similar study with children, three-year-olds did just the opposite: they preferentially chose the collaborative option even when both options led to identical payoffs (Rekers, Haun, and Tomasello 2011). Furthermore, two other studies also demonstrate children's high motivation to participate in joint collaborative interactions and how intrinsically rewarding is for them. From two years of age, children try to reengage a recalcitrant partner who stops interacting in a joint activity, even when children could still play the game alone or the partner is not actually needed for goal attainment (Gräfenhain et al. 2009; Warneken, Grafenhain, and Tomasello 2012).

To sum up, chimpanzees are capable of working together with others to obtain mutually beneficial goals. They intentionally coordinate their actions with those of a partner and can flexibly overcome different obstacles (i.e. opening doors to recruit the partner or transferring the necessary tools to the partner) to guarantee coordination and successful goal achievement. They understand the instrumental role that the partner plays in the joint collaborative activity. However, they are less tolerant, egalitarian, and motivated to engage in joint activities to achieve resources than children are.

Young children are highly motivated to do things with others, which facilitates collaborative problem solving in a wider range of contexts; at the same time they exhibit a natural tendency towards equality when distributing the jointly acquired resources, which is crucial to maintain collaboration over time. However, despite their tendency to share equally after collaboration, children at these young ages still exhibit a self-serving bias when it comes to sharing windfall resources, and it is only later in ontogeny when they consistently incorporate norms of fairness into their interactions with others. In the following I review the line of studies investigating children's and chimpanzees' cooperative behavior when selfish benefits can be ruled out, and when children or chimpanzees can altruistically provide others with a service (i.e. helping).

Altruistic behavior

Although not very often, occasionally we read in the newspapers about heroic acts from people, such as jumping onto the train tracks to save another person who fell onto them. However, it is not necessary to look for such extreme behaviors to realize that in our daily social interactions we continually do things and intervene on behalf of others. We help our neighbor carry shopping bags, give directions to a lost person, donate blood, and even send money across the world to victims of natural catastrophes. In most of these situations it costs us nearly nothing to help, but in some others situations we incur real costs. Even if we do not risk our lives donating blood or money, we do pay a cost in terms of time or giving away money that we could keep for ourselves. At the same time we know that the motivation underlying these behaviors can vary enormously, from tactically helping others in anticipation of future reciprocation to genuine concern for the welfare of others, even when these are strangers.

Theoretical and empirical studies have shown that ultimately these behaviors can be evolutionarily advantageous if, in the long term, actors obtain return benefits that offset the initial cost. There are several ways in which this can happen (see Bshary and Bergmuller 2008 for a review), but two main mechanisms are direct and indirect reciprocity. In direct reciprocity, individuals who interact repeatedly alternate their roles as actor and recipient of altruistic acts (Trivers 1971). In indirect reciprocal interactions, the actor helps a recipient but is paid back by a third party (Alexander 1987). Here, reputation is the force that sustains cooperation in the long run. Individuals who help others gain good reputations and are more likely to be helped by third parties in the future (Leimar and Hammerstein 2001; Nowak and Sigmund 1998). It is important to distinguish between the two levels of explanation: proximate and ultimate. At a proximate level we can have an altruistic or a selfish motivation to help others, but the evolutionary mechanism maintaining the behavior could still be reciprocity. For example, two good friends who really care about each other may help each other in alternating occasions, as opposed to a cold, calculating businessman that behaves nicely to another business partner because he anticipates a future favor from this partner. Reciprocity could still be the underlying mechanism sustaining this type of behavior, but the underlying motivations, or proximate explanation, would be very different.

Because from a certain age on humans can plan ahead and understand the long-term consequences of exchanging favors, often these two levels of explanations are mixed up, and reciprocal interactions, which ultimately benefit the actor as well, are interpreted as selfishly motivated. However, as mentioned previously, although humans can engage in reciprocal interactions in a strategic way (motivated by the prospect of selfish benefits), this is not necessarily always the case, and it is unlikely that this capacity is present in young children or nonhuman animals.

In the following I review a series of studies suggesting that humans have a natural predisposition to help others selflessly, truly motivated by a concern for others. Evidence supporting this view comes from both human developmental studies and comparative studies with chimpanzees (e.g. Warneken and Tomasello 2006).

Warneken and Tomasello (2009) suggested a classification of altruistic behaviors based on the currency actors provided the recipient with. An actor can altruistically provide others with goods (sharing), services (helping), or information (informing). In the previous section I reviewed how children share resources in the special case of collaboratively produced resources. In this sharing context three-year-olds behaved more pro-socially than chimpanzees, even if in windfall situations equality does not emerge until later in ontogeny.

The main piece of evidence supporting the hypothesis that humans have a biological predisposition to altruistically help others comes from the series of experiments on instrumental helping. When 14- to18-month-old children see an adult stranger struggling to reach something or trying to place something in a specific location, in general failing to reach his/her goal, they intervene in various ways, such as picking up the object and giving it back to the adult, or opening a cabinet to help the adult put the objects inside (Warneken and Tomasello 2006, 2007). Interestingly, they do this spontaneously, without being asked for help or encouraged to intervene, and sometimes even when helping is associated with some costs, as for example when it requires the interruption of some other fun activity (Warneken et al. 2007). A further study by Warneken and Tomasello (2008b) also showed that extrinsic rewards undermine helping, suggesting that children are intrinsically motivated to help and that external rewards can undermine this tendency (the overjustification effect; see Lepper, Greene, and Nisbett 1973). A more recent study also shows similar physiological reactions (pupil dilation) when 24-month-olds help somebody in need or see this person being helped by a third party, but a different level of arousal when the person is not being helped by anybody (Hepach, Vaish, and Tomasello 2012). This again suggests a natural and intrinsic motivation to see others being helped.

Surprisingly and importantly, chimpanzees help others in similar situations as well. Warneken and Tomasello (2006) presented three human-raised chimpanzees with the same type of problems as the children. A caregiver struggled trying to reach an object, and without being asked for it (no eye contact or calling the subject's name), chimpanzees retrieved the object and gave it back to the care-giver. These results were replicated with a different group of chimpanzees who had nearly no relationship to the human who needed help, and also when helping was associated with some costs, such as climbing some meters up the testing room to retrieve the object. Furthermore, the chimpanzees (as well as the children) did not help more often when the recipient rewarded the subjects after every trial in which they helped (Warneken et al. 2007). The main difference between the children and the chimpanzees was that the children helped in a wider range of situations, whereas the chimpanzees only helped in the out-of-reach tasks in which they had to retrieve an object. This raised the possibility that chimpanzees were not actually helping but were just doing something, i.e. retrieving objects is often reinforced in captivity. Therefore they were presented with a completely new situation that they had never encountered before, and in the more ecologi-cally valid context of helping a conspecific. A conspecific struggled opening a door, and subjects could help him/her release the chain that was blocking the door. Chimpanzees helped in this new situation as well, releasing the chain in the test condition but not in the control condition, in which the recipient was not in the room or was trying to open a different door (Melis, Hare, and Tomasello 2008; Warneken et al. 2007). Several studies have since then replicated these findings, showing that chimpanzees are willing and have the capability to help others who are struggling to reach various goals. Yamamoto, Humle, and Tanaka (2009) dem-onstrated that chimpanzees helped a conspecific by handing over a tool he/she needs, and Melis et al. (2011) demonstrated that chimpanzees helped a conspe-cific who was struggling to pull a reward within reach (Figure 4.3). In all these situations the helpers could not profit in any way by helping, and control condi-tions ruled out that subjects were acting just out of boredom or without a full understanding of the consequences of their actions. It is important to emphasize, however, that a basic prerequisite for this type of instrumental helping is that potential recipients provide clear signals or overt cues (intentional or uninten-tional) of what they need or are trying to achieve. Both Yamamoto et al. (2009) and Melis et al. (2011) found that chimpanzees helped only when the recipient actively communicated his/her need of help. This *reactive* helping, i.e. in reaction to the overt cues by the helpee, contrasts with the *proactive* helping typical of children, who are able to discern from situational cues (and in the absence of communicative or behavioral cues from the helpee) that others need help (Warneken 2013; Warneken and Tomasello 2008a).

Importantly, children's willingness to intervene on behalf of others also extends to other contexts. From 12 months of age, children point and provide helpful information to others, even when they do not gain anything out of it (Liszkowski et al. 2006; Lisz-kowski, Carpenter, and Tomasello 2008). However, in interactions with relevant human partners chimpanzees only imperatively gesture or indicate what they want the human to do for them, but do not altruistically inform them (Bullinger et al. 2011; Rivas 2005; Tomasello 2008). So, even though we share with chimpanzees a basic capacity and motivation to help others achieve their goals, chimpanzees are limited in the range of their pro-social behavior. The level of empathy and sympathy underlying

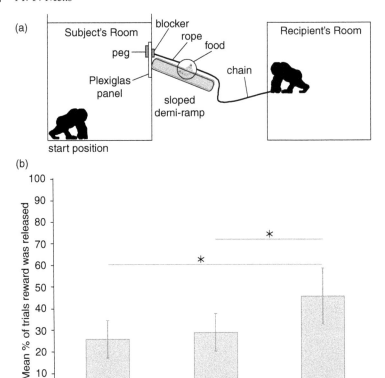

Figure 4.3 Chimpanzees help a conspecific to achieve his/her goal. Experimental set-up and results.

(a) Set up of the study. The subject on the left can help the recipient by releasing the peg that blocks the reward from sliding down the platform to the recipient, (b) Mean percentage of trials (± SEM) in which subjects released the reward as a function of whether the recipient was absent, present but passive, or present and actively providing some kind of signals about what he/she wanted (e.g. reaching, pulling the chain). Adapted from Melis et al. (2011).

chimpanzees' pro-social behaviors is currently still unclear (and a topic that deserves further research), but the studies reviewed here support the hypothesis that their empathic responses probably go beyond mere emotional contagion and are also based on a certain level of cognitive appraisal (see de Waal 2008; Koski and Sterck 2010; Preston and de Waal 2002 for reviews of the topic).

Young children, however, behave altruistically in various different ways, instrumentally helping others, sharing resources with others after joint collaborative work, and providing helpful information to others. Furthermore, there is evidence of sympathy-based pro-social behavior even in the absence of overt emotional signals from 18 months of age (Vaish, Carpenter, and Tomasello 2009).

Conclusions

The series of studies reviewed in this chapter show that although both species, chimpanzees and humans, possess skills and motivations to cooperate with others, cooperation comes more naturally to human children long before they have undergone intensive socialization practices. We share with chimpanzees skills to coordinate efforts to obtain otherwise inaccessible goals, and skills and motivations to altruistically help others achieve their goals in situations in which helping is low cost. This shows that there is a biological predisposition in humans to behave cooperatively. Our cooperative skills have probably evolved from skills that were already present in the last common ancestor of chimpanzees and humans. Cooperation, just like competition, is another strategy that helps individuals to maximize their fitness, so it is not surprising to find shared skills with another highly social and closely related primate species. Yet we humans are much better equipped than our primate cousins to engage in and maintain cooperative relationships with others, as evidenced by the developmental studies, showing the high tolerant nature of children, the tendency of young children to share rewards in an egalitarian way after joint collaborative work, and the wider range of helpful acts, including instrumental helping, pointing, and in general informative communication, that children engage in.

From an evolutionary perspective it is important that cooperative individuals are not exploited by free-riders, who do not cooperate themselves but who reap the benefits from others' cooperative behavior. We have seen that our closest primate relatives are not particularly good at rewarding collaborative partners after joint work, which suggests a lack of mechanisms to enforce collective actions. In a volunteers' dilemma scenario, in which one or two chimpanzees were needed to produce a collective good that a whole group could profit from, we found that in small-size groups dominance was the main factor predicting action, since dominant individuals were capable of securing a share of the spoils at the end. However, in larger groups individuals producing the benefits missed out opportunities to profit from them. In this situation levels of volunteering decreased in general, including volunteering by the dominant individuals in the group (Schneider, Melis, and Tomasello 2012). The most likely mechanism maintaining chimpanzees' cooperative behavior in dyadic interactions is direct reciprocity. The evidence so far suggests that when chimpanzees occasionally help others they do it without strategically planning future benefits, since they seem incapable of anticipating the benefits of alternating helpful acts (Brosnan et al. 2009; Yamamoto and Tanaka 2009). However, there is also good evidence suggesting that chimpanzees keep track of past interactions with others (de Waal 1997; Gomes et al. 2009; Melis et al. 2008; Mitani 2006), so it is possible that they are capable of a more emotionally based form of reciprocity in which individuals choose to preferentially interact or cooperate with partners who have behaved pro-socially to them in the past (attitudinal reciprocity sensu Brosnan and de Waal 2002).

Humans from a young age exhibit a wide range of psychological mechanisms that serve to enforce cooperation at a dyadic level and, what is more difficult, in large groups of anonymous individuals. By two years of age children keep track of past interactions with others and engage in direct reciprocity by being more helpful towards those who were helpful to them in the past (Dunfield and Kuhlmeier 2010). By age three to four years they engage in indirect reciprocity, learning from third-party interactions about others and demonstrating a preference to interact with pro-social individuals and to avoid uncooperative individuals (Hamlin and Wynn 2011; Olson and Spelke 2008; Vaish, Carpenter, and Tomasello 2010). Around the same age they start acquiring the specific social norms of their group and, what is more important, they actively intervene in third-party situations to help maintain these social norms (e.g. conventional norms: Rakoczy, Warneken, and Tomasello 2008; moral norms: Vaish, Missana, and Tomasello 2011). That is, even when they themselves are not directly affected by the norm violation, they are motivated to set things right, conforming to their group's expectations of social and moral conduct and demonstrating that they understand the general applicability of the norms beyond themselves. Slightly later in ontogeny, at five to six years of age, children start managing their own reputations, behaving more collaboratively in the presence of others and demonstrating an understanding of the potential future benefits (or avoidance of costs) of conforming to norms of social conduct (Engelmann, Herrmann, and Tomasello 2012; Piazza, Bering, and Ingram 2011).

In this way children become increasingly integrated into a society based on mutually agreed norms, which culminate in the complex institutions typical of all modern states. In these societies free-riders and norms' non-followers are criticized, ostracized, and directly punished. Furthermore, the institutionalization of punishment, in the form of police forces and laws, creates a solution to the second-order free-riding problem of individuals willing to cooperate but unwilling to punish others. Therefore, by paying 'taxes' individuals support organizations that punish and more generally work to preserve social coordination on a large scale (Traulsen, Rohl, and Milinski 2012).

So, although humans are more cooperative than other species, it is clear that cooperation, and especially cooperation in large groups of individuals, is not easy. Selfish interests are still part of the equation, and temptations to cheat and/or favor those closest to us (e.g. nepotism) will always threaten the stability of cooperation unless there are good enforcement mechanisms in place. However, there are different types of cooperation, and not all cooperation scenarios are equally threatened by selfish motives and free-riders. We need to understand that many of the serious global problems we currently face resemble more a coordination game than a prisoner's dilemma game, where free-riding is not the best possible strategy anymore, since it is only through cooperating that we can avoid catastrophic consequences for all.

Cooperation on a global scale will probably require changes at the individual, societal, and institutional levels. At an individual level, it is not surprising the lack of planning for collective goals in a distant future, knowing how much humans discount the future and our inhibitory control problems when it comes to simple personal decisions that could strongly improve our lives some few years from now (i.e. healthy diet and life style, or enough savings). If we can use the help of soft 'nudges' (Thaler and Sunstein 2008) to make the right decisions when it comes to our own lives, it seems reasonable to accept that we probably also need 'nudges' when it comes to global collective goals (e.g. consuming and polluting less). We also know that from a young age humans start assimilating the social norms of their group, so another important approach will be to influence and produce changes at the societal level by increased communication, information, public awareness, and education. Finally, in the same way that all individual societies require institutions that regulate social life and guarantee minimal levels of coordination and cooperation between individuals, international cooperation will also depend on well-organized institutions that can maintain cooperation between individual states, rewarding cooperators and punishing free-riders.

The evidence reviewed shows that human cooperation not only is the result of socialization and cultural norms, but also relies on a natural predisposition to cooperate that has its roots in the more basic forms of cooperation we share with our primate living relatives. Furthermore, humans have evolved a myriad of ways to enforce cooperation in small and large groups of individuals, although possibly not at such global scale. Therefore, we are at a critical stage in which we need to extend and use our knowledge about what motivates, helps sustain, and hinders human cooperation to design new ways to solve the global problems we face.

References

Alexander, R. D. (1987). *The Biology of Moral Systems*, New York, NY: Walter de Gruyter.

Benenson, J. F., Pascoe, J. and Radmore, N. (2007). 'Children's Altruistic Behavior in the Dictator Game', *Evolution and Human Behavior*, 28 (3): 168–75.

Birch, L. L. and Billman, J. (1986). 'Preschool Children's Food Sharing with Friends and Acquaintances', *Child Development*, 57 (2): 387–95.

Blake, P. R. and McAuliffe, K. (2011). ' "I Had So Much It Didn't Seem Fair": Eight-Year-Olds Reject Two Forms of Inequity', *Cognition*, 120 (2): 215–24.

Boesch, C. (1994). 'Cooperative Hunting in Wild Chimpanzees', *Animal Behaviour*, 48: 653–67.

Boesch, C. and Boesch, H. (1989). 'Hunting Behavior of Wild Chimpanzees in the Tai National Park', *American Journal of Physical Anthropology*, 78 (4): 547–73. doi: 10.1002/ajpa.1330780410.

Boesch, C. and Boesch-Achermann, H. (2000). *The Chimpanzees of the Taï Forest*, Oxford: Oxford University Press.

Boyd, R. and Richerson, P. J. (2009). 'Culture and the Evolution of Human Cooperation', *Philosophical Transactions of the Royal Society B: Biological Sciences*, 364 (1533): 3281–8.

Brauer, J., Call, J. and Tomasello, M. (2006). 'Are Apes Really Inequity Averse?', *Proceedings of the Royal Society: Biological Sciences*, 273 (1605), 3123–8. doi: 10.1098/rspb.2006.3693.

Brosnan, S. F. and de Waal, F. B. (2002). 'A Proximate Perspective on Reciprocal Altruism', *Human Nature*, 13 (1): 129–52.

Brosnan, S. F., Schiff, H. C. and de Waal, F. B. (2005). 'Tolerance for Inequity May Increase with Social Closeness in Chimpanzees', *Proceedings of the Royal Society B: Biological Sciences*, 272 (1560): 253–8. doi: 10.1098/rspb.2004.2947.

Brosnan, S. F., Silk, J. B., Henrich, J., Mareno, M. C., Lambeth, S. P. and Schapiro, S. J. (2009). 'Chimpanzees (Pan troglodytes) Do Not Develop Contingent Reciprocity in an Experimental Task', *Animal Cognition*, 12 (4): 587–97. doi: 10.1007/s10071–009–0218-z.

Bshary, R. and Bergmuller, R. (2008). 'Distinguishing Four Fundamental Approaches to the Evolution of Helping', *Journal of Evolutionary Biology*, 21 (2): 405–20. doi: 10.1111/j.1420–9101.2007.01482.x.

Bullinger, A. F., Melis, A. P. and Tomasello, M. (2011). 'Chimpanzees (Pan Troglodytes) Prefer Individual over Cooperative Strategies toward Goals', *Animal Behaviour*, 82 (5): 1135–41.

Bullinger, A. F., Zimmermann, F., Kaminski, J., and Tomasello, M. (2011). 'Different Social Motives in the Gestural Communication of Chimpanzees and Human Children', *Developmental Science*, 14 (1), 58–68. doi: 10.1111/j.1467–7687.2010.00952.x.

Camerer, C. F. and Fehr, E. (2006). 'When Does "Economic Man" Dominate Social Behavior?', *Science*, 311 (5757): 47–52. doi: 10.1126/science.1110600.

Chalmeau, R. and Gallo, A. (1996). 'Cooperation in Primates: Critical Analysis of Behavioural Criteria', *Behavioural Processes*, 35 (1–3): 101–11.

Crawford, M. P. (1937). 'The Cooperative Solving of Problems by Young Chimpanzees', *Comparative Psychology Monographs*, 14: 1–88.

Damon W. (1977). *The Social World of the Child*, London: Jossey-Bass.

Damon, W. (1980). 'Patterns of Change in Children's Social Reasoning: A Two-Year Longitudinal Study', *Child Development*, 51 (4): 1010–17.

de Waal, F. B. M. (1997). The Chimpanzee's Service Economy: Food for Grooming. *Evolution and Human Behavior*, 18: 375–86.

de Waal, F. B. M. (2008). 'Putting the Altruism Back into Altruism: The Evolution of Empathy', *Annual Reviews of Psychology*, 59: 279–300.

Dunfield, K. A. and Kuhlmeier, V. A. (2010). 'Intention-Mediated Selective Helping in Infancy', *Psychological Science*, 21 (4): 523–7. doi: 10.1177/0956797610364119.

Ehrlich, P. R. and Ehrlich, A. H. (2013). 'Can a Collapse of Global Civilization be Avoided?', *Proceedings of the Royal Society B: Biological Sciences*, 280 (1754): 20122845. doi: 10.1098/rspb.2012.2845.

Engelmann, J. M., Herrmann, E. and Tomasello, M. (2012). 'Five-Year Olds, but Not Chimpanzees, Attempt to Manage Their Reputations', *PLoS One*, 7 (10): e48433. doi: 10.1371/journal.pone.0048433.

Fehr, E., Bernhard, H. and Rockenbach, B. (2008). 'Egalitarianism in Young Children', *Nature*, 454: 1079–83.

Gilby, Ian C. (2006). 'Meat Sharing Among the Gombe Chimpanzees: Harassment and Reciprocal Exchange', *Animal Behaviour*, 71 (4): 953–63.

Gomes, C. M., Mundry, R. and Boesch, C. (2009). 'Long-Term Reciprocation of Grooming in Wild West African Chimpanzees', *Proceedings of the Royal Society B: Biological Sciences*, 276 (1657): 699–706.

Gräfenhain, M., Behne, T., Carpenter, M. and M. Tomasello (2009). One-year-olds' understanding of nonverbal gestures directed to a third person. Cognitive Development 24: 23–33.

Hamann, K., Warneken, F., Greenberg, J. R. and Tomasello, M. (2011). 'Collaboration Encourages Equal Sharing in Children but Not in Chimpanzees', *Nature*, 476 (7360): 328–31. doi: 10.1038/nature10278.

Hamlin, J. K. and Wynn, K. (2011). 'Young Infants Prefer Prosocial to Antisocial Others', *Cognitive Development*, 26 (1): 30–9. doi: 10.1016/j.cogdev.2010.09.001.

Hare, B., Melis, A. P., Woods, V., Hastings, S. and Wrangham, R. (2007). 'Tolerance Allows Bonobos to Outperform Chimpanzees in a Cooperative Task', *Current Biology*, 17 (7): 619–23.

Henrich, J., Boyd, R., Bowles, S., Camerer, C., Fehr, E., Gintis, H. and Tracer, D. (2005). ' "Economic Man" in Cross-Cultural Perspective: Behavioral Experiments in 15 Small-Scale Societies', *Behavioral Brain Science*, 28 (6): 795–815; discussion 815–55.

Hepach, R., Vaish, A. and Tomasello, M. (2012). 'Young Children Are Intrinsically Motivated to See Others Helped', *Psychological Science*, 23 (9): 967–72. doi: 10.1177/0956797612440571.

Jensen, K., Call, J. and Tomasello, M. (2007). 'Chimpanzees are Rational Maximizers in an Ultimatum Game', *Science*, 318 (5847): 107–9. doi: 10.1126/science.1145850.

Kanngiesser, P. and Warneken, F. (2012). 'Young Children Consider Merit When Sharing Resources with Others', *PLoS One*, 7 (8): e43979. doi: 10.1371/journal.pone.0043979.

Koski, S. E. and Sterck, E. H. M. (2010). 'Empathic Chimpanzees: A Proposal of the Levels of Emotional and Cognitive Processing in Chimpanzee Empathy', *European Journal of Developmental Psychology*, 7 (1): 38–66.

Langergraber, K. E., Mitani, J. C. and Vigilant, L. (2007). 'The Limited Impact of Kinship on Cooperation in Wild Chimpanzees', *Proceedings of the National Academy of Science of the USA*, 104 (19): 7786–90.

Leimar, O. and Hammerstein, P. (2001), 'Evolution of Cooperation through Indirect Reciprocity', *Proceedings of the Royal Society B: Biological Sciences*, 268 (1468): 745–53. doi: 10.1098/rspb.2000.1573.

Lepper, M. R., Greene, D. and Nisbett, R. E. (1973). 'Undermining Children's Intrinsic Interest with Extrinsic Rewards: A Test of the "Overjustification" Hypothesis', *Journal of Personality and Social Psychology*, 28 (1): 129–37.

Liszkowski, U., Carpenter, M., Striano, T. and Tomasello, M. (2006). 'Twelve- and 18-Month-Olds Point to Provide Information for Others', *Journal of Cognition and Development*, (2): 173–87.

Liszkowski, U., Carpenter, M. and Tomasello, M. (2008). 'Twelve-Month-Olds Communicate Helpfully and Appropriately for Knowledgeable and Ignorant Partners', *Cognition*, 108 (3): 732–9. doi: 10.1016/j.cognition.2008.06.013.

LoBue, V., Nishida, T., Chiong, C., DeLoache, J. S. and Haidt, J. (2011).'When Getting Something Good Is Bad: Even Three-year-olds React to Inequality', *Social Development*, 20 (1): 154–70.

Melis, A. P. (2013) 'The Evolutionary Roots of Human Collaboration: Coordination and Sharing of Resources', *Annals Of The New York Academy Of Sciences*, 1299: 68–76. doi: 10.1111/nyas.12263.

Melis, A. P., Altrichter, K. and Tomasello, M. (2013). 'Allocation of Resources to Collaborators and Free-Riders in 3-Year-Olds', *Journal of Experimental Child Psychology*, 114 (2): 364–70. doi: 10.1016/j.jecp.2012.08.006.

Melis, A. P., Hare, B. and Tomasello, M. (2006a). 'Chimpanzees Recruit the Best Collaborators', *Science*, 311 (5765): 1297–1300. doi: 10.1126/science.1123007.

Melis, A., Hare, B. and Tomasello, M. (2006b). 'Engineering Cooperation in Chimpanzees: Tolerance Constraints on Cooperation', *Animal Behavior*, 72 (2): 275–86.

Melis, A. P., Hare, B. and Tomasello, M. (2008). 'Do Chimpanzees Reciprocate Received Favors?', *Animal Behaviour*, 76 (3): 951–62.

Melis, A. P., Hare, B. and Tomasello, M. (2009). 'Chimpanzees Coordinate in a Negotiation Game', *Evolution and Human Behavior*, 30 (6): 381–92.

Melis, A., Schneider, A. C. and Tomasello, M. (2011). 'Chimpanzees (Pan Troglodytes) Share Food in the Same Way After Individual and Collaborative Acquisition', *Animal Behaviour*, 82 (3): 485–93.

Melis, A. P. and Semmann, D. (2010). 'How is Human Cooperation Different?', *Philosophical Transactions of the Royal Society B: Biological Sciences*, 365 (1553): 2663–74. doi: 10.1098/rstb.2010.0157.

Melis, A. P. and Tomasello, M. (2013). 'Chimpanzees' (Pan Troglodytes) Strategic Helping in a Collaborative Task', *Biological Letters*, 9 (2): 20130009. doi: 10.1098/rsbl.2013.0009.

Melis, A. P., Warneken, F. and Hare, B. (2010). 'Collaboration and Helping in Chimpanzees', in E. V. Lonsdorf, S. R. Ross, and T. Matsuzawa (eds.) *The Mind of the Chimpanzee: Ecological and Experimental Perspectives*, Chicago, IL: University of Chicago Press, 265–82.

Melis, A. P., Warneken, F., Jensen, K., Schneider, A. C., Call, J. and Tomasello, M. (2011). 'Chimpanzees Help Conspecifics Obtain Food and Non-Food Items', *Proceedings of the Royal Society B: Biological Sciences*, 278 (1710): 1405–13. doi: 10.1098/rspb.2010.1735.

Mitani, J. C. (2006). 'Reciprocal Exchange in Chimpanzees and Other Primates', in P. Kappeler and C. van Schaik (eds.) *Cooperation in Primates: Mechanisms and Evolution*, Heidelberg: Springer-Verlag, 101–13.

Mitani, J. C. and Watts, D. P. (1999). 'Demographic Influences on the Hunting Behavior of Chimpanzees', *American Journal of Physical Anthropology*, 109 (4): 439–54.

Mitani, J. C. and Watts, D. P. (2001). 'Why do Chimpanzees Hunt and Share Meat?', *Animal Behaviour*, 61 (5): 915–24.

Muller, M. N. and Mitani, J. C. (2005). 'Conflict and Cooperation in Wild Chimpanzees', *Advances in the Study of Behavior*, 35: 275–331.

Nowak, M. A. and Sigmund, K. (1998). 'Evolution of Indirect Reciprocity by Image Scoring', *Nature*, 393 (6685): 573–7. doi: 10.1038/31225.

Olson, K. R. and Spelke, E. S. (2008). 'Foundations of Cooperation in Young Children', *Cognition*, 108 (1): 222–31. doi: 10.1016/j.cognition.2007.12.003.

Piazza, J., Bering, J. M. and Ingram, G. (2011). ' "Princess Alice Is Watching You": Children's Belief in an Invisible Person Inhibits Cheating', *Journal of Experimental Child Psychology*, 109 (3): 311–20.

Povinelli, D. J. and O'Neill, D. K. (2000). 'Do Chimpanzees Use Their Gestures to Instruct Each Other?', in S. Baron-Cohen, H. Tager-Flusberg, and D. J. Cohen (eds.) *Understanding Other Minds: Perspectives from Developmental Cognitive Neuroscience*, Oxford / New York, NY: Oxford University Press, 459–87.

Preston, S. and de Waal, F. B. M. (2002). 'Empathy: Its Ultimate and Proximate Bases', *Behavioral and Brain Sciences*, 25 (1): 1–72.

Rakoczy, H., Warneken, F. and Tomasello, M. (2008). 'The Sources of Normativity: Young Children's Awareness of the Normative Structure of Games', *Developmental Psychology*, 44 (3): 875–81. doi: 10.1037/0012–1649.44.3.875.

Rekers, Y., Haun, D. B. and Tomasello, M. (2011). 'Children, but Not Chimpanzees, Prefer to Collaborate', *Current Biology*, 21 (20): 1756–8.

Rivas, E. (2005). 'Recent Use of Signs by Chimpanzees (Pan Troglodytes) in Interactions with Humans', *Journal of Comparative Psychology*, 119 (4): 404–17. doi: 10.1037/0735–7036.119.4.404.

Rochat, P., Dias, M. D. G., Guo, L., Broesch, T., Passos-Ferreira, C., Winning, A. and Berg, B. (2009). 'Fairness in Distributive Justice by 3- and 5-Year-Olds Across Seven Cultures', *Journal of Cross-Cultural Psychology*, 40 (3): 416–42.

Schneider, A. C., Melis, A. P. and Tomasello, M. (2012). 'How Chimpanzees Solve Collective Action Problems', *Proceedings of the Royal Society B: Biological Sciences*, 279 (1749): 4946–54. doi: 10.1098/rspb.2012.1948.

Thaler, R. H. and Sunstein, C. (2008). *Nudge: Improving Decisions about Health, Wealth and Happiness*, New Haven, CT: Yale University Press.

Tomasello, M. (2008). *The Origins of Human Communication*, Cambridge, MA/London: MIT Press.

Tomasello, M. (2009). *Why We Cooperate*, Cambridge, MA: MIT Press.

Tomasello, M., Melis, A. P., Tennie, C., Wyman, E. and Herrmann, E. (2012). 'Two Key Steps in the Evolution of Human Cooperation: The Interdependence Hypothesis', *Current Anthropology*, 53 (6): 673–92. doi: 10.1086/668207.

Tomasello, M. and Vaish, A. (2013). 'Origins of Human Cooperation and Morality', *Annual Review of Psychology*, 64: 231–55. doi: 10.1146/annurev-psych-113011-143812.

Traulsen, A., Rohl, T. and Milinski, M. (2012). 'An Economic Experiment Reveals that Humans Prefer Pool Punishment to Maintain the Commons', *Proceedings of the Royal Society B: Biological Sciences*, 279 (1743): 3716–21. doi: 10.1098/rspb.2012.0937.

Trivers, R. (1971). 'The Evolution of Reciprocal Altruism', *The Quarterly Review of Biology*, 46 (1): 35–57.

Vaish, A., Carpenter, M. and Tomasello, M. (2009). 'Sympathy through Affective Perspective Taking and Its Relation to Prosocial Behavior in Toddlers', *Developmental Psychology*, 45 (2): 534–43.

Vaish, A., Carpenter, M. and Tomasello, M. (2010). 'Young Children Selectively Avoid Helping People with Harmful Intentions', *Child Development*, 81 (6): 1661–9. doi: 10.1111/j.1467–8624.2010.01500.x.

Vaish, A., Missana, M. and Tomasello, M. (2011). 'Three-Year-Old Children Intervene in Third-Party Moral Transgressions', *British Journal of Development Psychology*, 29 (Pt 1): 124–30. doi: 10.1348/026151010X532888.

Walker, B., Barrett, S., Polasky, S., Galaz, V., Folke, C., Engstrom, G. and de Zeeuw, A. (2009). 'Environment: Looming Global-Scale Failures and Missing Institutions', *Science*, 325 (5946): 1345–6. doi: 10.1126/science.1175325.

Warneken, F. (2013). 'Young Children Proactively Remedy Unnoticed Accidents', *Cognition*, 126 (1): 101–8. doi: 10.1016/j.cognition.2012.09.011.

Warneken, F., Chen, F. and Tomasello, M. (2006). 'Cooperative Activities in Young Children and Chimpanzees', *Child Development*, 77 (3): 640–63.

Warneken, F., Grafenhain, M. and Tomasello, M. (2012). 'Collaborative Partner or Social Tool? New Evidence for Young Children's Understanding of Joint Intentions in Collaborative Activities', *Developmental Science*, 15 (1): 54–61. doi: 10.1111/j.1467–7687.2011.01107.x.

Warneken, F., Hare, B., Melis, A. P., Hanus, D. and Tomasello, M. (2007). 'Spontaneous Altruism by Chimpanzees and Young Children', *PLoS Biol*, 5 (7): e184. doi: 10.1371/journal.pbio.0050184.

Warneken, F., Lohse, K., Melis, A. P. and Tomasello, M. (2011). 'Young Children Share the Spoils after Collaboration', *Psychological Science*, 22 (2): 267–73. doi: 10.1177/0956797610395392.

Warneken, F. and Melis, A. (2012). 'The Ontogeny and Phylogeny of Cooperation', in T. K. Shackelford and J. Vonk (eds.) *The Oxford Handbook of Comparative Evolutionary Psychology*, Oxford / New York, NY: Oxford University Press, 3–16.

Warneken, F. and Tomasello, M. (2006). 'Altruistic Helping in Human Infants and Young Chimpanzees', *Science*, 311 (5765): 1301–3. doi: 10.1126/science.1121448.

Warneken, F. and Tomasello, M. (2007). 'Helping and Cooperation at 14 Months of Age', *Infancy*, 11 (3): 271–94.

Warneken, F. and Tomasello, M. (2008a). 'Extrinsic Rewards Undermine Altruistic Tendencies in 20-Month-Olds', *Developmental Psychology*, 44 (6): 1785–8. doi: 10.1037/a0013860.

Warneken, F. and Tomasello, M. (2008b). 'Roots of Human Altruism in Chimpanzees', *Primate Eye*, 96 (Special Issue: Abstracts of the XXII Congress of IPS, Edinburgh, UK): 16.

Warneken, F. and Tomasello, M. (2009). 'Varieties of Altruism in Children and Chimpanzees', *Trends in Cognitive Science*, 13 (9): 397–402. doi: 10.1016/j.tics.2009.06.008.

Yamamoto, S. and Tanaka, M. (2009). 'Do Chimpanzees (Pan Troglodytes) Spontaneously Take Turns in a Reciprocal Cooperation Task?', *Journal of Comparative Psychology*, 123 (3): 242–9. doi: 10.1037/a0015838.

Yamamoto, S., Humle, T. and Tanaka, M. (2009). 'Chimpanzees Help Each Other upon Request', *PLoS ONE*, 4: e7416. doi:10.1371/journal.pone.0007416.

5 Cooperation among humans[1]

David G. Rand and Martin A. Nowak

Cooperation is the third fundamental principle of evolution, beside mutation and selection. Mutation generates variation upon which selection acts.
Cooperation leads to the integration of competing units and allows the formation of higher levels of organization. The emergence of the first cells, of
eucaria, of multi-cellular organisms, of animal societies, and of humankind
are the consequences of cooperation. Cooperation is the creative force of
evolution, which allows the emergence of complexity and structure and ultimately human life. Cooperation is never fully stable, but waxes and wanes.
Natural selection tends to oppose cooperation unless specific mechanisms for
evolution of cooperation are operative in a population (Nowak 2006). Pres-
ently five such mechanisms are known: direct reciprocity, indirect reciprocity,
spatial selection, group selection, and kin selection. This chapter will discuss
theoretical and empirical evidence for each of those mechanisms (Rand and
Nowak 2013).

The importance and fragility of cooperation is evident in human interactions.
We attempt to cooperate and to realize the potential benefits of cooperation, but
the temptation to defect is always present. Humans are 'SuperCooperators'
(Nowak and Highfield 2011) in the sense that they can utilize and know all five
mechanisms for evolution of cooperation. Knowledge of this research endeavor,
which exists at the interface of mathematics, evolutionary biology, psychology,
and economics, is especially relevant in situations that see a breakdown of human
cooperation at the global level and at a time when cooperation would be most
needed to solve the world's pressing problems (Messner and Weinlich in this
volume).

In a cooperative (or social) dilemma, there is a tension between what is
good for the individual and what is good for the population. The population
does best if individuals cooperate, but for each individual there is a temptation to defect. A simple definition of cooperation is that one individual pays
a cost for another to receive a benefit. Cost and benefit are measured in terms
of reproductive success, where reproduction can be cultural or genetic. A
more detailed definition can be provided by game theory. Consider a game

DOI: 10.4324/9781315691657-7

between two strategies, C and D, and the payoff matrix (indicating the row player's payoff):

	C	D
C	R	S
D	T	P

When does it make sense to call strategy C 'cooperation' and strategy D 'defection'? The following definition (Hauert et al. 2006: 195; Nowak 2012) is useful: the game is a cooperative dilemma if (1) two cooperators get a higher payoff than two defectors, R > P, yet (2) there is an incentive to defect. This incentive can arise in three different ways: (2a) if T > R, then it is better to defect when playing against a cooperator; (2b) if P > S, then it is better to defect when playing against a defector; and (2c) if T > S, then it is better to be the defector in an encounter between a cooperator and a defector. If at least one of those three conditions holds, then we have a cooperative dilemma. If none hold, then there is no dilemma and C is simply better than D. If all three conditions hold, we have a Prisoner's Dilemma, T > R > P > S (Axelrod 1984; Rapoport and Chammah 1965).

The Prisoner's Dilemma (PD) is the most stringent cooperative dilemma. Here defectors dominate cooperators. In a well-mixed population natural selection always favors defectors over cooperators. For cooperation to arise in the PD we need a mechanism for the evolution of cooperation. Cooperative dilemmas which are not the PD could be called 'relaxed cooperative dilemmas'. In these games it is possible to evolve some level of cooperation even if no mechanism is at work. One such example is the snowdrift game, given by T > R > S > P. Here we find a stable equilibrium between cooperators and defectors even in a well-mixed population.

There are a few other conditions that one could consider. For example, it might be natural to demand that it is always better to meet a cooperator than a defector (regardless of your own strategy). This implies R > S and T > P. Moreover, if 2R > T + S, then the total payoff of the population is maximized if everyone cooperates; otherwise a mixed population achieves the highest total payoff.

The definition of a cooperative dilemma can be generalized to more than two people, which brings us to the theory of n person games. Denote the payoffs for cooperators and defectors by P_i and Q_i, respectively, in groups that contain i cooperators and $n - i$ defectors. For the game to be a cooperative dilemma we require that (1) an all-cooperator group gets a higher payoff then an all-defector group, $P_n > Q_0$, yet (2) there is some incentive to defect. The incentives to defect can take the following form: (2a) $P_i < Q_{i-1}$ for $i = 1 \ldots n$ and (2b) $P_i < Q_i$ for $i = 1 \ldots$ $n - 1$. The conditions (2a) mean that an individual can increase its payoff by switching from cooperation to defection. The conditions (2b) mean that in any mixed group, defectors have a higher payoff than cooperators. If only some of these incentives (2) hold, than we have a relaxed cooperative dilemma. In this case some evolution of cooperation is possible even without a specific mechanism. But a mechanism would typically enhance the evolution of cooperation by increasing the equilibrium abundance of cooperators, increasing the fixation probability of cooperators, or reducing the invasion barrier that needs to be overcome. The volunteer's dilemma is an example of a relaxed situation (Archetti 2009). If all incentives hold, we have the n person equivalent of a Prisoner's Dilemma, called the 'Public Goods Game' (PGG) (Hardin 1968), and a mechanism for evolution of cooperation is needed.

In a well-mixed population, where each individual is equally likely to interact and compete with each other, individual, natural selection favors defection in the PD. Defectors always out-earn cooperators, and in a population that contains both cooperators and defectors, the latter have higher fitness. Selection therefore reduces the abundance of cooperators until the population consists entirely of defectors. For cooperation to arise, a mechanism for the evolution of cooperation is needed. Such a mechanism is an interaction structure that can cause cooperation to be favored over defection (Nowak 2006). These interaction structures specify how the individuals of a population interact to receive payoffs and how they compete for reproduction. Previous work has identified five such mechanisms for the evolution of cooperation: direct reciprocity, indirect reciprocity, spatial selection, multi-level selection and kin selection.

It is important to distinguish between interaction patterns that are mechanisms for the evolution of cooperation and behaviors that are not mechanisms but instead require an evolutionary explanation themselves. Three examples are upstream reciprocity, strong reciprocity, and parochial altruism. Upstream (or generalized) reciprocity refers to the phenomenon of 'paying it forward', by which an individual who has just received help is more likely to help others in turn. Strong reciprocity refers to individuals rewarding cooperation and punishing selfishness even in anonymous interactions with no promise of future benefits. Parochial altruism (or in-group bias) describes the behavior whereby people are more likely to help members of their own group than members of other groups.

None of these concepts explain the evolution of cooperation: adding one or more of these elements to a PD will not cause selection to favor cooperation. Instead, these concepts are descriptions of behavior which require an evolutionary explanation. Group selection, spatial structure, or some chance of direct or indirect reciprocity can lead to the evolution of upstream reciprocity (Nowak and Roch 2007; Rankin and Taborsky 2009), strong reciprocity (Boyd et al. 2003; Nakamaru and Iwasa 2005; Ohtsuki et al. 2009), and parochial altruism (Choi and Bowles 2007; Fu et al. 2012; García and van den Bergh 2011; Hammond and Axelrod 2006; Masuda 2012).

In this chapter we build a bridge between theoretical work that has proposed the mechanisms for the evolution of cooperation, and experimental work exploring how and when people actually cooperate. We present evidence from experiments that implement each mechanism in the laboratory. We discuss why cooperation arises in some experimental settings where no mechanisms are apparent. Finally, we consider the cognitive underpinnings of human cooperation. We show that intuitive, automatic processes implement cooperative strategies that reciprocate, and that these intuitions are affected by prior experience. We argue that these results support a key role for direct and indirect reciprocity in human cooperation and emphasize the importance of culture and learning.

Theoretical basis of the five mechanisms

(1) Direct reciprocity arises if there are repeated encounters between the same two individuals (Binmore and Samuelson 1992; Fudenberg and Maskin 1986; Sigmund 2010; Trivers 1971). Because they interact repeatedly, individuals can use 'conditional strategies', where behavior depends on previous outcomes. Direct reciprocity allows the evolution of cooperation if the probability of another interaction is sufficiently high (Axelrod 1984). Under this 'shadow of the future' I may pay the cost of cooperation today in order to earn your reciprocal cooperation tomorrow. The repeated game can occur with players making simultaneous decisions in each round or taking turns (Nowak and Sigmund 1994). Successful strategies for the simultaneous repeated PD include tit for tat (TFT), generous tit for tat (Nowak and Sigmund 1992), and win-stay, lose-shift (Nowak and Sigmund 1993). TFT is an excellent catalyst for the emergence of cooperation, but when errors are possible it is quickly replaced by strategies that sometimes cooperate even when the opponent defects (Generous TFT) (Nowak and Sigmund 1992).

(2) Indirect reciprocity operates if there are repeated encounters within a population and third parties observe some of these encounters or find out about them. Information about those encounters can spread through communication, affecting the reputations of the participants. Individuals can thus adopt conditional strategies that base their decisions on the reputation of the recipient (Nowak and Sigmund 1998, 2005). My behavior towards you depends on what you have done to me and to others. Cooperation is costly but leads to the reputation of being a helpful individual, and therefore may increase your chances of receiving help from others. A strategy for indirect reciprocity consists of a social norm and an action rule (Brandt and Sigmund 2006; Ohtsuki and Iwasa 2006; Ohtsuki et al. 2009). The social norm specifies how reputations are updated based on interactions between individuals. The action rule specifies whether or not to cooperate given the available information about the other individual. Indirect reciprocity enables the evolution of cooperation if the probability of knowing someone's reputation is sufficiently high. In the context of indirect reciprocity, increasing scale and complexity of interactions is beneficial for cooperation, as more interactions allow greater flow of reputational information.

(3) Spatial selection can favor cooperation without the need for strategic complexity (Nowak and May 1992; Nowak et al. 2010a). When populations are structured rather than randomly mixed, behaviors need not be conditional on previous outcomes. Because individuals interact with those near them, cooperators can form clusters which prevail even if surrounded by defectors. The fundamental idea is that clustering creates assortment, where cooperators are more likely to interact with other cooperators. Therefore, cooperators can earn higher payoffs than defectors. More generally, population structure affects the outcome of the evolutionary process, and some population structures can lead to the

evolution of cooperation (Tarnita et al. 2009b; Tarnita et al. 2011). Population structure specifies who interacts with whom to earn payoffs and who competes with whom for reproduction. The latter can be genetic or cultural. Population structure can represent geographic distribution (Hauert and Doebeli 2004; Hauert and Imhof 2012) or social networks (Skyrms and Pemantle 2000), and can be static (Lieberman et al. 2005; Ohtsuki et al. 2006; Szabo and Fath 2007) or dynamic (Cavaliere et al. 2012; Fu et al. 2008; Perc and Szolnoki 2010; Santos et al. 2006; Skyrms and Pemantle 2000; Tarnita et al. 2009a). Population structure can also be implemented through tag-based cooperation, where interaction and cooperation are determined by arbitrary tags or markers (Antal et al. 2009; Riolo et al. 2001; Traulsen and Schuster 2003). In this case, clustering is not literally spatial but instead occurs in the space of phenotypes (Antal et al. 2009). Models of spatial selection generally suggest that as the scale interaction and degree of interconnectedness increase, it becomes more difficult to maintain cooperation: interconnection undermines clustering.

(4) Multi-level selection operates if, in addition to competition between individuals in a group, there is also competition between groups (Bowles 2009; Bowles and Gintis 2011; Boyd et al. 2003; Boyd and Richerson 1990; Sober and Wilson 1998; Traulsen and Nowak 2006; Wilson 1975). It is possible that defectors win within groups but that groups of cooperators outcompete groups of defectors. Overall such a process can result in the selection of cooperators. Darwin wrote in 1871,

> There can be no doubt that a tribe including many members who . . . were always ready to give aid to each other and to sacrifice themselves for the common good, would be victorious over other tribes; and this would be natural selection.
>
> (Darwin 1871: 159)

Interestingly, multi-level selection relies on competition between distinct groups, and thus may be challenged in the face of an increasingly interconnected and global world.

(5) Kin selection can be seen as a mechanism for the evolution of cooperation if properly formulated. In our opinion, kin selection operates if there is conditional behavior based on kin recognition: an individual recognizes kin and behaves accordingly. Much of the current kin selection literature, however, does not adhere to this simple definition based on kin recognition. Instead kin selection is linked to the concept of inclusive fitness (Hamilton 1964). Inclusive fitness is a particular mathematical method to account for fitness effects. It assumes that personal fitness can be written as a sum of additive components caused by individual actions. Inclusive fitness works in special cases, but it makes strong assumptions that prevent it from being a general concept (Nowak et al. 2010b). A straightforward mathematical formulation describing the evolutionary dynamics of strategies or alleles without the detour of inclusive fitness is a more universal, and more meaningful, approach. This position, which is critical of inclusive

fitness, is based on a careful mathematical analysis of evolution (Nowak et al. 2010b). Nevertheless it has been challenged by proponents of inclusive fitness (Abbot et al. 2011), but without engaging the underlying mathematical results (Nowak et al. 2011). In our opinion, a clear understanding of kin selection can only emerge once the intrinsic limitations of inclusive fitness are widely recognized. In the meanwhile it is useful to remember that no phenomenon in evolutionary biology requires an inclusive fitness–based analysis (Szabo and Fath 2007).

Each of the five mechanisms applies to human cooperation. Over the course of human evolution it is likely that they were (and are) all in effect to varying degrees. Although each mechanism has traditionally been studied in isolation, it is important to consider the interplay between them. In particular, when discussing the evolution of any pro-social behavior in humans, one cannot exclude direct and indirect reciprocity. Early human societies were small, and repetition and reputation were always in play. Even in the modern world most of our crucial interactions are repeated, such as those with our coworkers, friends, and family. Thus spatial structure, group selection, and kin selection should be considered in the context of their interactions with direct and indirect reciprocity. Surprising dynamics can arise when mechanisms are combined. For example, direct reciprocity and spatial structure can interact either synergistically or antagonistically, depending on the levels of repetition and assortment (van Veelen et al. 2012). Further exploration of the interactions between mechanisms is a promising direction for future research.

Experimental evidence for the five mechanisms

Theoretical work provides deep insight into the evolution of human cooperation. Evolutionary game theory allows us to explore what evolutionary trajectories are possible and what conditions may give rise to cooperation. To move from this space of possibilities towards an understanding of which particular path human cooperation has followed (and is currently following), theory must be complemented with empirical data from experiments (Rand 2012). Theory suggests what to measure and how to interpret it, whereas experiments provide actual empirical evidence.

Experiments illuminate human cooperation in two different ways: by examining what happens when particular interaction structures are imposed on human subjects, and by revealing the human psychology shaped by mechanisms that operate outside of the laboratory.

The first type of experiment seeks to recreate the rules of interaction prescribed by a given model. By allowing human subjects to play the game accordingly, researchers test the effect of adding human psychology. Do human agents respond to the interaction rules similarly to the agents in the models? Or are important elements of proximate human psychology missing from the models, revealing new questions for evolutionary game theorists to answer? Note that these experiments focus on learning rather than genetic evolution, but in doing so test the robustness of mechanisms for promoting cooperation proposed by theory.

The second type of experiment explores behavior in experiments where no mechanisms that promote cooperation are present (for example, one-shot anonymous games in well-mixed populations). By examining play in these artificial settings, we hope to expose elements of human psychology and cognition that would ordinarily be unobservable. For example, in repeated games it can be self-interested to cooperate. When we observe people cooperating in repeated games, we cannot tell if they have a predisposition towards cooperating or are just rational selfish maximizers (Dreber et al. 2014). It requires one-shot anonymous games to reveal social preferences. The artificiality of these lab experiments is therefore not a flaw, but rather can make such experiments valuable. It is critical, however, to bear this artificiality in mind when interpreting the results: these experiments are useful because of what they reveal about the psychology produced by the outside world, rather than themselves being a good representation of that world.

We now present both kinds of experimental evidence. First we describe experiments designed to test each of the mechanisms for the evolution of cooperation in the laboratory. We then discuss the insights gained from cooperation in one-shot anonymous experiments. For comparability with theory, we focus on experiments that study cooperation using game theoretic frameworks. Most of these experiments abide by the conventions of experimental economics. They are incentivized: the payout people receive depends on their earnings in the game. Subjects are told the true rules of the game, and deception is prohibited: in order to explore the effect of different rules on cooperation, subjects must believe that the rules really apply. Finally, interactions are typically anonymous, often occurring via computer terminals or over the Internet. This anonymity reduces concerns about reputational effects outside of the laboratory, creating a baseline from which to measure the effect of adding more complicated interaction structures.

Direct reciprocity

Across many experiments using repeated PDs, people typically learn to cooperate more when the probability of future interaction is higher (Dal Bó 2005; Dal Bó and Fréchette 2011; Dreber et al. 2008; Duffy and Ochs 2009; Fudenberg et al. 2012; Murninghan and Roth 1983; Roth and Murninghan 1978) (in these games, there is typically a constant probability that a given pair of subjects will play another round of PD together). Repetition continues to support cooperation even if errors are added (the computer sometimes switches a player's move to the opposite of what she intended) (Fudenberg et al. 2012), which is consistent with theoretical results (Fudenberg and Maskin 1990; Nowak and Sigmund 1992). More quantitatively, theoretical work using stochastic evolutionary game theory (modeling that incorporates randomness and chance) finds that cooperation will be favored by selection if TFT earns a higher payoff than the strategy 'always defect' (ALLD) in a population where the two strategies are equally common (when TFT is 'risk-dominant' over ALLD) (Nowak et al. 2004). More generally, as the payoff of TFT relative to ALLD in such a mixed population increases, so too does the predicted frequency of cooperation. Indeed, this prediction does an excellent job of organizing the experimental data across a number of repeated game experiments (Rand and Nowak 2013). This is one of numerous situations in which stochastic evolutionary game theory (Nowak et al. 2004) successfully describes observed human behavior (Manapat et al. 2012b; Rand and Nowak 2012; Rand et al. 2009a; Rand et al. 2013a).

Repetition promotes cooperation in dyadic interactions. The situation is more complicated if groups of players interact repeatedly (Levin 2000). Such group cooperation is studied in the context of the Public Goods Game (PGG) (Hardin 1968), an n-player PD. The PGG is typically implemented by giving each of n players an endowment and having them choose how much to keep for themselves versus how much to contribute to the group. All contributions are multiplied by some constant r, with $1 < r < n$, and split equally by all group members. The key difference from the two-player PD is that in the PGG targeted interactions are not possible: if one player contributes a large amount while another contributes little, a third group member cannot selectively reward the former and punish the latter. The third player can choose either a high contribution, rewarding both players, or a low contribution, punishing both. Thus, although direct reciprocity can in theory stabilize cooperation in multi-player games, this stability is fragile and can be undermined by errors or a small fraction of defectors (Boyd and Richerson 1988): for example, if I know that others will only contribute next period so long as all players contribute this period, then I maximize my payoff by contributing; but as soon as one person accidentally defects (or decides to experiment with defection), all players switch to defection. As a result, cooperation almost always fails in repeated PGGs in the laboratory (Fehr and Gächter 2000; Ostrom et al. 1992; Rand et al. 2009c).

Does this mean that mechanisms other than direct reciprocity are needed to explain cooperation among groups? We argue that the answer is 'no'. One must only realize that group interactions do not occur in a vacuum, but rather are superimposed on a network of dyadic personal relationships. In these personal pairwise relationships, people can condition their behavior on the other's previous conduct in the group. This allows for the targeted reciprocity that is missing in the PGG, giving us the power to enforce group-level cooperation. Dyadic relationships can be represented by adding pairwise rewards or punishment opportunities to the PGG. After each PGG round, subjects can pay to increase or decrease the payoff of other group members based on their contributions: high contributors are typically rewarded, and low contributors punished (Ellingsen et al. 2012; Fehr and Gächter 2000, 2002; Rand et al. 2009c). Thus the possibility of targeted interaction is reintroduced, and direct reciprocity can once again function to promote cooperation.

Numerous laboratory experiments demonstrate that pairwise reward and punishment are both effective in promoting cooperation in the repeated PGG (Choi and Ahn 2013; Fehr and Gächter 2000; Ostrom et al. 1992; Rand et al. 2009c; Sefton et al. 2007; Sutter et al. 2010). Naturally, given that both implementations of direct reciprocity promote cooperation to an equal extent, higher payoffs are achieved when using reward (which creates benefit) than punishment (which destroys it). Rewarding also avoids vendettas (Dreber et al. 2008; Niki-forakis 2008) and the possibility of 'antisocial punishment', where low contributors pay to punish high contributors. Antisocial punishment has been demonstrated to occur in cross-cultural laboratory experiments (Gächter and Herrmann 2009, 2011; Herrmann et al. 2008), and can prevent the evolution of cooperation in theoretical models (García and Traulsen 2012; Powers et al. 2012; Rand and Nowak 2011; Rand et al. 2010). These cross-cultural studies add a note of caution to previous studies on punishment and reward in the PGG: targeted interactions can only support cooperation if they are used properly. Antisocial punishment undermines cooperation, as does rewarding of low contributors (Ellingsen et al. 2012). With repetition and the addition of pairwise interactions, cooperation can be a robust equilibrium in the PGG, but populations can nonetheless get stuck in other less efficient equilibria or fail to equilibrate at all (Ellingsen et al. 2012).

Taken together, the many experiments exploring the linking of dyadic and multi-player repeated games demonstrate the power of direct reciprocity for promoting large-scale cooperation. Interestingly, this linking also involves indirect reciprocity: if I punish a low contributor, then I reciprocate a harm done to me (direct reciprocity) as well as a harm done to other group members (indirect reciprocity, Panchanathan and Boyd 2004). Further development of theoretical models analyzing linked games is an important direction for future research, as is exploring the interplay between direct and indirect reciprocity in such settings.

Indirect reciprocity

Indirect reciprocity is a powerful mechanism for promoting cooperation among subjects who are not necessarily engaged in pairwise repeated interactions. To study indirect reciprocity in the lab, subjects typically play with randomly matched partners and are informed about these partners' choices in previous interactions with others (Milinski et al. 2002; Wedekind and Milinski 2000). Most subjects condition their behavior on this information: those who have been cooperative previously, particularly towards partners who have behaved well themselves, tend to receive more cooperation (Bolton et al. 2005; Jacquet et al. 2011; Milinski et al. 2002; Pfeiffer et al. 2012; Rockenbach and Milinski 2006; Seinen and Schram 2006; Semmann et al. 2005; Sommerfeld et al. 2007; Ule et al. 2009; Wedekind and Milinski 2000). Thus having the reputation for being a cooperator is valuable, and cooperation is maintained: it is worth paying the cost of cooperation today in order to earn the benefits of a good reputation tomorrow.

Reputation effects have also been shown to promote pro-social behavior outside of the laboratory. Field experiments, conducted in real-world settings with participants that do not know they are part of an experiment, find that publicizing the names of donors increases the level of blood donation (Lacetera and Macis 2010) and giving to charity (Karlan and McConnell 2012). Non-financial incentives involving reputation have also been shown to outperform monetary incentives in motivating participation in an energy blackout prevention program in

California (Yoeli et al. 2013) and the sale of condoms on behalf of a health organization in Namibia (Ashraf et al. 2012).

Indirect reciprocity relies on peoples' ability to effectively communicate and distribute reputational information. Not surprisingly, people spend a great deal of their time talking to each other (gossiping) about the behavior of third parties (Dunbar et al. 1997; Sommerfeld et al. 2007). In addition to this traditional form of transmitting reputational information, the Internet has dramatically expanded our ability to maintain large-scale reputation systems among strangers. For example, online markets such as eBay have formalized reputation systems in which buyers rate sellers. As predicted by indirect reciprocity, there is a large economic value associated with having a good eBay reputation (Resnick et al. 2006). Similarly, business rating websites such as Yelp.com create a global-level reputation system, allowing people without local information to reliably avoid low-quality products and services and creating economic incentives for businesses to earn good reputations (Luca 2011).

A fascinating question that these studies raise is why people bother to leave evaluations at all. Or, even when people do provide information, why be truthful? Providing accurate information requires time and effort and is vital for reputation systems to function. Thus rating is itself a public good (Suzuki and Kimura 2013). However, indirect reciprocity may be able to solve this 'second order free-rider' problem itself: to remain in good reputation, you must not only cooperate in the primary interactions but also share truthful information. Exploring this possibility further is an important direction for future research.

Enforcement poses another challenge for indirect reciprocity. Withholding cooperation from defectors is essential for the reputation system to function. Yet doing so can potentially be damaging for your own reputation. This is particularly true when using simple reputation systems such as image scoring (Nowak and Sigmund 1998), which is a first order assessment rule evaluating actions only (cooperation is good, defection is bad). But it can apply even when using more complex reputation rules, where defecting against someone with a bad reputation earns you a good reputation: if observers are confused about the reputation of your partner, defecting will tarnish your name. Here we suggest a possible solution to this problem. If players have the option to avoid interacting with others, they may shun those with bad reputations. Thus they avoid getting exploited, while also not having to defect themselves. Such a system should lead to stable cooperation using even the simplest of reputation systems. This solution brings indirect reciprocity together with theories of partner choice (Fu et al. 2008; Manapat et al. 2012a; Skyrms and Pemantle 2000). Another interesting possibility involves intermediation: if you employ an intermediary to defect against bad players on your behalf, this may help to avoid sullying your reputation. Consistent with this possibility, experimental evidence suggests that the use of intermediaries reduces blame for selfish actions (Coffmann 2011; Paharia et al. 2009). We expect that researchers will explore these phenomena further in the coming years, using theoretical models as well as laboratory and field experiments.

Finally, there is evidence for the central role of reputational concerns in human evolution. Infants as young as six months of age take into account others' actions toward third parties when making social evaluations (Hamlin et al. 2007; Hamlin et al. 2011). This tendency even occurs between species: capuchin monkeys are less likely to accept food from humans who were unhelpful to third parties (Anderson et al. 2013). Humans are also exquisitely sensitive to the possibility of being observed by third parties (Milinski and Rockenbach 2007). For example, people are even more pro-social when being watched by a robot with large fake eyes (Burnham and Hare 2007), or when a pair of stylized eye-spots are added to the computer's desktop background (Haley and Fessler 2005). In the opposite direction, making studies double-blind such that the experimenters cannot associate subjects with their actions increases selfishness (Hoffman et al. 1996).

Spatial selection

Unlike direct and indirect reciprocity, experimental evidence of spatial selection among humans is less clear. (There is good evidence for spatial selection in unicellular organisms; Gore et al. 2009.) Experiments that investigate fixed spatial structure typically find no increase in cooperation. These experiments assign subjects to locations in a network and have them play repeatedly with their neighbors. Cooperation rates are then compared to a control where subjects' positions in the network are randomly reshuffled each round, creating a well-mixed population. As in the theoretical models, subjects in these experiments are usually given a binary choice – either cooperate with all neighbors or defect with all neighbors – and are typically presented each round with the payoff of each neighbor, as well as that neighbor's choice. Yet unlike the models, cooperation rates in these experiments are no higher in structured populations than in randomly shuffled populations (Gracia-Lázaro et al. 2012; Grujić et al. 2012; Grujić et al. 2010; Suri and Watts 2011; Traulsen et al. 2010).

Various explanations have been advanced for this surprising set of findings. One suggestion is that subjects in laboratory experiments engage in high rates of experimentation, often changing their strategies at random rather than copying higher-payoff neighbors (Traulsen et al. 2010). Such experimentation is analogous to mutation in evolutionary models. High mutation rates undermine the effect of spatial structure: when players are likely to change their strategies at random, then the clustering that is essential for spatial selection is disrupted (Allen et al. 2011). Without sufficient clustering, cooperation is no longer advantageous.

Another explanation involves the way subjects choose which strategy to adopt. Theoretical models make detailed assumptions about how individuals update their strategies, and whether network structure can promote cooperation in these models depends critically on these details (Tarnita et al. 2009b). It is possible that human subjects in the experimental situations examined thus far tend to update rules that cancel the effect of spatial structure (Traulsen et al. 2010). A related argument involves the confounding of spatial structure and direct reciprocity that occurs in these experiments (Semmann 2012). Subjects in the experiments know that they are interacting repeatedly with the same neighbors. Thus they can play conditional strategies, unlike the agents in most theoretical models. Because players must choose the same action towards all neighbors, players in these experiments cannot target their reciprocity (like in the PGG). Thus the tendency to reciprocate may lead to the demise of cooperation.

Here we offer a possible alternative explanation. Theoretical work has shown that cooperation is not *always* expected to succeed in structure populations. Instead, particular conditions are required. For example, under a particular set of assumptions about strategy updating, cooperation is only predicted to be favored when the PD's benefit-to-cost ratio exceeds the average number of neighbors in the network (Ohtsuki et al. 2006). Thus it may be that previous experiments found no effects of networked interaction because they did not explore the right combinations of payoffs and network structures. Exploring this possibility is an important direction for future study.

In contrast to these negative results using static networks, dynamic networks robustly promote cooperation in the laboratory (Fehl et al. 2011; Jordan et al. 2013; Rand et al. 2011; Wang et al. 2012). In these experiments subjects can make or break connections with others, and the network evolves over time. This dynamic character allows subjects to engage in targeted action via 'link reciprocity': players can choose to severe links with defectors or to make links with cooperators. The importance of dynamic assortment based on arbitrary tags has also been demonstrated in lab experiments using coordination games: associations between tags and actions emerge spontaneously, as does preferential interaction between players sharing the same tag (Efferson et al. 2008).

More generally, there is substantial evidence that social linkages and identity are highly flexible. Minimal cues of shared identity (such as preference for similar types of paintings, i.e. the 'minimal groups paradigm') can increase cooperation among strangers (Tajfel et al. 1971). Alternatively, the introduction of a higher-level threat can realign coalitions, making yesterday's enemies into today's allies (Rand et al. 2009b; Sherif et al. 1961). Such plasticity is not limited to modern humans: many early human societies were characterized by fission-fusion dynamics, where group membership changed regularly (Marlowe 2005). Developing evolutionary models that capture this multifaceted and highly dynamic nature of group identity is a promising direction for future work. Models based on changing set memberships (Fu et al. 2012; Tarnita et al. 2009a) and tag-based cooperation (Antal et al. 2009; Riolo et al. 2001; Traulsen and Schuster 2003) represent steps in this direction.

Finally, studies examining behavior in real-world networks also provide evidence for the importance of population structure in cooperation. For example, experiments with hunter-gatherers show that social ties predict similarity in cooperative behavior (Apicella et al. 2012). A nationally representative survey of American adults found that people who engage in more pro-social behavior have more social contacts, as predicted by dynamic network models (O'Malley et al. 2012). There is also evidence that social structure is heritable (Fowler et al. 2011), as is assumed in many network models.

In sum, there is evidence that spatial selection is an important force in at least some domains of human cooperation. However, further work is needed to clarify precisely when and in which ways spatial selection promotes cooperation in human interactions.

Multi-level selection

In the laboratory, multi-level selection is typically implemented using interaction structures where groups compete over resources. For example, two groups play a PGG and compete over a monetary prize: the group with the larger total contribution amount wins, and each member of that group shares equally in the prize. Thus the incentive to defect in the baseline PGG is reduced by the potential gain from winning the group competition, although defection is typically still the payoff-maximizing choice. Numerous such experiments have shown that competition between groups increases cooperation substantially (Bornstein et al. 1990; Erev et al. 1993; Gunnthorsdottir and Rapoport 2006; Puurtinen and Mappes 2009; Sääkusvuori et al. 2011; Tan and Bolle 2007). Furthermore, just phrasing the interaction as a competition between groups, without any monetary prize for winning, also increases cooperation (Böhm and Rockenbach 2013; Tan and Bolle 2007). Experience with real-world inter-group conflict also increases cooperation (Gneezy and Fessler 2012; Voors et al. 2012). In sum, there is ample evidence that inter-group competition can be a powerful force for promoting within-group cooperation.

Critics of multi-level selection argue that, empirically, the conditions necessary for substantial selection pressure at the level of group were not met over the course of human history (Williams 1966): concerns include low ratios of between-group versus within-group variation due to factors such as migration, mutation/experimentation, and infrequency of group extinction or lethal inter-group warfare. The laboratory experiments discussed above do not address these concerns: in these studies the interaction structure is explicitly constructed to generate group-level selection. Instead, anthropological and archaeological data have been used to explore when in human history the conditions necessary for multi-level selection have been satisfied, either at the genetic (Bowles 2009; Bowles and Gintis 2011) or cultural level (Bell et al. 2009).

Kin selection

Kin selection is the least studied mechanism when it comes to human cooperation. Research on humans largely focuses on cooperation between non-kin. In part this is because cooperation between related individuals is seen as expected and therefore uninteresting. Furthermore, humans cooperate with unrelated partners at a much higher rate than other species, and thus non-kin cooperation is an element of potential human uniqueness. There are also substantial practical hurdles to studying kin selection in humans. The effect of kinship is difficult to measure, as relatedness and reciprocity are inexorably intertwined:

we almost always have long-lasting reciprocal relationships with our close genetic relatives.

Nonetheless, understanding the role of kinship and kin selection in the context of human cooperation is important. It is essential to remember that parents helping children is *not* an example of kin selection, but rather straightforward selection maximizing direct fitness. Kin selection, however, may be at work in interactions between collateral kin (family members who are not direct descendants). In this context, some scholars have investigated the cues used for kin recognition. For example, in predicting self-reported altruistic behavior an interaction has been found between observing your mother caring for a sibling ('maternal perinatal association', MPA) and the amount of time spent living with a sibling (co-residence) (Lieberman et al. 2007): MPA is a strong signal of relatedness, and thus co-residence does not predict altruism in the presence of MPA. In the absence of MPA (for example, if you are a younger sibling that did not observe your older siblings being cared for), however, co-residence does predict altruism. This interaction suggests that co-residence is used as an indication of relatedness rather than as an indication of the probability of future interaction.

More studies on this topic are needed, in particular developing experiments that tease apart the roles of kinship and reciprocity. Progress in this area would be aided by theoretical developments combining evolutionary game theory and population genetics, thereby overcoming the limitations of inclusive fitness (Nowak et al. 2010b).

Cooperation in the absence of any mechanisms

How can we explain cooperation in one-shot anonymous interactions between strangers? Such cooperation is common (Bowles and Gintis 2011; Camerer 2003; Nowak and Highfield 2011; Rand and Nowak 2013; Tomasello 2009), yet it seems to contradict theoretical predictions because none of the five mechanisms appear to be in play: no repetition or reputation effects exist, interactions are not structured, groups are not competing, and subjects are not genetic relatives. Yet many subjects still cooperate. Why? Because the intuitions and norms that guide these decisions were shaped outside the laboratory, by mechanisms for the evolution of cooperation.

How exactly this happens is a topic of debate. There are two main dimensions along which scholars disagree: (1) whether cooperation in one-shot interactions was explicitly favored by evolution (through spatial or multi-level selection), or whether such altruistic cooperation is the result of overgeneralizing strategies from settings where cooperation is long-run self-interested (e.g. due to direct and indirect reciprocity); and (2) the relative importance of genetic evolution versus cultural evolution in shaping human cooperation.

On the first dimension, one perspective argues that multi-level selection and spatial structure specifically favored cooperation in one-shot anonymous settings (Bowles and Gintis 2011; Boyd et al. 2003; Choi and Bowles 2007). Thus, although laboratory experiments may not explicitly include these effects, they have left their mark on the psychology that subjects bring into the laboratory by giving rise to altruistic preferences. The alternative perspective argues that direct and indirect reciprocity were the dominant forces in human evolution. By this account, selection favors cooperative strategies because most interactions involve repetition or reputation. As cooperating is typically advantageous, we internalize cooperation as our default behavior. This cooperative predisposition is then sometimes overgeneralized, spilling over into the unusual situations where others are not watching (Delton et al. 2011; Haley and Fessler 2005). In this view, cooperation in anonymous one-shot settings is a side effect of selection for reciprocal cooperation rather than an active target of selection itself. Note that in both views evolution gives rise to people who are truly altruistic and who cooperate even when there are no future benefits from doing so: the disagreement is over whether or not one-shot cooperation was directly favored by selection or whether it is a byproduct of selection in non-anonymous interactions.

Turning to the second dimension, all of the mechanisms can function via either genetic evolution or cultural evolution. In the context of cultural evolution, traits spread through learning, often modeled as imitation of strategies which earn higher payoffs or are more common (Richerson and Boyd 2005). Multi-level selection has been argued by some to promote cooperation through genetic evolution (Sober and Wilson 1998), while others posit an important role of culture (Bowles and Gintis 2011; Bowles et al. 2003; Boyd and Richerson 1982; Chudek and Henrich 2011). The same is true of reciprocity: we might have genetic predispositions to cooperate because our ancestors lived in small groups with largely repeated interactions (Cosmides and Tooby 2005; Delton et al. 2011). Or we might have learned cooperation as a good rule of thumb for social interaction because most of our important relationships are repeated, and thus cooperation is typically advantageous – the 'Social Heuristics Hypothesis' (Peysakhovich and Rand in press; Rand et al. 2012; Rand et al. 2013a). Thus one's position in this second area of debate need not be tied to one's belief about the first.

Intuitive reciprocation

To help distinguish between these different possibilities, we examine the cognitive basis of cooperation. Experiments using economic games have shown that automatic, intuitive processes support cooperation in one-shot games, while reflection and deliberation lead to selfishness. Inducing an intuitive mindset through priming or time pressure can increase cooperation relative to a more reflective mindset (Rand and Kraft-Todd 2014; Rand et al. 2012; Rand et al. 2013b; Rand et al. 2014). Increasing the role of intuition through cognitive load augments generosity in a resource allocation game (Roch et al. 2000) and in a unilateral money division task (i.e. dictator game; Cornelissen et al. 2011; Schulz et al. 2014). Affective, emotional responses play an important role in prosocial decision making (Bartlett and DeSteno 2006; DeSteno 2009; DeSteno et al. 2010). These findings suggest that cooperation in one-shot anonymous interactions involves some overgeneralization: intuitive, emotional processes favor the *typically* advantageous behavior of cooperation, while reflection and reasoning adjust toward the behavior that is payoff maximizing in the *specific* context of one-shot games (i.e. selfishness). Direct evidence of such spillovers comes from a study in which subjects play a series of either long or short repeated PDs, and then a battery of one-shot anonymous games (Peysakhovich and Rand in press). Subjects randomized into the long PD condition are dramatically more pro-social in the subsequent one-shot games compared to subjects randomized into the short PD condition.

These experiments support the argument that cooperative strategies develop in the context of direct and indirect reciprocity, and are then misapplied to one-shot games. We now evaluate a further prediction of this line of reciprocity-based reasoning: cooperation should not *always* be intuitive. A key element of direct and indirect reciprocity is *conditional* cooperation. As exemplified by the strategy of tit for tat, reciprocal interactions should lead to intuitions that favor cooperation at the outset of a relationship, and cooperation in response to a cooperative partner. But in response to a selfish partner, the automatic response should reverse to selfishness. Put differently, reciprocity-based hypotheses for the evolution of human cooperation predict intuitive *reciprocation* rather than intuitive cooperation.

Support for this prediction comes from experiments using the Ultimatum Game (UG). In the UG, one player (the proposer) makes an offer of how to split a sum of money with a second player (the responder). If the responder rejects, neither receives anything. Both behavioral experiments and neuroimaging studies suggest that when responders are confronted with unfair offers, the intuitive decision is to reject, while reflection leads to increased acceptance (Gospic et al. 2011; Grimm and Mengel 2011; Sanfey et al. 2003; Sutter et al. 2003) (although evidence from transcranial magnetic stimulation experiments suggests that deliberative processes also play some role in rejections; Knoch et al. 2006; Wout et al. 2005). Thus intuition again favors reciprocation (in this case, paying a cost to retaliate against selfishness). As with cooperation in one-shot interactions, rejecting unfair offers in the UG is not payoff maximizing in the one-shot games studied in the lab, but is adaptive in the context of reciprocal interactions (Nowak et al. 2000).

This evidence of intuitive reciprocation supports the argument that strategies selected in the context of repeated games spill over into one-shot anonymous interactions. But are these intuitions the result of genetic hardcoding, or of learning and experience? Several additional results support the latter hypothesis. Some experiments find no effect of promoting intuition on cooperative behavior in one-shot games (Hauge et al. 2009; Rand et al. 2013b; Tinghög et al. 2013), suggesting that cooperative intuitions are not universal. Specific moderators of the intuitive cooperation effect have also been demonstrated. One-shot cooperation is only intuitive among people from communities where most others are trustworthy and cooperative themselves (Rand et al. 2012; Rand and Kraft-Todd 2014). If you grow up in a non-cooperative equilibrium, where cooperation is not payoff maximizing, you internalize defection as your default. Prior experience with behavioral experiments also moderates the role of intuition in cooperation. Individual-differences studies show that intuitive responses are more cooperative among naïve subjects, but that intuition does not promote cooperation among experienced subjects (Rand et al. 2012; Rand et al. 2014; Rand and Kraft-Todd 2014). At the study level, the effect of an increasingly experienced subject pool was explored by analyzing a series of experiments conducted over two years using the online labor market Amazon Mechanical Turk (Rand et al. 2014). During that period, behavioral experiments became dramatically more common on Mechanical Turk, resulting in a subject pool that is highly experienced with study participation. As predicted by the Social Heuristics Hypothesis, decisions made under time pressure became steadily less cooperative (as intuitions were eroded), while reflective responses remained constant. These findings suggest that intuitions are malleable rather than hardcoded. Thus we find support for the Social Heuristics Hypothesis and for the importance of learning and culture in human cooperation.

Conclusion

Understanding the evolutionary dynamics of cooperation has important implications for our conceptualization of ourselves as human beings. Research in this field helps to explain the widespread cooperation that is a cornerstone of our existence as a supremely social species. It also provides concrete guidance for individuals, organizations, and policy makers seeking to promote cooperation in settings where it is currently lacking.

In this review we shed light on human cooperation by synthesizing theoretical research on evolutionary dynamics with experiments examining human behavior. We provide empirical evidence for five mechanisms for the evolution of human cooperation: direct reciprocity, indirect reciprocity, spatial selection, multi-level selection, and kin selection. We also highlight areas where theory and experiments diverge and where more empirical and theoretical work is needed.

We also consider cooperation in one-shot anonymous settings where no mechanisms are explicitly present. We provide evidence that cooperative strategies developed in the context of reciprocal interactions 'spill over' into one-shot games. We show that this inclination toward intuitive reciprocation is malleable. Together, these results highlight the importance of reciprocity for human cooperation, as well as the powerful role played by learning and culture. The evidence we present does not rule out the possibility that (1) some level of one-shot cooperation *was* specifically favored by selection, or that (2) genetic evolution played an important role in the evolution of human cooperation (in support of the latter point, for example, babies seem to have reciprocal preferences [Hamlin et al. 2007; Hamlin et al. 2011] and young children are often willing to help others [Warneken and Tonasello 2006, 2009; Warneken et al. 2007]). Conducting experiments to further distinguish between these hypotheses for the origins of human cooperation in one-shot interactions is a fundamental challenge for the field. Critically, all of the perspectives on the evolution of human cooperation outlined in this chapter share a central message: selective forces from outside the laboratory influence play inside, effecting behavior in one-shot anonymous games. This key insight is often overlooked, particularly in the economics literature. Behavior in the laboratory cannot be explained without considering the environment in which that behavior evolved.

Our conclusion regarding the important of reciprocity for human cooperation complements the recently proposed 'hexagon of cooperation' (Messner, Guarín, and Haun in this volume). Here we have discussed the five mechanisms for the evolution of cooperation, interaction structures that can allow selection to favor cooperation when added to the PD. Rather than examining mechanisms per se, the hexagon of cooperation explores factors that are important for the successful functioning of mechanisms involving reciprocity. Some of these factors may be particularly important for direct reciprocity, such as trust. Others may be particularly important for indirect reciprocity, such as communication. Thus the hexagon of cooperation can provide a useful set of guidelines for those trying to use reciprocity to promote human cooperation.

Finally, we consider the implications for each mechanism of the modern world's ever-increasing scale and complexity of interaction. Spatial selection and multilevel selection rely on segregation: clusters of cooperators supporting each other, or groups of cooperators outcompeting groups of defectors. The global interconnections and interdependencies of the 21st century are therefore challenging for these mechanisms, making it harder for them to promote cooperation. Yet the opposite is true of mechanisms based on reciprocity (and, in particular, indirect reciprocity). Greater interdependence increases the power of reciprocity, both by increasing information flow regarding others' past behavior and by increasing the value of maintaining good relationships in the future. Thus, consistent with the hexagon of cooperation (Messner et al. in this volume), we may see an ever greater emphasis on reciprocity as our world becomes increasingly complex and interdependent. Although many may believe that selfishness is the essence of the human condition, this is not so: in a world where we depend on each other ever more, cooperation is clearly the winning strategy.

Note

1 Funding from the John Templeton Foundation is gratefully acknowledged.

References

Abbot, P., et al. (2011). 'Inclusive Fitness Theory and Eusociality', *Nature*, 471 (7339): E1–E4.

Allen, B., et al. (2011). 'How Mutation Affects Evolutionary Games on Graphs', *Journal of Theoretical Biology*, 299: 97–105.

Anderson, J. R., et al. (2013). 'Third-Party Social Evaluation of Humans by Monkeys', *Nature Communications*, 4: 1561.

Antal, T., et al. (2009). 'Evolution of Cooperation by Phenotypic Similarity', *Proceedings of the National Academy of Sciences*, 106 (21): 8597–600.

Apicella, C. L., et al. (2012) 'Social Networks and Cooperation in Hunter-Gatherers', *Nature*, 481 (7382): 497–501.

Archetti, M. (2009). 'The Volunteer's Dilemma and the Optimal Size of a Social Group', *Journal of Theoretical Biology*, 261 (3): 475–80.

Ashraf, N., et al. (2012) 'No Margin, No Mission? A Field Experiment on Incentives for Pro-Social Tasks', *Harvard Business School Working Papers*, No. 12–008.

Axelrod, R. (1984). *The Evolution of Cooperation*, New York, NY: Basic Books.

Bartlett, M. Y. and DeSteno, D. (2006). 'Gratitude and Prosocial Behavior: Helping When It Costs You', *Psychological Science*, 17 (4): 319–25.

Bell, A. V., et al. (2009). 'Culture Rather than Genes Provides Greater Scope for the Evolution of Large-Scale Human Prosociality', *Proceedings of the National Academy of Sciences*, 106 (42): 17671–4.

Binmore, K. and Samuelson, L. (1992). 'Evolutionary Stability in Repeated Games Played by Finite Automata', *Journal of Economic Theory*, 57 (2): 278–305.

Böhm, R. and Rockenbach, B. (2013). 'The Inter-Group Comparison – Intra-Group Cooperation Hypothesis: Comparisons between Groups Increase Efficiency in Public Goods Provision', *PLoS ONE*, 8 (2): e56152.

Bolton, G. E., et al. (2005). 'Cooperation among Strangers with Limited Information about Reputation', *Journal of Public Economics*, 89 (8): 1457–68.

Bornstein, G., et al. (1990). 'Intergroup Competition as a Structural Solution to Social Dilemmas', *Social Behaviour*, 5 (4): 247–60.

Bowles, S. (2009). 'Did Warfare Among Ancestral Hunter-Gatherers Affect the Evolution of Human Social Behaviors?', *Science*, 324 (5932): 1293–8.

Bowles, S. and Gintis, H. (2011). *A Cooperative Species: Human Reciprocity and Its Evolution*. Princeton, NJ / Woodstock: Princeton University Press.

Bowles, S., et al. (2003). 'The Co-Evolution of Individual Behaviors and Social Institutions', *Journal of Theoretical Biology*, 223 (2): 135–47.

Boyd, R. and Richerson, P. J. (1982). 'Cultural Transmission and the Evolution of Cooperative Behavior', *Human Ecology*, 10 (3): 325–51.

Boyd, R. and Richerson, P. J. (1988). 'The Evolution of Reciprocity in Sizable Groups', *Journal of Theoretical Biology*, 132 (3): 337–56.

Boyd, R. and Richerson, P. (1990). 'Group Selection among Alternative Evolutionarily Stable Strategies', *Journal of Theoretical Biology*, 145 (3): 331–42.

Boyd, R., et al. (2003). 'The Evolution of Altruistic Punishment', *Proceedings of the National Academy of Science USA*, 100 (6): 3531–5.

Brandt, H. and Sigmund, K. (2006). 'The Good, the Bad and the Discriminator – Errors in Direct and Indirect Reciprocity', *Journal of Theoretical Biology*, 239 (2): 183–94.

Burnham, T. and Hare, B. (2007). 'Engineering Human Cooperation', *Human Nature*, 18 (2): 88–108.

Camerer, C. F. (2003). *Behavioral Game Theory: Experiments in Strategic Interaction*, Princeton, NJ / Woodstock: Princeton University Press.

Cavaliere, M., et al. (2012). 'Prosperity Is Associated with Instability in Dynamical Networks', *Journal of Theoretical Biology*, 299: 126–38.

Choi, J.-K. and Ahn, T. K. (2013). 'Strategic Reward and Altruistic Punishment Support Cooperation in a Public Goods Game Experiment', *Journal of Economic Psychology*, 35: 17–30.

Choi, J. K. and Bowles, S. (2007). 'The Coevolution of Parochial Altruism and War', *Science*, 318 (5850): 636–40.

Chudek, M. and Henrich, J. (2011). 'Culture Gene Coevolution, Norm-Psychology and the Emergence of Human Prosociality', *Trends in Cognitive Sciences*, 15 (5): 218–26.

Coffman, L. C. (2011). 'Intermediation Reduces Punishment (and Reward)', *American Economic Journal: Microeconomics*, 3 (4): 77–106.

Cornelissen, G., et al. (2011). 'Are Social Value Orientations Expressed Automatically? Decision Making in the Dictator Game', *Personality and Social Psychology Bulletin*, 37: 1080–90.

Cosmides, L. and Tooby, J. (2005). 'Neurocognitive Adaptations Designed for Social Exchange', in M. Buss (ed.) *The Handbook of Evolutionary Psychology*, Hoboken, NJ: John Wiley and Sons, 584–627.

Dal Bó, P. (2005). 'Cooperation under the Shadow of the Future: Experimental Evidence from Infinitely Repeated Games', *American Economic Review*, 95 (5): 1591–604.

Dal Bó, P. and Fréchette, G. R. (2011). 'The Evolution of Cooperation in Infinitely Repeated Games: Experimental Evidence', *American Economic Review*, 101 (1): 411–29.

Darwin, C. (1871). *The Descent of Man and Selection in Relation to Sex*, London: Murray.

Delton, A. W., et al. (2011). 'Evolution of Direct Reciprocity under Uncertainty Can Explain Human Generosity in One-Shot Encounters', *Proceedings of the National Academy of Sciences*, 108 (32): 13335–40.

DeSteno, D. (2009). 'Social Emotions and Intertemporal Choice "Hot" Mechanisms for Building Social and Economic Capital', *Current Directions in Psychological Science*, 18 (5): 280–4.

DeSteno, D., et al. (2010). 'Gratitude as Moral Sentiment: Emotion-Guided Cooperation in Economic Exchange', *Emotion*, 10 (2): 289.

Dreber, A., et al. (2008). 'Winners Don't Punish', *Nature*, 452 (7185): 348–51.

Dreber, A., et al. (2014) 'Who Cooperates in Repeated Games: The Role of Altruism, Inequity Aversion, and Demographics', *Journal of Economic Behavior & Organization*, 98: 41–55.

Duffy, J. and Ochs, J. (2009). 'Cooperative Behavior and the Frequency of Social Interaction', *Games and Economic Behavior*, 66 (2): 785–812.

Dunbar, R. I. M., et al. (1997). 'Human Conversational Behavior', *Human Nature*, 8 (3): 231–46.

Efferson, C., et al. (2008). 'The Coevolution of Cultural Groups and Ingroup Favoritism', *Science*, 321 (5897): 1844–9.

Ellingsen, T., et al. (2012). 'Civic Capital in Two Cultures: The Nature of Cooperation in Romania and USA', last accessed at *Social Science Research Network* August 12, 2015, at http://ssrn.com/abstract=2179575

Erev, I., et al. (1993). 'Constructive Intergroup Competition as a Solution to the Free Rider Problem: A Field Experiment', *Journal of Experimental Social Psychology*, 29 (6): 463–78.

Fehl, K., et al. (2011). 'Co-Evolution of Behaviour and Social Network Structure Promotes Human Cooperation', *Ecology Letters*, 14 (6): 546–51.

Fehr, E. and Gächter, S. (2000). 'Cooperation and Punishment in Public Goods Experiments', *American Economic Review*, 90 (4): 980–94.

Fehr, E. and Gächter, S. (2002). 'Altruistic Punishment in Humans', *Nature*, 415 (6868): 137–40.

Fowler, J. H., et al. (2011). 'Correlated Genotypes in Friendship Networks', *Proceedings of the National Academy of Sciences*, 108 (5): 1993–7.

Fu, F., et al. (2008). 'Reputation-Based Partner Choice Promotes Cooperation in Social Networks', *Physical Review E*, 78 (2): 026117.

Fu, F., et al. (2012). 'Evolution of In-Group Favoritism', *Scientific Reports*, 2: 460.

Fudenberg, D. and Maskin, E. S. (1986). 'The Folk Theorem in Repeated Games with Discounting or with Incomplete Information', *Econometrica*, 54 (3): 533–54.

Fudenberg, D. and Maskin, E.S. (1990). 'Evolution and Cooperation in Noisy Repeated Games', *American Economic Review*, 80 (2): 274–9.

Fudenberg, D., et al. (2012). 'Slow to Anger and Fast to Forgive: Cooperation in an Uncertain World', *American Economic Review*, 102: 720–49.

Gächter, S. and Herrmann, B. (2009). 'Reciprocity, Culture and Human Cooperation: Previous Insights and a New Cross-Cultural Experiment', *Philosophical Transactions of the Royal Society B: Biological Sciences*, 364 (1518): 791–806.

Gächter, S. and Herrmann, B. (2011). 'The Limits of Self-Governance when Cooperators get Punished: Experimental Evidence from Urban and Rural Russia', *European Economic Review*, 55 (2): 193–210.

García, J. and Traulsen, A. (2012). 'Leaving the Loners Alone: Evolution of Cooperation in the Presence of Antisocial Punishment', *Journal of Theoretical Biology*, 307: 168–73.

García, J. and van den Bergh, J.C.J.M. (2011). 'Evolution of Parochial Altruism by Multilevel Selection', *Evolution and Human Behavior*, 32 (4): 277–87.

Gneezy, A. and Fessler, D.M.T. (2012). 'Conflict, Sticks and Carrots: War Increases Prosocial Punishments and Rewards', *Proceedings of the Royal Society B: Biological Sciences*, 279 (1727): 219–23.

Gore, J., et al. (2009). 'Snowdrift Game Dynamics and Facultative Cheating in Yeast', *Nature*, 459 (7244): 253–6.

Gospic, K., et al. (2011). 'Limbic Justice – Amygdala Involvement in Immediate Rejection in the Ultimatum Game', *PLoS Biology*, 9: e1001054.

Gracia-Lázaro, C., et al. (2012). 'Heterogeneous Networks Do Not Promote Cooperation when Humans Play a Prisoner's Dilemma', *Proceedings of the National Academy of Sciences*, 109 (32): 12922–6.

Grimm, V. and Mengel, F. (2011). 'Let Me Sleep On It: Delay Reduces Rejection Rates in Ultimatum Games', *Economics Letters*, 111 (2): 113–5.

Grujić, J., et al. (2010). 'Social Experiments in the Mesoscale: Humans Playing a Spatial Prisoner's Dilemma', *PLoS ONE*, 5: e13749.

Grujić, J., et al. (2012). 'Consistent Strategy Updating in Spatial and Non-Spatial Behavioral Experiments Does Not Promote Cooperation in Social Networks', *PLoS ONE*, 7: e47718.

Gunnthorsdottir, A. and Rapoport, A. (2006). 'Embedding Social Dilemmas in Intergroup Competition Reduces Free-Riding', *Organizational Behavior and Human Decision Processes*, 101 (2): 184–99.

Haley, K.J. and Fessler, D.M.T. (2005) 'Nobody's Watching? Subtle Cues Affect Generosity in an Anonymous Economic Game', *Evolution and Human Behavior*, 26 (3): 245–56.

Hamilton, W.D. (1964). 'The Genetical Evolution of Social Behaviour. I.', *Journal of Theoretical Biology*, 7: 1–16.

Hamlin, J.K., et al. (2007). 'Social Evaluation by Preverbal Infants', *Nature*, 450 (7169): 557–9.

Hamlin, J.K., et al. (2011). 'How Infants and Toddlers React to Antisocial Others', *Proceedings of the National Academy of Sciences*, 108 (50): 19931–6.

Hammond, R.A. and Axelrod, R. (2006). 'The Evolution of Ethnocentrism', *The Journal of Conflict Resolution*, 50 (6): 926–36.

Hardin, G. (1968). 'The Tragedy of the Commons', *Science*, 162 (3859): 1243–8.

Hauert, C. and Doebeli, M. (2004). 'Spatial Structure Often Inhibits the Evolution of Cooperation in the Snowdrift Game', *Nature*, 428 (6983): 643–6.

Hauert, C. and Imhof, L.A. (2012). 'Evolutionary Games in Deme Structured, Finite Populations', *Journal of Theoretical Biology*, 299: 106–12.

Hauert, C., et al. (2006). 'Synergy and Discounting of Cooperation in Social Dilemmas', *Journal of Theoretical Biology*, 239 (2): 195–202.

Hauge, K. E., et al. (2009). 'Are Social Preferences Skin Deep? Dictators under Cognitive Load', *University of Gothenburg Working Papers in Economics*, No. 371.

Herrmann, B., et al. (2008). 'Antisocial Punishment Across Societies', *Science*, 319 (5868): 1362–7.

Hoffman, E., et al. (1996). 'Social Distance and Other-Regarding Behavior in Dictator Games', *The American Economic Review*, 86 (3): 653–60.

Jacquet, J., et al. (2011). 'Shame and Honour Drive Cooperation', *Biology Letters*, 7: 899–901.

Jordan, J. J., et al. (2013). 'Contagion of Cooperation in Static and Fluid Social Networks', *PLoS ONE*, 8 (6): e66199.

Karlan, D. and McConnell, M. A. (2012): 'Hey Look at Me: The Effect of Giving Circles on Giving', *National Bureau of Economic Research Working Paper*, No. 17737.

Knoch, D., et al. (2006). 'Diminishing Reciprocal Fairness by Disrupting the Right Prefrontal Cortex', *Science*, 314 (5800): 829–32.

Lacetera, N. and Macis, M. (2010). 'Social Image Concerns and Prosocial Behavior: Field Evidence from a Nonlinear Incentive Scheme', *Journal of Economic Behavior & Organization*, 76 (2): 225–37.

Levin, S. A. (2000). *Fragile Dominion: Complexity and the Commons*, New York, NY: Basic Books.

Lieberman, D., et al. (2007). 'The Architecture of Human Kin Detection', *Nature*, 445 (7129): 727–31.

Lieberman, E., et al. (2005). 'Evolutionary Dynamics on Graphs', *Nature*, 433 (7023): 312–6.

Luca, M. (2011). 'Reviews, Reputation, and Revenue: The Case of Yelp. com', *Harvard Business School NOM Unit Working Paper*, No. 12-016.

Manapat, M. L., et al. (2012a). 'Information, Irrationality and the Evolution of Trust', *Journal of Economic Behavior and Organization*, 90: S57–S75.

Manapat, M. L., et al. (2012b). 'Stochastic Evolutionary Dynamics Resolve the Traveler's Dilemma', *Journal of Theoretical Biology*, 303: 119–27.

Marlowe, F. W. (2005). 'Hunter-Gatherers and Human Evolution', *Evolutionary Anthropology*, 14 (2): 54–67.

Masuda, N. (2012). 'Ingroup Favoritism and Intergroup Cooperation under Indirect Reciprocity Based on Group Reputation', *Journal of Theoretical Biology*, 311: 8–18.

Milinski, M. and Rockenbach, B. (2007). 'Spying on Others Evolves', *Science*, 317 (5837): 464–5.

Milinski, M., et al. (2002). 'Reputation Helps Solve the "Tragedy of the Commons"', *Nature*, 415 (6870): 424–6.

Murnighan, J. K. and Roth, A. E. (1983). 'Expecting Continued Play in Prisoner's Dilemma Games A Test of Several Models', *Journal of Conflict Resolution*, 27 (2): 279–300.

Nakamaru, M. and Iwasa, Y. (2005): 'The Evolution of Altruism by Costly Punishment in Lattice-Structured Populations: Score-Dependent Viability versus Score-Dependent Fertility', *Evolutionary Ecology Research*, 7 (6): 853–70.

Nikiforakis, N. (2008). 'Punishment and Counter-Punishment in Public Goods Games: Can We Still Govern Ourselves?', *Journal of Public Economics*, 92 (1): 91–112.

Nowak, M. A. (2006). 'Five Rules for the Evolution of Cooperation', *Science*, 314 (5805): 1560–3.

Nowak, M. A. (2012). 'Evolving Cooperation', *Journal of Theoretical Biology*, 299: 1–8.

Nowak, M. A. and Highfield, R. (2011). *SuperCooperators: Altruism, Evolution, and Why We Need Each Other to Succeed*, New York, NY: Free Press.

Nowak, M. A. and May, R. M. (1992). 'Evolutionary Games and Spatial Chaos', *Nature*, 359 (6398): 826–9.

Nowak, M. A. and Roch, S. (2007). 'Upstream Reciprocity and the Evolution of Gratitude', *Proceedings of the Royal Society B: Biological Sciences*, 274 (1610): 605–10.

Nowak, M. A. and Sigmund, K. (1992). 'Tit for Tat in Heterogeneous Populations', *Nature*, 355 (6357): 250–3.

Nowak, M. A. and Sigmund, K. (1993). 'A Strategy of Win-Stay, Lose-Shift that Outperforms Tit-For-Tat in the Prisoner's Dilemma Game', *Nature*, 364 (6432): 56–8.

Nowak, M. A. and Sigmund, K. (1994). 'The Alternating Prisoner's Dilemma', *Journal of Theoretical Biology*, 168 (2): 219–26.

Nowak, M. A. and Sigmund, K. (1998). 'Evolution of Indirect Reciprocity by Image Scoring', *Nature*, 393 (6685): 573–7.

Nowak, M. A. and Sigmund, K. (2005). 'Evolution of Indirect Reciprocity', *Nature*, 437 (7063): 1291–8.

Nowak, M. A., et al. (2000). 'Fairness Versus Reason in the Ultimatum Game', *Science*, 289 (5485): 1773–5.

Nowak, M. A., et al. (2004). 'Emergence of Cooperation and Evolutionary Stability in Finite Populations', *Nature*, 428 (6983): 646–50.

Nowak, M. A., et al. (2010a). 'Evolutionary Dynamics in Structured Populations', *Philosophical Transactions of the Royal Society B: Biological Sciences*, 365 (1537): 19–30.

Nowak, M. A., et al. (2010b). 'The Evolution of Eusociality', *Nature*, 466 (7310): 1057–62.

Nowak, M. A., et al. (2011). 'Nowak et al. Reply', *Nature*, 471 (7339): E9–E10.

Ohtsuki, H. and Iwasa, Y. (2006). 'The Leading Eight: Social Norms that Can Maintain Cooperation by Indirect Reciprocity', *Journal of Theoretical Biology*, 239 (4): 435–44.

Ohtsuki, H., et al. (2006). 'A Simple Rule for the Evolution of Cooperation on Graphs and Social Networks', *Nature*, 441 (7092), 502–5.

Ohtsuki, H., et al. (2009). 'Indirect Reciprocity Provides Only a Narrow Margin of Efficiency for Costly Punishment', *Nature*, 457 (7225): 79–82.

O'Malley, A. J., et al. (2012). 'Egocentric Social Network Structure, Health, and Pro-Social Behaviors in a National Panel Study of Americans', *PLoS ONE*, 7 (5): e36250.

Ostrom, E., et al. (1992). 'Covenants with and without a Sword: Selfgovernance Is Possible', *The American Political Science Review*, 86 (2): 404–17.

Paharia, N., et al. (2009). 'Dirty Work, Clean Hands: The Moral Psychology of Indirect Agency', *Organizational Behavior and Human Decision Processes*, 109 (2): 134–41.

Panchanathan, K. and Boyd, R. (2004). 'Indirect Reciprocity Can Stabilize Cooperation without the Second-Order Free Rider Problem', *Nature*, 432 (7016): 499–502.

Perc, M. and Szolnoki, A. (2010). 'Coevolutionary Games – A Mini Review', *Biosystems*, 99 (2): 109–25.

Peysakhovich, A. and Rand, D. G. (in press). 'Habits of Virtue: Creating Norms of Cooperation and Defection in the Laboratory', *Management Science*.

Pfeiffer, T., et al. (2012). 'The Value of Reputation', *Journal of the Royal Society Interface*, 9 (76): 2791–7. doi: 10.1098/rsif.2012.0332.

Powers, S. T., et al. (2012). 'Punishment Can Promote Defection in Group-Structured Populations', *Journal of Theoretical Biology*, 311: 107–16.

Puurtinen, M. and Mappes, T. (2009). 'Between-Group Competition and Human Cooperation', *Proceedings of the Royal Society B: Biological Sciences*, 276 (1655): 355–60.

Rand, D.G. (2012). 'The Promise of Mechanical Turk: How Online Labor Markets Can Help Theorists Run Behavioral Experiments', *Journal of Theoretical Biology*, 299: 172–9.

Rand, D. G. and Kraft-Todd, G. T. (2014). 'Reflection Does Not Undermine Self-Interested Prosociality', *Frontiers in Behavioral Neuroscience*, 8 (300): 1–8.

Rand, D.G. and Nowak, M.A. (2011). 'The Evolution of Antisocial Punishment in Optional Public Goods Games', *Nature Communications*, 2: 434.

Rand, D.G. and Nowak, M.A. (2012). 'Evolutionary Dynamics in Finite Populations Can Explain the Full Range of Cooperative Behaviors Observed in the Centipede Game', *Journal of Theoretical Biology*, 300: 212–21.

Rand, D.G. and Nowak, M.A. (2013). 'Human Cooperation', *Trends in Cognitive Sciences*, 17 (8): 413–25.

Rand, D.G., et al. (2009a). 'Direct Reciprocity with Costly Punishment: Generous Tit-for-Tat Prevails', *Journal of Theoretical Biology*, 256: 45–57.

Rand, D.G., et al. (2009b). 'Dynamic Remodeling of In-Group Bias during the 2008 Presidential Election', *Proceedings of the National Academy of Sciences USA*, 106 (15): 6187–91.

Rand, D.G., et al. (2009c). 'Positive Interactions Promote Public Cooperation', *Science*, 325 (5945): 1272–5.

Rand, D.G., et al. (2010). 'Anti-Social Punishment Can Prevent the Co-Evolution of Punishment and Cooperation', *Journal of Theoretical Biology*, 265 (4): 624–32.

Rand, D.G., et al. (2011). 'Dynamic Social Networks Promote Cooperation in Experiments with Humans', *Proceedings of the National Academy of Sciences*, 108 (48): 19193–8.

Rand, D.G., et al. (2012). 'Spontaneous Giving and Calculated Greed', *Nature*, 489 (7416): 427–30.

Rand, D.G., et al. (2013a). 'Evolution of Fairness in the One-Shot Anonymous Ultimatum Game', *Proceedings of the National Academy of Sciences*, 110 (7): 2581–6.

Rand, D.G., et al. (2013b). 'Rand et. al. Reply', *Nature*, 497 (7452): E2–E3.

Rand, D. G., et al. (2014). 'Social Heuristics Shape Intuitive Cooperation', *Nature Communications*, 5 (3677): 1–12.

Rankin, D.J. and Taborsky, M. (2009). 'Assortment and the Evolution of Generalized Reciprocity', *Evolution*, 63 (7): 1913–22.

Rapoport, A. and Chammah, A.M. (1965). *Prisioner's Dilema: A Study in Conflict and Cooperation*, Ann Arbor, MI: University of Michigan Press.

Resnick, P., et al. (2006). 'The Value of Reputation on eBay: A Controlled Experiment', *Experimental Economics*, 9 (2): 79–101.

Richerson, P.J. and Boyd, R. (2005). *Not by Genes Alone: How Culture Transformed Human Evolution*, Chicago, IL / London: University of Chicago Press.

Riolo, R.L., et al. (2001). 'Evolution of Cooperation without Reciprocity', *Nature*, 414 (6862): 441–3.

Roch, S.G., et al. (2000). 'Cognitive Load and the Equality Heuristic: A Two-Stage Model of Resource Overconsumption in Small Groups', *Organizational Behavior and Human Decision Processes*, 83 (2): 185–212.

Rockenbach, B. and Milinski, M. (2006). 'The Efficient Interaction of Indirect Reciprocity and Costly Punishment', *Nature*, 444 (7120): 718–23.

Roth, A.E. and Murnighan, J.K. (1978). 'Equilibrium Behavior and Repeated Play of the Prisoner's Dilemma', *Journal of Mathematical Psychology*, 17 (2): 189–98.

Sääksvuori, L., et al. (2011). 'Costly Punishment Prevails in Intergroup Conflict', *Proceedings of the Royal Society B: Biological Sciences*, 278 (1732): 3428–36. doi: 10.1098/rspb.2011.0252.

Sanfey, A. G., et al. (2003). 'The Neural Basis of Economic Decision-Making in the Ultimatum Game', *Science*, 300 (5626): 1755–8.

Santos, F. C., et al. (2006). 'Cooperation Prevails when Individuals Adjust Their Social Ties', *PLoS Computational Biology*, 2 (10): e140.

Schulz, J. F., et al. (2014). 'Affect and Fairness: Dictator Games Under Cognitive Load', *Journal of Economic Psychology*, 41: 77–87.

Sefton, M., et al. (2007). 'The Effect of Rewards and Sanctions in Provision of Public Goods', *Economic Inquiry*, 45 (4): 671–90.

Seinen, I. and Schram, A. (2006). 'Social Status and Group Norms: Indirect Reciprocity in a Repeated Helping Experiment', *European Economic Review*, 50 (3): 581–602.

Semmann, D. (2012). 'Conditional Cooperation Can Hinder Network Reciprocity', *Proceedings of the National Academy of Sciences*, 109 (32): 12846–7.

Semmann, D., et al. (2005). 'Reputation is Valuable Within and Outside One's Own Social Group', *Behavioral Ecology and Sociobiology*, 57 (6): 611–6.

Sherif, M., et al. (1961). *Intergroup Conflict and Cooperation: The Robbers Cave Experiment*, Norman, OK: Institute of Group Relations, University of Oklahoma.

Sigmund, K. (2010). *The Calculus of Selfishness*, Princeton, NJ / Woodstock: Princeton University Press.

Skyrms, B. and Pemantle, R. (2000). 'A Dynamic Model of Social Network Formation', *Proceedings of the National Academy of Sciences*, 97 (16): 9340–6.

Sober, E. and Wilson, D. S. (1998). *Unto Others: The Evolution and Psychology of Unselfish Behavior*, Cambridge, MA / London: Harvard University Press.

Sommerfeld, R. D., et al. (2007). 'Gossip as an Alternative for Direct Observation in Games of Indirect Reciprocity', *Proceedings of the National Academy of Sciences*, 104 (44): 17435–40.

Suri, S. and Watts, D. J. (2011). 'Cooperation and Contagion in Web-Based, Networked Public Goods Experiments', *PLoS ONE*, 6 (3): e16836.

Sutter, M., et al. (2003). 'Bargaining under Time Pressure in an Experimental Ultimatum Game', *Economics Letters*, 81 (3): 341–7.

Sutter, M., et al. (2010). 'Choosing the Stick or the Carrot? Endogenous Institutional Choice in Social Dilemma Situations', *Review of Economic Studies*, 77 (4): 1540–66.

Suzuki, S. and Kimura, H. (2013). 'Indirect Reciprocity is Sensitive to Costs of Information Transfer', *Scientific Reports*, 3: 1435.

Szabo, G. and Fath, G. (2007). 'Evolutionary Games on Graphs', *Physics Reports*, 446 (4): 97–216.

Tajfel, H., et al. (1971). 'Social Categorization and Intergroup Behavior', *European Journal of Social Psychology*, 1 (2): 149–78.

Tan, J. H. W. and Bolle, F. (2007). 'Team Competition and the Public Goods Game', *Economics Letters*, 96 (1): 133–9.

Tarnita, C. E., et al. (2009a). 'Evolutionary Dynamics in Set Structured Populations', *Proceedings of the National Academy of Sciences*, 106 (21): 8601–4.

Tarnita, C. E., et al. (2009b). 'Strategy Selection in Structured Populations', *Journal of Theoretical Biology*, 259 (3): 570.

Tarnita, C. E., et al. (2011). 'Multiple Strategies in Structured Populations', *Proceedings of the National Academy of Sciences USA*, 108 (6): 2334–7.

Tinghög, G., et al. (2013). 'Intuition and Cooperation Reconsidered', *Nature*, 497 (7452): E1–E2.

Tomasello, M. (2009). *Why We Cooperate*, Cambridge, MA : MIT press.

Traulsen, A. and Nowak, M. A. (2006). 'Evolution of Cooperation by Multilevel Selection', *Proceedings of the National Academy of Sciences USA*, 103 (29): 10952–5.

Traulsen, A. and Schuster, H. G. (2003). 'Minimal Model for Tag-Based Cooperation', *Physical Review E*, 68 (4): 046129.

Traulsen, A., et al. (2010). 'Human Strategy Updating in Evolutionary Games', *Proceedings of the National Academy of Sciences*, 107 (7): 2962–6.

Trivers, R. (1971). 'The Evolution of Reciprocal Altruism', *Quarterly Review of Biology*, 46 (1): 35–57.

Ule, A., et al. (2009). 'Indirect Punishment and Generosity Toward Strangers', *Science*, 326 (5960): 1701–4.

van Veelen, M., et al. (2012). 'Direct Reciprocity in Structured Populations', *Proceedings of the National Academy of Sciences*, 109 (25): 9929–34.

Voors, M. J., et al. (2012). 'Violent Conflict and Behavior: A Field Experiment in Burundi', *American Economic Review*, 102 (2): 941–64.

Wang, J., et al. (2012). 'Cooperation and Assortativity with Dynamic Partner Updating', *Proceedings of the National Academy of Sciences USA*, 109 (36): 14363–8.

Warneken, F. and Tomaselo, M. (2006). 'Altruistic Helping in Human Infants and Young Chimpanzees', *Science*, 311 (5765): 1301–3.

Warneken, F. and Tomasello, M. (2009). 'Varieties of Altruism in Children and Chimpanzees', *Trends in Cognitive Sciences*, 13 (9): 397–402.

Warneken, F., et al. (2007). 'Spontaneous Altruism by Chimpanzees and Young Children', *PLoS Biology*, 5 (7): e184.

Wedekind, C. and Milinski, M. (2000). 'Cooperation Through Image Scoring in Humans', *Science*, 288 (5467): 850–2.

Williams, G. C. (1966). *Adaptation and Natural Selection: A Critique of Some Current Evolutionary Thought*, Princeton, NJ / Chichester: Princeton University Press.

Wilson, D. S. (1975). 'A Theory of Group Selection', *Proceedings of the National Academy of Sciences USA*, 72 (1): 143–6.

Wout, M. V. T., et al. (2005). 'Repetitive Transcranial Magnetic Stimulation Over the Right Dorsolateral Prefrontal Cortex Affects Strategic Decision-Making', *Neuroreport*, 16 (16): 1849–52.

Yoeli, E., et al. (2013). 'Powering Up with Indirect Reciprocity in A Large-Scale Field Experiment', *Proceedings of the National Academy of Sciences USA*, 110 (S 2): 10424–9.

6 Can we think of the future?

Cognitive barriers to future-oriented decision making

Elke U. Weber and Eric J. Johnson

Introduction

Planning for the future is an ever more necessary requirement for the continued survival and long-term well-being of the human species, as is local and global cooperation to implement such plans. Yet resource depletion, species depletion in both flora and fauna, threats of catastrophic climate change, and extreme weather – to name only a few ways in which we are inflicting potentially irreversible damage on crucial ecosystems – indicate that the human ability to plan and coordinate for tomorrow may be severely limited and may indeed become outpaced by the speed of technological innovation and globalization of production and commerce. Whereas previous chapters in this book have described the evolutionary pressures for cooperation and the many forces that contribute to its emergence and success, this chapter will provide a counterweight to that position and argue that there are also many obstacles to cooperation.

A 'glass-half-full' perspective suggests that human evolution towards our current ability to cooperate is remarkable, as indeed it is. The 'glass-half-empty' perspective of this chapter suggests that our ability to cooperate may be adequate to solve the types of problems typical of the time and environment under which this ability evolved, but that the complexity and timescale of current individual as well as societal challenges severely challenge the human ability for cooperative and proactive problem solving. The names of common economic games that exemplify cooperation tasks (e.g. 'battle of the sexes', 'stag hunt') describe stylized settings for cooperation or competition that involve a small number of players and well-specified, riskless outcomes that become available to the contestants immediately. The proverbial 'real world' of course rarely comes in such simplicity.

Games like the 'Prisoner's Dilemma' have been devised with nation states as actors in mind, for example to model the Cold War of the 1950s. However, instances in which rational selection of the individually and socially worst option are the only Nash equilibrium, the *tragedy* of the commons (Hardin 1968) can be turned into a mere *drama* of the commons, where cooperation may be difficult but often prevails (Ostrom et al. 2002) and tends to be found primarily in smaller contexts, where individual actors or small collectives know each other and have repeated interactions. It is in precisely such settings that the factors of the

DOI: 10.4324/9781315691657-8

cooperation hexagon (e.g. we-identity, trust, communication, reputation; Messner, Guarín, and Haun in this volume) allow for cooperation can emerge.

We first review insights from psychology and behavioral economics on the way people actually make decisions (as opposed to the rational-economic view of how such decisions ought to be made and thus are assumed to be made), and describe the cognitive and motivational processes and constraints that prevent us from keeping the future on our processing horizon in the way rational models suggest. We then apply these insights more specifically to strategic decisions and describe obstacles that limit our ability to arrive at cooperative plans to ensure our future well-being. We conclude with a discussion on how to translate the actual decision processes of *homo sapiens* from liabilities into opportunities with the design of decision environments ('choice architecture') that increase the chances for cooperative decisions.

Insights from psychology and behavioral economics

Bounded rationality

Homo economicus – the rational decision maker who maximizes expected utility by evaluating all available choice options for all present and future consequences, appropriately discounted to present value with perfect information and infinite processing capacity – is at best a convenient fiction or aspiration (Weber 2013). *Homo sapiens* has the ability (i.e. the 'hardware') for rational deliberation and choice and rational updating of beliefs based on new information, but such processes need to be taught explicitly (i.e. the 'software' needs to be programmed). Even when such processes are in play, they are frequently overridden by automatic and faster processes that use shortcuts based on associations, emotions, and rules to arrive at judgments and decisions (Kahneman 2011; Marx et al. 2007; Weber and Lindemann 2007). The need for such cognitive shortcuts originates in people's attention and information processing limitations, often referred to as bounded rationality (Simon 1982).

Behavioral decision research shows that humans often construct their preferences while making their decisions, using processes that are typically different from the as-if calculations implicitly assumed by rational-economic models of choice (Lichtenstein and Slovic 2006), as described in the next section. As already discussed, choices are not purely deliberative but also involve automatic inference and decision processes of which people are unaware. These processes are elicited by features and conditions in the external environment that interact with internal states such as prior experience, expectations, and goals (Engel and Weber 2007; Weber and Johnson 2012).

In addition, choices do not follow purely from the valuation of choice options (i.e. choosing the one with the highest subjective value), but also involve temptation from prepotent response options, i.e. options, like immediate rewards, that are hardwired to be favored (ceteris paribus) and that require willpower and self-control to be overridden (Figner et al. 2010).

Preferences are constructed

Contrary to the assumptions of rational-economic models of choice, preferences are typically not preexisting and constant across contexts, but instead are constructed in real time at the time of decision, making them responsive to the choice context (Weber and Johnson 2009). This can be seen either as a liability (e.g. leading to inconsistency and preference reversals; Grether and Plott 1979) or as an asset (e.g. allowing preferences to be shaped and influenced; Thaler and Sunstein 2008).

Cognitive myopia

Given that attention and processing capacity are scarce, they need to be allocated wisely and strategically. With immediate survival being a necessary condition for achieving more distant and abstract goals (Maslow 1943), goals and constraints that are immediate in both time (now vs. later) and social distance (me vs. close others vs. distant others) tend to take precedence over more distant ones. The reinforcement of attention to immediate goals and constraints at the individual and cultural level sets up mechanisms that result in prepotent responses, i.e. responses that are being favored, all other things being equal, by attention or processing capacity being disproportionally allocated to them. The result is a type of cognitive myopia or shortsightedness that has been used to explain many real-world phenomena, including the equity premium puzzle in finance, i.e. the puzzling fact that investors hold bonds to the degree that they do given that the returns on stocks are significantly larger, albeit risky. The behavior, which is inconsistent with reasonable assumptions about risk aversion, can be explained by the assumption that investors do not apply sufficiently long-time horizons to their investment decisions, but instead compare and contrast the outcomes of risk-free and risky investment opportunities on a quarterly basis and get disproportionately agitated by losses (Benartzi and Thaler 1995).

Cognitive myopia prevents people from accurately perceiving the future benefits of a wide range of other actions that have immediate costs or reduce immediate benefits. Thus people fail to buy more energy-efficient appliances or a host of other energy-efficiency investments whose greater upfront purchase costs are more than compensated by future energy savings (Gillingham, Newell, and Palmer 2009). In negotiation settings, people favor immediate gains at great costs to their reputations (Malhotra and Bazerman 2007).

Status quo bias

Cognitive myopia also focuses attention on actions or regimes that are in place, at the cost of considering available alternatives that may increase individual or public welfare (Weber and Johnson 2009). This gives rise to a widely observed status quo bias (Samuelson and Zeckhauser 1988) that has been shown to influence consequential financial (Johnson et al. 1993; Kempf and Ruenzi 2006) and social decisions like organ donation (Johnson and Goldstein

2003). Public policy interventions and their implementation can be seen as the process of shifting an established status quo towards a legislated or incentivized new state perceived as preferable by domain experts using analytic assessment tools not subject to status quo bias (Weber 2015). We will revisit how judicious choice architecture can help overcome status quo bias at the end of the chapter.

Large and inconsistent time discounting

Future costs and benefits ought to be discounted in value (e.g. by the current rate of interest offered by banks), ideally at a constant rate per period of time delay, described by an exponential discount function. Empirical research shows, however, that people apply sharp discounts to costs or benefits that will occur at some point in the future relative to obtaining them immediately (e.g. a year into the future vs. now), but discount much less when both time points are in the future, with one occurring later than the other (e.g. two vs. only one year into the future) (Loewenstein and Elster 1992). Such behavior has been described by a hyperbolic discount function, which shows its steepest decrement in value as we defer immediate consumption (Ainslie 1975).

The discount rates implicit in both financially incentivized lab studies (Weber et al. 2007) and real-world decisions (Meier and Sprenger 2010) are often far larger than current interest rates, a result that is consistent with the existence of societal problems like the current obesity epidemic in the US and other countries, the popularity of balloon mortgages during the recent US subprime mortgage crisis, insufficient pension savings in countries that do not mandate such savings, and a general unwillingness by individuals, organizations, and governments to engage in environmental preservation and damage prevention. Actions to mitigate negative environmental consequences are unattractive because they require immediate sacrifices in consumption that are compensated only by heavily discounted and highly uncertain benefits at a much later point in time.

Cognitive myopia and excessive discounting are arguably the biggest hurdles to rational choice in individual, organizational, or societal decisions that involve long-term planning and consequences that occur over extended periods of time. Contrary to economic discounting of future and distant costs and benefits (e.g. by the rate of interest offered by financial institutions) as a function of the time delay, people are inconsistent in their discounting. They show a strong present bias (i.e. strongly preferring immediate benefits), as described earlier. They also apply different discount rates to outcomes in different domains (e.g. financial, health, or environmental outcomes; Hardisty and Weber 2009), and discount future benefits far more than future costs (Gong, Krantz, and Weber 2014; Hardisty, Appelt, and Weber 2013).

Egocentric biases

Shortsightedness is not restricted to time, but extends to other dimensions. It explains a variety of egocentric biases (Plous 1993a), where people use their own perceptions and reactions as a starting point when trying to predict the behavior of others, and where myopia prevents them from adjusting sufficiently for differences between themselves and others. Such egocentric biases become relevant in strategic situations, described further in the following section, where they result in an incomplete search of the decision space.

Query theory

Query theory (Johnson, Häubl, and Keinan 2007; Weber et al. 2007) is a framework that incorporates attentional limitations and a role for past experience into preference construction. Query theory conceives of preference construction and choice as an automatic and unconscious process of arguing with oneself (Weber and Johnson 2011), where people sequentially generate arguments for selecting each of the different choice options and where the first option considered has a large advantage, all other things being equal. In the context of an intertemporal choice, where the decision maker must select between an immediate benefit or a larger benefit at a future point in time, query theory assumes that people first assess the evidence arguing for immediate consumption and only then assess evidence that argues for delaying consumption. Query theory postulates that in order to help people reach a decision, evidence generated for an initially favored action (e.g. immediate consumption) tends to inhibit or reduce the subsequent generation of evidence arguing against that action and for other actions. Weber et al. (2007) provided empirical support for both conjectures. While it is true that in unaided decisions of this sort decision makers will initially search for reasons for the prepotent immediate choice option, the decision can be reframed in ways that direct initial attention to the delayed outcome choice option, e.g. by making the 'larger later' option the explicit default, i.e. the option that will be obtained if no active decision is made to switch away from it. Weber et al. (2007) show that this framing of the two choice options succeeds in drastically reducing decision makers' impatience, i.e. the discount rate applied to the later outcome implicit in their choices, and that this increase in patience and future orientation is mediated by the fact that they first generate evidence in favor of deferring consumption. Weber et al. (2007) succeeded in drastically reducing people's discounting of future rewards by prompting them to first generate arguments for deferring consumption, followed by a prompt to generate arguments for immediate consumption. Specifying a default option (i.e. an option that will be implemented unless a different option is actively selected) directs decision makers' attention to that option, getting them to consider arguments for this option first.

Other interventions that direct attention more equally to both the future and the present and that remind decision makers of the implicit tradeoff between time and money also succeed in reducing the discounting of future outcomes (Radu et al. 2011). One such intervention is the explicit (vs. hidden) zero framing of intertemporal choice options, which spells out that receipt of an immediate reward means that no future reward will be forthcoming (Magen, Dweck, and Gross 2008). Another intervention modifies the response methodology, asking respondents to distribute 100 tokens between the two intertemporal choice options, which will pay off at different rates and time points (rather than asking for one choice or the other), thus also directing attention more evenly to both choice options and making choices less impulsive and more dynamically consistent (Andreoni and Sprenger 2012).

Social norms and/or positive or negative affective reactions to a choice option also determine which option is considered first, especially in those situations where no default action exists (Johnson et al. 2007; Weber et al. 2007). Thus Hardisty, Johnson, and Weber (2010) found that 65 per cent of Republicans were willing to pay a CO_2 emission reduction fee on such purchases as airline tickets when the fee was labeled as a carbon offset (and first generated arguments for purchasing it), but that this percentage dropped to 27 per cent when the fee was labeled as a carbon tax, a label that generated negative visceral reactions in this group and led them to first generate arguments for purchasing a ticket without any carbon fee.

Lessons for strategic decisions

In this section we will examine the implications that insights from behavioral decision research on riskless and risky decisions have for strategic decisions, which are the focus of this book. Most behavioral decision research has focused on non-strategic decisions that involve only the evaluation of decision makers' own preferences for different choice options, with their risky or riskless resolutions. In contrast strategic choice is significantly more complex, as the outcomes of each decision maker's action depend also on the actions of his or her strategic opponent(s) or counterpart(s). This adds an important and difficult task, namely the prediction of the other side's preferences, which are in turn dependent on the opponents' evaluations of the first decision maker's preferences and choice.

Theories like prospect theory (Tversky and Kahneman 1992) provide behavioral 'band-aids' to the normative model for risky choice, namely expected utility theory (von Neumann and Morgenstern 1944), modifying it in parts to improve its fit to observed choice behavior. In this same way, behavioral game theory (Camerer 2003) generalizes and updates traditional game theory with more realistic assumptions about how strategic decision makers evaluate choice options and in the process anticipate the preferences and responses of their strategic opponent(s). There are three major assumptions of traditional non-cooperative game theory, namely about (1) the sole importance of the personal utility of the outcomes of joint actions and absence of other-regarding preferences, either positive or negative; (2) the absence of trust; and (3) the futility of communication, with any kind of verbal agreement or promise being described as unenforceable and hence untrustworthy 'cheap talk'. If these assumptions made by the normative model were behaviorally correct, this would knock most if not all of the components of the cooperation hexagon (Messner et al. in this volume) out of court, making them completely irrelevant to strategic decisions. Cooperation in strategic games only arises when groups of players may enforce cooperative behavior, and hence the game is a competition between coalitions of players rather than between individual players, thus building on the only component of the cooperation hexagon tenable within this normative game theory framework, namely 'enforcement'.

The balance of this book fortunately suggests, however, that these assumptions of the normative game-theoretical framework do not typically apply. As we will see in the remainder of this section, attentional limitations already encountered in the context of non-strategic decision making also play an important role in strategic decisions, and not necessarily always in detrimental ways – instead at times also contributing to more cooperative decisions and beneficial outcomes.

Failure to consider the actions of others

The first such instance where cognitive myopia may have a positive effect occurs in the context of the Prisoner's Dilemma, already mentioned earlier. In this game, two prisoners can each decide whether (a) to cooperate and deny all charges about their joint crime or (b) to defect and turn state witness, implicating his or her friend in the crime. The payoff matrix is such that mutual defection is the only Nash equilibrium (see Table 6.1). The tragedy of the situation is that this outcome is far inferior to the mutual cooperative choice, yet seems completely out of reach for rational decision makers (Hardin 1968). Many real-world resource utilization decisions have this payoff structure, often referred to as social dilemmas when the decision involves depletion of the resource (e.g. grass on the village commons, fish in the oceans) and as public goods dilemmas when the decision involves contribution to the resources (e.g. National Public Radio, blood bank reserves). In such situations, defection (involving either resource depletion or free-loading, i.e. resource use without contributions) tends to be the equilibrium choice. Fortunately, this is not always the dominant or even majority response observed in many real-world situations or lab experiments involving stylized, but often material, payoffs (Ostrom et al. 2002).

There are many reasons for this discrepancy between game theoretic predictions and observed responses (Attari, Krantz, and Weber 2014). One of them involves cognitive myopia, in this case resulting in a failure to realize that one is facing a strategic decision and treating it instead as a decision where only one's own action matters. This tendency to cut short the reasoning process about the best course of action by not considering the strategic element of these decisions, namely the consequences of the action of one's counterpart, was documented by the following study by Shafir and Tversky (1992). Participants in a single-round two-participant Prisoner's Dilemma game, seeing, for example, the payoff matrix in Table 6.1, were randomly assigned to one of three conditions. In the first

Table 6.1 Prisoner's Dilemma payoff matrix

"Prisoner's Dilemma/Arms Race"	**USSR** *cooperates (unilaterally disarms)*	**USSR** *defects (continues to arm)*
USSR cooperates (unilaterally disarms)	(2, 2)	(-8, 4)
USSR defects (continues to arm)	(4, -8)	(-6, -6)

condition they were told that their counterparts had decided to defect; in this condition 97 per cent also decided to defect, thus minimizing their losses. In the second condition they were told that their counterparts had decided to cooperate; in this condition 84 per cent decided to defect, thus maximizing their payoffs. In the third condition nothing was said about their counterparts' intended actions. However, since defection is the dominating action, i.e. the rational choice for both possible decisions by their counterpart, at least 84 per cent should have decided to defect. Instead, only 37 per cent made that decision, suggesting that well over half of respondents must have failed to take the extra step to think strategically about the impact of their counterpart's decision, focusing instead on the desirability of the cooperate-cooperate cell. In this case, cognitive myopia contributed to more cooperative behavior, resulting in an individually good and collectively excellent outcome.

Obstacles to predicting others' preferences

Even in situations where decision makers understand and appreciate that they are in a strategically interdependent situation, making strategic decisions is not as straightforward as the stylized framework of game theory would suggest. Few real-world decisions between cooperative vs. competitive action alternatives come with unambiguous payoff tables, and often not even with a well-defined action space. Instead, both parties need to generate their sets of possible actions and those of their counterparts, with the two not always being symmetric sets. They then need to construct their own utilities for finding themselves in each of the m-by-n cells, created by crossing their possible m actions with the n possible actions by their counterparts. And finally, and most difficult, they need to predict what their counterparts' utilities might be for ending up in each of the m-by-n cells.

Projection (egocentric biases) and stereotyping

How do people make such predictions about the preferences of others? Past behavior in the same or similar situations provides useful information. In the absence of such information, there are two general strategies, namely social projection or the use of stereotypes (Ames, Weber, and Zou 2012). Ames et al. show that participants in social dilemmas shift between social projection (using one's own preferences between courses of action to intuit a counterpart's preferences) and stereotyping (using general assumptions about a group to intuit a counterpart's preferences) as a function of the perceived similarity. Higher levels of perceived similarity between themselves and their counterparts are associated with increased projection and reduced stereotyping.

In addition to switching being projection and stereotyping, participants in strategic games can also be influenced in their assumptions of their counterparts' motives, and thus preferences, by manipulation of the reference class to which stereotypes are applied. Thus Libermann, Samuels, and Ross (2004) found that decisions in a Prisoner's Dilemma game could be influenced by the name assigned to that game. People who played 'The Community Game' cooperated approximately twice as frequently as participants who played an identical game entitled 'The Wall Street Game', presumably because they made different assumptions about their counterparts' motives, and thus their utilities, for different game cells.

Perceptual dilemmas

In international contexts, players in strategic games are typically antagonists, e.g. the USSR vs. the US during the Cold War. The Prisoner's Dilemma in Table 6.1 was designed to capture the assumed preferences of both sides regarding nuclear arming vs. disarming. There is, however, evidence to suggest that the arms race was more accurately modeled by a perceptual dilemma. In a perceptual dilemma, both sides prefer mutual arms reductions to all other outcomes; they want above all to avoid disarming while the other side arms, but they perceive the other side as preferring unilateral armament to all other outcomes. Plous (1993b) used surveys and interviews with US senators and European politicians with ties to Russian politicians during the time of the Cold War to show that the nuclear arms race should have been more appropriately modeled by a perceptual dilemma, a situation open to easier solutions than those required for a Prisoner's Dilemma. In this case, stereotyping of the other side and failure to see similarities between the two parties' situations led to potentially quite tragic misperceptions of the other side's motivations and preferences.

Greater use of some of the tools of the cooperation hexagon (Messner et al. in this volume) – in particular, communication – could, at least in principle, be used to avoid such errors. Communication, in combination with both initial trust and enforcement (when trust is violated), lies at the basis of creative paths to cooperation, even in Prisoner's Dilemma situations. Communication by action (rather than by 'cheap talk') is provided by the tit-for-tat strategy for repeated Prisoner's Dilemma interactions, which starts out with cooperation and then matches the other side's action on the previous trial, a simple and empirically winning strategy against a broad range of other strategies (Axelrod, 1984).

Failure to think forward and to backward induct

In what other strategic situations and tasks may cognitive limitations and resulting processing shortcuts have favorable consequences? The failure to think forward and to backward induct sufficiently in the context of some dynamic economic games provide other examples where cognitive myopia can lead to greater cooperation in some settings, even if it reduces the match between game theoretic predictions and observed behavior. Game theory has been a very powerful influence on understanding how forward thinking and backward induction ought to be used. However, descriptive *behavioral* game theory may prove to be more useful in understanding the presence or absence of cooperation in applied settings.

Evidence for a lack of forward thinking is perhaps most dramatically supplied by what is called the *Keynesian p-beauty contest*, a well-explored competitive game based on the ideas of John Maynard Keynes (1936: 156) when analyzing the dynamics of the stock market. The basic rules are that all members of a group need to guess a number between 0 and 100. The person whose number is closest to a proportion *p* of the mean of the guesses of all members will win a prize. The equilibrium solution to this game is provided by forward thinking, as follows: if everyone were to guess randomly a number between 0 and 100, then the mean would be 50. If *p* were 2/3, the winning number would be 33. But, of course, knowing that everyone would pick 33 would make the winning number 22, and so on. The eventual outcome of this iterative process, if forward thinking went to its logical conclusion, is that everyone would pick 0.

However, two things are true: (1) Data do not match this prediction. As shown by Nagel (1995) and by Ho, Camerer, and Weigelt (1998), choices are never, in initial rounds, 0. In fact they often reflect limited looking ahead, with peaks in responses reflecting the number of levels of forward thinking. For example, Level 1 (looking forward one level) at 33 in the game above, Level 2 at 22, Level 3 at 11, and so on. (2) Guessing the game theoretical equilibrium solution does not win the game. Instead, to guess the winning number one needs to think one level ahead of most people, but not further than that. To win in this game or to predict behavior, it is more important to understand the levels of rationality possessed by the other players than to follow the prescriptions of game theory.

Other evidence of myopia and limited future thinking is provided by studies that look at information searched for by competitors in economic games. Such work uses an analogue to eye movement recording to capture the attention and cognition of players. The basic payoff matrix is presented on a computer screen to participants, with the payoffs behind a label. When a cursor controlled by a mouse enters a cell, the payoff is revealed, and it is hidden again when the cursor exits. This technology has been extensively used to study individual choice, as well as more recently to study strategic choices (e.g. Costa-Gomes, Crawford, and Broseta 2001; Costa-Gomes and Crawford 2006; Johnson et al. 2002). Such methods can provide converging evidence about decision processes used in specific situations, including the use of backward induction, a basic tool for identifying equilibrium solutions in multi-stage games. The basic idea of backward induction is to focus first on the final round of the game and to then identify best responses to earlier stages from that perspective. One classic game to be solved in this fashion is the alternating offers or shrinking pie game (Rubenstein 1982), an analogy to management vs. labor union disputes, where the pie that needs to be distributed between two parties by alternating offers shrinks after each round, during which no agreement is reached. The game should be solved by backward induction. There are three rounds, and people should think first about what the payoffs are in the last round and work backwards from there to arrive at first and second round offers. However, significant amounts of data suggest that this is not an adequate descriptive model, since first-round offers are typically much higher than the game theoretical equilibrium. Johnson et al. (2002) hypothesized that this was due, in large part, to people failing to backward induct, suggesting that they instead only look one or occasionally two stages ahead, further evidence of cognitive myopia.

The advantage of using information acquisition data in this case is that such data provide direct evidence of the degree of consideration of future stages. Process data show that most players' information acquisition concentrated on the first round, with some not even looking at the payoff for the last round, and these looking patterns were closely related to the offers made. In addition, when players were explicitly instructed and trained to use backward induction, their offers were much closer to the equilibrium, and they spent much more of their time considering the final round payoff.

The limited nature of forward thinking in the beauty contest game and the failure of people to use backward induction to reason from end states in the shrinking pie game together suggest that cognitive myopia plays a key role in strategic contexts. Both of these examples also show that following the prescriptions of rational choice theory (in this case, game theory) would not necessarily or even typically improve the accuracy of predictions or the degree of cooperation – for example, backward induction in management: labor disputes would polarize the opening offers made by either side, probably making it less likely that a cooperative solution (i.e. an agreement rather than a strike) would be found. In this sense, cognitive myopia can again be seen as contributing to more cooperation in at least some settings.

Conclusions and takeaway

It is time to return to the title question of this chapter: can we think of the future? The evidence presented in this chapter paints both a 'glass-half-full' and a 'glass-half-empty' picture. The evidence tips more in the 'glass-half-empty' direction for decisions under risk, uncertainty, and time delay. A variety of interventions have evolved to help *homo sapiens* overcome existing barriers to future-oriented thought and decisions that do not exist for *homo economicus*. Historically, such interventions have involved paternalistic delegation of long-term planning decisions to experts (e.g. financial planners) and/or institutions (e.g. mandatory retirement savings plans).

More recently libertarian paternalism has been in greater favor, replacing compulsory mandates with choice architecture interventions, in settings from health care to retirement savings choices (e.g. Johnson et al. 2013), that gently assist and guide individual longer-term-planning decisions past the siren calls of immediate gratification and present bias (Elster 1979).

The fact that preferences are constructed can be a liability (making preferences context specific and leading to potential choice inconsistencies), but, as we showed earlier, they can also be an asset that provides tools to choice architects to help individuals achieve long(er)-term goals.

Evolution may have equipped us well to respond to risks and challenges in earlier and simpler choice environments (Weber 2006), with prepotent responses that favor immediate needs and result in present bias. Decisions that override the draw or 'temptation' exerted by such choice options require self-control, a resource that is in short supply (Figner et al. 2010). At the same time it has become very evident that the ability to override more impulsive, prepotent responses – i.e. choice of the immediate marshmallow in Mischel, Shoda, and Rodriguez's (1989) iconic developmental study with Stanford preschoolers – is correlated with a broad range of important life outcomes many years later, including educational attainment, salary, and marital satisfaction (Casey et al. 2011). Myopic choices do not always serve us well in the long run and are often regretted after the fact. While intertemporal tradeoffs and preferences are highly subjective, and one needs to be careful before calling any single decision incorrect or problematic, in many situations shortsighted individual decisions are resulting in social problems, from the obesity epidemic in many developed countries, to insufficient pension savings, to environmental crises that include resource and species depletion and climate change (Weber 2013).

Fortunately, different ways of presenting decision makers with choice options allow them to override temptation with more or less effort and thus more or less successfully. Interventions that focus attention first on choice options that are not automatically attended have been shown to increase consideration of arguments for larger later returns and to mediate greater patience (Weber et al. 2007; Zaval, Markowitz, and Weber 2015). Making forward-looking, future-oriented response options the choice default is an intervention that has been shown to be effective in a broad range of contexts, from organ donation (Johnson and Goldstein 2003) to retirement savings (Benartzi and Thaler 2004).

Cultural context also matters by influencing the chronic activation of different goals, and thus different attentional foci (Weber and Morris 2010). Hershfield, Bang, and Weber (2014) show that older countries (i.e. nation states that have been in existence longer) are more environmentally aware and have better environmental records. They explain this result by assuming that a longer past suggests a longer future, and that a longer perceived future motivates more forward-looking, future-oriented planning and action. In support of this country-level conjecture, the authors primed American respondents to perceive the US as either an old or a new country by showing them a time line that places the 237 years of US existence either as the major part of a time line, starting with Christopher Columbus's arrival in America, or at the very end of a time line, starting with the Roman empire. Respondents primed to perceive the US as an older country donated more of their experimental earnings to an environmental NGO.

The effects of cognitive myopia were not as uniformly negative in our review of strategic decision making. Here the general conclusion was that, at least at times, a myopic focus on one's own interests and actions and a failure to consider the interdependence of actions of two or more players may lead to more cooperation than predicted by classic game theory.

When decision makers do have the skill and expend the energy to think strategically, cooperation in social dilemma situations can be increased in other ways. Accurate assumptions about the utilities of different action cells in the game theoretic matrix are important to making sure that participants know what game needs to be solved. Perceptual dilemmas (Plous 1993b) may be relatively common. Misprediction of the other side's utilities can be the result of stereotyping, or at least stereotyping of an incorrect reference class. Global cooperation in a game theoretic sense may require an 'us' frame that may be politically infeasible, especially in contexts (e.g. climate change action) that lack a visible and imminent common enemy who can motivate a common front, and thus cooperation. Nevertheless, interventions that provide labels for such strategic interactions that prime cooperation, that suggest similarities, and that promote communication between the different parties can all help in smaller ways.

References

Ainslie, G. (1975). 'Specious Reward: A Behavioral Theory of Impulsiveness and Impulse Control', *Psychological Bulletin*, 82 (4): 463–96.

Ames, D. R., Weber, E. U. and Zou, X. (2012). 'Mind-Reading in Strategic Interaction: The Impact of Perceived Similarity on Projection and Stereotyping', *Organizational Behavior and Human Decision Processes*, 117 (1): 96–110.

Andreoni, J. and Sprenger, C. (2012). 'Estimating Time Preferences from Convex Budgets', *American Economic Review*, 102 (7): 2222–56.

Attari, S., M., Krantz, D. H. and Weber, E. U. (2014). 'Reasons for Cooperation or Defection in Real-World Social Dilemmas', *Judgment and Decision Making*, 9: 316–34.

Axelrod, R. (1984). *The Evolution of Cooperation*, New York, NY: Basic Books.

Benartzi, S. and Thaler, R. H. (1995). 'Myopic Loss Aversion and the Equity Premium Puzzle', *Quarterly Journal of Economics*, 110 (1): 73–92.

Benartzi, S. and Thaler, R. H. (2004). 'Save More Tomorrow: Using Behavioral Economics to Increase Employee Saving', *Journal of Political Economy*, 112 (S1): 164–87.

Camerer, C. F. (2003). *Behavioral Game Theory: Experiments in Strategic Interaction*, Princeton, NJ: Princeton University Press.

Casey, B. J., Somerville, L. H., Gotlib, I. H., Ayduk, O., Franklin, N. T., Askren, M. K., Jonides, J., Berman, M. G., Wilson, N. L., Teslovich, T., Glover, G., Zayas, V., Mischel, W. and Shoda, Y. (2011). 'From the Cover: Behavioral and Neural Correlates of Delay of Gratification 40 Years Later', *Proceedings of the National Academy of Sciences*, 108 (36): 14998–15003.

Costa-Gomes, M. A. and Crawford, V. P. (2006). 'Cognition and Behavior in Two-Person Guessing Games: An Experimental Study', *American Economic Review*, 96 (5): 1737–68.

Costa-Gomes, M., Crawford, V. P. and Broseta, B. (2001). 'Cognition and Behavior in Normal-Form Games: An Experimental Study', *Econometrica*, 69 (5): 1193–235.

Elster, J. (1979). *Ulysses and the Sirens*, Cambridge, UK: Cambridge University Press.

Engel, C. and Weber, E. U. (2007). 'The Impact of Institutions on the Decision of How To Decide', *Journal of Institutional Economics*, 3 (3): 323–49.

Figner, B., Knoch, D., Johnson, E. J., Krosch, A. R., Lisanby, S. H., Fehr, E. and Weber, E. U. (2010). 'Lateral Prefrontal Cortex and Self-Control in Intertemporal Choice', *Nature Neuroscience*, 13 (5): 538–9.

Gillingham, K., Newell, R. G. and Palmer, K. (2009). 'Energy-Efficiency Policies', *Discussion Papers Resources For the Future*, dp-04–19.

Gong, M., Krantz, D. H. and Weber, E. U. (2014). 'Why Chinese Discount Future Financial and Environmental Gains but Not Losses More than Americans', *Journal of Risk and Uncertainty*, 49: 103–24.

Grether, D. and Plott, C. (1979). 'Economic Theory of Choice and the Preference Reversal Phenomenon', *American Economic Review*, 69 (4): 623–8.

Hardin, G. (1968). 'The Tragedy of the Commons', *Science*, 162 (3859): 1243–8.

Hardisty, D. H., Appelt, K. C. and Weber, E. U. (2013). 'Good or Bad, We Want It Now: Fixed-Cost Present Bias for Gains and Losses Explains Magnitude Asymmetries in Intertemporal Choice', *Journal of Behavioral Decision Making*, 26 (4): 348–61.

Hardisty, D. H., Johnson, E. J. and Weber, E. U. (2010). 'A Dirty Word or a Dirty World? Attribute Framing, Political Affiliation, and Query Theory', *Psychological Science*, 21 (1): 86–92.

Hardisty, D. H. and Weber, E. U. (2009). 'Discounting Future Green: Money vs. the Environment', *Journal of Experimental Psychology: General*, 138 (3): 329–40.

Hershfield, H. E., Bang, H. M. and Weber, E. U. (2014). 'National Differences in Environmental Concern and Performance Predicted by Country Age', *Psychological Science*, 25 (2): 152–60.

Ho, T. H., Camerer, C. and Weigelt, K. (1998). 'Iterated Dominance and Iterated Best Response in Experimental "P-Beauty Contests" ', *American Economic Review*, 88 (4): 947–69.

Johnson, E. J., Camerer, C. F., Sen, S. and Rymon, T. (2002). 'Detecting Failures of Backward Induction: Monitoring Information Search in Sequential Bargaining', *Journal of Economic Theory*, 104 (1): 16–47. doi :10.1006/jeth.2001.2850.

Johnson, E. J. and Goldstein, D. (2003). 'Do Defaults Save Lives?', *Science*, 302 (5649): 1338–9.

Johnson, E. J., Hassin, R., Baker, T., Bajger, A. T. and Treuer, G. (2013). 'Can Consumers Make Affordable Care Affordable? The Value of Choice Architecture', *PLoS ONE*, 8(12): e81521.

Johnson, E. J., Häubl, G. and Keinan, A. (2007). 'Aspects of Endowment: A Query Theory of Loss Aversion', *Journal of Experimental Psychology: Learning Memory and Cognition*, 33 (3): 461–74.

Johnson, E. J., Hershey, J., Meszaros, J. and Kunreuther, H. (1993). 'Framing, Probability Distortions, and Insurance Decisions', *Journal of Risk and Uncertainty*, 7(1): 35–51.

Kahneman, Daniel (2011). *Thinking, Fast and Slow*, New York, NY: Farrar, Straus and Giroux.

Kempf, A. and Ruenzi, S. (2006). 'Status Quo Bias and the Number of Alternatives: An Empirical Illustration from the Mutual Fund Industry', *Journal of Behavioral Finance*, 7 (4): 204–13.

Keynes, J. M. (1936). *The General Theory of Interest, Employment and Money*, London: Macmillan.

Libermanm, V., Samuels, S. M. and Ross, L. (2004) 'The Name of the Game: Predictive Power of Reputations vs. Situational Labels in Determining Prisoner's Dilemma Game Moves', *Personality and Social Psychology Bulletin*, 30 (9): 1175–85.

Lichtenstein, S. and Slovic, P. (eds.) (2006). *The Construction of Preference*, New York NY: Cambridge University Press.

Loewenstein, G. and Elster, J. (eds.) (1992). *Choice Over Time*, New York, NY: Russell Sage Foundation.

Magen, E., Dweck, C. S. and Gross, J. J. (2008). 'The Hidden-Zero Effect: Representing a Single Choice as an Extended Sequence Reduces Impulsive Choice', *Psychological Science*, 19 (7): 648–9.

Malhotra, D. and Bazerman, M. H. (2007). *Negotiation Genius*, New York NY: Bantam Books.

Marx, S. M., Weber, E. U., Orlove, B. S., Leiserowitz, A., Krantz, D. H., Roncoli, C. and Phillips, J. (2007). 'Communication and Mental Processes: Experiential and Analytic Processing of Uncertain Climate Information', *Global Environmental Change*, 17 (1): 47–58.

Maslow, A. H. (1943). 'A Theory of Human Motivation', *Psychological Review*, 50 (4): 370–96.

Meier, S. and Sprenger, C. (2010). 'Present-Biased Preferences and Credit Card Borrowing', *American Economic Journal*, 2 (1): 193–210.

Mischel, W., Shoda, Y. and Rodriguez, M. L. (1989). 'Delay of Gratification in Children', *Science*, 244 (4907): 933–8.

Nagel, R. (1995). 'Unraveling in Guessing Games: An Experimental Study', *American Economic Review*, 85 (5): 1313–26.

Ostrom, E., Dietz, T., Dolsak, N., Stern P. C., Stonich, S. and Weber, E. U. (eds.) (2002). *The Drama of the Commons*, Washington, D.C.: National Academies Press.

Plous, S. (1993a). *The Psychology of Judgment and Decision Making*, New York, NY: McGraw Hill.

Plous, S. (1993b). 'The Nuclear Arms Race: Prisoner's Dilemma or Perceptual Dilemma?', *Journal of Peace Research*, 30 (2): 163–80.

Radu, P. T., Yi, R., Bickel, W., Gross, J. J. and McClure, S. M. (2011). 'A Mechanism for Reducing Delay Discounting by Altering Temporal Attention', *Journal of the Experimental Analysis of Behavior*, 96 (3): 363–85.

Rubinstein, A. (1982). 'Perfect Equilibrium in a Bargaining Model', *Econometrica*, 50 (1): 97–109.

Samuelson, W. and Zeckhauser, R. (1988). 'Status Quo Bias in Decision Making', *Journal of Risk and Uncertainty*, 1 (1): 7–59.

Shafir, E. and Tversky, A. (1992). 'Thinking through Uncertainty: Nonconsequential Reasoning and Choice', *Cognitive Psychology*, 24 (4): 449–74.

Simon, H. A. (1982). *Models of Bounded Rationality: Behavioral Economics and Business Organization*, Vol. 2, Cambridge, MA: MIT Press.

Thaler, R. H. and Sunstein, C. R. (2008). *Nudge: Improving Decisions about Health, Wealth and Happiness*, New Haven, CT: Yale University Press.

Tversky, A. and Kahneman, D. (1992) 'Advances in Prospect Theory, Cumulative Representation of Uncertainty', *Journal of Risk and Uncertainty*, 5 (4): 297–323.

von Neumann, J. and Morgenstern, O. (1944). *Theory of Games and Economic Behavior*, Princeton, NJ: Princeton University Press.

Weber, E. U. (2006). 'Experience-Based and Description-Based Perceptions of Long-Term Risk: Why Global Warming Does Not Scare us (Yet)', *Climatic Change*, 77 (1–2): 103–20.

Weber, E. U. (2013). 'Doing the Right Thing Willingly: Behavioral Decision Theory and Environmental Policy', in E. Shafir (ed.) *The Behavioral Foundations of Policy*, Princeton, NJ: Princeton University Press, 380–97.

Weber, E. U. (2015). 'Climate Change Demands Behavioral Change: What Are the Challenges?', *Social Research: An International Quarterly*, 82 (3): 17–24.

Weber, E. U. and Johnson, E. J. (2009). 'Mindful Judgment and Decision Making', *Annual Review of Psychology*, 60 (1): 53–86.

Weber, E. U. and Johnson, E. J. (2011). 'Query Theory: Knowing What We Want by Arguing with Ourselves', *Behavioral and Brain Sciences*, 34 (2): 91–2.

Weber, E. U. and Johnson, E. J. (2012). 'Psychology and Behavioral Economics Lessons for the Design of a Green Growth Strategy', White Paper for Green Growth Knowledge

Platform (OECD, UNEP, World Bank), *World Bank Policy Research Working Paper Series*, No. 6240.

Weber, E. U., Johnson, E. J., Milch, K., Chang, H., Brodscholl, J. and Goldstein, D. (2007). 'Asymmetric Discounting in Intertemporal Choice: A Query Theory Account', *Psychological Science*, 18 (6): 516–23.

Weber, E. U. and Lindemann, P. G. (2007). 'From Intuition to Analysis: Making Decisions with our Head, our Heart, or by the Book', in H. Plessner, C. Betsch, and T. Betsch (eds.) *Intuition in Judgment and Decision Making*, Mahwah, NJ: Lawrence Erlbaum, 191–208.

Weber, E. U. and Morris, M. W. (2010). 'Culture and Judgment and Decision Making: The Constructivist Turn', *Perspectives on Psychological Science*, 5 (4): 410–19.

Zaval, L., Markowitz, E. M., and Weber, E. U. (2015). 'How Will I Be Remembered? Conserving the Environment for Legacy's Sake', *Psychological Science*, 26 (2): 231–236.

7 Approaching cooperation via complexity

Jürgen Kurths, Jobst Heitzig, and Norbert Marwan

A universal experience of our society is the increasing complexity of our life. Technological progress is the fundament of an increased connectivity around the world, not only of rapid growth of knowledge and understanding about the mechanisms affecting our world and the major challenges we are facing (international conflicts, limited resources, climate change, population growth), but also of a growing quality of life. Whereas on the one hand cooperation is one of the key ingredients to form complex behavior, on the other hand the increasing complexity in our daily life calls for cooperation in order to manage specific problems, but which also makes cooperation more and more difficult. In this chapter we will therefore first give an introduction into complex systems science, highlighting how cooperation and other interaction between systems in general can lead to complexity due to feedbacks, and then we will focus more specifically on systems of cooperating humans, show how complexity arises there, and discuss its implications.

Complex systems science

The characterization of a system exhibiting complex behavior goes back only a few decades and is related to the rapid development of nonlinear sciences, the rapid progress in the available computer power, and a consequent cross-fertilization of the related disciplines, including statistical physics and mathematics. Before, it was a general and widely accepted concept that rather simple physical rules and natural laws (first principles) would be enough to explain the whole world – presumably enough information about the states and rules would be available, strongly related to Laplace's Demon. For a long period, this approach has been successful, e.g. the discovery of the accepted laws such as Ohm's law or Navier-Stokes equation for turbulence, as well as for their various uses in engineering.

However, it was found out that dynamics in the living world is more complicated. An instructive example is population dynamics. In a first attempt to model the Earth's human-carrying capacity at the end of the 18th century, Thomas Malthus suggested a two-component model by using an exponential growth of humankind but a linear growth of agricultural production. As soon as the exponential growth of humankind outpaces food supply, a further growth of humankind would

DOI: 10.4324/9781315691657-9

be limited and would result in the so-called Malthusian catastrophe. However, experience has shown that some of the basic assumptions of Malthus are too simple, e.g. the agricultural production could be substantially increased by new fertilizers and improved knowledge about plants and biology. In general, a better model for investigating the carrying capacity for a biological species would be to consider the birth rate r depending on the population size and a mortality rate depending on the population size as well as on the carrying capacity of the habitat. One famous model for such a dynamics is the logistic map, $x(t+1) = r\,x(t)\,(1 - x(t)/K)$, proposed already in 1838 by P.-F. Verhulst. For a very small population $x(t_0)$ at time t_0, far away from the carrying capacity K, the population $x(t)$ grows only slowly (because only a few species are available). The more species are available, the faster their population will increase, but close to the carrying capacity K the growth will slow down until it reaches an *equilibrium* value. This simple conceptual model already has a *feedback* mechanism. The feedback in this low-dimensional well-studied model causes, for higher birth rates, different dynamics, e.g. periodic variations of the population size or even highly complex, non-predictable (because of chaotic) variability. This behavior is related to the feedback, which is, in fact, the *nonlinear* part in the equation of the logistic map. It turns out that feedbacks are a crucial ingredient of complex systems.

When the system is chaotic, one important observation is that a very small difference between two initial conditions will cause, after some time, rapidly (exponentially) diverging results, although the difference between initial conditions might be so tiny that it would not be measurable. Such sensitivity to initial conditions is called deterministic chaos. Simple linear relationships or strong causalities are not able to show such behavior; the nonlinearity is a necessary condition and it may lead to weak causality. The emergence of nonlinear science is connected to the rising interest in complex systems and has strongly contributed to the understanding of them.

Another important property related to the sensitivity to initial conditions is the *stability* of the dynamics. Stability is important because although real world systems are usually exposed to perturbations, such as abrupt load changes in a power grid, an extreme weather event decreasing the population of a species, or a mistake made by a human decision maker, they nevertheless come back to some kind of 'normal' behavior. From a more formal point of view, we consider a small perturbation δ_0 at time t_0 and quantify the rate of change by comparing the initial perturbation with the divergence from the non-perturbed system δ_t after some time t, in practice by calculating the logarithm of the rate $\ln(\delta_t/\delta_0)$, which finally leads to the definition of the so-called *Lyapunov exponent* (Kantz and Schreiber 2003; Sprott 2003). If the Lyapunov exponent is positive, the system diverges and is considered to be unstable, and such a system is then called chaotic (Figure 7.1). Conversely, zero or negative Lyapunov exponents would result in *locally* stable dynamics (i.e. stable against small perturbations), such as periodic *oscillations* or stable fixpoints. Stable systems in which the perturbations are damped and then return to a specific state are asymptotically stable. A stable dynamics might not be the desired solution every time. In some special cases, synchronization and

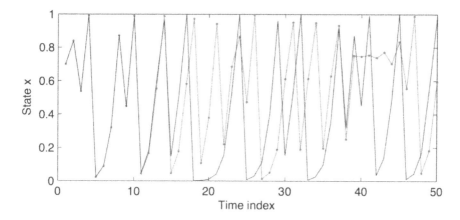

Figure 7.1 Two realizations of the logistic map for *r* = 4.

Two realizations of the logistic map for *r* = 4 (chaotic regime), where the initial value differs only by 10^{-5}. After 15 time steps the dynamics diverges rapidly and leads to completely different evolution. Knowing the initial state up to some certainty it is not possible to predict the long-term future of the system, although it is completely deterministic.

resonance can have dramatic consequences, as during epileptic seizures (related to synchronization in the brain) or for destabilizing civil engineering constructive works like a bridge due to resonance catastrophe.

The second approach to stability is perturbations of the system's parameter because dynamical systems can undergo rapid changes between different *regimes* by certain parameter changes. *Transitions* between steady states and periodic regimes, or between different periodic regimes, have been well known for a long time (Figure 7.3a). However, by studying nonlinear systems it has become clear that there are also further transitions, such as between order and chaos (Figure 7.2b). Coming back to the logistic map we easily find such behavior for different values of the control parameter *r* (for simplification we consider *K* = 1). For *r* smaller than 3, the system is in a steady state regime; for larger *r*, but yet smaller than some critical value $r_c \approx 3.57$, the dynamic is periodic. With $r > r_c$, chaotic behavior sets in. But even for larger *r*, the system can have again some periodic behavior, such as the periodic window between 3.83 and 3.85, where the system reveals a period-3 behavior (Figure 7.2a). The discovery of such transitions has opened new ways for understanding evolution.

This concept of stability and divergence is a core element for analyzing complex systems, as it allows a quantitative characterization of the dynamics and conclusions about predictability. We should note that locally stable systems might well be unstable against larger perturbations. When the perturbation is too strong, the system's dynamics can be pushed to another regime. In such cases only a certain region of states allows the dynamics to converge to the stable regime. Such a region is called the basin of attraction and also needs to be considered when discussing stability. This is of particular interest for so-called tipping elements, i.e.

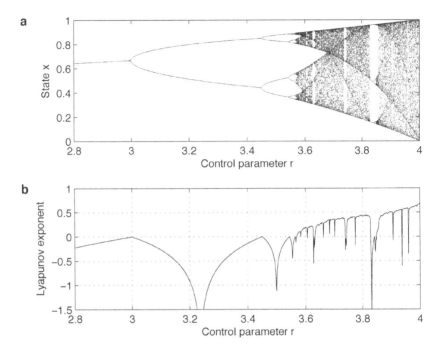

Figure 7.2 Bifurcation diagram and corresponding Lyapunov exponent of the logistic map.

(a) Bifurcation diagram of the logistic map $x(i+1) = r\,x(i)\,(1 - x(i))$ and (b) corresponding Lyapunov exponent. In periodic regimes, the Lyapunov exponent is negative, at bifurcation points zero, and during chaos positive.

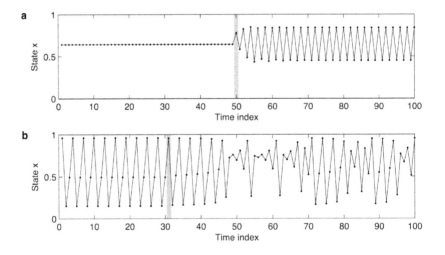

Figure 7.3 Transitions between different dynamical regimes of the logistic map.

(a) The steady state regime ($r = 2.8$) changes after 50 time steps (grey line) to a periodic regime ($r = 3.4$); (b) a period-3 regime ($r = 3.835$) changes after 30 time steps (grey line) to a chaotic regime ($r = 3.825$). The Lyapunov exponent for both regimes in situation (a) is negative, but in situation (b) it changes from negative to positive after time step 30.

multistable components of a system that may tip between several coexisting locally stable states, which occurs frequently in large-scale natural systems such as the climate system (Scheffer et al. 2009). A corresponding concept of stability against large perturbations is the recently introduced *basin stability* (Menck et al. 2013).

When discussing stability and perturbations, *stochasticity* is another important phenomenon that could be considered. However, stochastic processes form a different kind of processes (namely nondeterministic) that also reveal complex behavior. The study of stochastic dynamics requires different approaches related to probability theory and time series analysis. Although we focus here more on deterministic processes, stochasticity and randomization are sometimes helpful and necessary to explain real world processes. It is important to emphasize that stochastic influences do not always exert destructive effects on a system, but they can become constructive, i.e. noise can induce order. Basic phenomena are stochastic resonance (Gammaitoni et al. 1998) and coherent resonance (Pikovsky and Kurths 1997). Such effects can be generated by nonlinear systems only.

Dynamical systems usually are not formed by only one physical property, one state variable. Instead many variables $(x_1, x_2, \ldots, x_n)$ define the state $\mathbf{x}$ of the system. In the continuous deterministic case a state is determined by a set of differential equations, $d\mathbf{x}/dt = \mathbf{F}(\mathbf{x}, q)$, where $\mathbf{x}$ and $\mathbf{F}$ are vectors and functions defined in the n-dimensional space and q can be some parameters. The representation of the states $\mathbf{x}$ in an n-dimensional abstract space, the phase space, where the variables $x_1, x_2, \ldots, x_n$ are the coordinates of a state is another important approach to investigate the dynamics of a system (Figure 7.4) (Sprott 2003). The time evolution of the state $\mathbf{x}$ forms the phase space trajectory. For periodic dynamics, such a trajectory forms a closed loop (e.g. circle, ellipse, or torus). However, phase space trajectories of more complex dynamics can reveal a very complex feature. The trajectories are not closed loops anymore but run after some time very close to previously visited regions in the phase space. In fact, topological analysis shows that such trajectories can form higher-dimensional objects than a one-dimensional closed cycle, e.g. can densely fill a two-dimensional surface or even have a fractal (i.e. non-integer) dimension between 1 and 2 or larger, and are therefore called strange attractors. Nonlinear processes (such as a stretching, folding, and twisting process) causing chaotic dynamics are related to fractal properties. In such complex systems, a state in the phase space will never come back to the same state but only to some other, though very close, state. The difference can be infinitesimal small, thus filling the space almost completely. But the space covered by all states has, therefore, a fractal dimension.

This is related to another basic property of complex systems: *recurrence*. By studying the recurrence properties we can get deep insights into the dynamics (Marwan et al. 2007). For a chaotic regime, two of such very close states evolve almost in parallel for some time but then rapidly diverge with a rate corresponding to the maximum Lyapunov exponent.

Complex behavior is, of course, not limited to single systems. More interesting and challenging are connected and extended systems, where the complexity comes not only from the dynamics itself but also from the spatial distribution, as

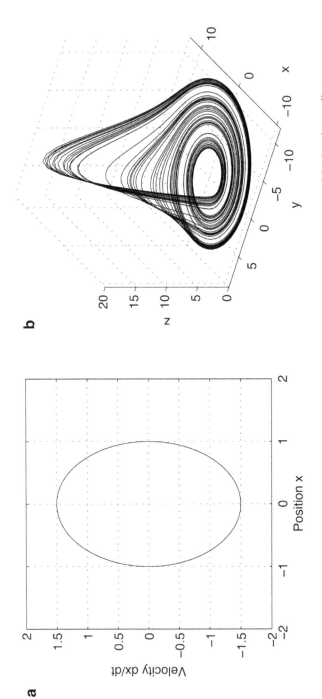

Figure 7.4 Phase space representation of the periodic dynamics of a pendulum and the chaotic dynamics of the Rössler oscillator.

Phase space representation of (a) the periodic dynamics of a pendulum and (b) the chaotic dynamics of the Rössler oscillator. The phase space trajectory of the Rössler oscillator has a fractal dimension ($D_2 \approx 1.8$) (Raab and Kurths 2001).

well affecting the dynamics of coupled systems. One challenge is to characterize and analyze various aspects of such spatiotemporal complexity. A novel but promising tool for such kinds of investigation is the *complex network* approach.

Complex networks

Complex networks have their origin in graph theory and have been exploited to investigate the relationships and topology in social networks (Boccaletti et al. 2006). Such networks have typically an irregular, complex structure that can even change over time. In the last two decades, this approach has received an increasing interest and growing number of applications in many different scientific disciplines, because it has the power to uncover hidden mechanisms and to study stability and failures, *collective* behavior and synchronization, and self-organization. Complex networks help to study complex systems from another perspective. Besides the traditional application for social networks, complex networks have been used to study, for example, stability, vulnerability, and cascading failures in infrastructure such as power grids or air traffic (Figure 7.5). By using measurements of the electrical activities at the human brain (by electroencephalography), functional networks of the brain can be reconstructed and shed light on the functioning of the brain during cognitive processing or seizure spreading. Brain regions which highly cooperate are closely connected in such a network. A more recent development exploits complex networks for the investigation of complex climate phenomena, e.g. to study moisture pathways and characteristic convergence zones during extreme rainfall events, to uncover hidden trigger regions in the global climate system, and to study convergence patterns or establish new prediction schemes (Boers et al. 2014). Again, closely connected

Figure 7.5 US American airline connections as an example for a complex network.

regions in such a climate network can be interpreted as cooperatively producing emergent system behavior that would not be observed without their strong interaction. Later we will see that also abstract entities, such as the incomplete preferences of a single agent, can be interpreted as a complex network.

A complex network is a set of vertices V and edges E forming a graph $G=(V, E)$. Such a network can be formed from directed or undirected edges and could have weights assigned to edges or vertices. The network can be represented by its adjacency matrix $\mathbf{A}$. Statistical measures have been introduced to characterize the vertices and also the network at whole.

The simplest measure for a network is the degree of a vertex that is the number of edges assigned to this vertex. The frequency of these degrees of the entire network, called degree distribution, can be used to analyze the network with respect to scale-free (self-similar) vs. random properties (Figure 7.6d and c). Vertices with high degree are called hubs. The implication of such findings (e.g. scale-free distribution, where the degree follows a very heavy-tailed power-law distribution) for real-world networks is that their formation is not simply by a random process, but that there are some rules behind the connecting process. Another essential measure considering the relationship between neighbors of a node is the clustering coefficient. The idea is to measure the usual aspect of 'two people I know most likely also know each other'. The clustering coefficient is the probability that we have such a triangle situation. This property is relevant with respect to topological order and the small-world property (Figure 7.6b). Other measures are based on shortest paths connecting one node with another. We can analyze the distribution of the length of shortest paths or count the number of shortest paths passing a certain node, which is called betweenness centrality.

Related to the distribution of shortest path lengths is the intriguing small-world (SW) property (Watts and Strogatz 1998). It characterizes such network topologies where we can reach any node from any other node by passing only a few edges. This phenomena is well known as the 'six degrees of separation', meaning that we are connected to any other people in the world by a chain of personal relationships in a maximum of six links. Networks with SW property are topologically different from regular (grids) and random ones. However, in the real world we find very

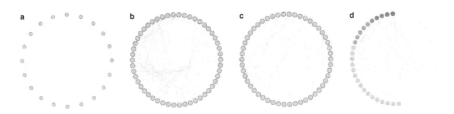

Figure 7.6 Basic network types.

(a) Regular, (b) small-world (SW), (c) random, and (d) scale-free networks. In a scale-free network, the higher the degree the lower frequent such nodes appear; the degree is color-coded (the darker the higher the degree).

often networks with the SW property, although at a first glance other network configurations seem to be more preferable because of simplicity, higher stability, or even better synchronizability. It has turned out that the SW property is obviously a trade-off between networks of high stability (regular grids) and high synchronizability (random networks) (Menck et al. 2013). Agents which are connected in such a SW manner can exchange information or form trust much faster, which can increase the level of cooperation considerably.

With complex networks the time evolution of a complex system can also be studied. Such an evolving network is formed by a time-varying ensemble of elements (nodes) and interrelations (connections). Under the effects of external influences or as a consequence of the local dynamics on each node, new elements may emerge to join the network or old ones may disappear, while the strength of each individual interaction may also fluctuate or even vanish. Such evolving or adaptive networks are marked by the emergence of information, rich dynamics, and structure formation, e.g. collective behavior between some of the elements. They can switch between stability and instability, leading to new qualitative behavior like robustness or vulnerability. As an example we analyze the Asian monsoon region. The investigation of a possible evolution of the monsoon dynamics is of high interest as this climate phenomenon has a huge socioeconomic impact in this region, e.g. by providing water for farming and, hence, ensuring sufficient food supply for a third of humankind. Past monsoon variation can be studied by using certain historical archives, such as tree rings, lake sediments, and speleothems. By comparing the variability of such records from different geographical locations, e.g. by correlation measures, we can construct a paleoclimate network that reflects the spatiotemporal dynamics of the Asian monsoon in the past (Figure 7.7). By separating cold and warm climate epochs, we find that the number of links connecting the eastern part with the western part of the paleoclimate network decreases during cold periods (Figure 7.7a). This suggests that during colder periods the Indian summer monsoon (mainly influencing the central

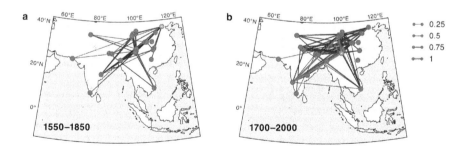

Figure 7.7 Paleoclimate network of the Asian monsoon system for the Little Ice Age and the recent warming period.

Paleoclimate network of the Asian monsoon system for (a) the Little Ice Age (1550–1850) and (b) the recent warming period (1700–2000), uncovering an increasing interlinking between the different monsoon branches. (Courtesy of Kira Rehfeld).

Asian region) is less active and does not influence the eastern Asian region (Rehfeld et al. 2013). Adaptive networks also play a role in models of coalition formation between humans (see following).

In this section we have considered different aspects of complexity. Nevertheless, this collection is far from complete. Complexity has many manifestations, but there is no clear definition of it. There are various classification possibilities by measures of complexity. We prefer to distinguish between traditional and alternative ones (Wackerbauer et al. 1994):

(1) Traditional measures refer highest complexity to the most disordered state and lowest complexity to the most regular one. Famous examples are *Shannon entropy*, *maximum Lyapunov exponent*, or *algorithmic complexity*, which quantifies the minimal description of a system. Such measures are minimum for a steady state regime and maximum for uncorrelated noise. They are widely used. (2) Alternative measures emphasize interplay of order and disorder as most complex. Important examples are some recurrence-based measures (Marwan et al. 2007), basin stability (Menck et al. 2013), or effective measure complexity (Wackerbauer et al. 1994). In contrast to case (1), they enable us to identify chaos-chaos transitions and, for applications, have advantages in early recognition of cardiovascular or bone diseases (Marwan et al. 2009; Wessel et al. 2000) and in finding the most stable synchronized complex network (Menck et al. 2013).

In applications, further and more specific classifications can be helpful to identify different complex behavior. In the analysis of decision making and cooperative behavior that we will study here, we can encounter the previously mentioned order-related form of complexity, e.g. in the preferences of agents if these preferences are incomplete or not transitive. Preferences also give rise to what we call *combinatorial* complexity, which relates to the large number of possible states of a system (here the preferences of the agent) and to the large structural variety of these. Combinatorial complexity is situated between the traditional and the alternative interpretation; for example, if preferences are basically unordered since they are incomplete but have at least some degree of order since they are transitive, then not only is their number very large, but also both the exact number and its exact order of magnitude are even yet unknown. Another less traditional and more alternative form of complexity that is especially useful in *modeling* is what we here call *conceptual* complexity. It refers to the number and complexity of concepts and notions used in the definition of a model and might be measured in a similar way as algorithmic complexity. For example, a partial differential equation is more conceptually complex than an ordinary differential equation, and a stochastic model is more conceptually complex than a deterministic one since it requires the notion of probability. Finally, we will use the alternative notion of *analytical* complexity if the analysis of a model or system (that may itself be conceptually simple) is complex, e.g. because it requires advanced methods or the distinction of large numbers of special cases. This form of complexity is also related to *emergent* complex behavior in conceptually simple systems. In the next section we will exploit the complex system approach for investigating this area of application in detail.

Complexity in rational decision making and cooperation

While other contributions in this volume rightfully explore bounds of rationality or pursue behavioral paradigms other than rational choice, the aim of this section is to show that one need not dispense with rationality in order to explain or predict cooperation. Although many popular examples of theoretical results or models based on rational choice exist that seem to imply low hopes for cooperation, we will see that these results and models are typically too simple and that models that take various forms of complexity into account can perfectly well predict high levels of cooperation, especially if they take into account time evolution and stochasticity. We will conclude that observed cooperation is rarely a falsification of the assumption of rationality but rather a falsification of too simple models. This is not to say that rationality is always a good assumption – there are indications both for and against it in different situations (e.g. Tversky and Kahneman 1986) – but that cooperation can be explained in many ways. One of them is rational behavior (others being heuristic learning rules, evolutionary selection and mutation of inherited behavior, altruism, and many more).

As illustrations we will in particular study the paradigmatic example of bilateral cooperation problems, the Prisoner's Dilemma; an example from decision making in large groups, the emergence of consensus; and an example from multilateral cooperation, the dynamic formation of coalitions. These will also reveal some nontrivial relationships between different forms of complexity: in particular that a small increase in one form may cause a large increase or decrease in another form of complexity; very similar complexity behavior is found in deterministic complex systems, as described in the previous two sections. But to understand the forms of complexity related to rational cooperation, we shortly have to look at the very foundations of rational choice first.

Individual decision making

While many forms of complexity arise from the dynamic interaction of more than one agent over time, some forms of complexity already arise in the context of a decision taken by one agent at one particular point in time. To make our point, the following working definition seems sufficient: we call an individual, i, *rational* if she makes choices that appear *optimal* (i.e. with no better choice existing) given her current *beliefs* about her *options*, their *consequences*, and her *preferences* (whatever they be, selfish, other-regarding, altruistic, . . .) regarding those consequences. Her options are given by an *action set* A, and the consequences of action a are given by a probability distribution (a *lottery*) $p(x \mid a)$ on a set X of m many possible *outcomes* x.

Complexity in preferences over outcomes

Much of the arising complexity is related to i's preferences over these outcomes, represented by a binary relation R on X, where xRy denotes a *weak* preference and is here vaguely interpreted as '*i* considers *x* as at least as desirable as *y*'. While most authors assume *R* to be a *complete, strict, linear ordering* (a ranking from 1 to *m*), the necessity of being able to make a rational choice requires much less regularity, and indeed one can easily find incomplete, non-strict, nonlinear examples of preferences. A good compromise level of assumed regularity arises from assuming only reflexivity (*xRx*) and transitivity (if *xRyRz* then *xRz*), which makes *R* a *quasiorder* (e.g. Fishburn 1968), an example of which is given in Figure 7.8, showing possible preferences regarding the following options: *x* = eating a small apple, *y* = eating a small apple and then a large one, *y'* = eating a large apple and then a small one, and *z* = eating a pear. Quasiorders arise whenever *i* compares outcomes along several linear but incommensurable criteria (such as quantity and taste) and weakly prefers *x* over *y* if *x* scores no lower than *y* on all *dimensions* (each quasiorder is hence an intersection of at most *m* many weak linear orderings; Fishburn 1968). Due to transitivity, each nonempty subset of outcomes has at least one optimal element, allowing *i* to make rational choices. In contrast to rankings, a quasiorder allows for both *indifference* (not caring whether *x* or *y*) and *undecidedness* (caring but having conflicting criteria) so that more than one optimal choice can exist, which we will see makes consensus easier and may also explain satisficing behavior as a form of rationality. Quasiorders are conceptually complex: neither their number nor the number of their possible shapes ('topologies') is known for *m* > 18, but both grow superexponentially with ~ $2^{m^2/4}$ (Heitzig and Reinhold 2000; Kleitman and Rothschild 1975). To generate a random quasiorder, one can either form the reflexive-transitive hull of a random directed network or the intersection of some random weak linear orderings (as in Figure 7.8d). If not transitivity but rather completeness (always *xRy* or *yRx*) is assumed, preference cycles can occur and optimal elements may not exist, leading to much higher analytic complexity, e.g. in the theory of *Tournament Solutions* (studying e.g. round-robin sports tournaments) or that part of *Social Choice Theory* that deals with majority decisions (e.g. Laslier 1997). On the most general level of description, without the assumption of special properties such as transitivity or completeness, preferences may best be described by a complex directed network whose nodes are options and whose links point from more to less desired options (Figure 7.8a).

Complexity in preferences over lotteries

If one assumes rational behavior is guided by preferences over consequences of actions, i.e. over lotteries of outcomes, one faces more complexity. To study such preferences, most authors apply *Expected Utility Theory*, where outcome preferences are complete and linear and lottery *p* is weakly preferred to lottery *q*, written *pRq*, iff $u(p) \geq u(q)$. In this, *u* is a real-valued *utility function* for lotteries and outcomes and $u(p) = p(x)u(x) + p(y)u(y) + \ldots$, summing over all outcomes *x*, *y*, ... (e.g. Fishburn 1968). Due to this convenient linearity, *u* can always be maximized by a deterministic outcome rather than a probabilistic lottery. Other models take into account some empirically observable nonlinearity or even discontinuity in the dependence

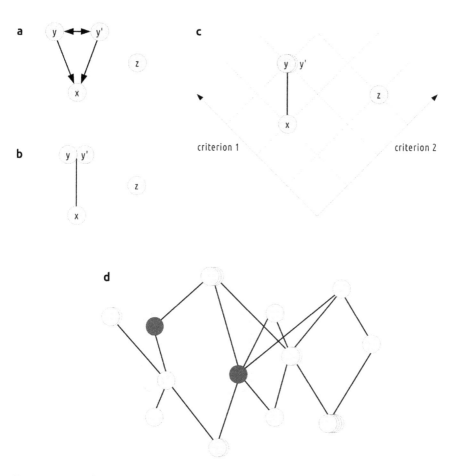

Figure 7.8 Simple example of nonlinear preferences.

Represented as (a) a directed network where $x \rightarrow y$ means x is weakly preferred to y, (b) a quasiorder (Hasse) diagram omitting the transitive edges and arrowheads (assumed to point downwards) of the network, and (c) as a consequence of two linear but incommensurable criteria. The three optimal elements are y and y', which the agent considers equivalent in all relevant respects (indifference), and z, which she finds neither consistently better nor worse than either of x, y, y' (undecidedness). (d) Larger example in quasiorder diagram form, showing optimal elements (dark) of some subset (dashed).

of choices on probabilities by assuming $u(p) = v(p(x))u(x) + v(p(y))u(y) + \ldots$ with some nonlinear function v (Prospect Theory, Kahneman and Tversky 1979), or by making other adjustments to the formula (e.g. Regret Theory, Loomes and Sugden 1982; Rank-Dependent Expected Utility, Quiggin 1982), and u might then attain its maximum only at a nondeterministic lottery, or i is *risk-averse* in a way that lets her prefer both x and y to tossing a coin to decide between x and y, which we will see can also make consensus easier. Another variant keeps the linear dependence of $u(p)$ on p but allows outcome preferences to be incomplete and nonlinear by letting

u be real-vector-valued and putting $u(p) \geq u(q)$ iff $u_j(p) \geq u_j(q)$ for all components j. The use of real numbers implies the Archimedean property that there cannot be outcomes x, y, z so that i prefers x to y and y to any lottery that gives some positive probability to z and otherwise selects x. If this seems implausible (e.g. x = eat the apple on the table and the apple on the tree, y = eat only the first apple, and z = die by falling off the tree), one may further increase the conceptual complexity by either using nonstandard numbers having infinitesimal and infinite components of various magnitude or lexicographically ordered utility vectors (Fishburn 1968), and such models can help explain why cooperation can be easier if some outcome must be avoided 'by all means' as with a precautionary principle.

Similar techniques can be used to model *other-regarding* preferences, those of a decision maker representing a whole society, or the welfare of that society itself. Then *inequality-aversion* can play a similar role as risk-aversion, e.g. leading to *social welfare functions* W such as the non-smooth rank-dependent one based on the Gini coefficient of inequality that gives increased weight to less well-off individuals (similar to Sen 1974): $W = u_1 + 2u_2 + 3u_3 + \ldots$, where $u_1 > u_2 > u_3 > \ldots$ are the decreasingly sorted utilities of the individual members of society.

Complexity in preferences over time

If some consequences accrue at different points in time, additional complexity arises from the fact that i may have preferences over when things happen. Note that although there is a time component here, this is still not about dynamics or interaction. A typical model of such *time preferences* assumes that outcomes x correspond to 'payoff' streams $\pi(x,t)$ interpreted as the flow of utility at time t, and that the (overall) utility of x is a weighted ('discounted') sum (or integral), $u(x) = w(0)\pi(x,0) + w(1)\pi(x,1) + \ldots$, where $w(0) > w(1) > \ldots > 0$ are certain *discounting factors*. In case of *Exponential Discounting* with $w(t) = \exp(-rt)$, where $r > 0$ is the *pure rate of time preference*, the optimality of a choice is time consistent since it does not depend on the time of evaluation. In *Hyperbolic Discounting* (Ainslie and Haslam 1992), the ratio $w(t)/w(t+1)$ instead decreases with growing t. This can make cooperation more profitable if the benefits, B, of cooperation (or any other investment) accrue a time interval T later than the costs, C, e.g. as in climate policy. But it can also give an incentive to delay cooperation if that shifts both costs and benefits in time by the same interval. This occurs if $w(T+dt)B - w(dt)C > w(T)B - w(0)C$, i.e. if the cost-benefit ratio C/B is larger than the discounting *rate* ratio $w'(T)/w'(0)$, which is more likely for larger T. The optimal time to invest then seems to lie always the same time interval away, an example of *time inconsistencies* that increase analytical complexity.

If future utility flow is increasingly *risky*, i.e. given by a probability distribution reflecting *uncertainty* rather than by a deterministic value $\pi(x,t)$, many models put $u(x) = w(0)E[\pi(x,0)] + w(1)E[\pi(x,1)] + \ldots$, where $E[\cdot]$ denotes expected values and $w(t)$ is either hyperbolic (Weitzman 2001) or exponential with a risk-adjusted rate r^* that is typically smaller than r if i is risk-averse (Dasgupta 2008), which again may improve cooperation.

In the next section we will see how the described complexities in preferences such as indifference, undecidedness, non-expected utility, risk-aversion, non-Archimedean preferences, and hyperbolic discounting may, among other factors, help consensus and cooperation.

Bilateral cooperation

The analysis of decisions gets considerably more complex if two or more agents are involved, mainly because this almost always leads to some form of interaction and dynamics. Many aspects can be seen already in the paradigmatic *Prisoner's Dilemma (PD)* in which two players, Row and Col, each have two possible actions, C ('cooperative' behavior) or D ('defective' behavior), and their utility depends on the four possible combinations CC, CD, DC, DD, e.g. as given by Table 7.1, representing symmetric but *conflicting* preferences that make cooperation difficult because of a temptation to defect. Similar preference conflicts occur in many global systems, e.g. bilateral trade or the joint provision of public goods such as climate protection, ocean water quality, international security, and epidemics control, where noncompliance and free-riding incentives exist.

Many authors take it for granted that *Game Theory*, the mathematical study of multi-agent rational choice under conflicting preferences, must predict that both choose D and receive a suboptimal joint utility of 2 instead of the Pareto-optimal value of 8, this constituting the dilemma. But a real game-theoretical analysis depends strongly on further specifications:

- *Time* structure: at what time points (and in particular in what order) can or must which player make, revise, or finalize his/her choice, and at what time point(s) do the consequences occur? Is the situation singular ('one-shot') or repeated/iterated? Without knowing the time structure, the resulting dynamics cannot be studied.
- *Communication and information* structure: what means of communication do the players have at each time point and what do they know at each time point about the structure, the other players' previous choices, and the consequences? Without this knowledge, the possible interactions remain unclear.
- *Commitment/contract power:* can players commit themselves bindingly to later actions, either individually or mutually via an enforceable contract?

Table 7.1 Example payoffs in the Prisoner's Dilemma

(Row's utility, Col's utility)		Col's action	
		C	D
Row's action	C	4, 4	0, 5
	D	5, 0	1, 1

Only a full specification of all these defines a *game*. If the game is one-shot, if actions are chosen simultaneously and mutually unobservably, and if players cannot communicate or commit beforehand, then indeed the prediction is DD since D is then a *dominant strategy* for both players, which is optimal regardless of what they believe the other does. But real-world situations are rarely one-shot and rarely have dominant strategies, and optimal behavior will depend on other players' past and anticipated actions, often leading to *feedback dynamics*. For example, if the PD is repeated indefinitely (or a previously unknown number of times) and players discount exponentially or hyperbolically and know each others' previous actions ('complete information'), then very complex strategic interaction can occur in this repeated game (e.g. Sorin 1986). This can involve features very similar to other complex dynamical systems, e.g. *multistability* due to nonunique *equilibria*, the 'curse of *dimensionality*' due to infinite strategy spaces, punishment *oscillations* (feuds) triggered by *errors* and possibly *dampened* by deliberately *randomized* forgiveness, and even gradual escalations or *resonance catastrophes* if the action space is continuous. Because of these complexities, sharp predictions are then difficult and require a conceptually complex *Theory of Repeated Games* (e.g. Aumann 2006; Sorin 1986) that applies recursively defined or self-referential notions such as common knowledge of rationality, credible threats, or subgame-perfect, renegotiation-proof, trembling-hands-perfect, and evolutionarily stable equilibria. A typical result is that as long as discount rates are small enough (possibly helped by risk-aversion or hyperbolic discounting), all kinds of Nash equilibria exist (a popular but very basic and weak form of equilibrium) leading to various levels of cooperation, but that cooperation can be sustained as a very strong form of equilibrium by certain (not too) complicated strategies that involve empirically observable reactions such as punishment via *reciprocity* and reestablishment of cooperation via *forgiveness* (e.g. van Damme 1989). Hence players only need to be sufficiently patient and/or risk-averse, solve the problem of *equilibrium selection*, and *coordinate* at some time point on such a *socially optimal* equilibrium, e.g. by direct communication, indirect *signaling*, or social *norms*, but not necessarily by requiring any form of altruism.

In all this it is important to notice that in contrast to other notions of 'equilibrium' in other disciplines, a game-theoretic equilibrium does not at all imply that the system's *state* has come to rest and the dynamics has stopped. It only implies that the system's *equations* (given by the agents' behavioral rules) are in a specific sense consistent with each other. Hence equilibrium behavior can be very dynamic: e.g. the positive results on cooperation in the two-player PD have recently been generalized to PD-like games in which many players can repeatedly provide an arbitrary amount of a public good such as greenhouse gas emissions reductions; Figure 7.9 shows the dynamics arising when players apply a simple but very strong form of equilibrium strategy (Heitzig, Lessmann, and Zou 2011). This climate application also shows that additional complexity arises if over time the payoff matrix changes due to stock effects or if uncertainty is gradually resolved due to incoming information, which can give rise to *nonstationary* strategies and time inconsistencies. Also, the analysis of an *n* times–repeated game may turn out completely different depending on whether *n* is infinite or only large (a *finite-size effect*), and whether the action space is continuous or only finely discretized.

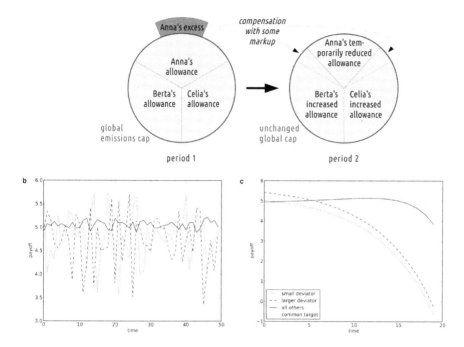

Figure 7.9 Sustaining cooperative levels of greenhouse gas emissions reductions.

(a) A very stable (renegotiation-proof and groupwise subgame-perfect) strategy to sustain coopera-tive levels of greenhouse gas emissions reductions (Heitzig et al. 2011). After a player's emissions exceed their allowances in some period, allowances are temporarily redistributed in the next period to compensate for this with some markup factor. (b) Resulting time evolution of payoffs if two of 10 players make random errors, leading to reduced average payoffs for the deviators and increased average payoffs for all others. (c) Time evolution if punishments escalate when two players devi-ate persistently, leading to exponentially decreasing deviators' payoffs and temporarily increasing others' payoffs.

While all this is well studied in the repeated PD, it is less well known that cooperation can also emerge between rational players in the *one-shot* PD, even if they cannot sign enforceable contracts. In many real-world situations the assump-tion of simultaneous, mutually unobservable choices is implausible since ultimate action requires observable preparation over time, possibly leading to strategic *feedbacks* already during preparations. An example is the analysis of the Cuban missile crisis with the *Theory of Moves* (Brams and Wittman 1981), where the eventual 'cooperation' emerged from rational dynamic adjustments leading to de-escalation. A similar analysis of the one-shot PD with observable preparations would model the situation as a game with more detailed time-structure, in which players can alternately switch between states C ('preparing for cooperation') and D ('preparing for defection') for an unknown but supposedly large number of times before actions are ultimately fixed (similar to Fang, Hipel, and Kilgour 1989; Willson 1998). This game has then a strong perfect equilibrium leading to mutual cooperation via the following simple strategy (Figure 7.10a): switch to D if you are currently at C and the other is currently at D, otherwise switch to C (i.e. prepare for cooperation unless when the current preparations put you in the 'sucker's position' of CD). This notion of equilibrium, however, assumes that each player *farsightedly anticipates* similar reactions from the other player, because then any change in her own strategy, e.g. to switch to D more often, only leads to a cycle involving state DD but only rarely or never visiting her preferred 'free-riding' state DC (Figure 7.10b, c).

But also if players *myopically* anticipate only the other's immediate reaction, cooperation may be an equilibrium, at least if uncertainty and nonlinear

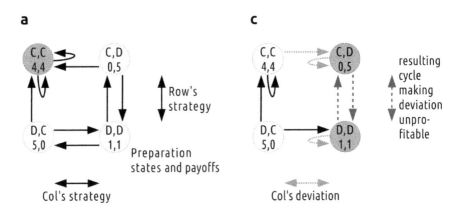

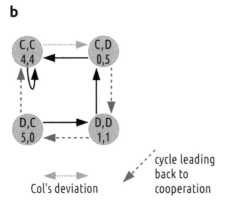

Figure 7.10 Dynamic *Theory of Moves* analysis of the Prisoner's Dilemma.

Dynamic *Theory of Moves* analysis of the Prisoner's Dilemma when preparations for action are observable and players dynamically change their preparations alternatingly. (a) Strong perfect equilibrium strategies leading to cooperation (darker state), with expected payoffs 4,4. (b) A unilateral deviation (dotted) leading to periodic cycling (dotted and dashed arrows, darker states), with unprofitable expected payoffs 11/4 < 4. (c) A larger deviation in Col's strategy (dotted) leading to a different cycle, with expected payoffs 6/2 < 4.

preferences are involved. For example, assume i's preparations imply a probability $p_i(t)$ of i eventually playing C, and that i can continuously but only smoothly adjust $p_i(t)$ to j's preparations by moving $p_i(t)$ into the direction where his/her utility of the resulting lottery $(p_i(t),p_j(t))$ ascends most steeply: $dp_i(t)/dt = \partial u_i(p_i(t),p_j(t))/\partial p_i$. If they weigh probabilities as in *Prospect Theory*, the resulting nonlinear dynamical system has four fixed points corresponding to CC, CD, DC, and DD, which may all be stable with different levels of basin stability.

Repeated games, the *Theory of Moves*, and the steepest ascent dynamics shown previously are just some examples of how *dynamic feedbacks* can induce cooperation, and hence why dynamic rather than static models are needed.

Multilateral decision making

After having seen much complexity already in bilateral interactions, let us now turn to multilateral cooperation, first studying the paradigmatic situation where a large group G of agents i has to jointly pick exactly one option x from a given set X when their preferences R_i over X may differ. *Social Choice Theory* studies preference aggregation rules and group decision methods to solve this problem. *Conceptual* and *analytical complexity* arises – e.g. since pairwise option comparisons can lead to majority cycles (Condorcet's 'paradox') that can be resolved in numerous ways, each having some drawbacks related to intuitive appeal, consistency under simple modifications, strategic equilibria, etc. Indeed, Arrow's famous 'impossibility theorem' seems to prove that no satisfactory solution to this exists, but it may simply use a too simple model, e.g. not allowing for randomization, and at the same time ask for too much, i.e. a complete ranking of all options instead of only an option selection rule.

Stochasticity

Surprisingly, while it is commonly known that deliberate stochasticity, i.e. *randomization*, may be required to achieve fairness when distributing indivisible goods (e.g. green card lotteries), social choice theory considers it only rarely although it can help solve the cooperation problem both in a majoritarian and a consensus decision making framework. The majoritarian framework's problem – that there may not be an option x in X that beats all others in pairwise majority comparisons – can be solved by noting that there is always a unique lottery p on X that beats all other lotteries q in the sense that the probability that an option drawn from p beats an option drawn from q is at least ½ (Laslier 1997). This shows that an increase in conceptual complexity (adding randomization) can reduce analytical complexity and make cooperation easier (by leading to a uniquely 'best' lottery to choose from).

Emergence of consensus

In the consensus decision making framework, a major problem is that when no consensus is reached after some time, a decision must be made anyway, typically employing a deterministic fallback method such as plurality or approval voting (picking the option getting the largest number of votes). This makes the whole procedure strategically equivalent to the fallback method, so that, for example, a majority desiring x has incentives to simply block consensus and then vote for x in the fallback method. Again, allowing for randomization can solve the problem and lead to cooperation, as can be seen by the simplest example of a voting method for which consensus is a game-theoretic equilibrium: each voter marks a potential consensus option on a green ballot and his/her favorite option on a blue ballot. If all green ballots have the same option marked, that one is picked, otherwise a randomized fallback is applied in which the option marked on a randomly drawn blue ballot is picked. It can be shown that under some weak conditions all strongly correlated equilibria of the resulting voting game will indeed result in picking a good consensus option, whereas the randomized fallback only serves as a threat that is never actually carried out (Heitzig and Simmons 2012). However, to make this prediction the conceptually complex notion of strong correlated equilibrium is needed, which considers that subgroups of voters may *coordinate* to act strategically (see also Aumann 1959, 2006; Gintis 2009). A simpler analysis, e.g. using pure-strategy equilibrium, would only reveal that this voting game has a huge number of weak equilibria and would not be able to select between them. Of course, this example of a voting rule is still impractical since already a mistake by a single voter would destroy consensus, and if several good potential consensus options exist voters have difficulties selecting between them. Only some additional conceptual complexity can resolve this, e.g. by allowing for partial consensus and introducing well-designed forms of communication that support feedbacks resulting in the convergence of voting behavior towards an emerging consensus.

Social hierarchies vs. networks

While the problem of making well-informed group decisions in large societies has traditionally been solved by some form of voluntary or involuntary centralization of decision power through a hierarchy of representatives or rulers, leading to complex but relatively static social structures, modern information and communication technology increasingly supports decentralized group decisions with less hierarchical but potentially even more complex interactions. For example, many organizations use *Proxy Voting*, where agents can dynamically transfer their voting power for individual decisions to other better informed agents that they trust, and some consider using *Delegable Proxy Voting*, where the voting power of an agent can be transmitted further through the social network, which can lead to complex delegation relationships and complex distributions of effective voting power strongly depending on the topology of the underlying social network and influencing the latter in turn, resulting in an *adaptive* network dynamics. But already without proxy voting systems similar effects can occur simply because of complex *opinion formation* or *learning* dynamics on social networks that influence the beliefs, preferences, and options of the agents (e.g. Holme and Newman

2006). Whether or not one understands the resulting convergence of opinions as cooperation in the wider sense, it also has profound effects on cooperation in a stricter sense.

Dynamics of coalition formation

Both the influence of nonlinear dynamics and complex networks on cooperation on the one hand, and the emergence of complexity from cooperation on the other hand, can probably best be seen in our final example, the question of how rational agents will form, join, or leave cooperative groups such as work teams, cooperatives, firms, political parties, cartels, etc., over time. We focus on *coalitions*, i.e. groups acting (in all respects important to the given context) like a single rational agent whose preferences represent some aggregate of the group members' preferences, e.g. via a social welfare function or a joint revenue.

Combinatorial complexity

Correspondingly, coalitions may contain subcoalitions (e.g. divisions, departments, party wings) but are otherwise nonoverlapping. Most generally, given N agents, the coalition formation's current *state* $C(t)$ is then given by a hierarchical tree-like structure of subsets of agents representing all coalitions existing at time t. This results in a finite but combinatorially complex state space of superexponential size in N (already >40,000 states for $N=6$). For example, the coalition structure code $C(t) = (AB)C,DE,F$ represents a state in which a three-element coalition ABC with a two-element subcoalition AB, another two-element coalition DE, and a single outsider F has formed. In reality, only agents sufficiently connected can form a coalition, so we may assume some social network $G(t)$ representing communication possibilities and/or trust relationships, and that only sets that are internally connected in $G(t)$ can become coalitions. Since networks are typically sparse, this reduces the number of possible coalition formation states $C(t)$ considerably but still leaves at least exponentially many and introduces exponentially many possible network states $G(t)$.

Conceptual complexity

Typically, both the membership of i in a certain coalition J as well as the existence of further coalitions besides J will have consequences on i because of externalities (e.g. if coalitions are economic output cartels in a *Cournot oligopoly*, the whole structure $C(t)$ influences i's revenues via the resulting market price), this being a form of nonlocal, *long-range interactions*. Depending on these consequences, their assumed effect on the network itself, and the assumed degree of farsightedness, one can specify a model of the dynamics of the joint system of $C(t)$ and $G(t)$ assuming that agents try to influence the coalition structure in accordance with their preferences, i.e. rationally, resulting in a stochastic dynamic process, like the one in Figure 7.11, with transitions of different probability. The model does not assume these probabilities upfront but rather derives them as a form of (unfortunately nonunique) game-theoretic equilibrium between these probabilities (representing the agents' beliefs about what will happen), the agents' evaluations of all states resulting from these beliefs via farsighted discounting, and the feedbacks that the rational behavior resulting from these evaluations has in turn on the probabilities (Heitzig 2012).

Limited predictability

One such model for the context of international climate protection through a cap-and-trade regime results in a bottom-up process (formally a Markov chain) in which smaller coalitions successively merge and can be proven to eventually form an efficient global coalition (Figure 7.11). In contrast, the typical nondynamic but static models of coalition stability popular in the economics literature miss

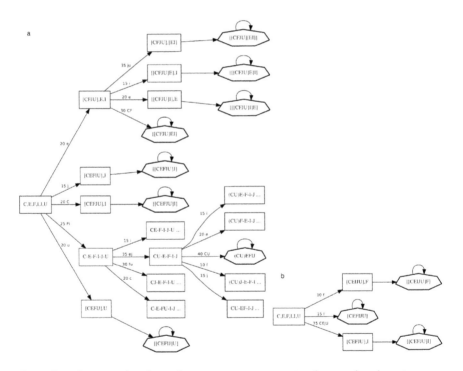

Figure 7.11 Dynamical coalition formation in an international cap and trade regime.

Dynamical coalition formation in an international cap and trade regime with six major emitters (C,E,F,I,J,U) and different types of coalitions (trade with or without immediate or delayed cap coordination). Transition probabilities are derived by solving a large number of nonlinear equations. The resulting process ends in one of a number of global coalitions. (a) Typical complex process (diagram truncated) when coalitions are irreversible. (b) Less complex process resulting from higher conceptual and analytical complexity when coalitions are reversible (from Heitzig 2012).

the dynamical effects and predict no significant level of cooperation. Predictability is, however, limited since the process is intrinsically stochastic and because the order of the mergers and the resulting cost sharing between the countries are initially unknown, becoming clearer from step to step. This also highlights the importance of modeling *transient behavior* instead of just identifying steady states in order to assess their relative likelihood.

Analytical complexity

Figure 7.11a shows the states, moves, and move probabilities for typical parameter values when coalitions are assumed to be irreversible, in which case the process can easily be derived by simple backwards induction. Surprisingly, when the conceptual and analytical complexity is raised by making coalitions reversible and thus allowing for cycles that require a more sophisticated *Kakutani fixed-point algorithm* to find the probabilities, the complexity of the resulting process is reduced considerably (Figure 7.11b), again an example for nontrivial relationships between different forms of complexity. Interestingly, agents' farsightedness keeps cycles from actually occurring.

Coevolution of social network and coalitions

The interaction between coalition formation and the underlying network can best be seen in a simpler model version that assumes myopic agents that do not anticipate the consequences of joining or leaving a coalition on the further coalition formation process. In one such model (Auer et al. 2015), the question of whether a global coalition does or does not emerge depends on parameters such as the initial type of network topology and the relative speed with which the network adapts to the coalition structure, showing complex nonlinear *phase transitions*, *scaling* behavior and *criticality* similar to Holme and Newman's (2006) model of opinion formation on adaptive networks and models of droplet growth (Blaschke and Lapp 2012).

Concluding remarks

We have discussed in this chapter the concept of complexity from two main perspectives: the rather general complex systems science and the more specified field of rational decision making and cooperation. Additionally, a few selected applications, ranging from population dynamics via infrastructure and climate to coalition formation, have been presented in this context. It turns out that this concept has a tremendous potential; it can be effectively used in a wide area of systems, from a very few coupled nonlinear systems to large networks with complex topology or multi-agent systems. We would like to emphasize that it is a well-accepted concept, although there is no general definition of complexity available and it is probably impossible to formulate one at all. This becomes very clear in the fact that measures of complexity known from complex systems science are rather context dependent. We have given some classification of such measures into traditional and alternative ones. Comparing them with combinatorial, conceptual, and analytical complexity, we have found that the latter ones are in between these two classes. Despite the lack of a general definition, one needs some basic ingredients for a system to become complex, mainly to mention some kind of feedback coupling, also called cooperation, and some nonlinearity. We have especially shown how coupling or cooperation generates complexity in various systems and how one can describe such behavior.

It is important to note that despite the strong recent progress of this approach, there are many challenging open methodological problems, i.e. in evolving systems, in networks of substantially different networks, in retrieving large complex systems from observations and experiments, or in modeling feedbacks and cooperation. Advancements in these directions would open new essential fields of application, such as coevolution of natural and socioeconomic subsystems of the Earth system and its relationship to planetary boundaries.

References

Ainslie, G., and Haslam, N. (eds.) (1992). 'Hyperbolic Discounting', in G. Loewenstein and J. Elster *Choice over Time*, New York, NY: Russell Sage Foundation, 57–92.

Auer, S., Heitzig, J., Kornek, U., Schöll, E., and Kurths, J. (2015). 'The dynamics of coalition formation on complex networks', *Nature Scientific Reports*, 5: 13386. doi:10.1038/srep13386

Aumann, R. J. (1959). 'Acceptable Points in General Cooperative n-Person Games', in *Contributions to the Theory of Games*, Vol. 4, Princeton, NJ: Princeton University Press.

Aumann, R. J. (2006). 'War and Peace', *Proceedings of the National Academy of Sciences of the United States of America*, 103 (46): 17075–8. doi:10.1073/pnas.0608329103.

Blaschke, J. and Lapp, T. (2012). 'Breath Figures: Nucleation, Growth, Coalescence, and the Size Distribution of Droplets', in *Fluid-Structure Interactions in Soft-Matter Systems: From the Mesoscale to the Macroscale*, Prato, Italy: Monash University, 103.

Boccaletti, S., Latora, V., Moreno, Y., Chavez, M. and Hwang, D. U. (2006). 'Complex Networks: Structure and Dynamics', *Physics Reports*, 424 (4–5): 175–308. doi:10.1016/j.physrep.2005.10.009.

Boers, N., Bookhagen, B., Barbosa, H. M. J., Marwan, N., Kurths, J. and Marengo, J. A. (2014). 'Prediction of Extreme Floods in the Eastern Central Andes Based on a Complex Networks Approach', *Nature Communications*, 5: 5199. doi:10.1038/ncomms6199.

Brams, S. J., and Wittman, D. (1981). 'Nonmyopic Equilibria in 2x2 Games', *Conflict Management and Peace Science*, 6 (1): 39–62. doi:10.1177/073889428100600103.

Dasgupta, P. (2008). 'Discounting Climate Change', *Journal of Risk and Uncertainty*, 37 (2–3): 141–69.

Fang, L., Hipel, K. W. and Kilgour, D. M. (1989). 'Conflict Models in Graph Form: Solution Concepts and Their Interrelationships', *European Journal of Operational Research*, 41 (1): 86–100.

Fishburn, P. C. (1968). 'Utility Theory', *Management Science*, 14 (5): 335–78.

Gammaitoni, L., Hänggi, P., Jung, P. and Marchesoni, F. (1998). 'Stochastic Resonance', *Reviews of Modern Physics*, 70 (1): 223–87. doi:10.1103/RevModPhys.70.223.

Gintis, H. (2009). *The Bounds of Reason: Game Theory and the Unification of the Behavioral Sciences*, Princeton, NJ / Woodstock, NY: Princeton University Press.

Heitzig, J. (2012). 'Bottom-Up Strategic Linking of Carbon Markets: Which Climate Coalitions Would Farsighted Players Form?', *SSRN Environmental Economics eJournal*, 5: 1–34. doi:10.2139/ssrn.2274724.

Heitzig, J., Lessmann, K. and Zou, Y. (2011). 'Self-Enforcing Strategies to Deter Free-Riding in the Climate Change Mitigation Game and Other Repeated Public Good Games', *Proceedings of the National Academy of Sciences of the United States of America*, 108 (38): 15739–44.

Heitzig, J. and Reinhold, J. (2000). 'The Number of Unlabeled Orders on Fourteen Elements', *Order*, 17 (4): 333–41. doi:10.1023/A:1006431609027.

Heitzig, J. and Simmons, F. W. (2012). 'Some Chance for Consensus: Voting Methods for Which Consensus Is an Equilibrium', *Social Choice and Welfare*, 38 (1): 43–57. doi:10.1007/s00355–010–0517-y.

Holme, P. and Newman, M. E. J. (2006). 'Nonequilibrium Phase Transition in the Coevolution of Networks and Opinions', *Physical Review*, E 74: 056108. doi:10.1103/PhysRevE.74.056108.

Kahneman, D. and Tversky, A. (1979). 'Prospect Theory: An Analysis of Decision Under Risk', *Econometrica: Journal of the Econometric Society*, 47 (2): 263–92.

Kantz, H. and Schreiber, T. (2003). *Nonlinear Time Series Analysis*, Cambridge, MA: Cambridge University Press.

Kleitman, D. J. and Rothschild, B. L. (1975). 'Asymptotic Enumeration of Partial Orders On a Finite Set', *Transactions of the American Mathematical Society*, 205: 205–20.

Laslier, J.-F. (1997). *Tournament Solutions and Majority Voting*, Berlin / New York, NY: Springer.

Loomes, G. and Sugden, R. (1982). 'Regret Theory: An Alternative Theory of Rational Choice Under Uncertainty', *Economic Journal*, 92 (368): 805–24.

Marwan, N., Kurths, J., Thomsen, J., Felsenberg, D. and Saparin, J. (2009). 'Three-Dimensional Quantification of Structures in Trabecular Bone Using Measures of Complexity', *Physical Review*, E 79: 021903. doi:10.1103/PhysRevE.79.021903.

Marwan, N., Romano, M. C., Thiel, M. and Kurths, J. (2007). 'Recurrence Plots for the Analysis of Complex Systems', *Physics Reports*, 438 (5): 237–329. doi:10.1016/j.physrep.2006.11.001.

Menck, P. J., Heitzig, J., Marwan, N. and Kurths, J. (2013). 'How Basin Stability Complements the Linear-Stability Paradigm', *Nature Physics*, 9 (2): 89–92. doi:10.1038/nphys2516.

Pikovsky, A. and Kurths, J. (1997). 'Coherence Resonance in a Noise-Driven Excitable System', *Physical Review Letters*, 78 (5): 775–8. doi:10.1103/PhysRevLett.78.775.

Quiggin, J. (1982). 'A Theory of Anticipated Utility', *Journal of Economic Behavior and Organization*, 3 (4): 323–43.

Raab, C. and Kurths, J. (2001). 'Estimation of Large-Scale Dimension Densities', *Physical Review*, E 64: 016216. doi:10.1103/PhysRevE.64.016216.

Rehfeld, K., Marwan, N., Breitenbach, S. F. M. and Kurths, J. (2013). 'Late Holocene Asian Summer Monsoon Dar and Peace', *Climate Dynamics*, 41 (1): 3–19. doi:10.1007/s00382–012–1448-3.

Scheffer, M., Bascompte, J., Brock, W. A., Brovkin, V., Carpenter, S. R., Dakos, V., Held, H., van Nes, E. H., Rietkerk, M. and Sugihara, G. (2009). 'Early-Warning Signals for Critical Transitions', *Nature*, 461 (7260): 53–9. doi:10.1038/nature08227.

Sen, A. (1974). 'Informational Bases of Alternative Welfare Approaches', *Journal of Public Economics*, 3 (4): 387–403.

Sorin, S. (1986). 'On Repeated Games with Complete Information', *Mathematics of Operations Research*, 11 (1): 147–60.

Sprott, J.C. (2003). *Chaos and Time-Series Analysis*, Oxford / New York, NY: Oxford University Press.

Tversky, A. and Kahneman, D. (1986). 'Rational Choice and the Framing of Decisions', *Journal of Business*, 59 (4): S251–78.

van Damme, E. (1989). 'Renegotiation-Proof Equilibria in Repeated Prisoners' Dilemma', *Journal of Economic Theory*, 47 (1): 206–17. doi:10.1016/0022–0531(89)90111–7.

Wackerbauer, R., Witt, A., Atmanspacher, H., Kurths, J. and Scheingraber, H. (1994). 'A Comparative Classification of Complexity Measures', *Chaos, Solitons & Fractals*, 4 (1): 133–73.

Watts, D.J. and Strogatz, S.H. (1998). 'Collective Dynamics of Small-World" Networks', *Nature*, 393 (6684): 440–2. doi:10.1038/30918.

Weitzman, M.L. (2001). 'Gamma Discounting', *American Economic Review*, 91 (1): 260–71.

Wessel, N., Ziehmann, C., Kurths, J., Meyerfeldt, U., Schirdewan, A. and Voss, A. (2000). 'Short-Term Forecasting of Life-Threatening Cardiac Arrhythmias Based on Symbolic Dynamics and Finite-Time Growth Rates', *Physical Review. E, Statistical Physics, Plasmas, Fluids, and Related Interdisciplinary Topics*, 61 (1): 733–9.

Willson, S.J. (1998). 'Long-Term Behavior in the Theory of Moves', *Theory and Decision*, 45 (3): 201–40.

8 The concrete utopia of the gift

A genuine sociological approach to interdisciplinary cooperation theory

Claus Leggewie

Introduction

Understood as intentional collaboration between individuals, groups, and larger collective actors with a common goal in mind, cooperation is being called into question at many levels within our culturally diverse global society. How can systems as complex as 'our' global society cultivate common interests (and is it 'our' society at all)? How do cultural differences hinder or facilitate this process? And how do we avoid social dilemmas and curb the selfish practice of free-riding? In today's knowledge systems and disciplines, opportunities for cooperation are generally determined by economic factors (as an expression of individual utility maximization) or psychological factors (with regard to positive or negative emotional disposition). On the one hand, they revolve around 'interests', which, in the best-case scenario, can be pooled to generate shared benefits and the moods that contribute thereto or detract therefrom. On the other hand, from a natural sciences perspective predispositions come into play that give varying impressions of how suited to cooperation individuals are.

While these observations are undoubtedly important when assessing opportunities for and barriers to global cooperation in the 21st century, there is a surprising lack of *genuine* social-sciences and cultural-studies approaches within interdisciplinary cooperation research. Such approaches must provide a plausible explanation of social interaction (the kind that could be considered cooperative or collaborative) from a sociological angle, that is, from the perspective of a person's '*social* nature', which expresses itself in specific social and cultural contexts (Tomasello 2014a, 2014b). Cooperative relationships are, after all, based not only on matching interests, tit for tat, shared expectations of benefits, and rigid mutual obligations of *homo economicus*. Cooperation is also and especially a mark of the 'pointless' play of children: for instance, a musical ensemble improvises not (only) because they want to sell a CD; the dancers in a *corps de ballet* work together for the sheer joy of it; and an amateur choir sings solely for the sake of singing together.[1] These small examples demonstrate the *intrinsic* value of cooperation as such, a value that is based on empathy and emerges from itself in the process of current interaction, often unintentionally or occasionally counter-intentionally.

DOI: 10.4324/9781315691657-10

It hardly needs stressing, then, that cooperation is originally a social-sciences topic. One foundational, now classic contribution to sociological cooperation research is the theory of gift exchange, which addresses non-utilitarian social relationships, interaction, and reciprocity between groups and communities of individuals. It was formulated by Marcel Mauss in the 1920s on the basis of ethnological field studies of people groups whose living conditions have since radically changed in the course of economic and cultural globalization. I would like to show in this chapter that 'the gift' can be employed effectively to describe and explain current cooperation relationships, too, and that it could even be used to overcome barriers to cooperation nowadays.

Such barriers are virtually ubiquitous nowadays. When the East-West conflict came to an end, it was expected that 'humankind', in the interests of a peace dividend following the end of the Cold War, would turn its attention to the problem of safeguarding global public goods, an issue supposedly transcending political differences. Instead, we have fallen back into territorial conflicts (in eastern Ukraine, for example) and religious wars (such as the one between Shias and Sunnis in the Middle East) that were thought to have been consigned to the past. For example, almost all actors in our world system see an urgent need for an agreement on averting the dangers of climate change, but we have so far failed to reach one. And our response to the bank collapses of 2008, which showed clearly just how dysfunctional the financial markets were, has been limited to short-term crisis management. States have also largely sidestepped their responsibility to protect (R2P) in the event of flagrant human rights abuses and crimes against humanity. The Syrian civil war with its many victims is just one example.

Within a multipolar world system, there is no hegemonic power to coerce others into acting cooperatively, nor is there an effective multilateral mechanism for achieving compromise, nor a global negotiating process that is not subject to the presentist practice of pursuing short-term interests.[2] Now more than ever, our global society appears to be stuck in a 'Prisoner's Dilemma' in which the short-term benefits to one player or a small number of players are favored over the medium and long-term benefits to all players. This chapter aims to show how a paradigm shift based on a sociological theory of cooperation can provide a way out of this dilemma.

The theory of the gift

The sociologist Marcel Mauss began his comparative studies on the exchange of gifts around 1900, elaborating systematically on his findings in *Essai sur le don* in 1923/4.[3] The explanandum comprised the inherent binding force of the gift and the paradox that, while a gift is given voluntarily, it *must* always be reciprocated, that is, there is an *obligation* to give a gift in return. A gift involves three obligations: to give, to receive, and to reciprocate. A fourth motive explicitly stated by Mauss, but one that has often been overlooked due to readers filtering out the study's socioreligious content, is that of giving gifts to the gods through animal sacrifice or self-sacrifice. Gifts do not have to be reciprocated directly to the giver. Instead, as the majority of Mauss's case studies show, they are reciprocated between collectives and even generations. Unlike the cooperation relationships examined in social psychology and game theory, the theory of the gift goes beyond direct reciprocity between A and B to emphasize generalized reciprocity $(A \rightarrow B \rightarrow C \ldots N \rightarrow A)$.

It is here that we find the key difference between gift exchange and the exchange of equivalences: from Mauss's perspective, the gift has less to do with economic and material exchange and more to do with material goods as a medium for the symbolic creation, articulation, and stabilization of social relationships. Mauss attributed the widespread loss of integrative power within modern gift-giving structures to the increasing lack of institutionalized and lifeworld-compatible structures of giving, receiving, and reciprocating; the reduction of the gift to an economic exchange of goods; and the spread of utilitarian individualism throughout society (Moebius 2012).

Mauss referred to the exchange of gifts as a 'total social fact' (*fait social total*):

> c'est-à-dire qu'ils mettent en branle dans certains cas la totalité de la société et de ses institutions (potlatch, clans affrontés, tribus se visitant, etc.) et dans d'autres cas seulement un très grand nombre d'institutions, en particulier lorsque ces échanges et ces contrats concernent plutôt des individus [Social phenomena that effect all (or a number of important) social institutions].
>
> (Mauss [1922–3] 2002: 102)

Giving always involves several religious, aesthetic, legal, political, and moral dimensions. Moreover, today, as in archaic times, the principle of the gift pervades the whole of society. Moebius (2006) highlights the social leverage effect of *mana*:

> The item that has been given away still carries with it a piece or an 'element' (*mana, hau*) of the giver. The recipient takes the giver into himself or herself, and the giver in turn takes possession of the recipient. Consequently, giving always involves individuals giving themselves or giving of themselves, that is, giving away a part of their person, spiritual power, *hau*, or 'spiritual essence' that transcends them as human beings. In this way, the circulation of gifts creates an obligation that at once constitutes and stabilizes the notion of sociality.

This means that '[t]he giver and the gift are not completely separated. In receiving a gift, recipients also receive into themselves the person who gave it'. As such, Moebius points out that Mauss's concept of giving and receiving in his theory of the gift has little to do with simple reciprocity, as is often assumed as a result of the study having been read primarily through a structuralist lens. Instead, it points to the ecstatic, self-transcending nature of the recipient's relationship with the giver and to the experience that the recipient upon receiving the gift has of being possessed by that item and its giver.

The final section of *Essai sur le don* is devoted to examining the current relevance of the practice of gift giving, and the moral and sociological conclusions that can be drawn for the 20th century from a historical and ethnological case study. Like (his uncle) Émile Durkheim, Mauss is looking for a principle to safeguard morality and solidarity in modern society. Consequently, he is seeking not only to describe and analyze the gift without making a value judgment, but also to prevent modern society from succumbing to interests of a purely profit-making nature.

Looking at the theory from a historical perspective, issues such as reciprocity, anti-utilitarian expenditure, and the state of being possessed can be examined. If Claude Lévi-Strauss (1999) and Pierre Bourdieu (2004) see in Mauss's theory of the gift forms of exchange that point to a super-subjective, symbolic structure constituting the exchange partners and objects, then proponents of 'anti-utilitarian' thought are primarily concerned with the moments of 'unproductive waste'[4] in the theory, placing particular emphasis on the generous nature of the gift exchange analyzed by Mauss and on a presentation of the social that is not predicated on economic benefit. Gifts do not create a legal basis for obligatory reciprocation or a symmetrical order in which reciprocity can be considered a certainty, nor do they have a monetary basis, which is ultimately the quantifying factor in a utilitarian benefit calculation. Instead of creating a legal obligation, the gift, according to Adloff and Mau (2005), bears witness to a symbolic order of 'expectations of expectations' that is above both the recipient and the giver and testifies that there is a shared world. It is therefore also able to initiate cooperation, to establish a relationship between strangers and – in the case of the extraordinary gift – to restore the realm of normality when trust and facticity are questioned. This theory is supported by linking the theory of the gift back to the ethnomethodological (or constructivist) theory, developed by Émile Durkheim and elaborated upon by Goffman, Garfinkel, Sacks, and Bergmann in the context of symbolic interactionism, that social 'facts' are only created through social cooperation. It is not only gifts, but also social actions, immaterial word plays, and tactical moves that circulate until a common worldview emerges (or does not emerge, as the case may be). As such, the *homo cooperativus* differs from the utility-maximizing *homo economicus*, just as it does from the value and role-motivated *homo sociologus* in structural-functional theory.[5]

In summary, giving creates (in Durkheim's terms) social facts *sui generis*, that is, it postulates a type of sociality that cannot be attributed solely to the actions and intentions of the actors involved. This emergent sociality creates its own obligations. The gift item demands something of its recipient; it is an act of communication that compels both parties to enter into the logic of sequential events and actions. Giving a gift limits the scope for contingency; something specific is communicated; and the gift item facilitates direct contact between ego and seniority. Giving is followed by receiving (or not, as the case many be), which is then followed by reciprocation (or not, as the case may be) (Bedorf 2010). This means that a universally applicable sphere of sociality can emerge in principle even in the absence of oral communication and a shared culture, that is, in the midst of 'otherness'. The oscillation of gifts creates a common order of interaction, which is typically accompanied by feelings of antagonism. Those who give gifts find honor and prestige, while those who receive them are put in an inferior position and thereby are shamed. Under egalitarian conditions, givers and recipients keep swapping positions, and so this exchange does not have to result in a permanent hierarchy. The feelings and obligations arising from the exchange of gifts can therefore be traced back to the inherent logic of the order of interaction itself and not primarily to the motives (be they selfish or altruistically normative) of the actors involved.

Put simply, in a global societal context cooperation cannot rely (solely) on utilitarian and culturally normative guarantees. Instead, it is a phenomenon that must bring about its own existence. According to Mauss, a 'culture of cooperation' can emerge from *practices* of cooperation and exchange, and these practices create specific, *affective* bonds that stabilize them. In forms of cooperation involving reciprocal giving, there is a joint focusing of attention that may produce shared emotions from which symbolizations of commonality can arise – in what one could call a secularized form of *mana* or emotional energy (Collins 2004). Thus cooperation is not brought about by the sheer maximization of individual utility or by an *a priori* shared culture in the form of stored knowledge and common values and norms. Instead, it arises from practices which generate their own emotional intensity from a common focus on a given activity, thereby bringing individuals together. Where a social unit is associated with positive emotions, an affective bond develops with that group (solidarity), and where it is associated with negative feelings a weak affective bond develops, in which case the cooperation relationship does not have an affective basis (Lawler 2001). The exchange of gifts can help to create a common cognitive and emotional focus, with normativity arising out of this form of shared intentionality. Values and norms can then be generated from common goals and emotions (though less so the other way around). While gifts may be able to institute new rituals with a shared focus on the 'sacred', even where there is a lack of common values and norms, they are still contingent in that they can succeed or fail in their purpose. At this point it is necessary to examine Mauss's theory from a theoretical and empirical perspective to ascertain whether gifts are able of their own accord to create opportunities for self-transcendence and self-commitment, thereby indirectly creating orders of cooperative interaction *sui generis*.

The global gift: Debt and guilt, forgiveness and adoption

It is now time to put cooperation theory to good use with regard to the current cooperation problems already mentioned. It is interesting to note that Mauss developed his ethnological theory against the backdrop of and with clear reference to a contemporary issue of his day, namely, as indicated by Mallard (2011), the repayment of debts and the reparations that the German Reich had to pay to the Allied Powers after its defeat in the First World War. As such, Mauss in his less well-known 'political writings' took the position that, while the German

Reich certainly had obligations to make repayments and reparations, it was possible to temper these obligations through moratoria and debt relief measures to prevent debtors (and creditors) rising up in an act of nationalistic defiance. Mauss also worked to promote a liberal socialist movement during the interwar period and saw the exchange of gifts as providing a matrix for cross-border solidarity, for example as part of the cooperative movement, which he held in high regard. Once again, the 'archaic' practices provided the thought patterns. For example, the Kula ring is understood as an intertribal, and therefore in some respects international, system of gift exchange. Oversimplifying matters a little, we could say that Durkheim understood solidarity as being intra-societal, while Mauss considered it to be inter-societal. For Mauss, societies were always fundamentally reliant on 'international', that is intercultural, exchange.

'The proof of the pudding is in the eating', as the old saying goes. It is possible to demonstrate the vitality and effectiveness of the gift paradigm if its structural elements can be traced in current cooperation processes or if it can be presented as a plausible alternative to failing cooperation. While this chapter is too short to achieve this, it will identify five empirically and conceptually promising areas of research.

(1) The focus is once again on the current issue of debt, budget deficits in the public and private sectors, and the national debt of wealthy OECD countries and, more particularly, peripheral countries in the global South. Compared with the sanctions imposed by the Treaty of Versailles, which were considered draconian, West Germany was dealt with relatively leniently after the Second World War. While the London Debt Agreement did enshrine German war guilt in law, it recognized the fledgling Federal Republic as an ally, giving it breathing space to rebuild and put its development on a self-sustaining footing, as this was in the (Western) Allied Powers' own interest.

In the case of the debt-ridden countries of southern Europe and the global South today, it is legitimate to ask the question of whether the creditors (states and banks) wish to force these countries to pay back their debts (at the cost in this case of an inexorable collapse) or to provide debt relief and grant moratoriums on payments, which should be linked to development measures, in order to enable self-sustaining development and to foster self-respect.[6]

It would appear that such generosity is destined to fail in the face of the sad realism of the 'debt crisis'. However, as the bargaining between the leftist government of Greece and the 'troika' and the European Union's ministers of finance in January/February 2015 may prove, it is those rescue plans that strive to take account of 'reality' but that fail to take account of any options involving generous debt relief measures that do not make any demands in return (such as compliance on the part of the Irish, Greeks, etc., in future) that have failed or are doomed to failure. The idea of debt forgiveness seems less bizarre if we take into account once more the fact that debtors and creditors are *mutually* entangled, and that this also entails a loss of freedom to act on the part of those who, in the event of the southern European economies collapsing under the weight of debt repayment demands, would have to wait *ad calendas graecas*, in the truest sense of the phrase, for the payment of interest and the repayment of debt, thereby being sucked into the maelstrom. We need to recognize that the current financial crisis was brought about by *both* sides.

The only way to prevent a collapse is paradoxically, only at first glance, to give *more* gifts in the hope that these investments will prove more fruitful. This is where another *to queue* argument comes into view. It is not only the economies of the global South, which now extends far into the European Union, that are up to their eyeballs in debt, but also the public and private sectors of the wealthy North, which has built its prosperity largely on credit. Incidentally, we find here an analogy between the financial and environmental crises. In both cases, current generations have conducted their business at the expense of future generations, to whom they will leave a legacy of enormous debt and damage. Since the 1960s in particular, the countries of central and northwestern Europe have eaten away at the future on the basis of questionable expectations. Consumers have acquired durable goods, public authorities have built expensive infrastructure, and social policy has evened out differences within capitalist class societies through transfer payments. Several decades on and it is not only a few municipalities operating on an emergency budget that are in trouble; many European cities and municipalities are already on the brink of ruin (this is the reality of life for most people, who cannot take refuge behind walls of super wealth). They will not be able to break out of the vicious cycle they are in by putting their hope in the dividends of growth that can only be financed on credit, but rather by means of a debt haircut, freeing both themselves and their creditors.

Despite markets and market actors appearing to be fundamentally unethical (a view promoted, for example, by Nikolas Lehmann (1988)), the capitalist economy is ethical not least because debt is its essential driver and is, as Karl Polanyi and most recently David Graeber (2011) have reminded us, very closely connected to guilt. 'Functionally differentiated societies', in which the economy, politics, and morality constitute discrete spheres and market prices alone regulate supply and demand, are considered amoral in social and economic theory.[7] However, it is not as if market actors entirely exclude emotions, ethical reasoning, and moral framework from their economic activities. Certainly one purchases a product where it is cheapest, but how can one be sure of being correctly informed? And would one buy from a seller who explicitly opposed one's own norms or used the funds from the sale for a harmful cause? One may well do so as long as such things are not spoken about during the transaction, but there are cases of boycotts against, for example, an ethnic group (Jews), a company (Shell), or a product (genetically modified food). Moralizing takes place in markets on all sorts of levels, ethical consumption being but one variety among others.

Moral considerations are ubiquitous in economic life, as anthropologist and Occupy activist David Graeber pertinently reminds us when drawing attention to the intensity with which notions of 'debt' are bound up with those of moral obligation, guilt, or even sin (Graeber 2011). The etymological connection is probably nowhere as tight as it is in German: the Middle High German 'schulden' means to be obliged, to have to thank, or to become indebted (see Grimm and Grimm

1870–94). The link persists in the monetization of moral obligations and in that monetary demands are backed up by moral claims. People are as a rule convinced that debts have to be repaid, and this conviction lies at the core of the relation between money and morals, although people tend to be mistrustful of professional moneylenders. Anti-Semitism is rooted in this attitude, as are general reservations about 'the bankers'.

The link is expressed in terms of money and its 'capacity to turn morality into a matter of impersonal arithmetic – and by doing so, to justify things that would otherwise seem outrageous or obscene' (Graeber 2011: 14; see also Simmel 1987). Thus argues David Graeber, who takes the thoughts of sociologist Georg Simmel and develops them into a theory of the relation between debt and moral obligation over the past 5,000 years. In 2006, Peter Sloterdijk posed a related question: 'Is there an alternative to the blind accumulation of value? Is there an alternative to the chronic trembling in the instant of taking stock? Is there an alternative to the unrelenting compulsion to pay off one's debts?' (Sloterdijk 2010: 29). The pressure to repay debts, which suffocates whole societies and does not, as Joseph Schumpeter's (1976) theory of creative destruction claims, engender in them a spirit of entrepreneurial optimism, and the treatment of 'the' Irish, Greeks, Argentines, and others by monetary funds, the mass media, and even well-meaning observers have shown that we have in a sense chained Greece as a whole nation to a troubled past that colonizes or eliminates its future potential.

Is there an alternative to this cycle of debt? Repayment would need to be replaced by forgiveness and debt bondage by freedom.

> In a transcapitalist economy, the progressive, creative, giving, and excessive gestures need to become constitutive. Only operations that are engaged for the sake of the future have the power to explode the law of exchanging equivalences, by way of forestalling becoming-guilty and going into debt.
>
> (Sloterdijk 2010: 30–1)

From this perspective, taking radical steps to end the ugly business of repayment is the only way to make a fresh start and is a move that would also set the victims free, presumably to their own astonishment. The hopeless entanglement of the wealthy debtor countries in the aporetic situation of the Greek debtor is the most recent evidence of this.

Though such reflections seem utopian, even insane to mainstream economists, they can be grounded in an alternative economic dogma: the before mentioned theory of gift exchange, which, while it appears to be formally related to the exchange of equivalences, also contrasts with it in some respects. As has already been established, the gift goes beyond simple reciprocity in that the voluntary act of giving to another is inherently ecstatic and self-transcending, and passes along increasingly anonymized chains of giving, receiving, and reciprocating. In accepting the gift, the recipient has the experience of being possessed by the giver and the thing given. As also mentioned, the paradox lies in the fact that there is no contractual or normative *obligation* to give, receive, or reciprocate. Each party can step out of this cycle at any point if they so desire. As such, the giver cannot assume from the outset that he or she will receive something back in return for his or her gift. While gifts *are* often reciprocated in reality, the motive for giving cannot be traced back to the expectation of receiving something in return. Consequently, freedom is just as constitutive for the gift as the obligation. It will not do to appeal to the sense of obligation that is often felt to arise from a gift.

A growing number of mainstream economists appear to be applying these concepts to whole economies. In John Geanakoplos's (2011) view, rather than waiting to get rid of debt through bankruptcies, governments should 'mandate debt forgiveness' (236), while the no less acclaimed Robert Skidelsky calls John Maynard Keynes (see also Cedrini and Marchionatti 2013), a stylite of economics, to the witness stand:

> Creditors and debtors alike would be better off with a comprehensive debt relief programme, as would citizens, whose livelihoods are being destroyed as a result of governments' desperate attempts to reduce their debt. From a philosophical perspective, the debt relief approach is based on the conviction that creditors share the blame for payment defaults with debtors, as it was the creditors who issued the rotten loans in the first place. Assuming the borrower did not deceive the lender at the time of accepting the loan, then the lender is at least partially responsible for the transaction. In 1918, Keynes appealed for measures to be taken to relieve the inter-Allied war debt that had accumulated during the First World War: 'We shall never be able to move again, unless we can free our limbs from these paper shackles'. And in 1923, his appeal turned into a warning that today's political decision-makers would do well to heed: 'The absolutists of contract . . . are the real parents of revolution'.
>
> (Skidelsky 2012: n.p.)

Gift-based resource transfer (as opposed to gestures/gifts of a purely symbolic nature) is fundamentally different to market exchange, as givers do not know whether they will receive anything in return, what is being reciprocated, or when something will be reciprocated. Each of these things is in the hands of the recipient. Conclusions can be drawn from this scenario for re-establishing solidary and economically ethical bodies and forms of action, such as cooperatives, charitable aid, non-profit organizations, gifts to charity, endowments, and civic involvement. These terms belong to a field that cannot be reduced to the logic of markets or state allocation. It involves the transfer of resources on the basis of trust with no expectation of any tangible remuneration, but instead a desire to contribute to a convivial moral economy and to create material benefits for all or for many.

This is not a sugar-sweet, idealistic approach, as opponents claim. Even Mauss pointed out that, in addition to promoting solidarity and respect, gifts can also give rise to and consolidate hierarchies, disdain, and inequality. This happens whenever there is a high degree of inequality in the amount of resources possessed by different groups, meaning that gifts cannot be reciprocated. In the first instance, it may be that privileged groups do not have to reciprocate the gifts of poorly resourced groups, such as when employers only pay their workers the bare minimum (exploitation). Second, perpetual debt and power imbalances develop if one social group has insufficient resources to reciprocate gifts – typical examples would be paternalism in giving to the poor (humiliation/dependency), or another state accumulating debt as Greece did. Third, certain groups can become excluded from the flow of sought-after materials and intangible goods. In all three cases, we see a failure to establish relationships based on *equality*.

For areas such as debt relief, development aid, humanitarianism, and philanthropy this means that the act of (unilateral, paternalistic, asymmetrical) giving could lead to humiliation and disdain if there is not at the same time a realization and recognition that the gift's recipients have something of value to give in return. Mutual respect requires a reciprocal recognition that all the parties involved are able to give something. When givers indicate that recipients can also give something of value in return, then the act of giving not only brings about equality but also creates a shared world, the 'communality' referred to by Pierre Rosanvallon (2013) or the 'conviviality' described by Ivan Illich (1973).

(2) The counterpart to financial 'generosity' within the gift paradigm is philanthropy in its various forms, a phenomenon that has seen explosive growth over the last few decades and that has become a factor in transnational policy, which is symbolized (and to some degree compromised) by immensely rich patrons such as Bill Gates and Warren Buffett. Modern philanthropy, which is currently expanding in an unprecedented way, abandons and contradicts an exclusive focus on reciprocity and exchange (Pulcini 2010a, 2010b, 2012). Empirical studies show that modern philanthropy is characterized by a marked asymmetry and a definite *lack* of reciprocity. However, instead of being the object of respect and admiration, philanthropy is constantly confronted with suspicion and is therefore in need of justification. According to Pulcini's reading, this illustrates the need to overcome a way of thinking in dichotomies such as reciprocity vs. non-reciprocity, spontaneity vs. obligation, etc., and instead to focus more on the plurality of 'worlds of worth'.[8] Even if a litany of 'egoistic' motivations and gains may be detected in the history and practice of philanthropy (etymologically 'love of humanity'), it should be used in the original sense of caring, nourishing, developing, and enhancing 'what it is to be human' on both the benefactors' (by identifying and exercising their values in giving and volunteering) and beneficiaries' (by benefiting) parts. In this regard philanthropy has to be distinguished from *business* (i.e. private initiatives for private good, focusing on material prosperity) and *government* (i.e. public initiatives for public good, focusing on law and order). Instances of *philanthropy* commonly overlap with instances of *charity*, though not all charity is philanthropy, or vice versa. The difference commonly cited is that charity relieves the pains of social problems, whereas philanthropy attempts to solve those problems at their root causes (the difference between giving a hungry man a fish, and teaching him how to fish for himself).

While in material terms philanthropy is characterized by a radical asymmetry in the order of interaction, this does not call into question its relation to the theory of the gift. The issue with philanthropy is, rather, that unlike tax-funded social transfers and like commercial transactions, selective and inegalitarian preferences can prevail, and there is generally a lack of public accountability. Ethnic, religious, aesthetic, and other prejudices and stereotypes may determine the way that 'neediness' is defined when choosing which groups to support. While this is not objectionable in and of itself, it could in the overall scheme of things intensify inequalities and promote discrimination unintentionally.

(3) In this context, it is worth mentioning one type of gift that would appear essential to the future of global cooperation: the practice of adoption, recast in collective terms. An adoption is a private initiative that takes place for partially selfish motives of self-actualization (the desire to have a child), but it also involves a strong component of loving care for an individual who has been literally or symbolically orphaned. In other words, adoption involves a high degree of altruism. Again, there is no *a priori* reason to view the aspect of personal gratification critically, even if it can become excessive on occasions. An increasing number of adoptions involve children from 'poor countries', following a North-South paradigm. As such, these adoptions have an indirect but inherent element of development cooperation to them, which, as is typical in such constellations, can be ambivalent. The structural element of adoption is something worth considering when looking at global cooperation relationships. This element is expressed not only in family relationships but also in programs such as Local Agenda 21, and exhibits asymmetrical yet reciprocal patterns of reference to public goods and superordinate and unifying aims of humankind. A similar structure is also seen in the generous admission of refugees to a country or in the awarding of stipends for interested overseas students who come to a wealthy nation to receive initial or further training in order, in most cases, to return to their native region to work, thereby extending the gift to local public issues, with the stipend now indirectly benefiting third and fourth parties.

We have now touched upon the problem of scale within global cooperation. Efforts to protect public goods (as part of climate-change negotiations, for example) are frequently hampered by the fact that a problem such as climate change appears temporally and spatially abstract, as people believe that it will take place 'far away' and 'in the distant future'. Built into the gift model of loose and long-term chains of reciprocity is a temporal dimension. As such, gifts always represent an 'investment in the future' that has the next generation, and the one after that, in mind. This brings the 'far away' issue of climate change closer in both spatial and temporal terms and makes future tasks in traceable socio-biological chains of reciprocity look plausible.

(4) A corresponding element of material compensation is thus the moral aspect of 'working through the past', a process in which 'atonement' is provided for damage caused, restitution is made for property, individual perpetrators and the states representing them acknowledge their responsibility for the crimes they have committed, and victims respond to these actions by extending forgiveness (an act that is voluntary and not to be automatically expected, much less demanded). It is interesting (and unsettling) to note in this context that during the intervention

initiated by Germany, or attributed to the German Government, to resolve Greece's debt crisis, old demands for reparations payments for war crimes committed by the German Reich resurfaced. The Germans, from their experience of repayments and paying compensation after 1918 and 1945 (without doubt rightly), must know how one feels in such a situation. It can therefore hardly come as a surprise that the Greeks, in their unwillingness to pay, have in turn reminded their German taskmasters of the Holocaust and Nazi occupation and are now making their own demands for compensation. These relate on the one hand to war crimes committed by the SS and the Wehrmacht, and on the other hand to the repayment of the 476 million reichsmark loan for the financing of occupation costs that the Deutsches Reich had forced the Greek National Bank to grant it in 1942. (Even the Nazi leadership itself had announced that it would repay the loan after the end of the war.) In contrast to assertions made in the German courts and official documents, every Greek government since 1950 has insisted that these demands have in no way been satisfied as a result of the London Debt Agreement of 1953 or of the Two Plus Four Treaty of 1990.

The best-known example of a Greek compensation claim for war crimes relates to the massacre of Distomo on 10 June 1944, an act that is as yet unatoned for. According to the findings of the Landgericht (regional court) in Bonn, the events in this central Greek village are as follows: in a 'retaliation measure', the 4th SS Polizei Panzergrenadier Division murdered 218 villagers who had not participated in partisan fighting. The village was razed to the ground, the victims were old people, women, children, and infants. The atrocities were beyond imagination, as *Der Spiegel* reported in January 1988:

> Men and children alike were shot at random, women raped and butchered, with soldiers hacking the breasts off of many of them. Pregnant women were slit open, some victims were executed with bayonets. Others were beheaded or had their eyes gauged out.

These deeds have still not been dealt with under criminal law, and compensation to the tune of 37.5 million euros remains outstanding, following a 1997 ruling against the Federal Republic of Germany by a court in Livadia, Greece, on behalf of the offspring of the victims of the massacre of Distomo; the Greek government has until now refused to grant its consent for a related foreclosure process to commence concerning assets belonging to the Federal Republic of Germany (including the seizure of the Goethe Institute in Athens). Regional courts in Bonn and Cologne, the Federal Court of Justice, and the Federal Constitutional Court, as well as international courts, have dismissed civil law actions. The highest German courts have argued that, when considered under the Hague Conventions, the massacre was a military operation; the Federal Constitutional Court does not therefore recognize it specifically as a Nazi crime. As such, what would today be considered a blatant breach of international law is considered a normal act of war when viewed in the context of the time in which it was committed.

An attempt to have a mortgage on German property in Italy recognized before the Italian Court of Cassation in Rome, as the highest Italian civil court, was declared inadmissible by the International Criminal Court in The Hague and state immunity was confirmed: states cannot be sued by individuals from foreign states. The Japanese president of the International Criminal Court, Hisashi Owada, expressed regret and astonishment at the outstanding compensation and recommended the commencement of political negotiations. Here the logic of the 'reciprocity of exchange' must come to bear. The French sociologist Marcel Mauss drew attention to this kind of logic, just as John Maynard Keynes did, with reference to the treatment of the Deutsches Reich after World War I. As such, the crux of the matter lies in requesting reparations to be paid, but at a rate that does not spawn revanchism and that casts the debtor who is forced to pay as both a future cooperative partner and an actor that can contribute to Europe's general well-being (Mallard 2011).

It is well known that the demands of the Treaty of Versailles were, up until 1932, exacted rather ruthlessly, such that the Weimar Republic could be disavowed by its opponents. After World War II, the western Allies applied a different logic: more important than payments was the contribution made to a supranational economic community that could also succeed politically as a community of peace and development and overcome European nationalisms. The London Conference of 1952/3 tailored obligations attached to the servicing debts in accordance with the capacities at the time of the young Federal Republic of Germany. 'Lenient' creditors thus paradoxically enabled a so-called *Wirtschaftswunder* or 'economic miracle' and, with that, Germany's comeback as an *économie dominante* in Europe, something that the creditors could have obstructed or delayed with higher demands, assuming they had foreseen it.

Germans carry a particular responsibility, as the historian Constantin Goschler (2015: 2; cf. Schwan 2015) explains:

> The German comeback after World War II had much to do with the generosity of their former adversaries, who could in turn count on profiting from the economic strength of the Federal Republic. However, conversely, the question of reparations should not be instrumentalized for the purposes of short-term political gains, particularly since the problem can only be properly handled in the context of Europe as a whole, given the large number of countries affected. There is an urgent need to discuss anew the basis for reciprocal exchange, upon which European integration and peace after 1945 were based.

Is there an alternative to the Greek debt cycle and that of other 'debtor countries'? Could there be forgiveness in lieu of repayments and freedom in lieu of debt bondage?

> In a transcapitalistic economy, the progressive, creative, giving and excessive gestures need to become constitutive. Only operations that are engaged

for the sake of the future have the power to explode the law of exchanging equivalences, by way of forestalling becoming-guilty and going into debt.

(Sloterdijk 2010: 30)

Only a radical break with the 'odious business of repayments' would pave the way for a new beginning that allows freedom to be restored – probably to the surprise of the injured parties themselves.

In Greece, a debt conference and debt relief in a form akin to the London negotiations of 1952/3 is repeatedly encouraged or suggested. But copycat solutions of this sort are impossible for many reasons: Greece has neither caused and lost a war, nor could negotiations of this kind be conducted behind closed doors as they were at the beginning of the 1950s, including with regard to compensating the state of Israel too (against the grain of public opinion in both countries) (Diner 2015; Fleischer and Konstantinakou 2006). And debt relief cannot be allowed to distract attention from demands for the domestic reform of Greek administrative organs. It is, however, likely that one will have to embed the current challenges surrounding Greek public debt and Germany's historical responsibility in a new kind of context for negotiations. The same applies to challenges presented by the share of responsibility that international financial markets and European banks now carry. In this new context debt relief and questions of tax justice would also have to be considered, as well as how to determine reparations and individual compensation.

Hannah Arendt extolled two abilities of the *zoon politikon* that the pure *homo faber* (or *economicus*) does not possess: the capacity to *forgive* (a remedy for the irreversibility of past actions) and the ability to make and keep *promises* (a remedy for the unforeseeable nature of the future).

> Drawing on Hannah Arendt's concept of action, which is in principle very closely related to that of Mauss' gift, it is possible to describe a general category that we could call 'constitutive action'. This kind of action unlocks and creates opportunities that did not previously exist and brings something into being where there was previously nothing.
>
> (Caillé 2006: 218)

Such action allows trust to be rebuilt where there was previously only mistrust. Arendt looked in depth at forgiveness as a concept providing a fresh start with multiple options and possibilities. In doing so, she picked up on a Christian theme, historicizing and secularizing the experience of Jesus's disciples in the early church. She interpreted the personal love of Jesus in 'thoroughly earthly terms' that extended beyond the individual and private relationship between a guilty party and the one by whom that party is forgiven. It was essential to Arendt that both sides receive the freedom to make a fresh start. Both those who are forgiven and those who forgive are freed from the long-term consequences of a wicked past or deed. Just like punishment, forgiveness does not deny the wrongfulness of a deed, but it does break the deadly cycle of fixating on this guilt-ridden past (see Kodalle's (2013) monograph).

Beginning with the Holocaust debate in the 1980s, the recognition of the relationship between reparations payments and the process of 'working through the past' or through transnational justice issues in the wake of war crimes, political crimes, ethnic cleansing, and so forth (that is, providing moral and material compensation for past wrongs) has given rise to a global reparations movement. This movement encompasses historical slavery, the removal and extermination of indigenous peoples, colonial crimes, and numerous genocides, but also extends to the ongoing campaign to secure restitution for various forms of stolen art. It is not possible to explore this issue in greater detail here, but it would likely prove fascinating not only to discuss these global interactions from an international-law, historical-political, and moral perspective, but also to view them *ex negativo* in the context of the gift theory, where violent theft and mass killings are 'atoned for' from an inclusive cooperation angle through acknowledgement of moral responsibility and material compensation.

(5) The naturalization of stateless persons, which the UN has encouraged and postulated in several conventions, shows what an indirect gift could look like from this angle. The UNHCR in Geneva estimates that there are at least 10 million stateless persons in 2014. These are individuals who do not have the nationality of the country in which they are living. Being stateless severely restricts their access to education, health care, and the labor market, as well as their freedom of movement, and they live in constant fear of deportation. Most stateless individuals are victims of recent ethnically and religiously motivated discrimination, and the overwhelming majority of them have fled (civil) war. The number of stateless persons is growing, not only because individuals are fleeing their countries but also because, according to the UNHCR, every 10 minutes a baby is born stateless somewhere in the world, with the extralegal status being inherited from one generation to the next, potentially on a permanent basis. It must be obvious to a European community, which has compromised its position historically as a result of colonial crimes and various forms of ethnic and political cleansing, some of them committed in the more recent past, that it needs to make it easier for individuals to be awarded citizenship in a European country and to put an end to statelessness.

In this chapter it was shown that the sociological paradigm of the gift could be used as a valuable pattern for global cooperation in a non-utilitarian, pragmatic way. The case of the Greek 'debt crisis' shows the entanglement of economic and moral obligations which should be linked together as a tool for current crisis management and debt regulation. The patterns of 'political adoption' (e.g. in the German program of sustainable development partnerships of the 'Lokale Agenda 21'), transnational citizenship and balanced philanthropy may be further institutionalizations of a non-utilitarian 'do-ut-des' paradigm in International Relations (Ramel 2004).

Notes

1 This aspect is stressed by Hyde (2007) and by the artist Jochen Gerz during the 'Gifts of Cooperation' Masterclass at the Centre for Global Cooperation Research in Essen from 22 to 26 September 2014.

2 As always, there are exceptions: one example of successful cooperation is the Montreal Protocol on Substances that Deplete the Ozone Layer, which paved the way for the Vienna Convention for the Protection of the Ozone Layer and which has been in force since January 1989.

3 Mauss built on the ethnographic research work of Robert Hertz, Bronislaw Malinowski, and Franz Boas, as well as on comparative studies of a range of national legal systems; see also Liebersohn 2010.

4 This is an aspect taken up by Georges Bataille, Michel Leiris, and other members of the *Collège de Sociologie*.

5 Also worthy of mention are Jacques Derrida's opposition to reciprocal theories of gift exchange and his emphasis on the obligation to give without any expected reciprocity. In a more recent interpretation of Mauss' gift study, Marcel Hénaff views the gift as a symbolic practice of performatively establishing social relationships and bonds at the level of recognition, cf. Hénaff 2009.

6 A case study is provided in Leggewie (2013); the following reflections build on and expand this illustration.

7 For discussion of this thesis, see Stehr (2007); cf. Luhmann (1988) and Polanyi (1944).

8 We here do not refer to the historical tradition of philanthropy since Antiquity, or the religious context of giving and receiving; in the Roman Catholic dogma the notions of gift, sacrifice, offering, and donation are omnipresent.

References

Adloff, F. and Mau, S. (2005): 'Zur Theorie der Gabe und der Reziprozität', in F. Adloff and S. Mau (eds.) *Vom Geben und Nehmen. Zur Soziologie der Reziprozität*. Frankfurt am Main: Campus, 9–57.

Bedorf, T. (2010) *Verkennende Anerkennung. Über Identität und Politik*, Suhrkamp: Berlin

Bourdieu, P. (2004). 'Marcel Mauss aujourd'hui', *Sociologie et Société*, 36 (2): 15–22.

Caillé, A. (2006). 'Weder methodologischer Holismus noch methodologischer Individualismus. Marcel Mauss und das Paradigma der Gabe', in S. Moebius and C. Papilloud (eds.) *Gift – Marcel Mauss' Kulturtheorie der Gabe*, Wiesbaden: Verlag für Sozialwissenschaften, 161–214.

Cedrini, M. A. and Marchionatti, R. (2013). 'On the Theoretical and Practical Relevance of the Concept of the Gift to the Development of a Non-Imperialist Economics', *The Department of Economics and Statistics 'Cognetti de Martiis' Working Papers Series*, No. 48/2013.

Collins, R. (2004). *Interaction Ritual Chains*, Princeton, NJ: Princeton University Press.

Diner, D. (2015). *Rituelle Distanz: Israels deutsche Frage*, München: Deutsche-Verlags-Anstalt.

Fleischer, H. and Konstantinakou, D. (2006). 'Ad calendas graecas? Griechenland und die deutsche Wiedergutmachung', in H. G. Hockerts, C. Moisel, and T. Winstel (eds.) *Grenzen der Wiedergutmachung: Die Entschädigung für NS-Verfolgte in West- und Osteuropa 1945–2000*, Göttingen: Wallstein Verlag, 375–457.

Geanakoplos J. (2011). 'Panel Statement: Endogenous Leverage and Default', in M. Jarocinski, F. Smets, and C. Thimann (eds.) *Approaches to Monetary Policy Revisited – Lessons from the Crisis, 6th ECB Central Banking Conference, 18–19 November 2010*, Frankfurt am Main: European Central Bank, 220–38.

Goschler, C. (2015). 'Schuld und Schulden', *Süddeutsche Zeitung*, 19 March, 2.

Graeber, D. (2011). *Debt: The First 5000 Years*, New York, NY: Melville House.

Grimm, J. and Grimm, W. (1870–94). 'Schuld', in J. Grimm and W. Grimm (eds.) *Deutsches Wörterbuch*, last accessed on April 26, 2015, at http://www.woerterbuchnetz.de/DWB?lemma=schuld.

Hénaff, M. (2009). *Der Preis der Wahrheit. Gabe, Geld und Philosophie*, Frankfurt am Main: Suhrkamp.

Hyde, L. (2007). *The Gift: Creativity and the Artist in the Modern World*, New York, NY: Vintage Books.

Illich, I. (1973). *Tools for Conviviality*, last accessed on April 26, 2015, at http://eekim.com/ba/bookclub/illich/tools.pdf.

Kodalle, K.-M. (2013). *Verzeihung denken. Die verkannte Grundlage humaner Verhältnisse*, Paderborn: Wilhelm Fink.

Lawler, E. J. (2001). 'An Affect Theory of Social Exchange', *American Journal of Sociology*, 107 (2): 321–52.

Leggewie, C. (2013). *Zukunft im Süden. Wie die Mittelmeerunion Europa wiederbeleben kann*, Hamburg: Edition Körber Stiftung.

Lehmann, N. (1988). *Die Wirtschaft der Gesellschaft*, Frankfurt am Main: Suhrkamp.

Lévi-Strauss, C. (1999). 'Einleitung in das Werk von Marcel Mauss', in *Marcel Mauss: Soziologie und Anthropologie*, Vol. 1, Frankfurt am Main: Fischer, 7–41.

Liebersohn, H. (2010). *The Return of the Gift: European History of a Global Idea*, Cambridge: Cambridge University Press.

Luhmann, N. (1988). *Die Wirtschaft der Gesellschaft*, Frankfurt am Main: Suhrkamp.

Mallard, G. (2011). 'The Gift Revisited: Marcel Mauss on War, Debt, and the Politics of Reparations', *American Sociological Association*, 29 (4): 225–47.

Mauss, M. [1922–3] (2002). *Essai sur le don. Formes et raisons de l'échange dans les sociétés primitives*, last accessed August 16, 2015, at http://classiques.uqac.ca/classiques/mauss_marcel/socio_et_anthropo/2_essai_sur_le_don/essai_sur_le_don.pdf

Moebius, Stephan (2006). *Marcel Mauss*, Konstanz: UVK.

Moebius, S. (2012). 'Art. Mauss, Die Gabe', in C. Leggewie et al. (eds.) *Schlüsselwerke der Kulturwissenschaften*, Bielefeld: Transcript, 47–9.

Polanyi, K. (1944). *The Great Transformation*, New York, NY: Farrar and Rinehart.

Pulcini, E. (2010a). 'The Responsible Subject in the Global Age', *Science and Engineering Ethics*, 16: 447–61.

Pulcini, E. (2010b). 'Le don à l'age de la mondialisation', in *Revue du Mauss*, No. 36 (Mauss vivant), Paris: La Découverte, 210–18.

Pulcini, E. (2012). *Care of the World: Fear and Responsibility in the Global Age*, Dordrecht: Springer.

Ramel, F. (2004). 'Marcel Mauss et l'étude des relations interationales: un héritage oublié', *Sociologie et sociétés*, 36 (2): 227–45.

Rosanvallon, P. (2013). *The Society of Equals*, Cambridge, MA: Harvard University Press.

Schumpeter, J.A. (1976) *Capitalism, Socialism, and Democracy*, London: Allen & Unwin.

Schwan, G. (2015). 'Das reiche Deutschland wirkt peinlich', *Spiegel Online*, 17 March, last accessed on March 17, 2015, at http://www.spiegel.de/politik/deutschland/griechenland-schwan-fordert-entschaedigung-fuer-ns-verbrechen-a-1023956.html.

Skidelsky, R. (2012). *Financial Times Deutschland*, 19 April.

Simmel, G. (1987). 'Gesamtausgabe in 24 Bänden', Vol. 6, in D. P. Frisby and Köhnke, K. C. (eds.) *Philosophie des Geldes*, Frankfurt am Main: Suhrkamp.

Sloterdijk, P. (2008, engl. 2010). *Zorn und Zeit. Politisch-psychologischer Versuch*, Frankfurt am Main: Suhrkamp.

Stehr, N. (2007). *Die Moralisierung der Märkte: Eine Gesellschaftstheorie*, Frankfurt am Main: Suhrkamp.

Tomasello, M. (2014a). 'The Ultra-Social Animal', *European Journal of Social Psychology*, 44 (3): 187–94.

Tomasello, M. (2014b). *A Natural History of Human Thinking*, Cambridge, MA: Harvard University Press.

Part III

Interdisciplinary approaches to global cooperation

9 The possibilities of global we-identities

Gianluca Grimalda

Introduction

Social identity, understood as an individual's sense of identification with and emotional attachment to a group, is widely regarded as a potent instrument to boost cooperation with others. However, groups are normally constructed in terms of what social psychologists call 'ingroups' and 'outgroups' (Brewer 1999), or what anthropologists call an 'ethnic psychology' (Henrich and Henrich 2007), that is, the tendency to treat favorably members of one's own group but to treat unfavorably outsiders. Such 'we' vs. 'them' mentality may be at the same time a strong trigger of cooperation within the ingroup but detrimental for cooperation across outgroups (Choi and Bowles 2007). This would be particularly worrisome for global cooperation, which calls for joint action on a planetary scale and thus involves widely dispersed and culturally different outgroups to come together for the common good.

In this chapter I address these issues reporting experimental results from a pioneering study[1] conducted in six countries at very different stages of their economic, social, and political involvement in globality. I analyze measures of individual identifications with the local, national, and global communities, as well as their level of active involvement in economic and social networks or relationships that are global in character. Experimental measures of an individual's propensity to cooperate with global others for the provision of public goods are also analyzed. The main message coming from the study is that global social identity seems to be a positive and strong trigger of global cooperation. People who report high levels of identification with the global community are significantly more likely to cooperate in experimental public goods problems. Moreover, social identity seems to act as a mediator in the positive effect that active participation in global networks has on cooperation. This is consistent with what has been called the 'cosmopolitan hypothesis' (Buchan et al. 2009). That is the idea that as the process of globalization spreads, individuals become more accustomed to think of others as being part of their own 'we-group' rather than being associated with the 'them-group'. Therefore, rather than being a force that radicalizes attachment to traditional groups and loyalties, this study suggests that globalization seems to favor the construction of inclusive sense of identities that are significantly associated with a heightened propensity to cooperate.

DOI: 10.4324/9781315691657-12

The chapter is organized as follows. I first offer an overview of the theoretical and empirical bases of social identity and sketch out theoretical accounts of why social identity is relevant for global cooperation. I then describe the design of this study and present the main results. First, I report an analysis of how social identities differ across countries and which demographic and attitudinal factors are associated with global social identity. Second, I report the results of a mediation analysis that supports the cosmopolitan hypothesis. Third, I analyze the reciprocal basis of cooperation and its correlation with global social identity. I then critically discuss the generalizability of these findings. To conclude I endeavor to put forward a tentative policy agenda for the 'globality-minded policy-maker'.

Defining the concepts: Social identity, cooperation, and globalization

A review of social identity theory

Social identity has been defined as *'a person's sense of self derived from perceived membership in social groups'* (Chen and Li 2009). According to the theory developed by Tajfel and Turner (1979), social identity has three major components. First, *categorization* is the psychological process of assigning people to categories. For instance, people may be described on the basis of their religion, their gender, or their occupation. Categorization is not limited to other people but can also be applied to the self. Second, *identification* is the process whereby an individual associates himself/herself with certain groups. The literature makes a key distinction between the 'ingroup', i.e. the group with which one identifies, and the 'outgroup', i.e. the group with which one does *not* identify. The outgroup may also be a residual category, i.e. all others not belonging to the ingroup. Third, *comparison* is the process whereby we compare our groups with other groups, generally creating a favorable bias toward the group to which we belong.

A large body of experimental evidence shows that social identity *means* something to individuals. Once a person categorizes himself/herself as part of a group, he/she adopts behaviors that are consistent with the stereotypes associated with that group identity in fields as disparate as performance in math tests, walking speed, and person perception (Akerlof and Kranton 2000; Bargh and Pietromonaco 1982; Shih, Pittinsky, and Ambady 1999). Moreover, once individuals identify with groups they tend to give preferential treatments to ingroup members over other people. This occurs even in so-called minimal groups (Tajfel and Turner 1979), where people are assigned to groups in the laboratory on the basis of arbitrary criteria, such as a participant's tastes in paintings. People rate other ingroup members as having more agreeable characteristics than people belonging to the outgroup, and assign more money to fellow ingroup members than to outgroup members. Such 'ingroup favoritism' also seems to carry over to strategic interactions such as coordination and cooperation problems. Although recent research has somehow reduced the relevance of ingroup favoritism in minimal groups (Yamagishi 2007; Charness, Rigotti, and Rustichini 2007), favoritism seems to lead to higher cooperation rates when groups are 'homogenous' – i.e. formed by people being assigned to the same group – rather than 'heterogeneous' (Brewer 1999; Charness et al. 2007; Chen and Li 2009; Eckel and Grossman 2005; Koopmans and Rebers 2009).

In experiments on cooperation conducted with naturally occurring groups, ingroup favoritism has been found to emerge when groups are assigned according to ethnicity (Bernhard, Fischbacher, and Fehr 2006; Fershtman, Gneezy, and Verboven 2005), nationality (Finocchiaro Castro 2008), community of residence (Falk and Zehnder 2013; Ruffle and Sosis 2006), or exogenous random assignment to groups (Goette, Huffman, and Meier 2006). However, ingroup favoritism does not seem to be a universal characteristic of human behavior. Other studies find either no or little ingroup bias effect between some ethnic groups (Fershtman and Gneezy 2001; Whitt and Wilson 2007), or even *outgroup* favoritism (Tanaka and Camerer 2010), which is linked to social status. Indeed, ingroup solidarity may be higher in some social groups than others (Hoff, Kshetramade, and Fehr 2011) and may be linked to ethnic-specific social norms (Habyarimana et al. 2007).

This evidence suggests that ingroup favoritism is a primary psychological mechanism for individuals, but that a wide array of cultural and social factors may weaken, annul, or even reverse the ingroup phenomenon as observed in laboratories.

Does social identity matter for cooperation? And if it does, is it beneficial?

Although a number of alternative mechanisms have been proposed in the literature, I focus here on two accounts that have received the most attention (see also Buchan et al. 2011). One theory of ingroup cooperation is based on the idea that shared group membership gives rise to group-based trust, namely, the general expectancy that others will be cooperative within the ingroup (Brewer 1986; Yamagishi and Kiyonari 2000). Ingroup trust is the general expectation held by a group member that other group members will cooperate for the very fact of belonging to the same group. This expectation is grounded on norms of reciprocity that are strong in intra-group interactions and weaker or absent across group boundaries (Tanis and Postmes 2005). Reciprocity is defined here as the willingness to respond to beneficial (harming) actions to oneself *from* others with beneficial (harming) actions *to* others (Falk and Fischbacher 2006). Expecting that others will behave cooperatively reduces the fear that one's own cooperation will be wasted. It simply follows that the stronger one's expectations that others will cooperate, the higher one's propensity to cooperate. Fischbacher, Gächter, and Fehr (2001) elaborated an ingenious experimental method to disentangle possible distinct motivations in cooperation games. They conclude that reciprocity counts for as much as 50% of observed cooperation and selfish motivations account for 30% of the behavior, while remaining behavior follows other, sometimes unintelligible, patterns.

An alternative mechanism posits that social identification has a direct effect in transforming individuals' goals. By attaching their sense of self to their group, individuals see themselves as interchangeable components of a social collective. Not only does this result in affective attachment to the group, but also it engenders a shift of motives and values from self-interest to group interests. As a consequence of this re-definition of the self, the group's interest becomes a direct expression of self-interest. The group success becomes the individual's success. Group identity, therefore, involves a transformation of goals from the personal to the collective level, which does not hinge upon expectations that others in the group will reciprocate cooperation (De Cremer and van Dijk 2002; Kramer and Brewer 1986).

Once demonstrated that social identity can improve cooperation in ingroups, the next question is whether this is efficient *overall* for society. One needs to weigh up both the *increase* in the willingness to cooperate with one's ingroup – what social psychologists term 'ingroup love' – and the *decrease* in the willingness to cooperate with one's outgroup – that is, 'outgroup hate' (Brewer 1999). If the latter exceeded the former, then the existence of groups would overall be inefficient, as aggregate cooperation would decrease in spite of its increase within ingroup boundaries. Efficiency in this case would be maximized if social relationships were concentrated within ingroup boundaries. However, this would call for the segmentation of the society into the cleavages created by group belonging, which would constitute a rather undesirable social and political outcome (Bowles and Gintis 2002).

In experiments designed to address this issue, social psychologists conclude that ingroup love dominates 'outgroup hate' (Brewer 1999; Yamagishi 2007). In fact, outgroup hate, when it manifests itself, seems to be uncorrelated with ingroup attachment, pointing to the idea that the underlying reasons for experiencing ingroup love or outgroup hate are independent (Brewer 1999). However, recent evidence in experimental economics provides a bleaker view, as ingroup love turns out to be negligible and outgroup hate substantial, the overall net benefit of forming groups being negative (Chen and Li 2009; Hargreaves Heap and Zizzo 2009). This negative evidence has been gathered in laboratory experiments with so-called minimal groups. However, results may differ in real groups because social ties that are typical of real groups are likely to create emotional bonds among group members. Degli Antoni and Grimalda (2013) shows outgroup hate to be absent in a sample of associations members, but Fershtman et al. (2005) do find evidence of outgroup hate in a sample involving Flemish and Walloons Belgians. Again, it becomes an empirical issue to ascertain which of the two phenomena is prevalent.

Why social identity may matter for 'global' cooperation

Scholte (2002) conceptualizes globalization as 'the spread of transplanetary and . . . supraterritorial connections between people. Globalization involves reduction in barriers to transworld contacts. People become more able – physically, legally, culturally, and psychologically – to engage with each other in "one world"' (13–14). In this sense, globalization differs from the notions of internationalization, westernization, universalization, and liberalization, which have been proposed by others as the crux of globalization.

Two channels have been identified in Buchan et al. (2009) as possible mechanisms of the influence of globalization on cooperation. The main idea is that the social, cultural, and psychological engagement inherent in globalization has the effect of reshaping the 'boundaries' between the ingroup and the outgroup. According to one account, globalization facilitates convergence to a global identity that is expansive in character – i.e. includes other groups into the boundaries of the 'we-group' – or to where the very notion of the boundary between a 'we' and several 'them' is replaced by an all-encompassing 'global we'. In the words of Giddens (1991), 'with globalization humankind becomes a "we", where there are no others' (27). Some scholars argue that people around the world converge to a similar form of identity through a process of homogenization of culture, production, and values, partly as a consequence of the spread of capitalism and the Western way of life/culture (Tomlison 2003). Others suggest that the idea that people expand their group attachment to the whole of humankind as a result of globalization leads to the notion of a 'cosmopolitan' individual (Archibugi and Held 1995; Hannerz 1992; McFarland, Webb, and Brown 2012). The flourishing of several 'global' social movements around a variety of causes, such as human rights or the environment, and the growing importance of global humanitarian relief operations are all instances of this cosmopolitan conscience (Vertovec and Cohen 2002). I refer to this as the 'cosmopolitan hypothesis'.

According to a different account, globalization enhances even further the cleavage between the ingroup and outgroup. A 'resistant' individual, who attaches even further to local or national communities, emerges as a result of globalization (Arnett 2002; Castells 2004; Keating 2001). According to this stance, globalization triggers a reaction against global flows of objects, commodities, people, and ideas, which may lead to an entrenchment in the state-nation community. In terms of the 'ingroup-outgroup' model, this mechanism makes the presence of an 'other' more vivid to members of an ingroup, thus strengthening even further the constricted parochial boundary between 'us' and 'them'. If that were the case, the balance between ingroup love and outgroup hate would, in a global context, be likely to shift in favor of the latter. Several movements or groups have been deemed as being spawned by this 'backlash' against globalization. Examples are the surge of xenophobic political parties all around the world, the adhesion to religious fundamentalist groups, the revival in so-called ethno-nations (e.g. Basque, Scots, Catalans), and the birth of social movements opposing globalization (Scholte 2002; Smith 2013). I refer to this as the 'parochial hypothesis'.

Experimental design

An extensive description of the methods behind the project can be found in Buchan et al. (2009; Supplementary Online Materials (SOM)).

Experimental decisions

Participants in this research engaged in three experimental decisions that measured their propensity to cooperate in Public Goods Games (PGG). Here I focus on the last of the three decisions, which focuses on global level cooperation. People were endowed with 10 tokens, each worth an equivalent amount of money in terms of purchasing power parity across countries. In the US, a token was worth \$0.50. An option that individuals had was to allocate their tokens to a personal account, where money would maintain its monetary value intact. That is, the individual Marginal Per Capita Return (MPCR) is 1. The other options implied allocating tokens to some collective accounts. As standard in PGGs, the MPCR from collective accounts is less than 1 for an individual, but creates positive externalities for a group of other people. This is the case because each token allocated to a collective account is multiplied by the researcher by a factor greater than 1, and then is equally divided among the people making up the group. That is, each contribution to a collective account generates a Marginal *Social* Return (MSR) greater than 1.

The experimental design uses a nested PGG (Blackwell and McKee 2003; Wit and Kerr 2002). Individuals had the option of keeping their endowment for themselves, contributing some of it to a local account, and/or contributing some of it to a global account. The local account is comprised of the participant plus three other participants from the local area. Every token contributed to the local account is multiplied by 2 and shared among 4 people. Hence, a token contributed to the local account yields an MSR of 2 and an MPCR of 0.25. The global account consists of the participant's local group plus two other local groups of four people from two different countries. Every token contributed to the global account is multiplied by 3 and shared among 12 people. Hence, a token contributed to the global account yields an MSR of 3 and an MPCR of 0.25. Such a nested PGG allows us to study the impact of 'enlarging' the boundaries of individuals' social environment on their propensity toward cooperation. The design is seen schematically in Figure 9.1.

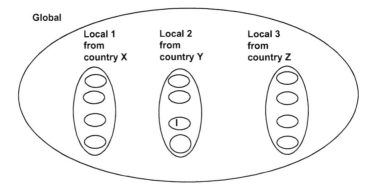

Figure 9.1 Representation of the nested social dilemma.

Note: I stands for "Individual". 'Local 1', 'Local 2', and 'Local 3' represent groups of people in the same locality in three different countries. 'Global' is the group encompassing the three local groups.

This design realistically maps onto the nature of local-global relations. Globalization does not exclude the local constituency but potentially expands the level of inclusion to both local and non-local participants. This design also captures the tension between the different incentives for giving to the local good vis-à-vis the incentives for giving to the global good. In this design MPCR from giving to the local public account is greater than MPCR from giving to the global account, but on the other hand the MSR is higher in the latter.

Measuring social identity and individual-level globalization

I analyze a set of three social identity measures, adapted from Yuki et al. (2004). They measure social identification at the levels of the local community (local social identity – LSI), the nation (national social identity – NSI), and the world (global social identity – GSI), drawing on the following three questions:

1) How strongly do you feel attachment to your community in *[name of location where participant lives]*?
2) How strongly do you define yourself as a member of your community in *[name of location where participant lives]*?
3) How close do you feel to other members *of* your community in *[name of location where participant lives]*?

Social identity at the national and global level was measured substituting the following expressions, respectively, for 'your community in [location where subject lives]': 'to your community in [country where subject lives]', and 'to the world as a whole'. Responses to each item were made on a four-item rating scale having as extreme options as 'not at all' and 'very much'.

A person scoring 1 in, say, the LSI answered that he/she feels very strong attachment to his/her local community, very strongly defines himself/herself as a member of his/her local community, and feels very close to other members of his/her local community. A person scoring 0 in the LSI answered that he/she feels no attachment to his/her local community, would not at all define himself/herself as a member of his/her local community, and does not at all feel close to other members of his/her local community.

I also analyze an individual participation in globalization index (PGI). This mirrors the existing country-level measurement of globalization as in, for instance, the country-level globalization index (CGI) of Lockwood and Redoano (2005) or the Foreign Policy index (Kerney 2004). The PGI measures participation in four different spheres, namely the social, cultural, political, and economic. The idea underlying the PGI is to measure an individual's *usage* of global networks of direct connection or interpersonal relations. Examples of such media of global connections or relationships are the Internet, mobile phones, satellite TV channels, international news agencies, credit cards, and multinational companies. Such media have a potentially global reach, but the actual scope is subject to individual choice. An individual could, for instance, access the Internet only to gather information about local issues. For this reason the PGI taps into both the frequency with which the individual accesses media of global connection and the territorial scope of the connection, distinguishing between connections carried out at the local, national, or global level. The PGI assigns higher scores to individuals who participate in the global network more frequently and on a larger scope than others. The whole list of the 30 items making up the PGI is reported in Buchan et al. (2009: SOM).

I derive from the PGI two sub-indexes. The Global Network (GN) index includes only the social aspect of global connections. This is based on subjects' use (frequency and geographic scope) of social media of global connections, such as the Internet, mobile phones, international travels, and the like. The index of exposure to economic globalization (EEG) is instead based on six questionnaire items asking participants whether access to products and services produced by foreign or multinational companies is available in the areas where they live. Such an index is a summative scale of dummy variables identifying whether a certain product is available in the area where the subject lives.

An additional measure that is used in the ensuing analysis is a global awareness (GA) index. This is based on the answers to four questions inquiring about the subject's awareness of four issues having a global character, such as global warming, the spread across the planet of potentially dangerous diseases, the action of the International Criminal Court, and the persistent gap in income inequality between the rich and the poor. This follows the emphasis given, e.g. by Robertson (1992), to the process of globalization being characterized as the 'consciousness of the world as a whole'.

Selection of research environments, sampling techniques, and implementation

The six countries being sampled span a relatively broad range of the globalization spectrum as measured by the CGI in the year 2004. The general strategy behind this project was to designate a large urban center as the 'hub' of the fieldwork and to encompass less globalized centers located within a relatively small radius from the hub. The hubs of the research in four countries were Columbus, OH (US), Milan (Italy), Buenos Aires (Argentina), and Kazan (Russia). In South Africa residents of four different (and widely diverse in economic and cultural terms) boroughs of Johannesburg were sampled. In Iran the research was instead conducted in the two largest cities of the country, Tehran and Shiraz.

Stratified samples of around 200 adults were recruited in each country. Participants were told that they were involved in a series of decisions involving people from their own local area and from other countries around the world. Which countries these were was not specified in order to avoid any biases in attitudes toward a specific country.

Results

Descriptive statistics of social identity scales

Table 9.1 reports descriptive statistics for the three social identity measures in the six countries. For most countries identification with the local and national levels appears to be similar and, on average, higher than at the global level. The

Table 9.1 Descriptive statistics for local, national, and global social identity per country

	Local Social Identity	National Social Identity	Global Social Identity
Iran			
Mean	0.66	0.69	0.40
Median	0.67	0.67	0.33
St. Dev.	0.24	0.21	0.24
Obs.	177	178	174
South Africa			
Mean	0.70	0.72	0.57
Median	0.67	0.78	0.56
St. Dev.	0.28	0.27	0.31
Obs.	149	144	143
Argentina			
Mean	0.75	0.78	0.48
Median	0.78	0.78	0.44
St. Dev.	0.26	0.22	0.29
Obs.	201	196	196
Russia			
Mean	0.71	0.67	0.54
Median	0.78	0.67	0.56
St. Dev.	0.26	0.25	0.29
Obs.	205	205	205
Italy			
Mean	0.74	0.80	0.65
Median	0.78	0.89	0.67
St. Dev.	0.25	0.21	0.22
Obs.	204	203	204
US			
Mean	0.63	0.65	0.59
Median	0.67	0.67	0.67
St. Dev.	0.29	0.27	0.26
Obs.	171	171	170
Total			
	0.70	0.72	0.54
	0.67	0.78	0.56
	0.27	0.24	0.28
	1107	1097	1092

country where the differences between local, national, and global social identity appear to be smallest is the US, where in fact the median levels of the three indexes coincide.

As reported in Grimalda, Buchan, and Brewer (2015), the lower scores observed for GSI in comparison with both the LSI and the NSI reach strong statistical levels of significance in all countries except the US, where levels of significance are only moderate. It can be concluded:

> **Result 1**: The global social identity scores are systematically lower than the local and national social identity scores in all countries. Differences are only moderate in the US.

Analysis of the possible determinants of GSI

This section draws on the econometric analysis developed in Grimalda et al. (2015). The goal is to examine which variables are most strongly correlated with GSI. Figure 9.2, Panel (a) offers a graphical representation of the values of the coefficients estimated in this econometric analysis for a set of relevant variables. The higher the value of the coefficient, the higher the estimated impact of an increase in the independent variable onto GSI. The coefficients have been standardized in order to make possible a direct comparison of their impact on GSI, regardless of their unit of measure (see the note to Figure 9.2).

A common phenomenon in social identity is that individuals who declare high attachment to one group (e.g. their neighbors) also declare high attachment to other groups (e.g. their co-citizens). This is also the case here, as both LSI and, particularly so, NSI show positive correlations with GSI. The same is found in McFarland et al. (2012). The econometric model includes both NSI and LSI to control for this aspect. The results of the present analysis should then be interpreted as accounting for GSI *relative* to LSI and NSI, rather than in *absolute* terms. In other words, the analysis examines the impact of some factors on the propensity of an individual to report GSI scores that are *higher* than LSI and NSI scores.

CGI exerts a positive and strongly significant effect on GSI ($p < 0.001$). This is also the case for EEG, albeit at weak levels of significance ($p = 0.067$). This implies that as a country increases its level of globalization, and as individuals become more exposed to the economic aspect of globalization, this model predicts an increase in a subject's identification with the global community. On the other hand, exposure to migrant groups has negligible effects ($p = 0.869$). As for demographic variables, females' GSI scores are, *ceteris paribus*, nearly 6% higher than men's scores, the difference being strongly significantly ($p = 0.001$). More educated people report significantly higher GSI scores than people with lower educational attainments ($p = 0.001$). The effect of income and age is not significant. Age would have been significant, with a negative sign, had one omitted LSI and NSI from the analysis. This denotes the tendency of older people to report higher scores than younger people across all social identity measures.

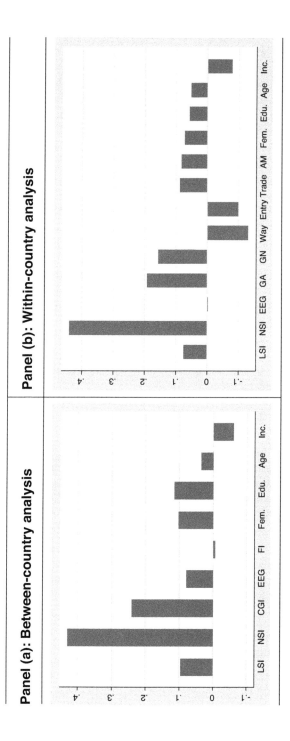

Figure 9.2 Estimated impact of selected variables on GSI.

Note: The two panels report the standardized coefficients estimated in two econometric models deployed to study the correlation between GSI and a set of variables possibly associated with GSI. The value that is reported in the graphs is given by $\beta^y_{xSTD} = \beta^y_x \frac{\sigma_x}{\sigma_y}$ where β^y_x is the coefficient estimated in a Tobit linear regression model.

Such a coefficient expresses the estimated impact that a variation in the independent variable x has on the dependent variable y (GSI in this case). The standardization permits the direct comparison of the coefficients so obtained for different variables because it expresses them in a common 'metrics'. Panels (a) and (b) report the results from a between-country analysis and a within-country analysis, respectively. The legend for the variables are as follows: LSI=Local Social Identity; NSI = National Social Identity; CGI = Country-level Globalization Index; EEG = Exposure to Economic Globalization index; FI = Foreign Immigrants; Fem. = Female; Edu. = Education; Inc. = Income; Age identifies subjects older than 50 years; GA = Global Awareness index; GN = Global Network index; Way = Belief that national way of life should be protected from foreign influence; Entry = Belief that entry to the country should be prohibited to foreigners; Trade = Belief that global business and trade are not a good thing; AM = Association Membership; Fem. = Female.

The analysis conducted thus far has taken a 'between-country' perspective. The following analysis introduces country fixed effects and thus takes a 'within-country' perspective. The introduction of such fixed effects comes at the cost of excluding all variables that are invariant within country, like, for instance, the CGI. This analysis should then be seen as complementary to the one carried out before.

Figure 9.2, Panel (b) reports the standardized coefficients of a model including additional variables measuring participants' connectivity and involvement with global networks. Both these measures are strongly significantly correlated with the GSI. This means that people who are more aware and more globally connected than others also score higher GSI.

I also analyze some attitudinal measures of globalization, derived from questions asking people's opinions on some aspects of globalization. The more a subject expresses identification with the world as a whole, the less he/she believes that his/her citizens' way of life needs to be protected against foreign influence ($p < 0.001$) and that entry of foreigners should be restricted ($p = 0.005$), and the more he/she agrees that trade and global business are a good thing ($p = 0.012$). Subjects scoring high in GSI are significantly more likely to be active in voluntary associations ($p = 0.012$).

Among the demographic variables, gender still exerts significant effects ($p = 0.007$), while education loses its impact ($p = 0.118$). This is likely caused by the high correlation between educational attainment and awareness of global issues. The variable identifying people with 'High Income' becomes significant with a *negative* sign ($p = 0.082$). Nevertheless, in Grimalda et al. (2015) it is argued that this is likely to be a spurious effect.

It can be concluded:

> **Result 2**: Individuals declaring higher identification with 'the world as a whole' generally live in more globalized countries, are more aware of global issues, are more globally interconnected, are against restricting their country to migration flows, do not feel that their way of life needs to be protected against foreign influence, and think that trade and global business are a good thing. Being exposed to facets of economic globalization is positively correlated with GSI, but only when the analysis focuses on differences *between* countries rather than *within* countries. Females and people having higher educational attainments express significantly higher identification with the global community. People declaring higher GSI are significantly more likely to be members of voluntary associations.

Analysis of the mediating effects of GSI between participation in global networks and cooperation levels

Buchan et al. (2009) demonstrated a strong effect of individual participation in the global network, as measured by the PGI and the propensity to cooperate at the world level in the experimental decision described previously. Buchan et al. (2011) showed that, on the other hand, GSI also had a strong positive effect on cooperation rates in the same decision. The question that I want to address here is whether GSI may be deemed as having a mediating effect on PGI. A formal definition and an extensive statistical analysis are reported in Grimalda et al. (2015). Intuitively, a variable y is said to mediate the effect of a variable x on a variable z when x has a significant predictive effect on z, and this effect is 'absorbed' by y when y is also inserted in the model.

At the theoretical level, PGI may have *direct* effects on propensity to cooperate at the world level, as it may lead the individual to become more accustomed to interacting with global others, it may increase individual's *trust* in global others, or it may make the individual aware of the possibility and opportunities arising from cooperating worldwide. Nonetheless, the 'cosmopolitan hypothesis' illustrated previously posits that participation in global networks may also have an *indirect* effect on cooperation with global others, inasmuch as it increases one's identification with the global community. Since social identity theory argues that increased identification with a group goes hand in hand with increased propensity to cooperate with that group, one can infer that increased identification with the global community will be accompanied by increased propensity to cooperate with global others. The mediation analysis can be seen as a test of the 'cosmopolitan hypothesis'. If such a hypothesis holds, then one should observe GSI mediating the effect between PGI and experimental cooperation at the world level in this study.

The econometric analysis carried out in Grimalda et al. (2015: 18–20) does indeed strongly support the existence of a mediation effect of GSI between PGI and propensity to cooperate at the global level. When GSI is omitted from the model, PGI exerts a significant predictive effect on world-level cooperation rates ($p = 0.043$). Nevertheless, when GSI is inserted into the model, PGI effect becomes insignificant ($p = 0.33$). On the contrary, GSI is shown to exert a strongly significant effect on GSI ($p < 0.01$). A Sobel (1982) statistical test confirms the existence of a significant mediating effect of GSI between PGI and propensity to cooperate at the world level (see Grimalda et al. 2015: Figure 9.1 for a graphical representation).

A final econometric model sheds more light on the nature of the relationship between GSI and propensity to cooperate. It introduces an interaction effect between the GSI and the three countries in this sample that have the highest level of globalization, i.e. Russia, Italy, and the US. This allows us to study whether GSI exerts differential effects in high-globalization countries and low-globalization countries. The answer is indeed positive. GSI exerts a significantly stronger effect in countries at *lower* stages of globalization. This means that higher identification with the world as a whole has larger effects on cooperative attitudes in countries that have a lower baseline level of globalization. For instance, increasing one's level of identification with the world in Iran has significantly larger effects on global cooperation than increasing one's level of identification with the world in the US.

It can be concluded:

> **Result 3**: The econometric and test analysis strongly supports the hypothesis that the global social identity has a mediating effect between the

participation in globalization and propensity to cooperate at the global level. This is consistent with the conjecture that participation in globalization increases the propensity to cooperate at the global level inasmuch as it also increases social identification with the world as a whole. The global social identity exerts larger effects in countries at lower stages of globalization than in countries at higher stages of globalization.

Evidence for reciprocity in cooperative behavior

Reciprocity is seen by many as a fundamental facet of cooperation (Messner, Guarín, and Haun in this volume; Nowak 2006). Reciprocity is normally conceptualized in a dynamic context, and refers to the propensity of individuals to cooperate with others conditional on the observation of past cooperative behavior by others. 'Tit for tat' is the simplest form of reciprocity (Nowak 2006). It simply prescribes to start a repeated interaction cooperating, and to replicate the counterpart's action in the previous interaction in all future interactions. Nevertheless, reciprocity can also be conceptualized in terms of expectation over others' behavior, rather than actual observed behavior. In this context, reciprocity can be defined as the propensity to cooperate under the *expectation* that others will cooperate. In this case, reciprocity can be understood as a propensity to replicate *future expected behavior* by the counterpart rather than past behavior. Indeed, the experimental literature has ascertained that expectation-based reciprocity is a fundamental motivation of cooperation, even in interactions that are not repeated over time, i.e. 'one-shot interactions' (Croson 2007; Fischbacher et al. 2001; Rand and Nowak in this volume).

I can test for the relevance of reciprocity in this study by analyzing the correlation between experimental cooperative behavior and a measure of expectations of others' behavior that was asked for after decisions were made[2]. Such a measure of expectations was not monetarily incentivized, neither was it relevant for actual decision, as in Fischbacher et al. (2001). Expectations measures taken after decisions have been criticized because they may be simple ex-post rationalization of one's own behavior, or because people may simply project their own behavior onto others' behavior (Ellingsen et al. 2010). In spite of these concerns, I still think that such ex-post belief elicitation has scientific validity and is a widely used instrument of analysis. As a matter of fact, only 16% of the sample had experimental choice coinciding with expectations, so the relevance of the concerns illustrated appears to be limited in the present study.

Figure 9.3(a) reports the scatterplots and the predicted correlation between expected contributions to the world account from other group members and one's own contribution. It reveals strikingly similar patterns across countries. First, reciprocity matters in all countries: the higher the expected contribution, the higher one's own contribution. However, the relationship is less than proportional. A 10% increase in expected contribution is associated with an increase in one's own contribution that is less than 10%. This confirms the evidence coming from other studies of a 'self-serving bias' in reciprocity patterns (Fischbacher et al. 2001).

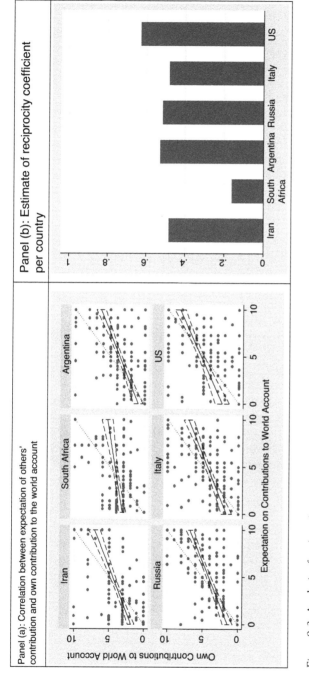

Figure 9.3 Analysis of reciprocity across countries.

Note: Panel (a) reports the scatterplot of pairs of observations for expectations of contributions to world account (horizontal axis) and one's own contribution to the world account (vertical axis). The solid line plots the best linear fit for the data, and the dashed lines around denote the 95% confidence intervals of the prediction. The dotted line is the 45° bi-sector line and represents the hypothetical condition of 'perfect' reciprocity – namely, the amount contributed equals the amount expected. Panel (b) reports the estimated coefficient for the 'Expectation of contributions to the world account' in each country, derived from a Tobit regression

Second, purely altruistic people are present in all countries. Those are people who contribute positive amounts even if they expect others to contribute nothing. This is in line with previous evidence (Fischbacher et al. 2001).

Figure 9.3(b) reports the value of the reciprocity coefficient estimated for each country. The country where reciprocity motives seem to be strongest is the US. This is reminiscent of the finding by Kocher et al. (2008) that US citizens are more sensitive to reciprocity motivations in a sample including US, Austria, and Japan. In the present sample, an increase in expected contributions of one token is associated with an increase in one's own contribution of 0.67 tokens in the US. Statistical tests indicate that the impact is significantly greater than zero in all countries except South Africa, where the relationship is only significant at the 10% level (p = 0.094). Statistical tests (available upon request) on the hypotheses that reciprocity coefficients are the same for pairs of countries never reject these hypotheses except for South Africa, whose coefficient is statistically lower than any other country.

Finally, I explore the relationship between GSI and reciprocity motivations. Is higher trust in global others correlated with higher GSI? I can test for this hypothesis using the variables elicited in the experiment. I insert trust in experimental cooperation at the world level by global others into the same econometric model used before to explore the determinants of GSI. The result of the analysis is that trust in cooperation by global others seems to exert small effects on GSI, once alternative explanatory variables are controlled for.

The general conclusion from the analysis of this section is:

> **Result 4**: Reciprocity – understood as the relationship between expectation of others' cooperation and one's own cooperation – seems to be an extremely strong and significant factor in this study. Reciprocity is a relevant factor of cooperation in all of the six countries studied, with the partial exception of South Africa, where the effect seems to be weak. Reciprocity motives are strongest in the US. Reciprocity and GSI seem to be little correlated once relevant explanatory factors are controlled for.

Discussion

Social identity and, more specifically, an individual's identification with a group have been deemed as a potent instrument to boost cooperation with others. However, groups are normally constructed in terms of an 'us' and a 'them', and it is still unclear whether the benefits of heightened identification with the 'us' exceed the potential costs of increased discrimination against the 'them'.

Global cooperation presents a scale of complexity that is arguably considerably higher than the forms of bilateral cooperation analyzed in laboratory experiments. Global cooperation demands millions of 'we' to take joint decisions that are expensive to the individual group (normally, the state), and beneficial for the global community. The risk that 'outgroup hate' dominate 'ingroup love' is concrete, especially in the face of massive asymmetries in wealth across groups and the consequent difficulty to pinpoint shared principles for the fair distribution of the burdens of global cooperation. Moreover, experimental evidence shows that individuals who are delegated to act on behalf of a group tend to act more selfishly than when acting as individuals (Charness et al. 2007). This result, transferred to the International Relations level, would entail that achieving large-scale cooperation is even more difficult when negotiations are carried out by people acting on behalf of large collectives.

Global social identity may offer an antidote to the troubles of global cooperation. The development of psychological attachment, identification, and willingness to act for the global community may radically restructure the 'us' vs. 'them' dynamics that is deemed crucial in cooperation problems. In other words, with globalization the demarcations between 'us' and 'them' may gradually disappear, as people come to realize the communality of their interests and the need to achieve global cooperative solutions. Global social identity may be inclusive in character, not excluding others but including broader and broader categories of people.

The empirical evidence on global social identity is scant, and this book chapter has been devoted to illustrating the results coming from the first experimental study addressing these issues. The main result has been a positive answer to the potential of global social identity. Global social identity is positively and highly significantly correlated with an experimental measure of cooperation with global others. The higher the identification with the global community, the higher the propensity to contribute to the global common good, relative to the basic propensity to cooperate with local others.

This result opens new avenues for not only policies seeking to improve global cooperation, but also challenging questions. The first fundamental question concerns the causality of the relationship between global social identity and cooperation. Can GSI be said to *cause* increased cooperation, or is an increased propensity to cooperate *leading to* higher probability to identify with the global community? It is clearly very difficult to ascertain neat causal relationships between unobservable psychological dispositions. Moreover, it is quite likely that the causal relationship goes either way, and that propensity to cooperate and GSI are both part of personality traits that mutually reinforce each other.

Econometric analysis is *prima facie* purely correlational, so it cannot be said to disentangle the causality issue. However, the mediation analysis that has been reported provides a strong test for the existence of a causal relationship going from increased participation in global networks, to global social identity, and then to cooperation. The fact that this theoretical model is supported (or not falsified) by the evidence reported here offers a strong indication that, to a significant extent, increasing GSI *will* lead to increased propensity to cooperate with others. Admittedly, only natural experiments relying on randomized assignment to control and treatment conditions may provide a truly conclusive proof of causality. These are obviously very difficult to implement because of the long time span needed to analyze the effects of the *explanans* on the *explanandum*. However, the evidence stemming from this investigation supports, or does not disconfirm, the existence of a causal relationship from GSI to a propensity to cooperate.

Another obvious word of caution concerns the use of experiments to derive these conclusions. Experiments permit the rigorous measurement of variables of interest under conditions of choice standardization and monetary incentives. However, this comes at the cost of implementing highly unnatural decisional situations, where individual behavior may be distorted under the lenses of the observing experimenter. Nonetheless, several studies have demonstrated the 'external validity' of experiments – i.e. the consistency of individual behavior within the laboratory and outside the laboratory (e.g. Fehr and Leibbrandt 2011) – although the extent of pro-social behavior may be magnified in the laboratory in comparison to pro-social behavior in real life. Assuming that people from different countries do *not* react to the experimental situation in a substantially different manner from each other – and at the moment there is no evidence that this may be the case – one can safely assume that the *difference* one observes across countries generalizes beyond the lab.

Conclusions: A tentative policy agenda for a globality-minded policy-maker

Even accepting, as tentatively as one may, that global social identity should be identified as a key target of policy, how and in which ways can it be really used to improve global cooperation? The results presented in this chapter offer some answers, although these are going to have a speculative character in the absence of a proof of causality relationships.

(A) Harness and exploit the positive effects of globalization

The first answer is that policy-makers may be moderately optimistic about the positive effects that exposure and participation in globalization may have on global social identity, and hence on the propensity to cooperate. Although causality issues are not fully disentangled in this analysis, I note that the exogenous character of exposure to globalization and its significant correlation with GSI supports the view that increased exposure *will* lead to increased GSI. To be sure, the same cannot be said about the PGI. But even those having a critical view of globalization should convene that no adverse consequence of increased globalization is found in this study. In particular, no instance of increased parochialism as a result of globalization emerges. The simple implication is that policies enhancing the exposure to and participation in global networks may at worst be ineffective, and at best be highly effective in instilling stronger identification with the global community. Such policies may take the form of encouraging contacts with people and cultural manifestations from other countries – for instance through travelling or facilitating access to global media of connection like the Internet – as well as increasing awareness of global issues. To be sure, opening a country to globalization in terms, for example, of trade and migration is going to create losers and winners, and a careful policy-maker should control the transition and compensate the temporary losers. Even so, the benefits that can be reaped from exposure to globalization appear to be positive.

(B) Propose the global community as a model for identification

The second consideration we would like to advance is that global social identity may be a *direct* target of policy. The main result of Buchan et al. (2011) is precisely that identification with the global community is strongly associated with the propensity to cooperate. Among the three measures of social identity, GSI is still the lowest – except in the US (see the 'Results' section). Therefore, there are potentially large margins for exploiting the potential of GSI. Even in this case, the direction of the causality relationship is uncertain. It may well be that highly cooperative people are also more inclined to embrace global communities in their radius of social identification. It is quite plausible that both variables co-vary and to some extent mutually influence each other. This should be undoubtedly the subject of future research. All the same, on the basis of the available evidence one can argue that policy-makers should be moderately optimistic about the fact that targeting global social identity will engender positive, or at least non-negative, consequences on the propensity to cooperate with global others. The danger may be that trying to manipulate people's natural dispositions by political authorities may be counterproductive and possibly contrary to democratic principles. Policy-makers should be careful in avoiding these dangers. Individuals seem to be eager to react to incentives very differently depending on whether the perceived *intention* of the actor setting the incentives is self-interested or other-regarding (Bowles and Polania-Reyes, 2012). The same concern applies to the present context. Policy-makers should engage in constructive dialogue with the populations, aiming at *proposing* global 'modes of thinking' rather than *imposing* them. A simple example may help to clarify this concern. Most of our history books are still ethnocentric in character, giving disproportionate emphasis to events that occurred in the continent where our country is situated. Giving global accounts of historical events would be, in my view, an effective way to propose to students to examine issues from a global standpoint rather than from a national one. The global perspective may easily accompany the national perspective.

(C) Frame problems of cooperation as global rather than as international

A related point has to do with the opportunity of 'framing' problems of collective actions in an explicitly global perspective, rather than in a multi-national or cross-national one[3]. The narrative that accompanies global agreements typically centers on national interests. Participation in international agreements is normally justified by policy-makers as being 'in the interests of the nation'. An alternative approach is to draw people's attention – or, in the words of Thaler and Sunstein (2008), to 'nudge' people – to think of the global interests when trying to build consensus for a policy. The recourse to national narratives is perhaps consistent with a narrow *homo economicus* view that citizens will not accept costly international agreements if these are not in their interests. However, the enormous body of evidence gathered in recent years that individuals very often depart from the *homo economicus* predictions should suffice to persuade globally minded policy-makers that 'nudging' people to think globally may be a successful approach in mobilizing people to comply with global agreements.

(D) Ensure that global agreements comply with the principle of reciprocity

An important caveat is, however, necessary. The model of human behavior that seems to be prevalent in explaining why humans cooperate even if it is not in their immediate self-interest is based on reciprocity (see the 'Results' section and Messner et al., this volume). Even in this study reciprocity was observed in all countries, although at variable degrees. Purely altruistic people – i.e. unconditional cooperators – do exist but are rare. Constructing global cooperative agreements on the idea that individuals will unconditionally help others is most likely going to be an unsuccessful strategy. Policy-makers need to devise institutions and agreements with which reciprocal individuals – or conditional cooperators – would comply. Not only does this require the *expectation* that others will cooperate, but also that the share of burdens and costs be *fairly* distributed among agents. To be sure, the enormous asymmetries in countries' starting conditions make this an extremely difficult problem to solve. The existence of 'self-serving biases', that is the over-weighting of one's own needs in relation to others' needs, complicates the possibility of finding shared principles of responsibility. As challenging as it may be, this research as well as others' unambiguously point to the need of constructing cooperation problems in which every agent involved is doing their fair share to address the problem. The perception that some agents are free riding on others will dramatically reduce the propensity of conditional cooperators to contribute to the common good.

(E) Focus on countries at low levels of globalization first

Result 4 entails that increases in GSI bear larger effects in less globalized countries. Therefore, priority in the efforts to spur a sense of global social identity should be given to this set of countries. This may be given by a 'saturation effect', as a 'learning curve' is always steeper in the earlier stages. The fact that normally low-globalized countries are also at low stages of economic development is somehow positive news, because policies are less costly in financial terms. However, the cultural opposition to change may be stronger in less globalized countries, as clearly shown by the fact that the US is the country with the highest level, in relative terms, of attachment to the global community.

Cooperating in a world of nine billion people (Messner et al. in this volume) is an immense challenge for humankind. It is also a game that 'we cannot afford to lose' (Pfeiffer and Nowak 2006). The scale of the problems facing humankind makes the current provision of global public goods to be much more limited than needed. In this chapter I have illustrated how global social identity is strongly associated with individual cooperation in an experiment involving people from different countries around the world. Consistent with the 'cosmopolitan hypothesis', global social identity seems to mediate the effect that participation in global network has on the propensity to cooperate. Globalization seems to expand the groups of people that an individual treats as the 'we' in opposition to the 'them', thus leading to stronger disposition to cooperate with them. Reciprocity also emerges as a strong driver of cooperation. The pioneering investigation presented in this chapter suggests that relying on global-we modes of thinking, combined with the necessity that the distribution of the burden is viewed by the agents as reciprocal in character, may – or should – be part of a comprehensive strategy to address these problems

Notes

1 I gratefully acknowledge the contributions of Nancy Buchan, Marilynn Brewer, Enrique Fatas, Margaret F. Foddy, and Rick K. Wilson, who were members of the research team from which this paper originated. I also thank Patricio Dalton, Iain Edwards, Saul Keifman, and Warren Thorngate for their valuable contribution during the fieldwork.
2 The text of the question was, 'How much do you think was put into all of the "World" envelopes by the other 11 people in your group (a maximum of 110 yellow tokens could be put into them)?'
3 I thank Eric Johnson for this suggestion.

References

Akerlof, G. and Kranton, R. (2000). 'Economics and Identity', *Quarterly Journal of Economics*, 115 (3): 715–53.
Archibugi, D. and Held, D. (eds.) (1995). *Cosmopolitan Democracy: An Agenda for a New World Order*, Cambridge: Polity Press.
Arnett, J. (2002). 'The Psychology of Globalization', *American Psychologist*, 57 (10): 774–83.
Bargh, J. and Pietromonaco, P. (1982). 'Automatic Information Processing and Social Perception: The Influence of Trait Information Presented outside of Conscious Awareness on Impression Formation', *Journal of Personality and Social Psychology*, 43 (3): 437–49.
Bernhard, H., Fischbacher, U. and Fehr, E. (2006). 'Parochial Altruism in Humans', *Nature*, 442 (7105): 912–5.
Blackwell, C. and McKee, M. (2003). 'Only for My Own Neighborhood? Preferences and Voluntary Provision of Local and Global Public Goods', *Journal of Economic Behavior and Organization*, 52 (1): 115–31.
Bowles, S. and Gintis, H. (2002). 'Social Capital and Community Governance', *Economic Journal*, 112 (483): F419–36.
Bowles, S. and Polania-Reyes, S. (2012). 'Economic Incentives and Social Preferences: Substitutes or Complements?', *Journal of Economic Literature*, 50 (2): 368–425.

Brewer, M. (1986). 'Ethnocentrism and Its Role in Interpersonal Trust', in M. Brewer and B. Collins (eds.) *Scientific Inquiry and the Social Sciences: A Volume in Honor of Donald T. Campbell*, San Francisco, CA: Jossey-Bass, 345–60.

Brewer, M. (1999). 'The Psychology of Prejudice: Ingroup Love or Outgroup Hate', *Journal of Social Issues*, 55 (3): 429–44.

Buchan, N., Brewer, M., Grimalda, G., Rick, W., Fatas, E. and Foddy, M. (2011). 'Global Identity and Global Cooperation', *Psychological Science*, 22 (6): 821–8.

Buchan, N., Grimalda, G., Rick, W., Brewer, M., Fatas, E. and Foddy, M., (2009). 'Globalization and Human Cooperation', *Proceedings of the National Academy of Sciences of the USA*, 106 (11): 4138–42.

Castells, M. (2004). *Power of Identity*, Malden, MA: Blackwell.

Charness, G., Rigotti, L. and Rustichini, A. (2007). 'Individual Behavior and Group Membership', American Economic Review, 97 (4): 1340–52.

Chen, Y. and Li, S. X. (2009). 'Group Identity and Social Preferences', *American Economic Review*, 99 (1): 431–57.

Choi, J.-K. and Bowles, S. (2007). 'The Coevolution of Parochial Altruism and War', Science, 318 (5850): 636–40.

Corson, R. (2007). 'Theories of Commitment, Altruism and Reciprocity: Evidence from Linear Public Goods Games', *Economic Inquiry*, 45 (2): 199–216.

De Cremer, D. and van Dijk, E. (2002). 'Reactions to Group Success and Failure as a Function of Identification Level: A Test of the Goal Transformation Hypothesis in Social Dilemmas', *Journal of Experimental Social Psychology*, 38 (5): 435–42.

Degli Antoni, G. and Grimalda, G. (2013). 'The Value of Real Voluntary Associations', *Working Papers, Economics Department Universitat Jaume I*, No. 2013/20.

Eckel, C. and Grossman, P. (2005). 'Managing Diversity by Creating Team Identity', *Journal of Economic Behavior and Organization*, 58 (3): 371–92.

Ellingsen, T., Johannesson, M., Tjøtta, S. and Torsvik, G. (2010). 'Testing Guilt Aversion', *Games and Economic Behavior*, 68 (1): 95–107.

Falk, A. and Fischbacher, U. (2006). 'A Theory of Reciprocity', *Games and Economic Behavior*, 54 (2): 293–315.

Falk, A. and Zehnder, C. (2013). 'A City-Wide Experiment on Trust Discrimination', *Journal of Public Economics*, 100: 15–27.

Fehr, E. and Leibbrandt, A. (2011). 'A Field Study on Cooperativeness and Impatience in the Tragedy of the Commons', *Journal of Public Economics*, 95 (9): 1144–55.

Fershtman, C. and Gneezy, U. (2001). 'Discrimination in a Segmented Society: An Experimental Approach', *Quarterly Journal of Economics*, 116 (1): 351–77.

Fershtman, C., Gneezy, U. and Verboven, F. (2005). 'Discrimination and Nepotism: The Efficiency of the Anonymity Rule', *Journal of Legal Studies*, 34 (2): 371–94.

Finocchiaro Castro, M. (2008). 'Where Are You From? Cultural Differences in Public Good Experiments', *The Journal of Socio-Economics*, 37 (6): 2319–29.

Fischbacher, U., Gächter, S. and Fehr, E. (2001). 'Are People Conditionally Cooperative? Evidence from a Public Goods Experiment', *Economics Letters*, 71 (3): 397–404.

Giddens, A. (1991). *Modernity and Self-Identity: Self and Society in the Late Modern Age*, Cambridge: Polity Press.

Goette, L., Huffman, D. and Meier, S. (2006). 'The Impact of Group Membership on Cooperation and Norm Enforcement: Evidence Using Random Assignment to Real Social Groups', *American Economic Review*, 96 (2): 212–6.

Grimalda, G., Buchan, N. and Brewer, M. (2015). 'Globalization, Social Identity, and Propensity to Co-operate: An Experimental Analysis of their Linkages and Effects', *Global Cooperation Research Papers*, No. 10.

Habyarimana, J., Humphreys, M., Posner, D.N. and Weinstein, J.M. (2007). 'Why Does Ethnic Diversity Undermine Public Goods Provision?', *American Political Science Review*, 101 (4): 709–25.

Hannerz, U. (1992). *Cultural Complexity: Studies in the Social Organization of Meaning*, New York, NY: Columbia University Press.

Hargreaves Heap, S.P.H. and Zizzo, D.J. (2009). 'The Value of Groups', *American Economic Review*, 99 (1): 295–323.

Henrich, J. and Henrich, N. (2007). *Why Humans Cooperate*, Oxford: Oxford University Press.

Hoff, K., Kshetramade, M. and Fehr, E. (2011). 'Caste and Punishment: The Legacy of Caste Culture in Norm Enforcement', *Economic Journal*, 121 (556): F449–75.

Keating, M. (2001). *Nations Against the State: The New Politics of Nationalism in Quebec, Catalonia and Scotland*, Basingstoke: Palgrave.

Kerney, A.T. (2004). *Foreign Policy Globalization Index*, accessed at http://foreignpolicy. com/2009/10/12/the-globalization-index-2007/

Kocher, M., Cherry, T., Kroll, S., Netzer, R. and Sutter, M. (2008). 'Conditional Cooperation on Three Continents', *Economic Letters*, 101 (3): 175–78.

Koopmans, R. and Rebers, S. (2009). 'Collective Action in Culturally Similar and Dissimilar Groups: An Experiment on Parochialism, Conditional Cooperation, and Their Linkages', *Evolution and Human Behavior*, 30 (3): 201–11.

Kramer, R.M. and Brewer, M.B. (1986). 'Social Group Identity and the Emergence of Cooperation in Resource Conservation Dilemmas', in H. Wilke, D. Messick, and C. Rutte (eds.) *Experimental Social Dilemmas*, Frankfurt: Peter Lang Verlag, 129–37.

Lockwood, B. and Redoano, M. (2005). 'The CSGR Globalization Index: An Introductory Guide', *CSGR Working Paper*, No. 155/04, last accessed on June 1, 2015, at http://www2. warwick.ac.uk/fac/soc/csgr/index/

McFarland, S., Webb, M. and Brown, D. (2012). 'All Humanity is My Ingroup: A Measure and Studies of Identification With all Humanity', *Journal of Personality and Social Psychology*, 103 (5): 830–53.

Nowak, M.A. (2006). 'Five Rules for the Evolution of Cooperation', *Science*, 314 (5805): 1560–3.

Pfeiffer, T. and Nowak, M.A. (2006). 'Climate Change: All in the Game', *Nature*, 441 (7093): 583–4.

Robertson, R. (1992). *Globalization: Social Theory and Global Culture*, Vol. 16, London / Thousand Oaks, CA / New Delhi: Sage Publication.

Ruffle, B. and Sosis, R. (2006). 'Cooperation and the In-Group-Out-Group Bias: A Field Test on Israeli Kibbutz Members and City Residents', *Journal of Economic Behavior and Organization*, 60 (2): 147–63.

Scholte, J.A. (2002). 'What Is Globalization? The Definitional Issue – Again' *Center for the Study of Globalisation and Regionalisation (CSGR)*, Working Paper No. 109/02.

Shih, M., Pittinsky, T.L. and Ambady, N. (1999). 'Stereotype Susceptibility: Identity, Salience and Shifts in Quantitative Performance', *Psychological Science*, 10 (1): 80–3.

Smith, A. (2013). *Nations and Nationalism in a Global Era*, Cambridge / Maiden: John Wiley and Sons.

Sobel, M. (1982). 'Asymptotic Confidence Intervals for Indirect Effects in Structural Equation Models', *Sociological Methodology*, 13: 290–312.

Tajfel, H. and Turner, J. (1979). 'An Integrative Theory of Intergroup Conflict', in W. Austin and S. Worchel (eds.) *The Social Psychology of Intergroup Relations*, Monterey, CA: Brooks/Cole, 34–47.

Tanaka, T. and Camerer, C. (2010). 'Patronizing Economic Preferences toward Low-Status Groups in Vietnam', Working paper, Mimeo: Arizona State University.

Tanis, M. and Postmes, T. (2005). 'A Social Identity Approach to Trust: Interpersonal Perception, Group Membership and Trusting Behavior', *European Journal of Social Psychology*, 35 (3): 413–24.

Thaler, R. H. and Sunstein, C. R. (2008). *Nudge: Improving Decisions about Health, Wealth, and Happiness*, New Haven, CT: Yale University Press.

Tomlinson, J. (2003). 'Globalization and Cultural Identity', in D. Held and A. McGrew (eds.) *The Global Transformations Reader*, Vol. 2, London: Polity Press, 269–77.

Vertovec, S. and Cohen, R. (eds.) (2002). *Conceiving Cosmopolitanism: Theory, Context and Practice*, Oxford: Oxford University Press.

Whitt, S. and Wilson, R. K. (2007). 'The Dictator Game, Fairness and Ethnicity in Postwar Bosnia', *American Journal of Political Science*, 51 (3): 655–68.

Wit, A. P. and Kerr, N. L. (2002). ' "Me Versus Just US Versus All" Categorization and Cooperation in Nested Social Dilemmas', *Journal of Personality and Social Psychology*, 83 (3): 616–37.

Yamagishi, T. (2007). 'The Social Exchange Heuristic: A Psychological Mechanism that Makes a System of Generalized Exchange Self-Sustaining', in M. Radford, S. Ohnuma, and T. Yamagishi (eds.) *Cultural and Ecological Foundation of the Mind*, Sapporo: Hokkaido University Press, 11–37.

Yamagishi, T. and Kiyonari, T. (2000). 'The Group as the Container of Generalized Reciprocity', *Social Psychology Quarterly*, 63 (2): 116–32.

Yuki, M., Maddux, W., Brewer, M. B. and Takemura, K. (2004). 'Cross-Cultural Differences in Relationship and Group-Based Trust', *Personality and Social Psychology Bulletin*, 31 (1): 48–62.

10 Diplomatic cooperation

An evolutionary perspective[1]

Iver B. Neumann

In 1937, Harold Nicolson, still the best-known modern writer on diplomacy, wrote a slim volume with the title *The Evolution of Diplomatic Method*. In 2011, Keith Hamilton and Richard Langhorne released the second edition of their book *The Practice of Diplomacy: Its Evolution, Theory, and Administration*. The last century has seen a series of books, essays, and even blog spots on diplomacy that advertise themselves as somehow evolutionary. However, almost all of them use the concept of evolution in the everyday sense of emergence.[2] They do not make reference to evolutionary theory, and they do not try to understand diplomacy as an institution evolved by the species. On the contrary, pre-Darwin style, they tend either to place the beginnings of history with writing or, following Hegel, with the emergence of what they refer to as states. Either way, they tend to treat diplomacy as something evolved not by the species in general, but by specific states or by diplomacy itself. As a result, 70 years after Nicolson the standard thing to do in the general literature is still to place the beginnings of diplomacy in ancient Greece (Kurizaki 2011; Nicolson 1939).

Within the multidisciplinary field of diplomacy studies that has emerged over the past three decades or so, there is a slight twist to this theme where the beginnings are concerned. Impressed by work carried out by the likes of Munn-Rankin and Raymond Cohen (Cohen and Westbrook 2000; Munn-Rankin 1956), the beginnings of diplomacy are now increasingly placed in the Eastern Mediterranean during the third millennium BC. It is certainly the fact that the first documented diplomatic system we know of, the so-called Amarna system, emerged in this geographical area some time around the middle of the second millennium BC. The word 'documented' should give their game away, however, for this way of dating the origins of diplomacy hangs on the 19th-century idea that history equals writing. The basic idea behind this dating is still that the institution of diplomacy follows the emergence of a particular political order, namely that sustained by what is usually but misleadingly referred to as pristine ancient states, such as Mesopotamia, China, and the Aztec polity (Fried 1967; cf. Renfrew and Cherry 1988).

The take in this chapter is different. Following the definitions made by Dirk Messner, Alejandro Guarín and Daniel Haun (2013), I treat diplomacy as a meso level of cooperation, with environmental factors understood as social selection

DOI: 10.4324/9781315691657-13

processes taking the role of macro level. Put differently, the perspective taken here is that diplomacy as an emergent institution is shaped by its social and material environment. Humanity shapes diplomacy, and diplomacy shapes humanity. The two are co-constitutive. The overall theme of this book is how cooperation in general, with diplomacy being one kind of cooperation, constitutes humanity, and this is a theme here as well. The stress is on the other story, however; how humanity evolves diplomacy. This is because one point of the exercise is to say something about how diplomacy is changing here and now, and in order to do that it is optimal to focus on how it has changed in the past.

There are obvious costs involved in using an evolutionary perspective on diplomacy. When the focus is on humanity's agency in general, the agency of specific humans is occluded. So are issues of power, and also of meaning. An evolutionary perspective is necessarily functionalist, which easily spells circularity if a causal reading is insisted upon. By the same token, organicism is a dangerous trap. Natural selection is guaranteed by biological factors that do not immediately translate into the social. There is no biological mutational logic in the social. When we speak of social mutations, we are speaking metaphorically. There is no such thing as social natural selection. Social selection processes are to do with factors such as density of habitat, social complexity, competition, and cooperation regarding resources. They give rise to social phenomena such as specific forms of signaling and communication. The emergence of language would be a key example. A more recent one would be the emergence of the World Wide Web. These are stochastic factors, as opposed to natural ones. These are all very good reasons why nobody has really applied an evolutionary way of thinking to diplomacy before. When I nonetheless think this is an exercise worth the candle, it is because an evolutionary frame gives us a kind of longue durée overview that is not readily available from elsewhere. It is in this spirit, and keeping in mind that evoking evolution may all too easily steer us down an asocial biologistic path, that I nonetheless find it useful to take evolutionary thinking to the case of diplomacy. In terms of beginnings, there is no reason why we should not begin our investigation as early as extant proof of human cooperation allows. The longue durée view allows us to speculate about further evolution of diplomacy from a wider and hence more solid base than if we think more short-term, say in centuries. Here we may already complement dominant approaches within diplomatic studies, which tend to see changes in diplomacy as a result of dynamics internal to diplomacy itself (but see Bátora and Hynek 2014; Der Derian 1987; Neumann 2011). Applying an evolutionary perspective to diplomacy is one way to demonstrate how diplomacy grows out of general social and environmental change.

I begin this chapter by discussing the general emergence of human cooperation and how it relates to diplomacy. Given the state of our knowledge, this part is necessarily speculative, and so I throw in some notes on method. Next comes a discussion of earlier evolutionary work, or, to be more precise, *the* earlier work, on diplomacy. I then attempt to move the discussion forward by introducing and applying the idea of evolutionary tipping-points to the study of diplomacy. Tipping-points are understood here as the moment when long-term selection processes crystallize in diplomatic institutionalization. To be absolutely clear, let me give an example of concrete procedure. I do not argue that, say, the founders of the League of Nations had no agency, or that questions of culture-specific power were not very important indeed to this process. Far from denying this, I use an evolutionary perspective to focus on the long-term preconditions for this tipping-point of multilateral diplomacy. Evolutionary thinking enables a focus on the line to be drawn from early gathering of tribes in a number of global locations, from Christian church meetings in the medieval period and so-called congress meetings by states, to the early stirrings of permanent multilateral diplomacy in 19th-century institutions such as the Central Commission for the Navigation on the Rhine and the International Telegraph Union. Having introduced the idea of tipping-points, I then look for moments when the institutionalization of diplomacy firmed historically and identify six such tipping-points. In conclusion, I speculate about the emergence of a seventh tipping-point, which challenges the present hierarchy of diplomatic agents.

Evolution and cooperation

If, in the spirit of evolutionary theory, we discard the idea that history starts with writing and that civilization somehow starts with the Ancient Greeks, and instead think of diplomacy as the institutionalized communication between groups, we get another picture. We must then start not from today and go back, genealogy fashion, but reverse temporality and ask how the species was able to evolve cooperation in the first place. Humanity evolves cooperation, and cooperation evolves humanity, in standard evolutionary circular fashion.

Homo sapiens has lived in foraging bands since it emerged some 200,000 years ago, and also has a prehistory of doing so. Such bands are dependent on a certain level of cooperation for finding and processing food, reproducing, etc. Note that inter-group relations were probably fairly intense:

> Contemporary foraging groups, which are probably not that different in migratory patterns from their prehistorical ancestors, are remarkably outbred compared to even the simplest farming societies, from which we can infer that dealing with strangers in short-term relationships was a common feature of our evolutionary history.
>
> (Gintis et al. 2005: 26)

By archaeological consensus, the level of cooperation increased radically as a response to an environmental factor, namely the possibility of capturing big game. Regardless of hunting method (driving animals into abysses, digging holes, spearing etc.), this would take a group rather than an individual. As demonstrated by a succession of scholars reaching from Peter Kropotkin (1902) via John Maynard Smith (1964) to Matt Ridley (1996) and Christopher Boehm (1999, 2011), the result of collaboration was pivotal in evolutionary terms because it immediately led to a change in the unit of natural selection. To quote Nowak (2006; see also

Messner et al. (2013: 8)), '[p]erhaps the most remarkable aspect of evolution is its ability to generate cooperation in a competitive world. Thus, we might add "natural cooperation" as a third fundamental principle of evolution beside mutation and natural selection' (1563).

When the species was young, selection was individual. With increased cooperation, the unit of selection changed from individual to group. I will follow Boehm and take the increased level of cooperation to follow on from the event of big game hunting, and to see big game hunting as ushering in a political revolution. For leading individuals this revolution posed a challenge, for the superior individual hunting skills which had made them leading were no longer an optimal environmental fit on their own, but had to be complemented by skills pertaining to leadership and collaboration. This change was driven by leveling behavior, which means that alpha males were lived down by coalitions who went in for sharing of food, group sanctions, and suchlike (cf. Shostak 1976).[3]

As is the rule in archaeology, if we want to date this, we are dependent on material findings. We have no guarantee that our findings equal the first occurrences of the phenomenon in question, for new findings may always antedate our oldest ones to date. Boehm talks about the explosion in cooperation as a 'Late Pleistocene revolution', and dates it to about 100,000 BC. This dating is not very convincing. In the mid-1990s, eight throwing spears were found together with thousands of horse bones in Schöningen, Germany (Thieme 2007). That find dated big game hunting to about 300,000 years ago. Big game hunting may be even older, however, with the find of stone-tipped spears used by *homo heidelbergiensis*, the common ancestor of *homo sapiens* and Neanderthals, that dates back more than half a million years (Wilkins et al. 2012). We simply do not know whether these spears were used for big game hunting. What is reasonably clear, however, is that the advent of big game hunting happened magnitudes before the time suggested by Boehm.

Note that even if qualitative increase in cooperation was immense, changes were rather limited in terms of group size. Our best estimate of the average size of hunter-gatherer groups based on anthropological studies of bands living under conditions roughly similar to those that dominated Pleistocene habitats would be around 37 (Marlowe 2005). Most groups would have been larger, however; so the Pleistocene human would probably have lived in a group numbering perhaps 70 to 120 individuals.[4]

All this is fairly well established by archaeologists. The key reason why this knowledge has not been applied to the study of diplomacy is probably to do with the focus on another social response to group selection, namely war. Extant evolutionary literature has focused on how cooperation may help one group outcompete another. In a primer on microeconomic foundations, Samuel Bowles and Herbert Gintis state that

> it has been conventional since Thomas Hobbes' *Leviathan* to attribute the maintenance of social order to states. But for at least 95% of the time that biologically modern humans have existed, our ancestors somehow fashioned

a system of governance that without the assistance of governments avoided the chaos of the Hobbesian state of nature sufficiently to become by far the most enduring of social orders ever. The genetic, archaeological, ethnographic, and demographic data make it quite clear that they did not accomplish this by limiting human interactions to a few close genetic relatives. [Rather, . . .] a particular form of altruism, often hostile toward outsiders and punishing toward insiders who violate norms, coevolved with a set of institutions – sharing food and making war are examples – that at once protected a group's altruistic members and made group-level cooperation the *sine qua non* of survival.

(Bowles and Gintis 2011: 5)

Following Darwin ([1873] 1998: 134–5), they argue that group conflict is an important driver of evolution, for it lays down an imperative that groups have to galvanize against other groups, and those who evolve the highest level of what they call parochial altruism will have an advantage that will crowd out other groups (Bowles and Gintis 2011: 133–47).[5]

The debate over whether war is an evolutionary necessity or not – and this debate is of interest to us, as its existence is arguably the main reason why so little attention has been paid to Pleistocene non-conflictual inter-group relations – is as old as the social sciences themselves. From Darwin there winds a continual line of thought that argues in favor of war's necessity, usually under the banner of conflict theory of the origin of the state. Conflict theorists tend to stress the key evolutionary advantage of effective leadership for war and war's key role in securing new ecological niches for certain groups at the expense of others.[6] Against these thinkers stand those who stress how war is but one of the institutions of social history. An early example is Kropotkin, author of a famous 1902 monograph on cooperation, but Kropotkin had little to say on intra-group relations. Another is the last of the post-war generation of evolutionists, Elman Service, whose work on the origins of large-scale political organization focused on the classical functionalist theme of systems maintenance rather than on conflict. But Service, too, no more than hints at the importance of what he refers to as external relations. Here is the key quote on the matter from his *magnum opus*:

[P]rimitive people recognize the danger of warfare and take measures to reduce its likelihood. These measures are various, of course, but they are all reducible to one generic mode of alliance-making, the reciprocal exchange. Reciprocal exchanges are the ways in which all kinship organizations extend or intensify the normal interpersonal bonds of kinship statuses. Any two relationships of kinship imply standardized obligations and rights that are symbolized by exchanges of goods and favors (as well as by prescribed forms of etiquette). Such exchanges are normally both utilitarian and symbolic. [. . . They are mainly of two kinds:] marriages and exchanges of goods.

(Service 1975: 60–1)[7]

Standardized obligations and rights, reciprocal exchange, prescribed forms of etiquette: here we have come to the subject at hand, namely diplomacy. With the partial exception of Ridley's (1996) already referenced book, later archaeological work has not followed up on Service's observation, however.

To sum up so far, for reasons that are to do with pre-Darwinian approaches to our past, the field of diplomatic studies has largely ignored the period before the third millennium BC. Whereas some kind of small-scale collaboration seems to be as old as the species itself, with the dawn of the late Pleistocene some 126,000 years ago, big game hunting inaugurated a political revolution based on heightened levels of cooperation. Pleistocene inter-group relations have, however, been largely studied in one aspect only, namely that of warfare. The observation is sometimes made that other environmental challenges, such as natural catastrophes, may make for inter-group collaboration, and it is acknowledged that gift-making, most basically in the Lévi-Staussian tapping of the exchange of women, is an ancient phenomenon. That, however, is where extant scholarship seems to stop.

Earlier work on diplomacy in evolutionary perspective

Well, not quite. As far as I am aware, there is one, and only one, scholar who breaks with this pattern. In the 1930s Ragnar Numelin left his native Finland to write his doctorate with his compatriot, evolutionary anthropologist and LSE professor in sociology Edvard Westermarck. The result was published in 1950 (when Numelin was working at the Finnish legation in Brussels) as *The Beginnings of Diplomacy: A Sociological Study of Intertribal and International Relations.*[8] Numelin is a bit shy, stating at the outset that he is

> not thinking in terms of evolutionary anthropology or history [. . . but only wants] to emphasize the sociological side of the question: that we should study also the social 'diplomatic' culture in the savage world and not, as has often been done, confine ourselves to conditions prevailing among 'historical' peoples.
>
> (Numelin 1950: 14)

Already on the next page, however, he states that 'it is an astonishing fact that we can observe, among savage peoples, the beginnings of a great many forms of development which actually belong to far higher stages of civilization' (Numelin 1950: 15). If this is not evolution-speak, then what is? There follow chapters that set out detailed catalogues of embryonic forms of hospitality, inter-group heralds and messengers, peace negotiators and war emissaries, and treaty-making and trade.

Numelin begins, in the tradition from Kropotkin, with a critique of other theorists, evolutionists included, for making the unwarranted assumption that war was the key political phenomenon of hunter-gatherer existence. For example, he notes that Herbert Spencer admitted 'the peaceful origin of primitive political organization', but nonetheless held the 'false conception' that war was key to it, simply because he had, by drawing on Ratzel and other German researchers, 'deliberately selected features from later savage and "barbarous" life as the starting-point of his political theories' (Numelin 1950: 67). Here Numelin is foreshadow-ing present-day attacks on the entire political canon from Hobbes to Pinker for having, willfully and on weak or even non-existent empirical grounds, created a prehistory which the archaeological evidence, such as it is, does not support (see any chapter in this book). Numelin goes on to note examples which were known at the time, such as pre-contact Tasmania. He sees what we may call an early tipping-point in totemism, as 'members of tribes with the same totem are generally well treated even if they should be strangers' (Numelin 1950: 111). Drawing on Malinowski's classical work on the Trobriand Islands, he notes the practice of cleansing strangers of their taboo by having a village girl 'act as the stranger's partner for the night' (Numelin 1950: 113). Another widespread practice was the presentation of (other) gifts (156). There is also the practice of the peace-invo-cating festival, such as the Mindarie-feasts of the Diery of Australia (141). The general practice on display here is hospitality, offered not least out of a fear of unknown supernatural powers.

Numelin (1950) goes on to detail the emergence of the messenger, who was personally inviolable and who was 'selected with great discrimination out of those members of the tribe or local group who enjoy general esteem and often belong to the most outstanding persons in the tribe' (130). Inviolability sometimes spread to commercial agents (152). War messengers are widespread amongst hunter-gatherer populations; Numelin (1950: 178) takes issue with older literature which held that formal declarations of war amongst 'primitives' were not necessary. The central case is the peace messenger, however.[9] Numelin gives as one example the Arunta of Australia:

> When a fight breaks out among the Arunta, and one of the parties wish to make it up, they send a man and his wife as messengers to the other camp. In order to try the adversaries' readiness to make peace the messenger has to put his wife at their disposal. If the offer is accepted and the men accordingly enter into intercourse with the messenger's wife – this act is called *Noa* (con-jux) or *Ankalla* ('cousinship') – a favorable issue of the political situation may be expected; if it is rejected, the fighting continues.
>
> (Numelin 1950: 170–71, cf. 214)

Note the use of kinship terminology here. A typical accoutrement of tribal messengers, which may be traced on all continents, is the message stick (Numelin 1950: 164) which served as identification and as a mnemonic aid for the mes-senger, a clear forerunner of the ancient Greek double-folded sheets framed and carried around the neck by messengers and called *diploun* – the phenomenon that has given diplomacy its name.

A key finding, from which Numelin (1950: 203) struggles in vain to find excep-tions, is the appearance of 'feasts and drinking bouts' when peace is negotiated.

The seemingly ubiquitous appearance of feasts gives the lie to those who see all the eating and drinking entered into by diplomats as an unnecessary luxury. The commensality of eating and drinking is an institution which can be observed amongst all known polities who do business with one another, and must therefore be seen as a historically necessary practice of diplomacy (Neumann 2013a). A special, and widespread, case is the blood-brotherhood, often sealed by the drinking of blood.[10] We need not heed Numelin's (1950: 211) speculation that this may be a forerunner of the drinking of one another's health, but do note that kinship terminology makes yet another appearance in the so-called pledging in blood.

To sum up, Numelin certainly looks at diplomacy as something that is being evolved by the species itself. He does identify a number of precursors of phenomena that we may trace down through written cultures (more on this later). As seen from the present, however, there is a key weakness in Numelin's method. His sources are, and had to be, given the time at which it was written, exclusively those of anthropologists who have studied hunters and gatherers during the 19th and 20th centuries, and he jumbles them all together. Some of these groups may be similar to pre-sedentary human polities in their material base, but we would not know, for Numelin does not discuss the matter. In their social organization, however, these groups have had just as much time, roughly 11,000 years, to evolve as have sedentary societies, and a number of them will have been marked by their contact with those sedentary societies. James C. Scott (2009), who has written insightfully on how states actually may *produce* non-state societies, has gone so far as to argue that 'we have virtually no credible evidence about the world until yesterday and, until we do, the only defensible intellectual position is to shut up' (Scott 2013: 15). This is clearly an overstatement. As demonstrated at the beginning of this article, archaeologists have excavated a lot of stuff that they have turned into evidence, although Scott is of course right that this evidence is tentative and so not necessarily credible, particularly to someone who does not seem to have taken the time to examine it. This is, however, a point one could wage against *all* knowledge about the social, as Scott himself has repeatedly underlined. Principally, it is therefore an untenable position for a working academic not to build on our scholarly knowledge such as it is and to try to widen and deepen that knowledge. Exit Scott.

A new approach to the history of diplomacy: Tipping-points

When Numelin is building exclusively on evidence culled from hunter-gatherer groups observed by anthropologists, this is because the data available at the time when he was writing, in the 1930s, made it very hard to do anything else. As a result, Numelin was condemned to stop at cataloguing relevant phenomena (as they were evident from the anthropological record) and could not go on to attempt much theorization. He does not look at what the evolutionist Morton

Fried (1967, in the context of the change from chiefdoms to states) refers to as 'leaps' of evolution. It seems to me that an attempt to pinpoint candidates for such leaps, tipping-points, or, to use evolution-speak, punctuated equilibrium effects (Eldredge and Gould [1972] 1985; for a recent critical assessment, see Scott 2007) must be the next logical step in applying evolutionary thinking to the case of diplomacy.[11]

For an illustration of how such leaps or tipping-points work analytically, let me reproduce an example from a much-used primer on game theory, whose subtitle is 'An Evolutionary Theory of Institutions' (Young 1998). The example concerns not diplomacy, but the rather less unwieldy (because it is binary) example of which side of the road to drive on:

> In the early stages, when there was relatively little traffic on the roads and its range was limited, conventions grew up locally; a city or province would have one convention, while a few miles down the road another jurisdiction would have the opposite one. As use of the roads increased and people traveled further afield, these local rules tended to congeal first into regional and then into national norms, though for the most part these norms were not codified as traffic laws until well into the nineteenth century. In areas with highly fragmented jurisdictions, the congealing process took longer, as an evolutionary model would predict. Italy, for example, was characterized by highly localized left-hand driving rules until well into the twentieth century. Once conventions became established at the national level, the interactions are between countries, who [*sic*] are influenced by their neighbors: if enough of them follow the same convention, it pays to follow suit. Over time, we would expect a single convention to sweep across the board. While this intuition is essentially correct, it ignores the effect of idiosyncratic shocks, which can displace one convention in favor of another. Remarkably, just such a shock occurred in the history of European driving: the French Revolution. Up to that time, it was customary for carriages in France as well as in many other parts of Europe to keep to the left when passing. This meant that pedestrians often walked on the right to face the oncoming traffic. Keeping to the left was therefore associated with the privileged classes, while keeping to the right was considered more 'democratic.' Following the French Revolution, the convention was changed for symbolic reasons. Subsequently Napoleon adopted the new custom for his armies, and it spread to some of the countries he occupied. From this point onward, one can see a gradual but steady shift – moving more or less from west to east – in favor of right-hand rule. For example, Portugal, whose only border was with right-driving Spain, converted after World War I. Austria switched province by province, beginning with Vorarlberg and Tyrol in the west and ending with Vienna in the east, which held out until the Anschluss with Germany in 1938. Hungary and Czechoslovakia also converted under duress at about this time. The last

continental European country to change from left to right was Sweden in
1967. Thus we see a dynamic response to an exogenous shock (the French
Revolution) that played out over the course of almost two hundred years.

(Young 1998: 16–17)

Since this is a multi-disciplinary volume and I have tipped my hat to economics
by quoting the likes of Samuel Bowles and Peyton Young, it is only fair that I now
be allowed a moment to blow my own horn: when Young the economist is looking
around for a key example, he comes up with stuff foregrounding politics: the
French Revolution, the Napoleonic Wars, the First World War, the Anschluss.
There is a pointer here to how tipping-points, understood as the culmination of
long-term trends, are institutionalized; it often happens in the context of
attempted learning once the victors (and sometimes the losers, too) have had the
chance to sit down and ponder what went wrong the last time. Note, however,
the contingent character of the social changes that brought on right-hand driving.
By the same token, I am not prepared to privilege any one set of factors that
determine diplomacy. Social evolution does not work like that. Stuff emerges,
becomes problematized and leads to cooperative and conflictual behavior without
the organic laws of biology to underpin the process, which therefore remains
stochastic.

Young's binary example (left-hand driving vs. right-hand driving) may only
help us part of the way, for it occludes the analogue nature of more complex social
changes such as those pertaining to diplomacy. Most social stuff is not like the
question of which side of the road to drive on, but rather preserves pre-tipping-
point stuff as part of the whole picture. The social is like a palimpsest, where older
practices shine through amongst the dominant and newest ones.[12] Specifically,
diplomacy may reach a tipping-point, and as seen from the time intervals between
them, history seems to be speeding up so that we now spend centuries or even
decades rather than millennia in reaching a new tipping-point. Once the tipping-
point has been reached, however, previous practices do not simply disappear, but
tend to hover. One contemporary example would be how a state like Russia is
markedly less involved in multilateral practices than is, say, Germany.

In the first part of this chapter, we already encountered one leap or tipping-
point that has been further evidenced by fossil findings, namely the late Pleistocene political revolution brought on by the possibility of big game hunting some
300,000 years ago. Here the selection process was driven by increased complexity
in signaling. While this revolution first and foremost had the effect of increasing
the value of ingroup cooperation, it also suggested the possibility of cooperation
between groups. Such cooperation would take diplomacy to come into being. Let
us call the Pleistocene revolution a proto-diplomatic tipping-point.

Note that 'cooperation' is a positively loaded word, and this occludes the importance of social relations for it to work. Every social scientist is, for example, familiar with Rousseau's fable of the stag hunt, where the point is that if only one of a
hunting party spots a hare and breaks rank by killing it, the cooperative scheme
to catch a stag will fall apart. The antidote to this is the wielding of social power.

To pick an example from the life of contemporary hunter-gatherers once again, in an ethnographic study of the !Kung, Shostak (1976) found that of the hours of quotidian conversation that she had recorded on tape, over one-third was spent on criticizing selected good hunters for not being cooperative enough, often within their earshot or even to their faces. If all known human settings display the use of power to keep cooperative schemes on the tracks, it is a safe assumption that the same went for the late Pleistocene revolution, and that it was, consequently, power laden.

This is important, for it should remind us of how cooperative schemes such as diplomacy are shot through with power relations. It is, for example, not the case that diplomacy is the opposite of war (see Barkawi, forthcoming). It is, rather, the opposite of not talking to the enemy. Diplomacy is attempts by socially designated representatives to handle difference on a group level by means of a cocktail of practices, with talk being paramount amongst them. The major importance of the late Pleistocene revolution to diplomacy, then, lies in the way it further institutionalized cooperative schemes as a standard *modus operandi* of human life in general. It enhanced the social space for action taken on bases other than at spear-point, as well as space for non-verbal and, in historical perspective, verbal communication of a non-violent but definitely power-laden kind.[13]

Numelin's work suggests a second tipping-point, namely totemism, which may serve as a template for turning living beings who were before considered impossible to talk to into *interlocateurs valable* by offering a ground on which to cooperate, namely the fact of sharing a common totem. While this is a highly tentative idea, if we fast-forward from hunter-gatherer groups to societies about which we have written knowledge, we do see a similar mechanism in operation. In all known early examples of diplomatic practices, kinship appears as a template. In the Amarna system, named after the findings of stone tablets documenting correspondence between 1300 BC polities such as Egypt, Babylonia, Assyria, and the Hittite polity Hatti, a key theme is the ongoing attempts by the other kings to have the Egyptians acknowledge them as brothers and not sons. The ancient Greek practice of 'discovering' kin, invariably groups of barbarians so strong that they could not be ignored but that somehow had to be dealt with, with the Macedonians being a prime example, brings out the logic (Neumann 2011). Kinship offers a language of categorization within which diplomatic maneuvering may take place. This still goes on within what is, appositely, often diplomatically called the 'family' of nations, i.e. the states system. Similar practices are known from other diplomatic systems, such as the Iroquois League which operated ca. 1300–1750. Given the overwhelming importance of kinship for all political organization, we are on fairly safe ground in assuming that the use of kinship-speak constituted a tipping-point of very old standing. How old, we have no way of knowing. Note that, contrary to the first tipping-point, which springs from a material factor, namely that the end of the Pleistocene ice age brought a warmer climate conducive to the emergence of edible megafauna, this tipping-point is brought on by social organization itself.

A third tipping-point is suggested by recent archaeological research and concerns the process of sedentarization. The selection processes that drove this was certainly habitat density, which led to increased competition between like units and also to cooperation amongst them. First, consider the emergence of villages. The earliest known cropped up in Anatolia some 7000 years ago and were not directly tied to agriculture. However, those that emerged in Sumer around 3500 BC were. For our purposes, the key thing to note is that there was more than one village. Thus a pattern was initiated where culturally similar but politically distinct entities emerged in the same place. Renfrew and Cherry (1986) have called these peer-group polities. These polities interacted on a regular basis from territorially stable positions. The result was institutionalized patterns of interaction, which we may see as the first embryonic diplomatic patterns. They have been studied first and foremost for their state-building results; Sumerian polities were united under a king already around BC 2900.

The Neolithic period is better understood than the earlier periods are because it overlapped with human memory in a sufficient degree to leave accounts in early writing, and because it left more material remnants. One example of these are the stone megastructures of what we now call Northern Europe, which have been interpreted as constituting a second variant of this third tipping-point. Some of these monuments have been read as representing the graveyards of different polities, gathered in one place, and serving not only as focal points for gatherings of the tribes, but also as material constitutive elements of what we may see as early diplomatic systems. For example, Renfrew (2007) interprets Stonehenge in this way. Noting that there was too much rainfall in Northern Europe for conditions to allow the kind of mud-hut-based villages that were in evidence in places like Sumer and further south in Europe, he postulates that the emerging sedentary culture needed a focus, and that 'the great henges would have served as ceremonial centres and perhaps also as pilgrimage centres for their parent communities . . . the end product was the emergence of a coherent larger community where none was before' (Renfrew 2007: 155–6).

If Renfrew is right, then there is a line to be drawn from the constitution of diplomatic relations centered on henges to the further rise of chiefs heading peer-group polities, and on to these chiefs vying for supremacy in early state building processes that resemble those found in Sumer. Examples include not only British kingdoms, but also Scandinavian ones and their offsprings, such as the Rus', arising around AD 800–1000 (Earle 1997; Neumann 2013b). What we may call the Viking world evolved stable patterns of diplomatic relations in the area stretching from Britain in the West to Rus' in the east, as well as diplomatic contact with dominating polities further south, such as the Byzantine empire.

Byzantium, with its patterned diplomatic relations with surrounding polities, was late to the ball, however, for the large-scale diplomatic relations between culturally distinct polities in evidence here were spearheaded in the area where Sumer was based, the East Mediterranean. Sumer's successor polity, Akkad, had regular diplomatic contacts with other kingdoms already in the third millennium BC, and eventually became a founder member of the first diplomatic system, the second-millennium BC Amarna system, consisting of polities such as Babylonia, Egypt, and Hatti, whose lingua franca was indeed Akkadian (Cohen and Westbrook 2000). The emergence of this first large-scale diplomatic system clearly constitutes a fourth tipping-point in the evolutionary history of diplomacy, driven by increased social complexity. Note that Greece, which is so often seen as the cradle of both Western civilization and diplomacy, constitute an example of the third tipping-point: culturally similar peer-group polities interacting at a time (the 4th century BC) when the fourth tipping-point had been in evidence elsewhere for 1500 years or so. Where diplomacy is concerned, the Greek *poleis* are an example of evolutionary re-emergence; it is not a tipping-point. The same would be the case for the already mentioned Iroquois diplomatic system in Turtle Island (ca. AD 1300–1750; see Neumann 2011).

A fifth tipping-point was reached as social interaction between large-scale polities intensified, and the need for more permanent exchanges than those afforded by messengers made itself felt. Once again, increased social complexity and more advanced signaling characterize the process. The answer was not only to base exchanges on messengers, but also to let people who were sedentary within one polity handle relations with other polities on a running basis. There are early examples on this – for example traders within the Amarna system, the institution of the *proximos* in ancient Greece (which involved citizens of one *polis* who were particularly close to some other Greek *polis*), and also in Africa. From the 4th century AD, different branches of Christendom evolved the institution of *apocrisiarii*, whereby some representative of the Catholic Church was resident in Byzantium. The first permanent, reciprocal, and so fully fledged, example of this institution, which came to be known precisely as permanent diplomacy, hails from the 14th-century Italian city-state system (Neumann 2011). After centuries of wrangling about reciprocity, permanent diplomacy went on to become a global phenomenon in the 20th century.

By then, a sixth tipping-point was already well in the making, driven not only by increased social complexity but also by technological innovation in the area of communication, particularly in infrastructure. We know it as internationalism. Its pre-history reached back to the institution of the gathering of the tribes, which we touched on already in our discussion of Stonehenge. A more elaborate form of this institution took the form of the irregular church meetings of the Catholic Church from the 4th century onwards and the *kurultais* that were called to choose successor rulers in the Turko-Mongol tradition of Eurasian steppe politics. The emergence of 'international' (that is, with states as members) organizations such as the Central Commission for the Navigation on the Rhine (1815) and the International Telegraph Union and International Postal Union during the second half of the 19th century brought permanence to what was soon to be called multinational diplomacy, just as permanence had been brought to bilateral diplomacy some centuries before. With the founding of the League of Nations in 1919, permanent multilateral diplomacy went global. The work of the thousands of international organizations in evidence today has increased the number of people doing diplomatic work enormously, and has lent to global diplomacy a much,

Table 10.1 Six tipping-points in the evolutionary history of diplomacy

	From when	Agents	Scale
1. Pleistocene revolution	BC 300,000 (?)	Individuals	Ingroup
2. Totemism	?	Nomads	Small-scale, classified kinship, culturally homogenous
3. Peer-group polities	BC 7500	Sedentaries	Small-scale, culturally homogenous
4. Amarna system	BC 1500 (?)	Kingdoms	Regional, culturally heterogenous
5. Permanent representation	AD 1430s	City States	Culturally homogenous, eventually international
6. Multilateral institutions	AD 1810s	States	International

much more socially dense quality than it had only a hundred years ago. Whereas the number of diplomats on the eve of the First World War could be counted in four-digit numbers, diplomats working for the state today are counted in six-digit numbers, and if we add international civil servants, activists in non-governmental organizations, consultants, spin doctors, and so on, we probably reach a seven-digit number.

To sum up, the evolutionary history of diplomacy may be told by way of identifying six tipping-points: the late Pleistocene political revolution 300,000 years ago; classificatory kinship as a template for regular cooperation (date unknown); regular and ritualized contacts between culturally similar small-scale polities (5,500 years ago); regular and ritualized contacts between culturally different large-scale polities (4,000 years ago); permanent bilateral diplomacy (five centuries ago) and permanent multilateral diplomacy (one century ago). This story is summed up in Table 10.1.

What's ahead?

The 19th century and early years of the 20th century saw a tipping-point in the evolution of diplomacy as it went permanently multilateral, and the years since then have seen an enormous quantitative increase, as the number of practitioners have gone from a five-digit to a seven-digit number. In evolutionary terms, diplomacy, as an institution of human cooperation, is a great success.

If asked whether today's diplomatic practices are optimal for the development of further cooperation given ongoing changes in environment, we may observe that today's diplomatic practices have primarily, but not exclusively, grown out of aristocratic European social institutions. Since the aristocracy was outmaneuvered by the bourgeoisie as the leading class more than two centuries ago, and Europe's century-and-a-half-long leading role in global politics ended about half a century ago, we may wonder whether the diplomatic institutions they spawned are not also being overtaken by other forms. There is certainly enough movement away from the stylized diplomacy of 18th-century Europe to make this a legitimate question. On the other hand, the changes in state-based diplomacy, be that in the bilateral diplomacy of states or in the multilateral diplomacy of international organizations whose members are states, have been incremental, and nothing suggests that the dynamism of change has been so slow that these institutions will simply be thrown away as a new tipping-point emerges.

As noted at the outset of this chapter, extant work on diplomacy tends to discuss change in the institution as a function of developments internal to it. However, diplomacy is embedded in everyday social life. One strength of an evolutionary approach is that it can clearly demonstrate this by directing attention to how diplomacy's social and material environment sets in motion developments which lead to tipping-points. So it is with possible future developments; their origins must be sought outside of the institution of diplomacy itself, in diplomacy's environment. There is little doubt that candidate number one is the shift away from a world centered around the states system toward a globalized world, with globalization referring to the increase in global social density and the condensation of spatiality and temporality. Like its forerunner, internationalism, the selection process is characterized by technological innovation in the area of communication, particularly software infrastructure and so-called social media. The explosion in public diplomacy is a key development here. As a result, and to an unprecedented degree, what happens in one local site is imbricated in developments elsewhere. As flows of people, ideas, trade, and services increase rapidly, the importance of boundaries between states changes. State discreteness is challenged, and with it state agency. To put it differently, the environment for state action changes rapidly, and this cannot but have repercussions on a diplomacy whose major agents are state, for it puts the centrality of the state system to global politics in question and raises the question of how states change as they try to optimize their role in the new environment.

There are two conventional answers to this question.[14] The first is that other, non-state agents threaten to overtake states. The second is that states keep on as before, with the one proviso that they delegate functions to other agents and become the principal agent of those other agents. In an evolutionary perspective, the first answer is wanting, for there is little or no evidence that the new environment fits other agents better than it does states. The second answer also comes up short, for in an evolutionary perspective state delegation means reshuffling, and reshuffling has recursive effects that will change the states that delegate. We must somehow account for all that, and I think the best way to do it is to grant the point that new agents become more important, and also the point that states seem to be able to harness most of the activity of these new agents for their own uses. What is about to happen, then, is that the former hierarchy of agents, with states firmly on top and with various kinds of non-state agents layered below them, is being condensed and hybridized. States retain their key status, but they become less like territorially bound entities that serve as containers for social life, and more like central nodes in networks of agents.

This has immediate repercussions for diplomacy, for it means that state agents may be found in other kinds of organizations. The posting of British and French diplomats to posts in ostensibly non-state development organizations dates back more than a decade. Non-governmental presence in Canadian and Norwegian negotiation teams emerged in the 1990s. Less formal use of seemingly free agents by key diplomatic agents is as old as institutionalized diplomacy itself. It also means that other organizations try to copy diplomatic organizational models for how to operate 'in the field'. Military attachés have done this for centuries. The 'expat' divisions of transnational companies are usually organized along lines first laid out by diplomats, and former diplomats are often employed by them. Non-governmental organizations specializing in development aid, humanitarian relief, peace and reconciliation work, and so on similarly organize their expatriates on models lifted from diplomatic services. The new tipping-point, which is already well advanced, is what we may call the hybridization of diplomacy; state and non-state actors become more similar, they face similar cooperation problems as did other constellations of diplomatic agents before them, and they partake of shifting alliances. The central role of states will probably not fade, but states will increasingly have to work *with* and *through* other kinds of agents rather than *on* them, as they usually did before. As always when a new tipping-point arises in social spheres, this is not totally new. In a social setting, as the example of how right-hand driving conquered Europe bore out, a tipping-point is something that is reached gradually. Britain and most of Asia still drives on the left-hand of the road. A tipping-point is not something that does away with previous practices overnight. When looking back at the emergence of diplomacy with a hunch that the next tipping-point is hybridization of agents, one spots plenty of forebodings. Neither – and this is where the digital example of left-hand vs. right-hand driving no longer speaks to the more complex social stuff such as diplomacy – do new practices totally eradicate old ones. The coming of hybridized diplomacy does not mean that a number of time-hallowed diplomatic practices will automatically disappear.

We may now, finally, turn to the question of how diplomacy relates to the more general question of human cooperation. Messner et al. (2013, see also Messner, Guarín, and Haun in this volume) write:

> Although all the elements in the cooperation hexagon are important, we contend that four of them are necessary to create conditions conducive to reciprocity: trust, communication (a key mechanism to develop trust), the ability to determine people's reputation as trustworthy partners, and the perception that the interaction is fair. In addition to these four mechanisms, we can use enforcement (via punishment or reward) as a means to rein in uncooperative partners. And finally, these mechanisms that enable reciprocation are much more likely to emerge within groups that are physically similar or that share a common narrative – in other words, with those with which we share a we-identity.
>
> (Messner et al. 2013: 16)

When run up against the case of diplomacy, this certainly holds. Punishment is famously costly (war) or ineffectual (sanctions, embargoes), as are rewards (development aid, intention agreements), but the logics are broadly the same as those we may identify for cooperation generally. As for the mechanisms concerned, while diplomacy is ubiquitous throughout human history, reciprocity was key to the formation of diplomatic systems such as the Sumer system, the Amarna system, the Iroquois system, and the European post-Renaissance system. While scattered cases of diplomacy based on symmetrical reciprocity may be observed elsewhere – Sverdrup-Thygeson (2011) looks at the Chinese case and highlights relations with the Liao in the 9th century and the relations with the Russian empire in the 17th century, and we could add relations with the Hsiung-nu during the last two centuries before our era – they were not permanent enough to take root. While power asymmetries between Europe and the rest of the world over the last 200 years are of course absolutely central to understanding how European practices became the major source for today's global diplomacy, and although examples of how European states drew on power asymmetries to ram through diplomatic rules and treaties are rife, the fact that there already existed a European system based on reciprocity that could be exported globally is, in the light of the introduction to this book, also a factor in understanding why it is that other origins have left so few marks on current diplomatic practices (Neumann 2012). A particularly illuminating example is the emergence of permanent representation, where powers such as the Ottoman Empire and China failed to reciprocate by not sending permanent representatives to European powers exactly *because* this would be a sign of accepting these powers on an equal basis, and therefore giving up on the claim to superiority. As late as 20 years ago, the importance of reciprocity was perhaps most easily observed in the quid pro quo practices of declaring foreign diplomats as personae non grata. Interestingly, since then there has been a movement away from host countries expelling people toward a practice where states which expect that the host country are about to take such action voluntarily send the diplomats involved back. In our perspective, such anticipation must be interpreted as yet another victory for cooperation because it forestalls overt quarrels.

The factors that create an institution are not necessarily the same as those that uphold it, however. When discussing the future of diplomacy, the relevant thing is not how trust, communication, the ability to determine people's reputation as trustworthy partners, and the perception that the interaction is fair played out in previous centuries, but rather what is the current state of play. Trust and communication are fairly well established. So, as is evident in the existence of an increasingly thick diplomatic culture, is we-feeling. To give but one example, Wille (2013) recently reported that, when asked why he taught diplomatic skills to young Eastern European diplomats that his own country would one day meet in negotiations, their German instructor answered that the higher the common understanding of the rules of the game, the easier the negotiations, and the higher the chance of getting to yes.

If present-day diplomacy scores highly on all these, we are still left with a major problem. In a situation where established and rising powers are in the middle of a prolonged face-off, the key problem is fairness. Emerging powers such as Brazil, China, and India complain that they are not given their due either in institutionalized terms or in terms of practices. This is obviously correct. To take a key example, there is no reason whatsoever why the country that is already a major player in Asia and that is about to become the most populous on earth, India, does not have a permanent seat in the UN Security Council. A good, if weaker, case may be made for Brazil. Further down the list, we find Nigeria. Conversely, there is no reason why Britain and France hang onto 40 per cent of the permanent seats, instead of the EU having one of, say, seven seats. By the same token, it is not immediately clear why the G7 decided intermittently to include Russia, a weak and probably fading power, while neglecting China. In a key arena of cooperation like global warming, rising powers rightly point out that established powers became established by burning off a lot of nonrenewable resources, and that this contributed to us landing where we are. Established powers rightly point out that, given where we are, things will certainly deteriorate if rising powers follow suit. Once again, the major stumbling block to cooperation in this area is fairness.

At certain historical junctures, diplomacy has been singled out as the root cause of the world's ills. After the First World War, many liberals pointed to secret diplomacy as the major cause for why war broke out. Revolutionary regimes from France via Russia to Iran have blamed diplomacy for why the world order was like it was. Today, we sometimes hear that diplomacy is not so much evil as it is out of touch with key issues that call for more cooperation. I would argue that all these views are mistaken. As I have tried to demonstrate in this chapter, diplomacy is a hard-won triumph of the species. In an evolutionary perspective, it is the recursive result, and not the cause, of cooperation between human polities. It has intensified from small-scale to large-scale, from intermittent to permanent, from bilateral to multi-lateral. Viewed closer up, all kinds of specific changes in diplomatic practices are in the making, with the articulation of sundry non-state agents to state agents being perhaps foremost amongst them. A new tipping-point is on its way. Since evolutionary explanations are by definition functionalist and long term, it makes little sense to apply an evolutionary perspective to small-scale changes. Suffice it to say, therefore, that it would be highly detrimental for the future of human cooperation to throw away the hard-won institution of diplomacy, for it would do no more than face us with the task of building something similar all over again.

Notes

1 I should like to thank Józef Bátora, Corneliu Bjola, Daniel Cadier, Thomas Hylland Eriksen, Håkon Glørstad, Silke Weinlich, and Ole Jacob Sending for comments on earlier drafts.
2 I will return to the one exception, namely the work by Ragnar Numelin.
3 'The regulation of social interactions by group-level institutions plays no less a role than altruistic individual motives in understanding how this cooperative species came to be. Institutions affect the rewards and penalties associated with particular behaviors, often favoring the adoption of cooperative actions over others, so that even the self-regarding are often induced to act in the interest of the group' (Bowles and Gintis 2011: 5). Where political theory is concerned, it is interesting to note (but not necessarily damning to Hobbes, since he is operating at the analytical plane) that these findings rather puncture Hobbes's thought experiment of the social contract, which turned on humans giving

up their freedom and uniting under a leader. Historically, it was the other way around; cooperation evolved exactly to take leaders down some notches, and not to exalt them. Exaltation came later with large-scale polities. On the other hand, Rousseau's thought experiment of the stag hunt overlaps with an absolutely essential evolutionary moment, for it is groups that are able to cooperate in bringing down big game and megafauna that gain an evolutionary edge by dint of which they crowd out less socially advanced groups.

4 '. . . during the Late Pleistocene [126,000 BC – 12,000 BC] a far greater fraction of hunter-gatherers than today lived in large, partially sedentary villages in the relatively densely populated resource-rich coastal and riverine environments from which they were subsequently expelled by Holocene farmers' (Bowles and Gintis 2011: 95).

5 Pointing to the frequent need for galvanizing against natural disasters, however, Bowles and Gintis do not see war as a necessary driver of social evolution, as did Darwin.

6 Service (1975: 41) notes a line running from Darwin via Spencer and Bagehot to sociologists such as Ludwig Gumplowicz, Franz Oppenheimer, Albion Small, and Lester Ward.

7 In a Kantian moment some pages later, he adds hospitality: '[I]ntersocietal relations are typically maintained by reciprocal exchanges of presents, people (in marriage), and hospitality. And if two groups can exchange local specialties that the other lacks, amiable relations are better assured' (Service 1975: 100).

8 Numelin also published a later and more detailed monograph about Australia and Oceania, as well as books in his native Swedish and articles in both languages, but they add little to his doctoral work.

9 Numelin (1950: 176) stresses its relative rareness in South America, though.

10 Numelin (1950: 213) also notes the Maasai habit of letting women from opposite parties in peace negotiations suckle one another's unweaned children.

11 Mention should be made here of Hendrik Spruyt's (1994a, 1994b: 188) work on the states system, which did bring the idea of punctuated equilibria to the study of IR. However, as Bátora and Hynek (2014) argue, 'since diplomacy is not seen [by Spruyt] as a specific institution, but rather as a centralized gatekeeping tool of newly formed political units, it cannot be linked to the discussion of social evolutionary change per se. This can be seen when Spruyt tackles adaptation to environmental demands in the context of evolving units in the international system but never in the context of diplomacy'. Finnemore and Sikkink (1998) talk about 'turning points' in the life cycle of a norm when enough states join its institutionalized form; this is an agency-focused use which is very different from an evolutionary take.

12 Sometimes, only a metaphorical echo remains. Where humans are concerned, the expression 'prick up your ears' would be an example of this.

13 The use of 'verbal' here may not be correct, for we do not know when language emerged, or even if it emerged suddenly or gradually. Most guesses places the event in the 100,000–70,000 BC range. One unresolved tension is the relationship between the actuality of big-game hunting, which demands advanced signaling, and the emergence of language.

14 This paragraph summarizes Neumann and Sending 2010.

References

Barkawi, T. (2015). 'Diplomacy, War and World Politics' in O.J. Sending, V. Pouliot, and I.B. Neumann (eds.) *The Future of Diplomacy*, Cambridge: Cambridge University Press, 55–79.

Bátora, J. and Hynek, N. (2014). *Fringe Players and the Diplomatic Order: Towards a 'New' Heteronomy?*, London: Palgrave.

Boehm, C. (1999). 'The Natural Selection of Altruistic Traits', *Human Nature*, 10 (3): 205–52.

Boehm, C. (2011). *Moral Origins: Social Selection and the Evolution of Virtue, Altruism, and Shame*, New York, NY: Basic.

Bowles, S. and Gintis, H. (2011). *A Cooperative Species: Human Reciprocity and Its Evolution*, Princeton, NJ: Princeton University Press.

Cohen, R. and Westbrook, R. (eds.) (2000). *Amarna Diplomacy: The Beginnings of International Relations*, Baltimore, MD: Johns Hopkins University Press.

Darwin, C. [1873] (1998). *The Descent of Man*, Amherst, MA: Prometheus.

Der Derian, J. (1987). *On Diplomacy. A Genealogy of Western Estrangement*, Oxford: Blackwell.

Earle, T. K. (1997). *How Chiefs Come to Power: The Political Economy in Prehistory*, Stanford, CA: Stanford University Press.

Eldredge, N. and Gould, S. J. [1972] (1985). 'Punctuated Equilibria: An Alternative to Phyletic Gradualism', in N. Eldredge (ed.) *Time Frames*, Princeton, NJ: Princeton University Press, 193–223.

Finnemore, M. and Sikkink, K. (1998). 'International Norm Dynamics and Political Change', *International Organization*, 52 (4): 887–917.

Fried, M. (1967). *The Evolution of Political Society*, New York, NY: Random House.

Gintis, H., Bowles, S., Boyd, R. and Fehr, E. (2005). 'Moral Sentiments and Material Interests: Origins, Evidence, and Consequences', in H. Gintis, S. Bowles, R. Boyd, and E. Fehr (eds.), *Moral Sentiments and Material Interests: The Foundations of Cooperation in Economic Life*, Cambridge, MA: MIT Press, 3–39.

Hamilton, K. and Langhorne, R. [1995] (2011). *The Practice of Diplomacy: Its Evolution, Theory and Administration*, 2nd edition, London: Routledge.

Kropotkin, P. (1902). 'Mutual Aid: A Factor of Evolution', last accessed August 13, 2015, at https://www.gutenberg.org/ebooks/4341

Kurizaki, S. (2011). 'A Natural History of Diplomacy', chapter 3 of a book manuscript titled *When Diplomacy Works*, 365, 1.3.

Marlowe, F. W. (2005). 'Hunter-Gatherers and Human Evolution', *Evolutionary Anthropology*, 14 (2): 54–67.

Maynard Smith, J. (1964). 'Group Selection and Kin Selection', *Nature*, 201 (4924): 1145–7.

Messner, D., Guarín, A. and Haun, D. (2013). 'The Behavioral Dimensions of International Cooperation', *Global Cooperation Research Paper Series*, No. 1, Duisburg: Käte Hamburger Kolleg / Center for Global Cooperation Research.

Munn-Rankin, J. M. (1956). 'Diplomacy in Western Asia in the Early Second Millennium BC', *Iraq*, 18 (1): 68–110.

Neumann, I. B. (2011). *At Home with the Diplomats: Inside a European Ministry of Foreign Affairs*, Ithaca, NY: Cornell University Press.

Neumann, I. B. (2012). 'Euro-Centric Diplomacy: Challenging But Manageable', *European Journal of International Relations*, 18 (2): 299–321.

Neumann, I. B. (2013a). *Diplomatic Sites: A Critical Enquiry*, London: Hurst.

Neumann, I. B. (2013b). 'Claiming the Early State for the Relational Turn: The Case of Rus' (ca. 800–1100)', in A. B. Tickner and D. L. Blaney (eds.) *Claiming The International*, London: Routledge, 78–97.

Neumann, I. B. and Sending, O. J. (2010). *Governing the Global Polity: Practice, Rationality, Mentality*, Ann Arbor, MI: University of Michigan Press.

Nicolson, H. [1939] (1963). Diplomacy, third edition, London: Oxford University Press.

Nowak, M. (2006). 'Five Rules for the Evolution of Cooperation', *Science*, 314 (5805): 1560–3.

Numelin, R. (1950). *The Beginnings of Diplomacy: A Sociological Study of Intertribal and International Relations*, London: Oxford University Press.

Renfrew, C. (2007). *Prehistory: The Making of the Human Mind*, London: Weidenfeld & Nicolson.

Renfrew, C. and Cherry, J. (eds.) (1986). *Peer Polity Interaction and Socio-Political Change*, Cambridge: Cambridge University Press.

Ridley, M. (1996). *The Origins of Virtue: Human Instincts and the Evolution of Cooperation*, New York, NY: Viking.

Scott, H. (2007). 'Stephen Jay Gould and the Rhetoric of Evolutionary Theory', *Rhetoric Review*, 26 (2): 120–41.

Scott, J. C. (2009). *The Art of Not Being Governed: An Anarchist History of Upland Southeast Asia*, New Haven, CT: Yale University Press.

Scott, J. C. (2013). 'Crops, Towns, Government', *London Review of Books*, 35 (22): 13–15.

Service, E. R. (1975). *Origins of the State and Civilization: The Process of Cultural Evolution*, New York, NY: Norton.

Shostak, M. (1976). *Nisa: The Life and Words of a !Kung Woman*, Cambridge, MA: Harvard University Press.

Spruyt, H. (1994a). 'Institutional Selection in International Relations: State Anarchy as Order', *International Organization*, 48 (4): 527–57.

Spruyt, H. (1994b). *The Sovereign State and Its Competitors*, Princeton, NJ: Princeton University Press.

Sverdrup-Thygeson, B. (2011). 'A Neighbourless Empire? The Forgotten Diplomatic Tradition of Imperial China', *The Hague Journal of Diplomacy*, 7 (3): 1–23.

Thieme, H. (ed.) (2007). *Die Schöninger Speere – Mensch und Jagd vor 400.000 Jahren*, Stuttgart: Konrad Theiss.

Wilkins, J., Schoville, B. J., Brown, K. S. and Chazan, M. (2012). 'Evidence for Early Hafted Hunting Technology', *Science*, 338 (6109): 942–6. doi: 10.1126/science.12276.

Wille, T. (2013). *The Diplomatisation of Kosovo*. Paper read at the London School of Economics, 2 December.

Young, H. P. (1998). *Individual Strategy and Social Structure: An Evolutionary Theory of Institutions*, Princeton, NJ: Princeton University Press.

11 Cognizing cooperation
Clues and cues for institutional design[1]

Siddharth Mallavarapu

Introduction

The objective of this chapter is to partake of recent developments in the field of cognitive neuroscience and to bring these into conversation with an important normative and practical concern – namely, the design of institutions that might further enhance the possibility of global cooperation. My interest here is specifically in institutions that help to overcome global collective action problems. The chapter is largely conceptual and does not intend to be policy prescriptive. However, it advances the case for renewed attention to invisible and often taken-for-granted premises in mainstream accounts in the field of International Relations that might eventually generate more inclusive institutional designs and desirable deliberative outcomes. While Barbara Koremenos, Charles Lipson, and Duncan Snidal have given considerable and careful thought to 'the rational design of international institutions', it is important to also contend with the drift of Alexander Wendt's claim that '[a]s a discipline international relations (IR) has barely begun to think about institutional design' (Koremenos, Lipson, and Snidal 2001; Wendt 2001: 1019).

Contemporary global governance discourse often entails an implicit or explicit repertoire of both substantive semantic quarrels and minor quibbles, along with the simultaneous interplay of affect and memory against diverse backdrops. If global history is seriously factored, we also have to contend with a potpourri of colonial wounds, injustices from the past, periodic allegations of reconfigured neo-imperialism, and/or less forcefully articulated claims of the retention of privilege by traditional powers at the expense of others.

The chapter is an invitation to revisit what could allow us to alter these 'framings' and make us more willing to encounter each other with a greater degree of confidence and belief in a common 'we' project (see Messner, Guarín, and Haun, this volume; Grimalda, this volume). It is perhaps also worth reflecting on ways in which coming to terms with the past might be as important a leitmotif as both principle and practice are. Can our modern foibles make way for a more intelligent use of language, memory, and affect, and depart from a rather restrictive invocation of instrumental rationalities and assumption of worst-case scenarios? None of this is amenable to easy simple translations, but even a non-specialist's foray into the

DOI: 10.4324/9781315691657-14

world of cognitive neuroscience reveals the urgency and need to acknowledge that language, memory, and affect might lie at the heart of any meaningful reconciliation towards genuinely global 'we' identities shorn of distrust and assorted inhibitions.

I begin this chapter by addressing definitional aspects relating to cooperation, explicating why cooperation matters and identifying what aspects of understanding relating to the human brain and its functioning might have a bearing on thinking more creatively about cooperation. I then proceed to discuss social cognition in some detail and, further, bring to bear state-of-the-art assessments (in cognitive neuroscience) of questions such as the employment of language, the role of analogies and memory, the relevant literature on 'heuristics and biases', affect, and their impact on political judgment formation, and eventually the impact of political decisions on outcomes (Tversky and Kahneman 1974). Further, I pursue the concept of brain plasticity and examine its correlate 'institutional plasticity' (Pierson 2004).

It would not be overstating the case to suggest that in the 21st century no discipline is likely to remain untouched by advances in the understanding of the human brain and associated theories of the human mind (Kandel 2007). Disciplines that remain smugly insular and carry on a pretense that nothing has changed are likely to be increasingly irrelevant, not by accident but by conscious neglect. However, some caution is also warranted. Many developments relating to the understanding of the human brain are still tentative, and there are vast arenas that we still do not fully comprehend. This suggests the need to eschew any hint of *hubris* and to embrace humility as a stance to approaching these developments while studying the implications for questions which directly interest us, such as the prospects, as well as limits, for cooperation.

Conceptualizing cooperation: Toward a working definition

The literature on cooperation is large, and the intent here is not to delve into the lineage of the concept, although that would merit another inquiry of its own. However, I do recognize the need to provide a working definition of cooperation that might help us navigate this rich and variegated field of inquiry. According to Brandon A. Sullivan, Mark Snyder, and John J. Sullivan, cooperation can be defined 'as behavior undertaken by individuals and groups of individuals in the service of a shared and collective goal and to promote collective well-being' (Sullivan, Snyder, and Sullivan 2008: 3). They further clarify that

> [c]ooperative processes are defined in turn as phenomena that characterize the implementation of cooperative behavior, many of which are involved in promoting cooperative behavior and determining when and where it will occur – causing such behavior to increase or decrease over time in response to changes in goals and environmental factors.
>
> (Sullivan et al. 2008: 3)

In some contrast, Sarah Coakley (a Divinity scholar) and Manfred Nowak (a biological mathematician) observe that '[c]ooperation is a form of working together in which one individual pays a cost (in terms of fitness, whether genetic or cultural) and another gains a benefit as a result' (Coakley and Nowak 2013: 4). For our immediate purposes here, I rely on the first of the two definitions. My preference for definition one over definition two stems from an interest in collective pooling behavior not restricted to zero sum scenarios. An enduring dimension of interest in problems relating to political cooperation at the macro-level is the question of global collective action. It is perhaps interesting to ask what obstacles to cooperation occur when large groups and not just individuals are likely to be beneficiaries of a particular human action. Since many global cooperation dilemmas that confront us, such as climate change dilemmas, among others, warrant a degree of collective action, it is perhaps worthwhile to ask how the collective good is perceived by different actors in the international system and what each of these actors is willing to bring to the table to achieve at least some of it. It is also plausible that not all social and political situations throw up clear and easily identifiable common goals, and a part of the cooperation challenge could relate to 'framing' inclusively (of which I shall have more to convey later) what this common set of objectives might be prior to inviting or eliciting material and intangible contributions from across the globe (Kahneman 2011).

On institutional design

An important dimension to address in the context of cooperation relates to institutions. Why do institutions matter? Institutions provide one crucible within which some explicit forms of cooperation reside and can be subsequently be reproduced. The great value associated with institutions and successful institutionalization oftentimes is that they generate stable expectations in the relevant domain. A working minimalist definition of institutions that I rely on for our purposes here states that '[a]n institution is a self-sustaining system of shared beliefs about how the game is played' (Aoki 2001: 26). This does not suggest automaticity or derogate from the fact that there are actors imbued with intentionality who are 'choice architects', and who generate an initial set of beliefs, eventually based on successful institutionalization, that morph into valid expectations (Sunstein and Thaler 2008).

While 'institutions constitute social reality in ways that are complex and multiform', they also 'shape the incentives and preferences of actors' (Katznelson and Weingast 2005: 15, 20). A useful backdrop against which institutions might be viewed is provided by Herbert Simon and his work on 'bounded rationality'. He reminds us of 'the limits upon the ability of human beings to adapt optimally, or even satisfactorily to complex environments. Attention to limits of human rationality help us understand why representation is important, and how policy statements imply representations' (Simon 1991: 132).

Ongoing research on institutional design

Institutional design is an indispensable element in thinking about the architecture of institutions. There are at least three dimensions that Robert E. Goodin, among others, regards as important to institutional design (Goodin 1996). These include 'revisability', 'sensitivity to motivational complexity', and the 'publicity principle' (Goodin 1996: 40–2). While the first principle speaks to the need for institutions to be nimble footed and to build on 'learning by doing', the second facet relates to the complex bases that inform human action and propel actors to behave in particular sorts of ways. A final dimension relates to the democratic viability of institutions that merits explanations to their publics (local, national, regional, or global) of the rationale(s) for their existence. While all these three dimensions are amenable to some scrutiny from a cognitive standpoint, the dimension of 'motivational complexity' to me remains the most vital to think through while designing optional institutions.

The challenge here is to begin grappling with serious gaps in the existing research. Paul Pierson laments the fact that

> social scientists have produced little sustained empirical work, organized around clear competing hypotheses, comparing institutional origins and change across different settings. Without this research, we are in no position to evaluate the impact of particular contextual features on institutional outcomes, or even to establish how prevalent such features are in our political world.
>
> (Pierson 2004: 130)

However, corrective action is possible. This would entail a willingness to 'consider dynamic processes that can highlight the implications of short time horizons, the scope of the unintended consequences, the efficacy or limitations of effects of institutions over extended periods. This requires *genuinely* historical research' (Pierson 2004: 130). Pierson argues that '[b]y genuinely historical research I mean work that carefully investigates processes unfolding over time, rather than simply mining history for illustrations of essentially static deductive arguments' (Pierson 2004: 130).

While bringing history back in to delve into actual processes of institutional origin and evolution could prove indispensable, it is perhaps equally important to tell the cognitive side of the story in terms of our species make up and predispositions to some forms of institutional design. How can we avoid some of the biases that come naturally to us by virtue of being human, and how can we tap into other intrinsic strengths that remain a part of our natural species evolutionary design that might be worth replicating in humanly crafted institutions?

Returning to the question of cooperation, there is much we can learn from the collaborative labors of a political scientist (Robert Axelrod) and a biologist (William Hamilton) in terms of thinking about cooperation. Axelrod claims that his 'framework is broad enough to encompass not only people but also nations and bacteria' (Axelrod 2006: 18). Or as they jointly claim,

> [a]s one moves up the evolutionary ladder in neural complexity, game-playing behavior becomes richer. The intelligence of primates including humans, allows a number of relevant improvements: a complex memory, more complex processing of information to determine the next action as a function of the interaction so far, a better estimate of the probability of future interaction with the same individual, and a better ability to distinguish between different individuals.
>
> (Axelrod and Hamilton 2006: 94)

One of the elements of human cognition that frequently resurfaces is our predisposition to cognize the world in terms of stories (Boyd 2010). Axelrod argues persuasively that human cooperation also has its own story to narrate. What does this story look like? Three claims are of particular relevance here in the context of disaggregating the different stages in a cooperative endeavor. First,

> [t]he beginning of the story is that cooperation can get started even in a world of unconditional defection. The development *cannot* take place if it is tried only by scattered individuals who have virtually no chance to interact with each other. However, cooperation can evolve from a small cluster of individuals who base their cooperation on reciprocity and have an even small proportion of their interactions with each other.
>
> (Axelrod 2006: 20–1)

Next, 'the middle of the story is that a strategy based on reciprocity can thrive in a world where many different kinds of strategies are being tried.' Finally, '[t]he end of the story is that cooperation, once established on the basis of reciprocity, can protect itself from invasion by less cooperative strategies. Thus, the gear wheels of social evolution have a ratchet' (Axelrod 2006: 20–1).

The implications of this are significant, especially when it comes to the scaling dimensions of human cooperation. The idea that collaboration begins with small groups, but eventually is bolstered by practices of reciprocity to the point at which it could be finessed among larger collectivities who see an intrinsic value in cooperative strategies over non-cooperative strategies, suggests that one has to proceed incrementally and patiently till this form of thinking is lodged in the very DNA of institutional design.

New insights from cognition studies

An emerging body of literature that is particularly pertinent to thinking about cooperation from the perspective of cognition relates to 'development precursors' (Sullivan et al. 2008). Nancy Eisenberg and Natalie D. Eggum study 'prosocial' forms of behavior and make a distinction between empathy, sympathy, and personal distress (Eisenberg and Eggum 2008). According to them empathy is 'an affective response that stems from the apprehensions or comprehension of another's emotional state or condition, and is similar to what the other person is feeling or would be expected to feel'. Sympathy, in contrast, 'is defined as an emotional response stemming from the apprehension of another's emotional state or condition'. Finally, personal distress refers to 'a self-focused, aversive affective reaction to the apprehension of another's emotion' (Eisenberg and Eggum 2008: 54). The larger point is that there appears to be a direct correlation between 'different motivational states' and 'different likelihoods of behaving in ways that benefit or harm others' (Eisenberg and Eggum 2008: 55). From the vantage point of politics in human collectivities, it becomes important to consider the possibilities of comprehending the predicaments of others. This translates into 'perspective taking' in the literature on cognition. From this vantage point it would be interesting to examine claims of humanitarianism, for instance in international affairs. A word of caution, though – the heady concoction of hard material interests and actual human capacities for altruism are not always obvious and easy to disentangle.

The term 'perspective taking' entails 'visualizing the impact a situation has on another person; it is often assumed to derive from the effort to put oneself in another's place'. What is the extent of 'affective attachment felt towards the other?' (Eisenberg and Eggum 2008: 61) The flip side of the story is prejudice. According to Stephan and Finlay, prejudice entails, 'negative attitudes towards social groups, to create a psychological distance between the prejudiced person and the target of his or her prejudice' (Eisenberg and Eggum 2008: 67). Such perceptions are antithetical to cooperation. Eisenberg and Eggum observe that '[i]ngroup members harboring prejudice towards outgroup members often have exaggerated perceptions of homogeneity within outgroups, as well as inflated perceptions of differences between groups. Perceived dramatic differences, in concert with dislike, may avert empathetic perspective taking' (Eisenberg and Eggum 2008: 67). One of the important takeaways from this study is that 'an important mediating variable between hereditary endowment or socialization experiences and peoples' empathy related responding is individual's ability to regulate their emotional arousal, including their vicariously induced emotion' (Eisenberg and Eggum 2008: 65). Ultimately 'associations of sympathy/empathy with moral reasoning, perspective taking, and an understanding of emotion have been demonstrated' (Eisenberg and Eggum 2008: 69).

What concrete implications might this carry for institutional design? Is institutional failure about the inability to successfully institutionalize 'perspective taking', and as a consequence confront serious legitimacy deficits? Will more active 'perspective taking' immunize institutions from other normative deficits? I would like to suggest here that one element of institutional innovation that might be factored in the actual design of institutions, is to actively incentivize an ability to gauge complexity and to forecast plausible responses that fare well in terms of 'perspective taking'. Institutional design intelligence needs to be judged not by its material corpus alone but by its ability to reproduce itself with sufficient legitimacy in the issue-area domain it chooses to focus on. My claims at this stage are largely suggestive, and there is no substitute for some hard empirical work to follow for anybody interested in pursuing these claims more rigorously.

Social cognition

Students of social science are no strangers to interpretive traditions. Hermeneutics, phenomenology, ethnography, critical epistemologies – both feminist and postcolonial have always been alive to the amenability of the social and political world to diverse registers of interpretation. A new and somewhat unlikely ally to the interpretive outlook now emerges from an unexpected quarter – cognitive neuroscience. Michael Gazzaniga is a key figure in this domain and is responsible for offering us a fresh perspective on how the brain cognizes the social world on a quotidian basis. As early as 1985 he authored *The Social Brain*, and has been credited with several other fundamental contributions, arguably engendering the field itself. In a volume paying tribute to the expanding oeuvre of ongoing work by Gazzaniga, Michael Posner, Mary K. Rothbrat, and Brad E. Sheese, drawing on his contributions, suggest that 'the human brain is unique in part, because through a left-hemisphere interpreter system highly related to language, it creates a narrative that forms the basis of a coherent self' (Posner, Rothbart, and Sheese 2010: 125).

Several exciting developments unraveling the working of the human brain are unfolding as part of cutting-edge scientific research made possible by technological developments that vastly improve our capacity for brain imaging (Kandel 2007). An important 'conceptual breakthrough has been the idea that we use overlapping neural systems in representing our knowledge, beliefs, intentions and actions as we use to understand others' (Aminoff et al. 2009: 1258). From my perspective, one of the most critical inflection points, as far as implications for social science approaches to the study of cooperation, is to reiterate the significance of context to interpret human behavior. However, context is understood more widely in this rendition than has traditionally been understood within the social sciences. It has been observed here that

> [o]ne can also consider context more broadly, such as the evolutionary forces that have shaped human and nonhuman primate brains and behavior, driven by ecological and environmental factors. From cellular systems to social neurosciences, there is no scarcity of examples demonstrating the importance of context.
> (Aminoff et al. 2009: 1259)

An important facet relates to how 'genes and experience are no longer considered to be polar opposite factors to influence but are instead viewed as dynamically interacting' (Aminoff et al. 2009: 1256). Daniel Lord Smail who is an advocate of 'deep history', argues that

> [g]enes alone are not enough to build deep grammar or a theory of mind in the absence of specific developmental experiences. These developmental

experiences are not only environmental; they are also cultural. In this way, culture can actually be wired in the human body. Since culture changes, human psychologies, in principle, can differ greatly from one era to the next.

(Smail 2008: 131)

Echoes of these ideas also find their way into thinking about institutional design.

There are three dimensions from the perspective of social cognition and institutional design that merit closer scrutiny. The first of these relates to language, the second to memory, and the third to the role of affect in the life of institutions. Cognitive neuroscience literature is persuading us to appraise ourselves of evolving assessments surrounding these questions. Anybody interested in the question of cooperation cannot afford to miss out on the excitement and insights that are emerging from this engagement. A caveat which I would like to reiterate at this stage is that we should treat these developments as clues and cues rather than definitive prescriptions in terms of institutional design. However, these clues and cues could find instantiation and acquire a deeper policy resonance with the passage and tests of time.

The criticality of language: Lessons for institutional design

Language is critical to understanding the grammar of both cooperation and conflict. What is the state of the art on language from the perspective of the brain-mind sciences? Alfonso Caramazza observes in this context that 'it is clear that we are still very far from an articulated theory of the biology of language. In some respects we are really only now beginning to develop the methodological and theoretical foundation for such a theory' (Caramazza 2009: 766). He argues that the work of Ramus and Fisher demonstrates that

> we have only begun to scratch the surface of many complicated factors that enter into a genetic theory. The same is true for cognitive neuroscience accounts of language, especially for the more complex functions such as synaptic processing and semantic integration. At this stage of the game we have many titillating insights but not yet articulated theories.
>
> (Caramazza 2009: 766)

From our perspective, it is important to distil what these 'insights' are and how we can draw on them intelligently to think about the design of institutions aimed at facilitating and furthering human cooperation. Lera Boroditsky from the perspective of linguistic relativism claims that

> a solid body of empirical evidence showing how language shapes thinking has finally emerged. The evidence overturns the long-standing dogma about universality and yields fascinating insights the origins of knowledge and the construction of reality. The result has important implications for law, politics and education.
>
> (Boroditsky 2011: 63)

Her labors are directed to 'uncovering how language shapes even the most fundamental dimensions of human experience: space, time, causality and relationship to others' (Boroditsky 2014: n.p.).

Three other thinkers who extensively draw on cognitive approaches to thinking about language are Douglas Hofstadter, Emmanuel Sander, and Steven Pinker. These accounts shall be robustly complemented in my account with the work of Daniel Kahneman on the issue of 'framing' and lessons from Yuen Foong Khong's empirical scrutiny of how 'historical analogies', a particular subset of analogies, have resulted in some fallacious foreign policy decisions from the perspective of the actors interested in those decisions. I shall synoptically present their arguments in the ensuing paragraphs and return to the question of what implications all of this might carry for institutional design that might incentivize cooperation. The thread running through our interest in language is again a curiosity about how we employ language and how that facilitates or inhibits cooperation, and why institutions should care about this.

In their most recent book, *Surfaces and Essences: Analogy as the Fuel and Fire of Thinking*, Hofstadter and Sander advance a fundamental claim. They argue that

> the spotting of analogies pervades every moment of our thought, thus constituting thought's core. To put it more explicitly, analogies do not happen in our minds just once a week or once a day or once an hour or even once a minute; no analogies spring up inside our minds numerous times every second. We swim nonstop in an ocean of small, medium-sized, and large analogies, ranging from mundane trivialities to brilliant insights.
>
> (Hofstadter and Sander 2013: 18)

What is perhaps more relevant from the perspective of thinking about cooperation and institutional design is the pervasiveness of categories that inform our social and political world. Succinctly stated, '[c]ategorization through analogy making drives thinking at all levels, from the smallest to the largest' (Hofstadter and Sander 2013: 25).

Two dimensions revealed about the analogies in the account by Hofstadter and Sander are particularly worth pondering over from the perspective of our interest in institutional design. The first relates to how we are 'manipulated' by analogies, and the second relates to how we do the same on occasion to analogy making. According to the first usage,

> analogies, because they are essentially invisible, manipulate us. We are unaware of being taken over by an analogical interpretation of a situation. In this sense, the invisible analogy manipulates us because it has simply imposed itself on us, willy-nilly. And it manipulates us in another sense – namely, it foists new ideas on us, pushing us around. Unsatisfied with being merely an agent that enriches our comprehension of a situation we are facing, the analogy rushes in and structures our entire view of the situation,

trying to make us align the newly encountered situation with the familiar old one.

(Hofstadter and Sander 2013: 31)

The most crucial finding is that analogy making and categorization are in the final analysis 'one and the same' (Hofstadter and Sander 2013: 32). We are all at one plane aware that unrelenting categorization does accomplish a lot more than being mere semantic placeholders. They designate peoples, cultures, histories, and objects that populate our universe in particular registers, eventually with implications for how we come to define the world and our place in it.

Yuen Foong Khong also takes analogies rather seriously and demonstrates reliance on analogies by foreign policy decision makers, particularly to navigate a complex world in crises moments. What appears clear from this account is that 'analogies exert their impact on the decision-making process, they make certain options more attractive and others less so' (Khong 1992: 252). Distilling three implications from his book-length account of the sway of historical analogies in foreign policy decision making, Khong points out that analogies 'matter most during the selection and rejection of policy options, and they exert their impact by influencing the assessments and evaluations that policymakers must make in order to choose between alternative options' (Khong 1992: 253). Further, he points out 'that a major source of the power of historical analogies is their heuristic or diagnostic versatility. The ability of analogies to perform several diagnostic functions at once allowed policymakers who used them to arrive at a comprehensive picture' (Khong 1992: 254). Finally, analogical thinking helps redress problems with other approaches. As Khong notes, '[a]lthough less parsimonious and more contingent, the analogical explanation is more accurate and more satisfying' (Khong 1992: 254).

Steven Pinker's account *How the Mind Works* complements his interest in understanding *The Language Instinct*. Language is far from an innocent act of mere communication; it is freighted with several potentialities for signaling both cooperation and alternatively reflecting a willingness to spar. Pinker observes that '[t]he games people play as they use language are anything but frivolous' (Pinker 2007: 422–3). Language use might contribute or ward off 'a damaging loss of face' (Pinker 2007: 425). Thus,

> the expressive power of language [is] a mixed blessing: its lets us learn what we want to know, but it also lets us learn what we don't want to know. Language is not just a window into human nature but a fistula: an open wound through which our innards are exposed to an infectious world. It's not surprising that we expect people to sheathe their words in politeness and innuendo and other forms of doublespeak.

(Pinker 2007: 425)

Finally, Kahneman and Amos Tversky have also contributed substantially to our appreciation of 'heuristics and biases' that might result in fallacious judgments based on our processing of information. The 'availability heuristic' reminds us of the fallacy of relying on too thin a sliver of evidence based upon the 'ease of recall' to make judgments. The 'perseverance heuristic' gestures to our unwillingness to retract our judgments even in the face of contrary evidence, while the 'anchoring heuristic' reminds us of how we fallaciously choose base lines to make comparisons when arriving at certain judgments (Tversky and Kahneman 1974). A key finding of Kahneman's more recent book *Thinking Fast and Slow* is that '[u]ltimately, a richer language is essential to the skill of constructive criticism. Much like medicine, the identification of judgment errors is a diagnostic task, which requires precise vocabulary' (Kahneman 2011: 418). From an institutional perspective, listening to diverse points of view is of paramount importance from this lens. To invoke an image

> there is a direct link from more precise gossip at the watercooler to better decisions. Decision makers are sometimes better able to imagine the voices of present gossipers with future critics than to hear the hesitant voice of their own doubts. They will make better choices when they trust their critics to be sophisticated and fair, and when they expect their decisions to be judged by how it was made, not only how it turned out.
>
> (Kahneman 2011: 418)

From the perspective of thinking about both cooperation and questions of institutional design, to the extent that institutions are a human construct, we need to be attentive to the manner in which language operates in these settings. How can institutions avoid 'narrow framings', evolve categories with care, and use analogies intelligently? Smart design must come to terms with these facets if it has to prove successful in terms of its stated objectives. Most crucially, it has to often secure compliance among its members and minimal acceptance from those located outside of these institutions, which potentially impact others who are not always a part of the deliberative process.

From Boroditsky we learn about the different valances particular institutional usages are likely to carry among their intended and unintended audiences. Institutions do not always speak in one voice, but when they do seek to establish a degree of coherence, they have to innovate in terms of how they wish to convey what they wish to convey. This is not a plea for cynical spin doctoring but a case for an active investment in rethinking the categories that slot and determine our worlds. The scholarship on analogies reinforces the need for institutions to be attentive to what parallels they pick in order to make decisions and, further, how sensibly they are deployed. One aspect that emerges strongly from cognitive work on analogies is the inevitability at some plane of taking recourse to these analogies. The real challenge appears to be picking the right ones and operationalizing them with imagination and nuance. How can institutions do this creatively and much more systematically merits further inquiry. Cognitive insights on language have reaffirmed the centrality of language in representation. It is quite clearly not simply a matter of semantics but often lays bare our epistemic and political commitments and the extent to which they are genuinely able to transcend more immediate and pedestrian gains. Our inability to speak the same language may also be the source of considerable unease in both lending legitimacy to specific institutional remedies, as well as ensuring their smooth translation of their specific visions in the rough and tumble of the real world.

'Brain plasticity', 'institutional plasticity', and 'memory malleability': Lessons for institutional design

One of the distinguishing traits of the human brain is its plasticity. Helen Neville and Mriganka Sur argue that 'the ability of the brain to change adaptively during learning and memory or in response to changes in the environment – is one of the most remarkable features of higher brain function' (Neville and Sur 2009: 89). Brain plasticity is evident in the manner in which 'maps' and 'visual pathways' are processed. Sam Horng and Mriganka Sur observe that

> [r]einotopic and feature selective maps constitute key organizational principles of the visual pathway. Intrinsic genetic programs and activity-dependent processes both play a role in setting up the structure and function of these maps. In addition, patterns of activity interact with programs of gene expression as they modulate signaling pathways within the cell. Understanding specific mechanisms of how visual stimulus feature maps are assembled and modified in response to experience is central to identifying fundamental processes of neural circuit development and plasticity.
>
> (Horng and Sur 2009: 102)

The work of Wu Li and Charles D. Gilbert demonstrates that '[v]isual cortical plasticity is not limited to postnatal development and to contingent reactions induced by anomalous experiences. It is a lifelong ongoing process accompanying visual perception, as shown in various cortical changes associated with perceptual learning' (Li and Gilbert 2009: 13).

Alvaro Pascual-Leone provides further evidence of the importance of plasticity to human survival. He observes

> [t]he brain is highly plastic, and that plasticity represents evolution's invention to enable the nervous system to escape the restrictions of its own genome (and its highly specialized cellular specification) and adapt to its rapidly shifting and often unpredictable environmental and experimental changes.
>
> (Pascual-Leone 2009: 151)

Courtney Stevens and Neville recognize a fair amount of diversity in this domain. They note in this context that '[d]ifferent brain subsystems and related sensory and cognitive abilities display different degrees and time periods ('profiles') of neuroplasticity. These may depend on the variable time periods of development and redundant connectivity displayed by different brain regions' (Stevens and Neville 2009: 165). This brings us back to the question of language. Stevens and Neville point out here that

> [i]t is reasonable to hypothesize that the same principles that characterize neuroplasticity of sensory systems – including different profiles, degrees, and mechanisms of plasticity – also characterize language. Here, we focus on the subsystems of language examined in our studies of neuroplasticity, including those supporting semantics, syntax, and speech segmentation.
>
> (Stevens and Neville 2009: 169)

To invoke an analogy, is there a correlate of brain plasticity in the world of institutions? If we think of plasticity as essentially an adaptive function which responds to a complex environment reflecting elements of gene-culture interactions, can institutions also reveal elements of plasticity that reflect their capacity to innovate, demonstrate a degree of nimbleness, and provide the wherewithal to navigate a complex world of collective action dilemmas? This brings us back to the work of Pierson on institutions, where he suggests that 'institutional plasticity' might have a life when it comes to the economic domain but will find it much harder to survive intact as an 'assumption' in the political sphere. His suspicion of its applicability in the political arena rests on 'the great complexity and ambiguity of the political world' (Pierson 2004: 125). He further asserts that 'causal chains between actions and outcomes are often very long' (Pierson 2004: 125).

In some contrast, in the world of economics he claims 'learning' is somewhat easier to accomplish. This is because of

> the central clarifying role of prices, the prevalence of repeated interactions, the absence of a need to coordinate many of one's economic decisions with those of large numbers of other actors, and the presence of relatively short causal chains between choices and results make it relatively easy for economic actors to correct mistakes over time. In other words, these features improve the prospects for learning.
>
> (Pierson 2004: 125)

Pierson, invoking the language of 'institutional plasticity', cautions us 'that efforts to translate theoretical arguments from the economic realm to the political one are more perilous than is often recognized. Such translations need to be done with care, with an appreciation of the limits of the analogy' (Pierson 2004: 130). I would like to argue that 'plasticity' as a principle in the natural and socio-political world has a larger life and is perhaps worth exploring with care in terms of questions relating to institutional design. Good institutions must reflect this vital trait in order to avoid the rigidities we have come to associate with defunct institutions. For instance, some would argue that the IMF is in a state of rigor mortis. In the absence of a dynamic interplay of existing and sometimes deeply anchored predispositions and changing realities, there is room to explore the grammar of plasticity and incessant change – usually incremental, sometimes opening up a hitherto undiscovered capacity to innovate.

Another example which bears a Wittgensteinian family resemblance to 'plasticity' is the notion of 'malleability'. The work of William Hirst builds on this dimension in the context of 'collective memory'. He argues that

> [a] memory cannot bear on collective identity if it is not shared in the first place, and this, a virtue of memory's malleability lies in the role this malleability plays in constructing shared memories. Shared memories may be valuable because they contribute to collective identity and facilitate social bonding, but this contribution is realized in large part because memory's malleability promotes their creation.
>
> (Hirst 2010: 140–1)

This could assume many forms – 'social cognition, induced forgetting, and resistance'. To Hirst '[s]ocial contagion refers to incidents in which speakers impose memories on listeners. Induced forgetting refers to incidents in which what the speaker says leads the listener to forget material.' In some contrast, '[r]esistance is the opposite of social contagion and induced forgetting. It occurs when people want the past to be their own, now what others want it to be'. Perhaps an important lesson from Hirst's account is to recognize that 'collective amnesias can produce social bonds just as effectively as collective memories' (Hirst 2010: 144).

Cognitive neuroscience is clear 'about what memory is *not*: it is not a single concept.' There is also an appreciation according to Daniel L. Schachter that 'memory can be divided into multiple forms or systems – collections of the processes that operate on different kinds of information and according to semantic, priming and procedural memory . . . all familiar to contemporary researchers' (Schachter 2009: 655). A final insight worth gleaning from emerging research in cognitive neuroscience on memory is the 'constructive nature of memory' building on the 1932 work of figures like F. C. Bartlett (Nader 2009: 700).

If institutions are also treated as storehouses of memory, then we might ask how these memories have been constructed, what of these memories are worth preserving, and how do we most importantly build on positive recollections and alter the negative connotations that also fight for attention in the same mnemonic space. Good institutional design aesthetics will need to grapple with these issues right from the outset if the right memories have to endure.

From the perspective of global cooperation, here it might be good to tap into shared histories of multilateralism. It would merit a more systematic empirical scrutiny of what were the conditions under which multilateralism thrived, and what explained its success in some formats and its relative failure in others. What the memory literature from cognition also does is reinforce the role of how we relate to the past and how that invariably shapes our current political ontologies. Goodin succinctly captures this sentiment when he argues that

> [m]uch of the point of studying institutions, after all, is to explore more precisely those ways in which the past leaves traces in the present and constrains our present actions and future options. So designers of institutions, of all people, should be particularly sensitive to the ways in which past inheritances will inevitably constrain them in their own design activities.
>
> (Goodin 1996: 30)

Viewed from this perspective, '[g]ood institutional design is not just a matter of pragmatics' (Goodin 1996: 39).

Thinking affect: Lessons for institutional design

A critical frontier of cognitive neuroscience research in recent years has been unraveling the life of emotions and their impact, particularly their impact on human judgments and decision-making. Todd F. Heatherton and Joseph E. Ledoux assert that

> [a]t the core of this emphasis on social cognition is the importance of emotional processing. The social and emotional aspects of the brain are inexorably linked, the adaptive significance of emotions being closely linked to their social value, and nearly all social interaction produces affective responses.
>
> (Heatherton and Ledoux 2009: 887)

This assumes particular salience when we acknowledge that

> [f]or humans, many of the most pernicious adaptive problems involve other humans, such as selecting mates, cooperating in hunting and gathering, forming alliances, competing over scarce resources, and even warring with neighboring groups. Interacting with other humans produces emotion, and these emotions serve as guidelines for successful group living.
>
> (Heatherton and Ledoux 2009: 888)

It appears clear that 'any true understanding of human nature will require a full consideration of both the emotional brain and the social brain' (Heatherton and Ledoux 2009: 888).

Jason P. Mitchell and Todd F. Heatherton identify four distinctive elements of the 'social brain'. These include 'self-awareness', 'mentalizing', 'self-regulation', and 'detection of threat' (Mitchell and Heatherton 2009). The first dimension has thrown up a number of exciting developments. As Mitchell and Heatherton reveal

> [m]ore recently, Neisser (1988) has described a number of distinct ways in which one can think of selfhood, such as a 'conceptual self' that represents

our sense of authoring our own actions in the environment, and a 'narrative self' that maintains our sense of personal history and autobiographical memory (also see Boyer, Robbins and Jack, 2005; S. Gallagher, 2000). Sedikides and Skowronski (1997) argue that this last sense of self is a widely shared human trait that leads to more efficient mental processing of personal and contextual information, thereby increasing the likelihood of survival and reproduction.

(Mitchell and Heatherton 2009: 954)

The second dimension is about our 'ability to infer the mental states of other people.' Referred to as 'mentalizing', it allows for 'the ability to empathize and cooperate with others, accurately interpret other people's behavior, and even deceive others when necessary'. It has been suggested that 'although one cannot directly perceive the mental states of another person, one does typically have access to a decent proxy system: oneself' (Mitchell and Heatherton 2009: 955). The third aspect relates to 'self-regulation'. Mitchell and Heatherton claim in this regard that

it helps people to control their behaviors and actions so that they remain in good standing within their groups. Throughout evolutionary history, people have faced the continuing struggle between satisfying personal desires and being a good member of the group.

(Mitchell and Heatherton 2009: 957)

Finally, '[o]ver the course of human evolution, a major adaptive challenge to survival was other people, both ingroup members and members of other groups. However, the nature of threats is distinctly different'. It is evident that 'the social brain requires mechanisms not only to detect threats posed by both ingroup and outgroup members, but also to differentiate between the specific nature of each kind of social threat' (Mitchell and Heatherton 2009: 957).

As we learn more about 'a suite of different mechanisms' by which people relate to each other, we could also consciously tap into these insights to encourage some forms of institutional design over others (Mitchell and Heatherton 2009: 959). All these dimensions suggested by Mitchell and Heatherton can find applicability while thinking about institutional design aimed to further cooperation. An awareness of self translates into a degree of overall institutional coherence. A distinct personality or identity for institutions is perhaps as critical to institutions as it is to individuals. Institutions flounder when they lack this broad coherence which also speaks to a lack of clarity of what goals – material and normative – they seek to accomplish. The second dimension, referred to here as 'mentalizing', is replaced by 'cognizing' when it comes to thinking of institutions and the attainment of their objectives, in this instance securing cooperation among disparate actors aimed at some commonly acknowledged public good. Self-regulation and anticipation of threats also involve coming to terms with both benign and malign intentions of actors in the real world.

Conclusion

To reiterate, the following sets of claims are relevant to this intervention. First, developments in the field of cognitive neuroscience offer us an interesting vantage point to revisit the question of institutional design and cooperation. We need to tread carefully though, because these findings are often tentative, although they point in interesting directions. I would like to argue at this stage that these insights have the capacity to complement rather than supplant thinking which is proceeding alongside questions of institutional design from within the social sciences. There is a need for more sustained empirical attention in this domain. The proof of the pudding will be in the eating. Tangible results that reflect institutional design alterations based on these new insights, with impact on both process and outcomes, will be the most relevant in this context.

Second, the chapter elicited developments in three specific, though interlinked, domains that cognition is helping us to illuminate further. These include language, memory, and affect. An underlying premise here has been that while thinking of institutions and institutional design, broader human predispositions and flaws need to be factored in more carefully. Research in the field of cognition makes explicit these inclinations and also forewarns us of increased awareness to deploy these predispositions with greater thought.

On language, I argue that institutions will also have to contend with how the language they use to represent their own selves and their relationship to the larger world is often likely to reflect deeper biases and prejudices. The importance of analogies in making decisions and the accompanying errors that might follow the employment of particular analogies over others, as well as the role categories play in defining our worlds and thereby engendering inclusions and exclusions, simultaneously merits emphasis. A final insight about language worth incorporating in terms of institutional design is that language both manipulates institutions and lends itself to manipulation as well. Simply put, language potentially impacts the overall ecology of institutional design.

With regard to memory from a cognitive standpoint, we are reminded about how memory (or its converse, shared amnesia) can actually bring human collectivities closer. From the perspective of institutional design, it is important to acknowledge that institutions also carry with them distinct memories of their own identities. For those of us interested in global cooperation, it could be worth asking how institutional design can echo deeper impulses of solidarity in forging agreement on some common concerns. Global cooperation is large-scale cooperation, but the history of multilateralism suggests that there also have been instances where multilateralism has not met with the same kind of success, and it is important to get more analytical traction on what also does not work in this context.

Finally, an aspect that is often universally acknowledged, but because of the hard science protocols of measurement and verifiability is given short shrift in most accounts of politics in general and institutional design specifically, is the role of affect. The key question here is how affect or emotions combines with memory and language to generate a distinctive grammar of cooperation or resistance to it.

Cognitive research has established the role of, mirror neurons, in empathetic responses (see, for instance, Ramachandran 2010). If we see a pedestrian being involved in an accident right before our eyes, it induces a nauseated response in us because we can put ourselves momentarily in the shoes of another person involved in an unfortunate accident. For me, the curiosity has been to think along these lines about the extent to which institutions carry within their design a similar ability in terms of responsiveness to external stimuli. Institutional designs flounder, in my assessment, when they lack or deny themselves the capacity or sensibility of 'perspective taking'. A UN that lacked the political resolve to act to stop the genocide in Rwanda would be a good illustration of what I have in mind here.

To immediately translate these arguments into concrete policy prescriptions is not my objective, and to do so at this stage would indeed be a stretch too far. However, I would like to argue that institutional design literature under the sway of *homo economicus* has tended by and large to ignore this apparently softer side of political conduct. However, this would be empirically inaccurate because we are aware through more recent work on cognition that language, memory, and affect are here to stay, and we have to find a way of both tapping into them creatively while also understanding their role and implications more clearly in terms of institutional design. I would even go further and suggest that the real challenge remains to be design institutions that are able to redress, if not considerably eliminate, perceived biases and prejudices in favor of one or the other social constellation, as well as also to find ways of allying with a contingent milieu that would trigger the right impulses and cooperative instincts perhaps already present in a more nascent form in evolutionary design (Coakley and Nowak 2013).

Note

1 I would like to acknowledge my gratitude to Dirk Messner, Thomas Fues, and Silke Weinlich for encouraging research in this direction. Many thanks to Tim Linka, Max Lesch, and Dennis Michels for their research assistance at various stages of this study, and Vineeta Rai for proofreading. A special word of gratitude to the Kate Hamburger Kolleg in Duisburg for its generous and intellectually stimulating multidisciplinary ecology.

References

Aminoff, E. M., Balslev, D., Borroni, P., Bryan, R. E., Chua, E. F., Cloutier, J., Cross, E. S., Drew, T., Funk, C. M., Gil-Da-Costa, R., Guerin, S. A., Hall, J. L., Jordan, K. E., Landau, A. N., Molnar-Szakacs, I., Montaser-Kouhsari, L., Olofsson, J. K., Quadflieg, S., Somerville, L. H., Sy, J. L., Uddin, L. Q. and Yamada, M. (2009). 'The Landscape of Cognitive Neuroscience: Challenges, Rewards, and New Perspectives', in M. S. Gazzaniga (ed.) *The Cognitive Neurosciences*, Cambridge, MA: The MIT Press, 1255–62.

Aoki, M. (2001). *Toward a Comparative Institutional Analysis*, Cambridge, MA: MIT Press.

Axelrod, R. (2006). *The Evolution of Cooperation*, New York, NY: Basic Books.

Axelrod R. and Hamilton, W. (2006). 'The Problem of Cooperation, in R. Axelrod (ed.) *The Evolution of Cooperation*, New York, NY: Basic Books, 88–106.

Boroditsky, L. (2011). 'How Language Shapes Thoughts', *Scientific American*, Februrary, last accessed on September 21, 2015 at psych.stanford.edu/~lara/papers/sci-am-2011.pdf, 63–65.

Boyd, B. (2010). *On the Origin of Stories: Evolution, Cognition, and Fiction*, Cambridge, MA: Harvard University Press.

Caramazza, A. (2009). 'Introduction' in M. S. Gazzaniga (ed.) *The Cognitive Neurosciences*, 4th edition, Cambridge, MA: The MIT Press, 765–6.

Coakley, S. and Nowak, M. (2013). 'Introduction: Why Cooperation Makes a Difference', in M. Nowak and S. Coakley (eds.) *Evolution, Games, and God: The Principle of Cooperation*, Cambridge, MA: Harvard University Press, 1–34.

Eisenberg, N. and Eggum, N. D. (2008). 'Empathy-Related and Prosocial Responding', in B. A. Sullivan, M. Snyder, and J. L. Sullivan (eds.) *Cooperation: The Political Psychology of Effective Human Interaction*, Malden: Blackwell, 53–74.

Goodin, R. E. (1996). 'Institutions and Their Design', in R. E. Goodin (ed.) *The Theory of Institutional Design*, Cambridge: Cambridge University Press, 1–53.

Heatherton, T. F. and Ledoux, J. E. (2009). 'Introduction', in M. S. Gazzaniga (ed.) *The Cognitive Neurosciences*, 4th edition, Cambridge, MA: The MIT Press, 887–8.

Hirst, W. (2010). 'The Contribution of Malleability to Collective Memory', in P. A. Reuter-Lorenz, K. Baynes, G. R. Mangun, and E. A. Phelps (eds.) *The Cognitive Neuroscience of Mind: A Tribute to Michael Gazzaniga*, Cambridge, MA: MIT, 139–53.

Hofstadter, D. and Sander, E. (2013). *Surfaces and Essences: Analogy as the Fuel and Fire of Thinking*, New York, NY: Basic Books.

Horng, S. and Sur, M. (2009). 'Patterning and Plasticity of Maps in the Mammalian Visual Pathway', in M. S. Gazzaniga (ed.) *The Cognitive Neurosciences*, 4th edition, Cambridge, MA: The MIT Press, 91–107.

Kahneman, D. (2011). *Thinking Fast and Slow*, London: Allen Lane.

Kandel, E. (2007). *In Search of Memory: The Emergence of a New Science of Mind*, New York, NY: W. W. Norton and Co.

Katznelson, I. and Weingast, B. R. (2005). 'Interactions between Historical and Rational Choice Institutionalism', in I. Katznelson and B. R. Weingast (eds.) *Preferences and Situations: Points of Intersection Between Historical and Rational Choice Institutionalism*, New York, NY: Russell Sage Foundation, 1–26.

Khong, Y. F. (1992). *Analogies at War: Korea, Munich, Dien Bien Phu, and the Vietnam Decisions of 1965*, Princeton, NJ: Princeton University Press.

Koremenos, B., Lipson, C., and Snidal, D. (2001). 'The Rational Design of International Institutions', *International Organization*, 55 (4): 761–99.

Li, W. and Gilbert, C. D. (2009). 'Visual Cortical Plasticity and Perceptual Learning', in M. S. Gazzaniga (ed.) *The Cognitive Neurosciences*, 4th edition, Cambridge, MA: The MIT Press, 129–40.

Mitchell, J. P., and Heatherton, T. F. (2009). 'Components of a Social Brain' in M. S. Gazzaniga (ed.) *The Cognitive Neurosciences*, 4th edition, Cambridge, MA: The MIT Press, 953–60.

Nader, K. (2009). 'Reconsolidation: A Possible Bridge between Cognitive and Neuroscientific Views of Memory', in M. S. Gazzaniga (ed.) *The Cognitive Neurosciences*, 4th edition, Cambridge, MA: The MIT Press, 691–703.

Neville, H. and Sur, M. (2009). 'Introduction', in M. S. Gazzaniga (ed.) *The Cognitive Neurosciences*, 4th edition, Cambridge, MA: The MIT Press.

Nowak, M. and Coakley, S. (eds.) (2013). *Evolution, Games, and God: The Principle of Cooperation*, Cambridge, MA: Harvard University Press.

Pascual-Leone, A. (2009). 'Characterizing and Modulating Neuroplasticity of the Adult Human Brain', in M. S. Gazzaniga (ed.) *The Cognitive Neurosciences*, 4th edition, Cambridge, MA: The MIT Press, 141–52.

Pierson, P. (2004). *Politics in Time: History, Institutions and Social Analysis*, Princeton, NJ: Princeton University Press.

Pinker, S. (2007). *The Stuff of Thought: Language as a Window into Human Nature*, New York, NY: Viking.

Posner, M. I., Rothbart, M. K. and Sheese, B. E. (2010). 'Genetic Variation Influences How the Social Brain Shapes Temperament and Behavior', in P. A. Reuter-Lorenz, K. Baynes, G. R. Mangun, and E. A. Phelps (eds.) *The Cognitive Neuroscience of Mind: A Tribute to Michael Gazzaniga*, Cambridge, MA: MIT, 125–38.

Ramachandran, V. S. (2010) *The Tell Tale Brain: A Neuroscientist's Quest for What Makes Us Human*, Noida: Random House India.

Simon, H. A. (1991). 'Bounded Rationality and Organizational Learning', *Organization Science*, Special Issue: Organizational Learning: Papers in Honor of (and by) G. James March, 2 (1): 125–34.

Smail, D. L. (2008). *On Deep History and the Brain*, Berkeley, CA: University of California Press.

Stevens, C. and Neville, H. (2009). 'Profiles of Development and Plasticity in Human Neurocognition', in M. S. Gazzaniga (ed.) *The Cognitive Neurosciences*, 4th edition, Cambridge, MA: The MIT Press, 165–81.

Sullivan, B. A., Snyder, M. and Sullivan, J. L. (ed.) (2008). *Cooperation: The Political Psychology of Effective Human Interaction*, Malden, MA: Blackwell.

Sunstein, C. and Thaler, R. H. (2008). *Nudge: Improving Decisions About Health, Wealth, and Happiness*, New Haven, CT: Yale University Press.

Tversky, A. and Kahneman, D. (1974). 'Judgment under Uncertainty: Heuristics and Biases', *Science*, 185 (4157): 1124–31.

Wendt, A. (2001). 'Driving with the Rearview Mirror: On the Rational Science of Institutional Design', *International Organization*, 55 (4): 1019–49.

Index